Christian Democracy and the Fall of Communism

CHRISTIAN DEMOCRACY and the FALL of COMMUNISM

Edited by

MICHAEL GEHLER
PIOTR H. KOSICKI
HELMUT WOHNOUT

LEUVEN UNIVERSITY PRESS

Cover: Austria's Foreign Minister, the Christian Democrat Alois Mock met Hungarian Foreign Minister Gyula Horn on 27 June 1989 to cut down barbed wire along the Iron Curtain – a symbol of the Cold War – at the Hungarian-Austrian border.
[Austrian National Library (ÖNB), Robert Jäger, APA-Archiv, picturedesk.com]

ISBN 978 94 6270 216 5
eISBN 978 94 6166 316 0
D/2019/1869/50
https://doi.org/10.11116/9789461663160
NUR: 697

GPRC
Guaranteed
Peer Reviewed
Content
www.gprc.be

TABLE OF CONTENTS

FOREWORD

Christian Democracy is one of the fundamental "families" of political modernity. It emerged as a movement in the last decades of the 19th century in Europe, incorporating older social Christian movements and their experiences. Partially encouraged by the Catholic Church, it developed into a political reality at the beginning of the 20th century, becoming a permanent and influential component of Catholic movements and parties in Germany, Belgium, France, Austria, Spain, Switzerland, the Netherlands, and Italy. Especially after the Second World War, Christian Democratic parties and movements developed into leading actors in the reconstruction of continental Europe, establishing stable democracies and building redistributive "welfare" regimes. At the same time, Christian Democracy was a central pillar of post-war European integration and identity, being a driving force behind the origins and development of the present-day European Union. Against the backdrop of the Cold War and post-war decolonization, it experienced a rapid globalization beyond Europe, extending its scope to what then became dubbed the "Third World" and experiencing a remarkable expansion in Latin America. With its resolute internationalism, grounded on a commitment to both supranational cooperation and a duty of solidarity concerning less fortunate peoples and countries, it played a decisive role in the creation of the United Nations and the development of an international ethos of human rights. Even today, Christian Democracy continues to be influential in Europe and Latin America (although it is also present in other parts of the world), remaining one of the fundamental forces for the future of democracy.

Notwithstanding its relevance, Christian Democracy is a challenging subject to study. Its identity is not easy to grasp. It is not a monolith of movements and parties but a house with many rooms, differentiated by origins, developments, conditions, and trends. The diversity of names of Christian Democratic parties (with their dissimilar references, besides democracy, to populism or social Christianity) alone demonstrates the difficulty of a definition. Furthermore, Christian Democracy, as an ideology, is not easy to pinpoint in the spectrum of modern politics. It does not fit squarely into categories of left and right. It incorporates both traditional Church and family values, as well as progressive ones such as social welfare and redistribution of wealth. It is based on a moral critique of capitalism, it rejects the individualist world view that underlies political liberalism and free-trade economics in favor of the dignity of the human person, and it recognizes the need for the state to intervene in the economy. Yet it opposes socialism and defends private property, resisting excessive intervention of the state in social life and education, again in the name of the sanctity of human life. It is based on Christian values and supported by believers. Yet Christian Democratic parties have often operated autonomously from ecclesiastical organizations, welcomed the support of non-believers, and adopted a secular discourse, privileging pragmatic policies over overtly religious themes.

Thus, many scholars have suggested interpretations that risk generalization. Does Christian Democracy have a conservative identity on cultural, social, and moral issues, and a progressive one on economy, environment, labor, and foreign policy? To what extent are national and regional differences blurred by a common identity and ideology? Likewise, the transformation of Christian Democratic parties after the end of the Cold War posed many questions about their identity and their future, which are difficult to answer. After the end of communism, the conditions of their power and hegemony radically changed, causing metamorphoses, fragmentation, and in some cases, decline. The European People's Party still receives millions of votes. However, it has reinvented itself, losing some of its traditional and original components and acquiring new ones that have limited links with Christian Democratic tradition and history.

Because of all these reasons, thorough and comparative historical research on Christian Democracy is key to comprehending contemporary history. It is badly needed if we want to understand Christian Democracy's real roots and its historical development over time and place. It is badly needed if we are going to fathom an essential part of our contemporary world and the memory of its citizens. It is badly needed if we want to make a necessary addition to the political culture of today.

It is these goals that the CIVITAS Series aims to support. CIVITAS – Forum of Archives and Research on Christian Democracy was founded in 2013 by the Istituto Luigi Sturzo (Rome), KADOC-KU Leuven – Documentation and Research Center on Religion, Culture and Society (Leuven) and the Konrad-Adenauer-Stiftung e. V. (Sankt Augustin). It is a platform of research and archival institutions, and of individual archivists and researchers, focused on the field of research and records of Christian Democracy at national and European levels, as well as worldwide. Its Series aims to present the outcome of its research initiatives and archival work to a broad but specialized academic audience. The CIVITAS Series publishes innovative studies dealing with the history and politics of Christian Democracy in a European and global context and, by doing so, wishes to foster international research and access to sources and to situate Christian Democracy in broader twentieth-century histories. The Series welcomes academic monographs, edited volumes and annotated editions of sources that deal with specific topics related to the history and politics of Christian Democracy. In addition to the assessment by the Scientific Committee of CIVITAS-FARCD, each volume is submitted to blind review.

As President of CIVITAS, it is my pride and joy to introduce, on behalf of the other members of the Steering Board, Prof. Kim Christiaens from KADOC-KU Leuven and Dr. Michael Borchard from the Konrad-Adenauer-Stiftung, the publication of this first volume of the Series. It is devoted to a central issue in the history of European Christian Democracy, analyzing its role in and responses to the collapse of communism and the ensuing transitions to democracy. Our satisfaction is doubled by the fact that the publication of this astonishingly exciting scholarly volume coincides with the thirtieth anniversary of the fall of the Berlin Wall.

The present volume would never have been completed, however, without the vision and the engagement of two colleagues I have the duty and the pleasure to thank with the most heartfelt conviction. Prof. Hanns Jürgen Küsters, former President and now Honorary President of CIVITAS, and Prof. Jan De Maeyer, Honorary Director of KADOC-KU Leuven, envisaged the Series, defined its goals and features, and placed it in the hands of an academic and internationally established publisher. Our gratitude for them is sincere. The Board would like to express special thanks to Dr. Godfried Kwanten and to all his colleagues at KADOC-KU Leuven who took the utmost care in the editing of the texts, including Luc Vints, Lieve Claes and Alexis Vermeylen.

I am sure that this will be the first book of a long and excellent Series.

Renato Moro
President CIVITAS – Forum of Archives and Research on Christian Democracy

ACKNOWLEDGMENTS

It is almost a commonplace to note that 1989, the celebrated *annus mirabilis* of the late 20th century, transformed the political face of the European continent. Yet this volume takes an entirely new approach to exploring what happened in 1989, what followed the events of that year, and why, looking both to Western Europe and to Central and Eastern Europe, as well as the broader global context that framed their interactions. From the perspective of countries formerly trapped behind the Iron Curtain, this volume explores the successes and failures of political party formation against the backdrop of ideas belonging to the broadly understood political family known as Christian Democracy. In addition, it addresses the efforts of established Christian Democratic parties to the west of the former Iron Curtain to make contact and establish networks with political parties in the new democracies and to influence party foundations on their behalf. Thus, the contributions contained in this book help to contextualize and explain mutual influences and their repercussions across transnational – and indeed, global – spaces.

It is the pleasant duty of the editors to offer their gracious thanks to the various individuals and institutions who, in their different roles and at different times, contributed to making the publication of this book possible.

This book draws heavily on the academic conference *The Opening of the East and the Fall of the Iron Curtain: The Role of Europe's Christian Democratic and Conservative Parties, 1989*, hosted by the Karl von Vogelsang Institute in Vienna on 9-11 November 2016, under the auspices of the annual conference series sponsored by the international scholarly network CIVITAS – Forum of Archives and Research on Christian Democracy. Meinhard Friedl and Johannes Schönner assured the conference's smooth operation. The Karl von Vogelsang Institute subsequently provided additional financing for the preparation of this volume. Idesbald Goddeeris (KU Leuven) and Kyrill Kunakhovich (University of Virginia) offered indispensable feedback in the process of review and revision. Gregory Weeks assured a smooth and expeditious process of copy editing.

Finally, this publication would not be possible without the deep commitment and generous support of CIVITAS – Forum of Archives and Research on Christian Democracy – and its partner, the Leuven University

Press. We acknowledge the initiative and work of the CIVITAS Steering Board, consisting of Renato Moro, Kim Christiaens, and Michael Borchard, as well as the three founding core institutions of CIVITAS: the Konrad-Adenauer-Stiftung, the KADOC Documentation and Research Center at KU Leuven, and the Istituto Luigi Sturzo. Special thanks also go to Hanns Jürgen Küsters, founding CIVITAS president *emeritus*, and Jan De Maeyer, founding CIVITAS treasurer *emeritus*, as well as to the entire CIVITAS Editorial Board. Kim Christiaens and Godfried Kwanten shepherded the volume to fruition at Leuven University Press.

Now, we are pleased to present a consolidated volume commemorating the revolutions of 1989, whose publication date coincides almost exactly with the 30th anniversary of the fall of the Berlin Wall.

Michael Gehler, Piotr H. Kosicki and Helmut Wohnout

INTRODUCTION

Michael Gehler

The European political family broadly known as Christian Democracy played an important role in the fall of communism in Central and Eastern Europe (hereafter, CEE) at the turn of the 1980s and the 1990s (often called "the revolutions of 1989"), even though the long-term legacy of that role proved to be more ambiguous or limited. This book deals with this topic in great depth, and its chapters cover a number of those detailed stories. The purpose of this introductory contribution is not only to explain the structure and content of the book, but also to highlight key aspects that outline the larger context for both aspects of the book's subject matter: the revolutions of 1989 and the trans-European legacy of Christian Democracy.

The Ambivalent Revolutions of 1989 in Perspective: the Before and the After

What were the origins and reasons for the revolutionary events and effects of the *annus mirabilis* of 1989?[1] Certainly, there were many: especially economic decline, the ideological and political erosion of communist rule, as well as the administrative and structural deficits of the so-called "really existing socialism" embraced by the 1970s within the Soviet Bloc. One decisive factor predominated, however, and his name was Mikhail Gorbachev.

1 For the relevant literature, see Timothy Garton Ash, *We the People: The Revolution of '89 Witnessed in Warsaw, Budapest, Berlin and Prague* (Cambridge: Granta, 1990); Id., *Ein Jahrhundert wird abgewählt: Aus den Zentren Mitteleuropas 1980–1990* (Munich-Vienna: Hanser, 1990); Id., *In Europe's Name: Germany and the Divided Continent* (London: Jonathan Cape, 1993); Id., *The File: A Personal History* (New York: Vintage Books, 1998); S. J. Ball, *The Cold War: An International History, 1947–1991* (London - New York - Sydney - Auckland: Arnold, 1998); Jost Dülffer, *Jalta, 4. Februar 1945: Der Zweite Weltkrieg und die Entstehung der bipolaren Welt* (Munich, DTV: 1998); Jeremy Isaacs and Taylor Downing, *Der Kalte Krieg. Eine illustrierte Geschichte* (Munich-Zurich: Wilhelm Heyne, 2001); Vladimir Tismăneanu, ed., *The Revolutions of 1989* (London: Routledge, 1999); Vladimir Tismăneanu and Sorin Antohi, eds., *Between Past and Future: The Revolutions of 1989 and their Aftermath* (Budapest: CEU Press, 2000); Wilfried Loth, *Die Teilung*

1. Gorbachev: an ambivalent revolutionary

Mikhail Gorbachev was an ambivalent revolutionary. He tried to bring the "old thinking" to an end and made the emergence of "new thinkers" possible. According to Andrei Grachev, he was an "unusual politician," "a dilettante statesman, an idealist, or a visionary." His policy was based on the well-calculated intention of replacing the old balance of power with a new one. Although Gorbachev did not encourage the opening of the Iron Curtain, he tolerated it and agreed with Germany's unification after the country's more than forty years of division. Gorbachev's "new political thinking" was not so different from George H.W. Bush's vision of an emerging "new world order." He also made decisive gestures toward globalization, and this would give him the status of a world revolutionary like Vladimir Ilyich Lenin or Joseph Stalin. Gorbachev created highly controversial new realities due to the ambivalence of his policies. During Gorbachev's time in power, it was not possible for the concept of "new political thinking" to be successful because the structural limitations of the Soviet Union were too deeply entrenched.[2]

2. Poland: the "self-limiting revolution" with a well-organized underground movement

From the late 1970s onward, Karol Józef Wojtyła, the first Polish pope, known as John Paul II, and his strong anticommunism had a decisive ideo-

der Welt: Geschichte des Kalten Krieges 1941–1955 (Munich: Taschenbuch Verlag, 4th ed., 1983, rev. ed., 2000); Odd Arne Westad, *The Global Cold War* (Cambridge: Cambridge University Press, 2005); John Lewis Gaddis, *The Cold War* (London - New York: Penguin, 2005); Rolf Steininger, *Der Kalte Krieg* (Frankfurt: Fischer-Taschenbuch-Verlag, 2006); Bernd Stöver, *Der Kalte Krieg: Geschichte eines radikalen Zeitalters 1947–1991* (Munich: C.H. Beck, 2007); Pierre Grosser, *1989: L'année où le monde a basculé* (Paris: Perrin, 2009); Victor Sebestyen, *Revolution 1989: The Fall of the Soviet Empire* (London: Phoenix, 2009); Stephen Kotkin with Jan T. Gross, *Uncivil Society: 1989 and the Implosion of the Communist Establishment* (New York: Vintage Books, 2010); Mary Elise Sarotte, *1989: The Struggle to Create Post-Cold War Europe* (Princeton, NJ: Princeton University Press, 2011); Robert Service, *The End of the Cold War, 1985–1991* (London: Pan Books, 2015); Michael Gehler, "The Fall of the Iron Curtain: Causes, Structures, Timelines and Effects," in *The Republic of Austria, 1918–2018: Milestones and Turning Points*, ed. Heinz Fischer, Andreas Huber and Stephan Neuhäuser (Vienna: Czernin, 2018), 185–200.

2 Andrei Grachev, "Gorbachev and the 'New Political Thinking,'" in *The Revolutions of 1989: A Handbook*, ed. Wolfgang Mueller, Michael Gehler and Arnold Suppan (Vienna: OAW, 2015), 33–46. In this handbook, one can also find all of the relevant literature from international scholarship until 2015.

logical impact on political developments and changes in his country.[3] The round-table talks of February through April 1989 and the first semi-free parliamentary elections in June constituted milestones in Poland's shift to democratic structures and rule. But bargaining had already started months before the Round Table was established. The Catholic Church served as a guarantor and legitimating factor in these talks from the very beginning. While the "self-limiting revolution" (Jadwiga Staniszkis) had been put to an end by Wojciech Jaruzelski's introduction of martial law in December 1981 – without legal basis and in grievous violation of human rights – in the end, de-legalizing and prohibiting the Solidarity trade union was counterproductive: it led to the development of a well-organized clandestine underground movement that, due to its decentralization, was more difficult to control than the public dissent that had taken place earlier.[4] Poland served as an icebreaker with regard to the ensuing revolutionary events – especially those in Hungary, but also in East Germany – yet the road to the first free elections in the still Soviet-bloc country was long and stony. Several influential pre-revolutionary events took place in Poland in the decades before 1981. Revolution and reform were two sides of the same coin (what Timothy Garton Ash described as "refolution"). Poland's ensuing transition to liberal democracy was negotiated and contained contradictions, failures, paradoxes, and setbacks.[5]

3. Hungary: the "negotiated revolution"

The fall of communism in Hungary must be understood with regard to the country's defeat by Soviet troops in 1956 and the ensuing collective memory of Soviet military intervention against a people's uprising.[6] In the second half of the 1980s, compromises were found, and in 1989, a political transition was achieved through what Rudolf L. Tökés called a "nego-

3 Andreas Englisch, *Johannes Paul II: Das Geheimnis des Karol Wojtyła* (Munich-Berlin: Ullstein, 2003); see also Piotr H. Kosicki, "Vatican II and Poland," in *Vatican II behind the Iron Curtain*, ed. Piotr H. Kosicki (Washington, DC: Catholic University of America Press, 2016), 127–198.

4 Jadwiga Staniszkis, *Poland's Self-Limiting Revolution*, ed. Jan T. Gross (Princeton, NJ: Princeton University Press, 1984).

5 Klaus Bachmann, "Poland 1989: The Constrained Revolution," in *The Revolutions*, ed. Mueller, Gehler and Suppan, 47–75; and before: Timothy Garton Ash, *The Polish Revolution: Solidarity, 1980–82* (London: Cape, 1983); August Pradetto, *Techno-bürokratischer Sozialismus: Polen in der Ära Gierek (1970–1980)* (Frankfurt/Main - Bern - New York - Paris: Lang, 1991); Id., *Bürokratische Anarchie: Der Niedergang des polnischen "Realsozialismu"* (Vienna-Cologne-Graz: Böhlau, 1992).

6 György Litván and János M. Bak, eds., *Die Ungarische Revolution 1956: Reform – Aufstand – Vergeltung* (Vienna: Passagen Verlag, 1994).

tiated revolution."[7] Party leader János Kádár stepped down in 1988, and the Soviet leadership remained silent. Gorbachev assured Prime Minister Miklos Németh on 3 March 1989 that there would be "no new 1956" as long as he was in power. The Kremlin also agreed to negotiations concerning the withdrawal of troops from Hungary; in November 1989, the USSR removed its nuclear warheads from Hungarian soil. Moscow did not protest the rehabilitation of Hungarian revolutionaries, the country's roundtable talks (modeled after Poland) or Hungary's decision to blow a hole in the Iron Curtain by opening its western border for East German refugees. While he opposed the introduction of a multiparty system in Hungary, Gorbachev did not take any measures to hinder it. Questions remained for a long time:

1. Who were the main actors in the political changes of 1989?
2. Who really shaped the decision-making at the round tables – reform-minded communists, or dissidents?[8]
3. Was the *annus mirabilis* really a revolution, or instead an evolution, or a transformation?
4. Were events driven by public pressure, or did societies remain largely passive?
5. Is the notion of "revolution from above" more appropriate when describing the Hungarian events of 1989?

Andreas Schmidt-Schweizer has argued that it was a peaceful transformation represented by reform communists and socialists while the population remained passive. Since the 1970s, the majority of the population as well as the opposition had accepted Kádár's "goulash communism." While freedom remained restricted, living conditions, albeit modest, were satisfactory. In the second half of the 1980s, the economy declined. A large majority of the population began to long for a replacement of the system. Only in the summer of 1989 did a nascent, fragmented opposition succeed in mobilizing the masses, which took part in demonstrations and campaigned for political issues such as the role of the Hungarian minority

7 Rudolf L. Tökés, *Hungary's Negotiated Revolution: Economic Reform, Social Change, and Political Succession 1957–1990* (Cambridge: Cambridge University Press, 1996).

8 Jon Elster, ed., *The Roundtable Talks and the Breakdown of Communism. Constitutionalism in Eastern Europe* (Chicago: University of Chicago Press, 1996).

in Romania or the rehabilitation of the 1956 Hungarian revolutionaries.[9] The funeral of Imre Nagy (deposed during the Soviet intervention in 1956, executed in 1958) on 16 June 1989 in Budapest was one of the clearest signs that the political climate had changed, when the young patriot and political spokesman of the Fidesz youth, Viktor Orbán, demanded Hungary's independence, liberty, and Soviet troop withdrawal.[10]

4. China: the bloody suppression of the revolutionary student movement

The Chinese student opposition movement of spring 1989 and the Tiananmen Square massacre in Beijing on 4 June 1989 – the same day as the semi-free elections in Poland – deeply imprinted both the leadership and the societies of Central and Eastern Europe. The year 1989 was not only a critical moment with regard to political developments in China, but was also a turning point for Sino-East European relations: the CEE countries experienced more or less peaceful and bloodless revolutions, while protest movements in China were violently suppressed. The developments in China strengthened the anti-socialist movements in the CEE countries, while the developments in these states alarmed the Chinese communist leaders. In the end, the Chinese government took brutal action against organized opposition groups in its country. The bloodless events in the CEE states were also a result of the bloody developments in China. There, the harsh oppression of the student protests in Tiananmen Square prevented a revolution from below and generated a policy of reforms from above. As a consequence of the political changes in the CEE states, Sino-East European bilateral relations collapsed. After the bloody events of 4 June 1989, in

9 Andreas Oplatka, *Der Eiserne Vorhang reißt: Ungarn als Wegbereiter* (Zurich: Neue Zürcher Zeitung, 1990); Id., "Hungary 1989: Renunciation of Power and Power-Sharing," in *The Revolutions*, ed. Mueller, Gehler and Suppan, 77–91; Andreas Schmidt-Schweizer, "Die politischen Auseinandersetzungen am 'Nationalen Runden Tisch': Systemtransformation auf dem 'Verhandlungsweg'?," *Südosteuropa* 46, no. 1/2 (1997): 37–64; Id., "Die Öffnung der ungarischen Westgrenze für die DDR-Bürger im Sommer 1989: Vorgeschichte, Hintergründe und Schlussfolgerungen," *Südosteuropa Mitteilungen* 37, no. 1 (1997): 33–53; Id., "Motive im Vorfeld der Demontage des 'Eisernen Vorhangs' 1987–1989," in *Grenze im Kopf*, ed. Peter Haslinger (Frankfurt am Main - Berlin - Bern: Lang, 1999), 127–139; Id., *Vom Reformsozialismus zur Systemtransformation: Politische Veränderungsbestrebungen innerhalb der Ungarischen Sozialistischen Arbeiterpartei (MSZMP) von 1986 bis 1989* (Frankfurt am Main - Berlin - Bern: Lang, 2000); Id., *Politische Geschichte Ungarns 1985–2002: Von der liberalisierten Einparteienherrschaft zur Demokratie in der Konsolidierungsphase* (Munich: Oldenbourg, 2007).

10 Karl P. Benziger, "The Funeral of Imre Nagy: Contested History and the Power of Memory Culture", *History and Memory* 12, no. 2 (2000): 142–164.

order to regain acceptance and legitimacy for the still-existing totalitarian system, the Chinese communist government proposed a political offensive of reform policies. In the early 1990s, the Chinese communist regime achieved economic growth and reestablished its relations abroad.[11]

5. The German Democratic Republic: the unintended and involuntary self-dissolution of East Germany and the Socialist Unity Party of Germany

The official opening of the Hungarian-Austrian border for East German refugees on 11 September 1989 was a "critical event." The decisive moment came, however, with the Monday demonstration by tens of thousands of protesters in Leipzig on 9 October, launching the East Germans' "October Revolution" (Hans Hermann Hertle). The televised reporting of these events enhanced their effect. Hungary's "hole in the wall" (so termed by Andreas Oplatka) demonstrated the weakness and loss of power of the regime of the Socialist Unity Party of Germany (SED).[12] As the exodus grew, protests against the government in the German Democratic Republic (GDR) exploded. Since 1961 the Berlin Wall had guaranteed the existence of the GDR. The quick opening of the border and "the fall of the Wall" on 9 November were not planned by the SED leaders. The revolutionary events were triggered largely by the media. In the three weeks after 9 November, the number of demonstrations did not decrease. Hertle describes the irony of the fact that the SED leaders had realized the state's bankruptcy already weeks before the revolution had begun and that, without West Germany's help, the GDR would not survive. Indeed, the East German communist politicians were ahead of their own people. Therefore it was a tragedy that the intellectual and political opposition dreamed of a new socialist GDR without knowing the details of its debts and deficits, while the majority of the population at the end of 1989 and the very beginning of 1990 claimed the rights of self-determination and German unity. Many civil rights activists marginalized themselves because of this contradiction. It was important for ordinary East Germans that the West German chancellor and Christian Democratic leader Helmut Kohl advocated Ger-

11 Peter Vámos, "The Tiananmen Square 'Incident' in China and the East Central European Revolutions," in *The Revolutions*, ed. Mueller, Gehler and Suppan, 93–112; Martin K. Dimitrov, "European Lessons for China: Tiananmen 1989 and Beyond," in *The Long 1989: Decades of Global Revolution*, ed. Piotr H. Kosicki and Kyrill Kunakhovich (Budapest: CEU Press, 2019), 61–88.

12 Andreas Oplatka, *Der erste Riss in der Mauer: September 1989 – Ungarn öffnet die Grenze* (Vienna: Paul Zsolnay Verlag, 2009).

man "reunification." But the main reason for the success of the revolutionary events was Gorbachev's policy of wait and see. If he had ordered a military intervention, this would have contradicted his "new thinking." This was something that the SED leader Erich Honecker ignored. He had not learned the lesson that Leonid Brezhnev had taught him in 1970: that the GDR could not exist without the power and support of the USSR.[13]

6. Czechoslovakia and the "Velvet Revolution": a double revolution within national frameworks leading to the state's division

The violent suppression of a peaceful student demonstration on 17 November 1989 by police forces in Prague provoked resistance and strikes the next day by artists and intellectuals. Opposition movements and parties were organized. The Ladislav Adamec government launched discussions with the opposition, but the concessions it offered had come too late. On 10 December, a new federal government was appointed and the communist Gustáv Husák resigned as state president. The former dissident Václav Havel became the new elected president.[14] However, his nomination caused problems with the Slovaks, who wanted as president Alexander Dubček, the Prague Spring leader of 1968 who was also an ethnic Slovak.

In Czechoslovakia, a double revolution took place: a Czech one and a Slovakian one. Both revolutions took place within a specific national framework and thus, they must be seen as weakened half-revolutions that led to the state's division. A small and temporary compromise was reached with the election of Dubček as chairman of the Federal Assembly. But a later round table resulted in a division of power that involved political fragmentation and conflicts. A fight against the communist past began, but attempts at creating a "Czech road to capitalism" as a way to

13 Jeffrey Kopstein, *The Politics of Economic Decline in East Germany 1945–1989* (Chapel Hill, NC: University of North Carolina Press, 1997); Kotkin with Gross, *Uncivil Society*; Hans-Hermann Hertle, "The October Revolution in East Germany," in *The Revolutions*, ed. Mueller, Gehler and Suppan, 113–135; Id., *Der Fall der Mauer: Die unbeabsichtigte Selbstauflösung des SED-Staates* (Opladen-Wiesbaden: VS Verlag, 2nd edition, 1999); Id., *Chronik des Mauerfalls: Die dramatischen Ereignisse um den 9. November 1989* (Berlin: Links Verlag, 2009); Id., *Der Tag, an dem die Mauer fiel: Die wichtigsten Zeitzeugen berichten vom 9. November, 1989* (Berlin: Nicolai, 2009); Mary Elise Sarotte, *The Collapse: The Accidental Opening of the Berlin Wall* (New York: Basic Books, 2014).

14 Milan Otáhal, "Die 'samtene' Revolution – ohne Alternative," in *Wandel durch Repräsentation – Repräsentation durch Wandel: Entstehung und Ausformung der parlamentarischen Demokratie in Ungarn, Polen, der Tschechoslowakei und der ehemaligen DDR*, ed. Uwe Thaysen and Hans Michael Kloth (Baden-Baden: Nomos, 1992), 125–130.

solve the chaotic political structures failed. Slovakia, guided by Vladmir Mečiar's national-populist coalition, separated from the Czech Republic, which was represented by a center-right coalition headed by Václav Klaus. The "Velvet Revolution" changed the communist regimes into democratically elected governments in both Prague and Bratislava. Slovakia's Christian Democratic prime minister Ján Čarnogurský missed his opportunity to reshape the political process. The national separation into the Czech and Slovak Republics was decided by the real political leaders of both sides: Klaus and Mečiar.[15]

7. Bulgaria: failed reforms from above and no revolution from below

The end of the communist system in Bulgaria was the product of a legitimacy crisis: economic problems and the alienation of Bulgaria's youth and labor forces played an important role. In the late 1980s, the socialist party started to reduce its visibility in order to extract itself from public criticism. Already in the summer of 1987, it gave more maneuvering room to state authorities and enterprises. It increased the autonomy of companies, allowed more worker self-management, and supported decentralization. These measures were designed to reduce the alienation of workers and increase their will to push productivity. But the reforms came too late. The party did not give up its power, and in the end its reforms were unsuccessful. The "Bulgarian pseudo-perestroika" (Ulrich Brunnbauer) involved spiraling administrative chaos and a regime that was unable to organize any successful political changes. The long-standing (since 1954) First Secretary of the Bulgarian Communist Party, Todor Zhivkov, even stated that the population had lost confidence in the party and that no one wished to get involved in the proclaimed political changes. As a result, Bulgaria experienced "a half-baked reform" that laid bare the self-created deficits of the communist political system. At the end of the 1980s, the question was no longer whether communist rule would end, but when and how. Its weak performance and the breakdown of the economy led to political collapse. In Bulgaria, a revolution did not arise from below, but instead resulted from the failed reforms from above.[16]

15 James Krapfl, *Revolution with a Human Face: Politics, Culture, and Community in Czechoslovakia, 1989–1992* (Ithaca, NY: Cornell University Press, 2013); Jiři Suk, "Czechoslovakia in 1989: Causes, Results, and Conceptual Changes," in *The Revolutions*, ed. Mueller, Gehler and Suppan, 137–160.

16 Ulrich Brunnbauer, "The End of Communist Rule in Bulgaria: The Crisis of Legitimacy and Political Change," in *The Revolutions*, ed. Mueller, Gehler and Suppan, 177–197.

8. Romania: a confiscated, corrupt, incomplete, and unfinished revolution

Romania faced the consequences of the world economic crises in the 1970s, the loss of Western support, and the emergence of domestic opposition. In contrast to the largely peaceful reformist developments elsewhere in the CEE, the popular uprising against Nicolae Ceaușescu in December 1989 cost many lives: over 1,000 civilians, officers and army conscripts were killed, with over 4,000 persons injured. Still many more died after 22 December, when Ceaușescu and his wife were taken out of Bucharest, arrested, and executed. The vast majority of Romanians even 25 years later believed that the revolution's casualties had died in vain, since the anti-communist people's uprising had been "stolen" or "diverted." The still unclear backgrounds of these violent events following the capture of Ceaușescu continued to influence the state's course of political, social, and economic transformation. Those who seized power after December 1989 did everything they could to prevent the investigation, prosecution and condemnation of those who were responsible for the bloody events. Thousands of people were investigated, but most were released or pardoned. A group of people around Ion Iliescu seized power in a military coup d'état following a popular uprising in Timișoara. They remained in power into the twenty-first century: although some of them were responsible for the bloodshed of December 1989, they escaped prosecution. To a greater degree than the other CEE revolutions, the Romanian revolution was supported by electronic media and Western radio stations broadcasting to Romania, above all the US-sponsored Radio Free Europe. This contributed to an anti-regime mobilization that delegitimized Ceaușescu's position and popularized regime dissidents from the 1980s. A "tele-revolution" took place, which in the end seems to have bred a mixture of a popular uprising and a coup d'état.[17]

17 Anneli Ute Gabanyi, *Die unvollendete Revolution: Rumänien zwischen Diktatur und Demokratie* (Munich: Piper, 1990); Id., *Systemwechsel in Rumänien: Von der Revolution zur Transformation* (Munich: Piper, 1998); Id., "The Romanian Revolution," in *The Revolutions*, ed. Mueller, Gehler and Suppan, 199–220; Peter Siani-Davies, *The Romanian Revolution of December 1989* (Ithaca, NY: Cornell University Press, 2005); Roman Hutter, *Revolution und Legitimation: Die politische Instrumentalisierung des Umbruchs 1989 durch die Postkommunisten in Rumänien* (Berlin: Frank & Timme, 2015).

9. The Baltic "singing revolution"

These revolutionary events spanning the years from 1987 to 1991 can be characterized by an extraordinarily high degree of youth engagement. Decisive was a collective consciousness of the past, notably of the secret annex to the Molotov-Ribbentrop Pact of 1939 and the Soviet occupation in 1940, as well as the persistence of an un-Sovietized Baltic culture shared by Estonia, Latvia, and Lithuania. Youth engagement grew into a mass movement in the streets that was visible to all.

Until 1990, the new Soviet leadership hesitated to intervene militarily, since this would have risked violating the image carefully crafted by Gorbachev. Nonetheless, Lithuania's declaration of independence on 11 March 1990 provoked negative feelings in Moscow. Also the Western powers were less than euphoric, fearing the destabilization of Gorbachev's position. But while the Baltic revolutionary changes were initially peaceful, they escalated into bloody confrontations in January 1991 when Soviet leaders decided to suppress the protests. This move also contributed to the further weakening of the Soviet Union. The erosion process of the USSR seems to have started in Poland at the beginning of the 1980s, moving on to Hungary and the GDR, but the collapse of the Soviet Union was not only caused by the economic and political decline of these countries whom it had long supported economically and infrastructurally. The mass demonstrations and "the singing revolution" in the Soviet republics of Estonia, Latvia and Lithuania constituted a new dimension: they were a decisive threat for the Soviet empire's cohesion from *within* the Union itself, rather than among the satellite states of the Soviet Bloc.[18] The Baltic states changed from being annexed and controlled districts at the empire's periphery into being a subversive and separatist region. But they should not be seen as unique cases. Their claims to emancipation and independence from the USSR in 1988–1989 demonstrated both the lack of appeal of the communist system and a resentment boiling over against Russian "imperial overstretch."[19]

18 Guntis Smidchens, *The Power of Song: Nonviolent National Culture in the Baltic Singing Revolution* (Seattle: University of Washington Press, 2014); see also Stephen Zunes, "Estonia's Singing Revolution (1986–1991)," April 2009, www.nonviolent-conflict.org/estonias-singing-revolution-1986-1991/ (quoted December 2018).

19 Stephen Kotkin, *Armageddon Averted: The Soviet Collapse* (Oxford: Oxford University Press, 2001); Karsten Brüggemann, "'One Day We Will Anyway': The 'Singing Revolution' in the Soviet Baltic Republics," in *The Revolutions*, ed. Mueller, Gehler and Suppan, 221–246.

10. Austria's adequate perceptions and mediating role

In the mid-1980s, the Austrian capital of Vienna was a "Western" city surrounded by Soviet "Eastern" Europe. For Polish, Czech, Slovak, Hungarian, Romanian, Bulgarian, Serb, Croat, and Slovene intellectuals, Vienna stood for "Central Europe" (*Mitteleuropa*),[20] an imagined community of cosmopolitan civility that Europeans had somehow mislaid in the course of the century.[21] Nevertheless, a great majority of the Austrian people, including the intellectuals, did not really recognize what was going on in the late 1980s in their region. They did not see the significance of the new nationalist movements in Serbia (from 1986), in Slovenia (from 1988), and in Croatia (from 1989); the increasing conflicts in Kosovo; and the fractures within the Union of the Yugoslav communists (in January 1990). They were also unaware of how important the reform processes within the Hungarian communist leadership (from 1987) had become, including the resignation of Kádár as Secretary General of the Party in May 1988 and the opening of the Iron Curtain, first in December 1988 for Hungarians, in August 1989 for some 600 East Germans at the Austro-Hungarian "border picnic," and then at midnight on 10–11 September for tens of thousands East German vacationers fleeing to West Germany. There is no doubt today that this mass exodus was the starting point of the disintegration of the communist regimes in East Germany and Czechoslovakia. Immediately after the "Velvet Revolution" in Prague, Austria also opened its border to Czechoslovakia. With the fall of the Iron Curtain, Austria's role at the periphery of the West was suddenly transformed into a position in the center of Europe.[22]

Austria responded early and positively to the reform efforts in the CEE countries. Its strongest sympathies were for the changes in Hungary. In contrast, the rapid end of East Germany surprised the Austrian leadership and had an entirely different impact, with the positive climate shifting quickly. Diplomats at the Ballhausplatz did not follow the changes in East

20 Erhard Busek and Emil Brix, *Projekt Mitteleuropa* (Vienna: Überreuter, 1986); Id., *Mitteleuropa Revisited: Warum Europas Zukunft in Mitteleuropa entschieden wird* (Vienna: K & S, 2018).

21 Arnold Suppan and Wolfgang Mueller, eds., *"Peaceful Coexistence" or "Iron Curtain": Austria, Neutrality, and Eastern Europe in the Cold War and Détente, 1955–1989* (Vienna–Berlin: Lit, 2009).

22 Arnold Suppan, "Austria and its Neighbors in Eastern Europe, 1955–89," in *The Revolutions*, ed. Mueller, Gehler and Suppan,419–436; Andrea Brait and Michael Gehler, eds., *Grenzöffnung 1989: Innen- und Außenperspektiven und die Folgen für Österreich* (Vienna: Böhlau, 2014); Michael Gehler and Andrea Brait, eds., *Am Ort des Geschehens in Zeiten des Umbruchs. Lebensgeschichtliche Erinnerungen aus Politik und Ballhausplatzdiplomatie vor und nach 1989* (Hildesheim: Georg Olms Verlag, 2018).

Germany merely by waiting and sitting still, but with a sense of urgency and concern. The end of the SED regime was perceived with surprise and mixed feelings. While the reaction of Austrian Social Democratic chancellor Franz Vranitzky toward a reform-oriented GDR was positive, his Christian Democratic foreign minister Alois Mock backed Kohl's policy of a quick solution to the "German Question" in the form of unification.

The differing positions were also due to different approaches toward Brussels. Mock's course focused on assuring Austrian accession to the European Communities (EC), for which he relied on the support of West Germany. Vranitzky moved more cautiously with regard to a possible Austrian EC membership. While the chancellor's attitude toward the CEE states was based on state decisions and the status quo, Mock was focused on humanitarian and cultural goals, despite being an anti-communist hardliner.[23]

In the end, Vienna proved to be accurate in its assessment of the interdependence and mutual interaction between *glasnost* and *perestroika* in the Soviet Union and the changes in the CEE countries, recognizing early Gorbachev's key role in the reform processes and the further opening of the CEE countries. That is why the stability of Gorbachev's government was seen as a top priority. In this regard, Austria's foreign policy was parallel to that of the Western powers. The reform movements in CEE were seen as a matter of realism rather than ideology, with the differences between the pioneering role of Poland and Hungary and the slower political changes in Bulgaria, East Germany, Czechoslovakia and Romania being evaluated dispassionately. The perception of the latter developments ranged from skepticism to disapproval. The Conference on Security and Cooperation in Europe (CSCE) process and especially the successor meetings in Vienna (1986–1989) offered an important stabilizing and conciliatory framework into which the dramatic upheavals could be placed.[24] The key way in which Austria intervened politically in the course of the events immediately preceding the fall of the Berlin Wall was through the symbolic cutting of the Iron Curtain and the assistance and support it gave to fleeing East German citizens. The Austro-Hungarian prologue in the summer of 1989 was decisive for the extreme speed that the developments in Germany took that autumn.[25]

23 Michael Gehler, "Paving Austria's Way to Brussels: Chancellor Franz Vranitzky (1986–1997): A Banker, Social Democrat and Pragmatic European Leader," *Journal of European Integration History* 18, no. 2 (2012): 159–182.

24 Matthias Peter and Hermann Wentker, eds., *Die KSZE im Ost-West-Konflikt: Internationale Politik und gesellschaftliche Transformation 1975–1990* (Berlin-Boston: De Gruyter, 2013).

25 Michael Gehler, "Austria, the Revolutions, and the Unification of Germany," in *The Revolutions*, ed. Mueller, Gehler and Suppan, 437–466; see also the chapter by Andrea Brait and Michael Gehler

11. Wait-and-see policy by the superpowers: international context, external influences, perceptions and reactions

While British prime minister Margaret Thatcher and French president François Mitterrand wanted the USSR to prevent Germany's unification in 1989, the general secretary of the Communist Party of the Soviet Union wanted the Western powers and the German chancellor to restrain the Americans from "interfering" in the CEE countries. The main concern of the US administration and George H.W. Bush was maintaining Gorbachev's reform policies as well as the political status quo in Europe. The wait-and-see attitude of the superpowers continued even when the CEE countries and the East Germans claimed a right of self-determination. When Hungary pulled down its barriers to Austria, thereby enabling East Germans to escape onward to West Germany, Moscow treated this as an affair that concerned only Hungary, the GDR, and the Federal Republic of Germany (FRG). When Polish communists made a power-sharing deal with the trade union movement Solidarity in the context of round-table discussions that contributed to the erosion of communism, this happened without Soviet interference.

Neither Moscow nor Washington stopped Kohl's moves toward German unification. Norman M. Naimark speaks of the "self-induced paralysis of the superpowers." This international context helped East German protesters and West German political decision makers alike to work to bring the postwar order in Germany to an end. Concerning the outcome of the revolutionary events, Naimark considers Gorbachev's role a decisive one. In the second half of the 1980s, his assurances that the CEE countries could make their own decisions supported the resulting political changes. *Perestroika* encouraged the opposition movements to articulate their claims. While it seems that Gorbachev did not have a policy concerning Germany, he nonetheless opposed the old "conservative" foreign policies such as the Brezhnev Doctrine. Due to various special interests, the su-

in this volume; Maximilian Graf, *Österreich und die DDR 1949–1990: Politik und Wirtschaft im Schatten der deutschen Teilung* (Vienna: VAW, 2016), 570–607; Id., "Österreich und das 'Verschwinden' der DDR: Ostdeutsche Perzeptionen im Kontext der Langzeitentwicklungen," in *Grenzöffnung 1989*, ed. Brait and Gehler, 221–242; Michael Gehler and Maximilian Graf, "Austria, German Unification, and European Integration: A Brief Historical Background," *Cold War International History Project/CWIHP Working Paper* 86 (March 2018), Wilson Center, Washington DC, www.wilsoncenter.org/publication/austria-german-unification-and-european-integration-brief-historical-background (quoted December 2018); Michael Gehler and Maximilian Graf, eds., *Österreich und die deutsche Frage: Vom Honecker-Besuch in Bonn bis zur Einheit 1987–1990* (Göttingen: Vandenhoeck & Ruprecht, 2018).

perpowers limited themselves to an observer's position and did not interfere. Naimark reflects that the congratulations they gave themselves about "1989" were "mostly about what they did not do rather than what they did."[26]

Philip Zelikow, a key US foreign policy and security advisor during the George H.W. Bush administration, spoke about "the generation of 1988," which included Ronald Reagan, George Shultz, Hans-Dietrich Genscher, and Margaret Thatcher. Despite having some differences, together with other experts they believed the Cold War had ended in 1988. This makes sense if one takes the INF-Treaty and the START talks into account. The end of the Cold War thus began with a European arms control agenda in 1987–1988, a period of transition from June to November 1989, and a phase of rapid changes from November 1989 to November 1990. When in December 1989 President George H.W. Bush assured the Europeans that US troops would remain in Europe as long as their presence was desired, he also frankly asserted that the United States would remain "a European power." Europe's leaders had nothing against such reassurances.[27]

French president François Mitterrand expressed hopes that European integration would reduce the influence of the United States and Russia in Europe, especially with regard to military questions. But the CEE governments thought NATO offered them a guarantee of security.[28] All of the following developments proved decisive: the reemergence of the German Question (from summer 1988 to autumn 1989); the attempts to keep the consequences of the fall of the Berlin Wall under control (from November 1989 to January 1990); the period of unification negotiations (from February to October 1990); and the debates concerning a new European balance after autumn 1990. By the summer of 1989, French politicians realized that the GDR system was eroding, but they still believed in an evolutionary development with a mid-range perspective. During talks in Latche on 4 January 1990, Mitterrand heard from Kohl that German unification would take years.

26 Norman M. Naimark, "The Superpowers and 1989 in Eastern Europe," in *The Revolutions*, ed. Mueller, Gehler and Suppan, 249–270.

27 Philip Zelikow and Condoleezza Rice, *Germany Unified and Europe Transformed: A Study in Statecraft* (Cambridge, MA: Harvard University Press, 1996); Philip Zelikow, "US Strategic Planning in 1989–90," in *The Revolutions*, ed. Mueller, Gehler and Suppan, 283–306; Christian F. Ostermann, "The United States and German Unification," in *Europa und die deutsche Einheit: Beobachtungen, Entscheidungen und Folgen*, ed. Michael Gehler and Maximilian Graf (Göttingen: Vandenhoeck & Ruprecht, 2017), 93–116.

28 Alexander von Plato, *Die Vereinigung Deutschlands – ein weltpolitisches Machtspiel: Bush, Kohl, Gorbatschow und die geheimen Moskauer Protokolle* (Bonn: Bundeszentrale für Politische Bildung, 2003); Id., "Opposition, Movements and Big Politics in the Reunification of Germany," in *The Revolutions*, ed. Mueller, Gehler and Suppan, 307–319.

Paris decided that Bonn should not pursue a unification policy alone: the EC should play an important role and the process should be "europeanized." Elisabeth Guigou, advisor to Mitterrand, emphasized the need to link unification with the deepening of European integration. It would allow immediate issues to be settled, but would also launch a new phase in the life of the European supranational community. According to Georges Saunier, the 1990 Charter of Paris was a "détente treaty" that paved the way for disarmament in a unified Europe. In view of future transatlantic relations, Paris considered NATO stability necessary in this period of European transition and thus that Germany should remain part of NATO. The evolution of NATO was a key element in the 1990 negotiations, with US policy aiming at its expansion. This was something France had opposed in former times and thus Paris was confronted with a dilemma. But due to the circumstances, France had to favor the revitalization of NATO. French policy, therefore, tried to introduce a reference to a future European defense structure within the formal framework of the alliance, although the German unification treaties did not contain any clauses providing for such structures. In 1990, it was too early for such concepts. The Quai d'Orsay had to accept that the other European partners were against any plans of this kind. Therefore NATO's development remained undecided. Mitterrand's policy followed a clear line that combined his own projects. Unified Germany was to be part of a unified Europe that was based on international agreements and organizations.[29]

29 Georges Saunier, "France, the East European Revolutions, and the Reunification of Germany," in *The Revolutions*, ed. Mueller, Gehler and Suppan, 385–401; Valérie Guérin-Sendelbach, *Frankreich und das vereinigte Deutschland: Interessen und Perzeptionen im Spannungsfeld* (Opladen: Leske + Budrich, 1999); Tilo Schabert, *Wie Weltgeschichte gemacht wird: Frankreich und die deutsche Einheit* (Stuttgart: Klett Cotta, 2002); Elke Bruck, *François Mitterrands Deutschlandbild – Perzeption und Politik im Spannungsfeld Deutschland-, Europa- und sicherheitspolitischer Entscheidungen 1989–1992* (Frankfurt/Main: Lang, 2003); Frédéric Bozo, *Mitterrand, la diplomatie française et la fin de la guerre froide*: *De Yalta à Maastricht* (Paris: Odile, 2005); Ulrich Lappenküper, *Mitterrand und Deutschland: Die enträtselte Sphinx* (Munich: Oldenbourg, 2011); Id., "Prekäres Vertrauen: François Mitterrand und Deutschland seit 1971," in *Diplomatie mit Gefühl: Vertrauen, Misstrauen und die Außenpolitik der Bundesrepublik Deutschland*, ed. Reinhild Kreis (Berlin: Oldenbourg, 2015), 83–96; Christian Wenkel, *Auf der Suche nach einem "anderen Deutschland": Das Verhältnis Frankreichs zur DDR im Spannungsfeld von Perzeption und Diplomatie* (Munich: De Gruyter, 2014), 497–504; Maurice Vaïsse and Christian Wenkel, eds., *La diplomatie française face à l'unification allemande. D'après des archives inédites* (Paris: Tallandier, 2011); Michèle Weinacher, ed., *L'Est et l'Ouest face à la chute du mur: Question de perspective* (Cergy Pontoise: CIRAC, 2013); Anne Kwaschik and Ulrich Pfeil, eds., *Die DDR in den deutsch-französischen Beziehungen / La RDA dans les relations franco-allemande* (Frankfurt am Main: Lang, 2013); Michael Gehler and Maximilian Graf, eds., *Europa und die deutsche Einheit: Beobachtungen, Entscheidungen und Folgen* (Göttingen: Vandenhoeck & Ruprecht, 2017).

Gorbachev's road toward German unity can be divided into three stages:

1. The retrospective approval for opening the Berlin Wall on 9 November 1989;
2. His consent, expressed in January-February 1990, with the two Germanys' right for self-determination regarding possible unification;
3. His acquiescence in May-July 1990 to Germany's proclaimed right to self-determination regarding a free choice of alliances.

Wolfgang Mueller argues that the Soviet leader made each of these decisions separately, a procedure that made each step easier to accept and, thus, influenced a final outcome that at the beginning had hardly been thinkable. Mueller demonstrates that the Soviet leadership communicated acceptance of the German right to self-determination with regard to German unification ten days earlier than hitherto thought, namely on 20 January 1990, in a conversation between the Soviet leader and the East German Foreign Minister Oskar Fischer.[30]

As a consequence of an internal party coup in November 1990, Margaret Thatcher had to give up her leadership of Britain's Conservatives and leave her post as prime minister. Her strict opposition to Germany's unification and European integration further contributed to her downfall. Thatcher's conservative, immobile, and narrow-minded policies concerning Germany and Europe also weakened the international position of Britain. The end of her career can be seen as a political tragedy: the anti-German Thatcher became a victim of Germany and its unification. Two months later, she lost her power entirely. After retiring, she attacked her successors from time to time and never forgave her party for its unceremonious farewell.[31]

30 Aleksandr Galkin and Anatolij Tschernjajew [i.e. Anatoly Chernyaev], eds., *Michail Gorbatschow und die deutsche Frage: Sowjetische Dokumente 1986–1991: Deutsche Ausgabe herausgegeben von Helmut Altrichter, Horst Möller und Jürgen Zarusky, kommentiert von Andreas Hilger* (Munich: Oldenbourg, 2001); Wolfgang Mueller, "The USSR and the Reunification of Germany, 1989–90," in *The Revolutions*, ed. Mueller, Gehler and Suppan, 321–353; Id., "'Die Lage gleitet uns aus den Händen': Motive und Faktoren in Gorbatschows Entscheidungsprozess zur Wiedervereinigung Deutschlands," *Zeitschrift des Forschungsverbundes SED-Staat* 39 (2016): 3–28; Hanns Jürgen Küsters, ed., *Der Zerfall des Sowjetimperiums und Deutschlands Wiedervereinigung: The Decline of the Soviet Empire and Germany's Reunification* (Cologne: Böhlau, 2016).

31 Klaus Larres, "Margaret Thatcher and German Unification Revisited," in *The Revolutions*, ed. Mueller, Gehler and Suppan, 355–384; Klaus-Reiner Jackisch, *Eisern gegen die Einheit: Margaret Thatcher und die deutsche Wiedervereinigung* (Frankfurt am Main: Lang, 2004); Dominik Geppert, "Isolation oder Einvernehmen? Großbritannien und die deutsche Einheit, 1989/90," *Geschichte in Wissenschaft und Unterricht* 67, no. 1/2 (2016): 5–22; Hinnerk Meyer, "Participation on limited cooperation – Großbritanniens schwierige Rolle im deutschen Einigungsprozess 1989–90," in *Europa und die deutsche Einheit*, ed. Gehler and Graf, 141–160.

12. Aftermath and consequences

What happened after 1989 with regard to economic integration and security policy? NATO's eastern enlargement was "successful" because it brought new democracies into the Euro-Atlantic partnership, but Stanley Sloan concedes that the process left a number of unanswered questions concerning the future of European security with regard to relations with Russia. Sloan draws attention to the fact that Russian officials used NATO's expansion toward the east as justification for their own foreign and domestic policies. The NATO and EU enlargement processes caused a double revolution: they stimulated first a new consciousness of European security and second, the democratization of former Soviet Bloc states and republics. Joining NATO was followed by active integration into the European Union: as former Warsaw Pact members joined the alliance, they became strong supporters of the transatlantic community within the EU. NATO enlargement therefore did not directly lead to a "new Cold War." Rather, political developments in Russia unconnected to NATO's enlargement process have turned out to be far more important to its relations with Europe than the acceptance of former Warsaw Pact allies and the Baltic republics by the transatlantic alliance. Moreover, NATO functions as a framework for coordinating responses to the defense and security needs of its new members.[32]

The EU's orientation to the east was accompanied with rather hesitant and grudging responses by the old members. The first round of new members – UK, Denmark, and Ireland (acceded in 1973) – had hardly been assimilated when the second round followed, with Greece (in 1981) and Spain and Portugal (in 1986) joining the then-European Communities. Following the German federal republic's absorption of the old GDR (in 1990), the third round was negotiated quickly, with Austria, Finland, and Sweden joining (in 1995), this causing nearly no problems. EU enlargement continued in 2004, after the EFTA states with the "return to Europe" (the so-called "big-bang" enlargement) of ten countries (mostly the Baltics, CEE, but also including Cyprus and Malta), which was combined with their peaceful transitions.[33]

32 Stanley Sloan, "NATO Enlargement in the Beginning: An American Perspective," in *The Revolutions*, ed. Mueller, Gehler and Suppan, 525–552; Michael Gehler, "Revolutionäre Ereignisse und geoökonomisch-strategische Ergebnisse: Die EU- und NATO 'Osterweiterungen' 1989–2015 im Vergleich," Zentrum für Europäische Integrationsforschung Discussion Paper C 239 (Bonn, 2017).

33 Jürgen Elvert, "A fool's game or a comedy of errors?," in *European Union Enlargement: A Comparative History*, ed. Wolfram Kaiser and Jürgen Elvert (London - New York: Routledge, 2004), 189–208.

John O'Brennan has shown that there was and is an ongoing process of unfinished enlargement, with accessions of new member states taking place although the assimilation of older members remains unconsolidated. But the enlargement to the east has differed significantly from previous rounds in terms of size, scale, and diversity. The year 1989 was also a starting point for changes in Western Europe, especially for the transformation of the EC into the EU, with the events of this year contributing to a revolution within the old European Communities. The Maastricht Treaty, signed in 1992, was a direct outcome of the revolutions of 1989 as well as a response to the unification of Germany.[34]

The EU's eastern enlargement has been tied to democratization, Europeanization, and modernization.[35] Following the initial political changes, however, euphoria and idealism disappeared; disappointment and a new realism took their place. This was a consequence of expectations that were too high, as well as the challenges of intra-state and inter-state supranational negotiations. With regard to new candidates from the Western Balkans, the controversies and struggles concerning widening the EU are back on the political agenda. The establishment of new institutional structures shows that there has been a successful adaptation of existing EU modes of decision-making, but the process has remained partial and incomplete in both a geographic and a normative sense. The democratic shortcomings of the CEE countries and of the EU itself have made it difficult to progress more quickly. The EU was and is confronted with a double challenge: on the one hand, serving as a welfare-boosting entity and on the other, a global geopolitical power. It has not been possible to reach both goals at the same time, which has led to the failure of consolidating the gains of the "1989 moment."[36]

34 Michael Gehler, *Europa: Ideen – Institutionen – Vereinigung – Zusammenhalt* (Reinbek-Hamburg: Lau Verlag, 2018), 325–359, here 349.

35 John O'Brennan (with a foreword by Pat Cox), *The Eastern Enlargement of the European Union* (New York: Routledge, 2006).

36 John O'Brennan, "EU Enlargement, 1989–2009," in *The Revolutions*, ed. Mueller, Gehler and Suppan, 553–571.

The Fall of Communism and the Impact of Christian Democracy, 1989–1990

The principal idea behind this volume is to marry the story of the revolutions of 1989 to that of the twentieth-century history of the European political family known as Christian Democracy. For this reason, the book includes contributions about Christian Democracy in a broader international context, which in turn frame both the internal stories of Christian Democracy in the decommunizing CEE and the transnational story of Western Europe's attempt to animate and shape the Christian Democracy of Central and Eastern Europe.

Three key questions guide this book, having been clearly formulated first at an international conference in Vienna in 2016 that has served as the point of departure for this project. The questions are as follows:

1. What was Christian Democrats' perception of Central and Eastern Europe before and after 1989?
2. What ideas, plans, and visions did Christian Democrats develop for the future of Europe before and after 1989?
3. What were the outcomes of Christian Democratic efforts and initiatives? Piotr H. Kosicki will return to these questions in his Conclusion at the end of this volume.

As previous studies of European Christian Democracy have shown, no clear and strong continuity existed between the Roman Catholic parties of interwar Europe and the post-World War II parties self-styled as Christian Democratic. The totalitarian experiences of Fascism, Nazism, and Stalinism, as well as the Second World War and the prevailing domestic socioeconomic, political, and external circumstances of the Cold War, imposed conditions under which Christian Democracy – depending upon geography – could or could not thrive in a divided continental Europe.[37] This happened due to the strong US economic, political, and military aid for

37 Vladimir Tismăneanu, ed., *Stalinism Revisited: The Establishment of Communist Regimes in East-Central Europe* (Budapest: CEU Press, 2009); Id., *The Devil in History: Communism, Fascism, and Some Lessons of the Twentieth Century* (Berkeley: University of California Press, 2012); "Introduction" to *Christian Democracy in Europe since 1945*, vol. 2, ed. Michael Gehler and Wolfram Kaiser (London - New York: Routledge, 2004), 1–9, here 7.

Western Europe[38] while this American support was impossible for Central and Eastern Europe.[39]

After the Second World War, Christian Democrats held a dominant position in Western Europe. Starting in the 1970s, and especially after 1989, the structural weaknesses of Christian Democracy continued because of the loss of its party-political core social, structural, and ideological strengths. These included, for example, previously cohesive and slowly-disappearing Catholic milieus, the diminishing significance of anti-communism following the Cold War's end, and Christian Democracy's deconfessionalization and consequent decrease in vitality in the form of "people's parties" functioning in many EC/EU member states.

Meanwhile, Christian Democratic parties that found themselves in the aftermath of the Second World War under Soviet military occupation and/or nascent communist dictatorship, as in Poland, Hungary, or Czechoslovakia, confronted with an omnipotent party, struggled to survive – and in most cases did not. By 1945, they had to position themselves under the constant threat of cooptation or annihilation by monopolistic Soviet-backed communist parties. The Central and Eastern European peoples and their societies suffered from their non-participation in Western European integration during the Cold War and its socializing effects. To the extent that Christian Democrats survived in CEE – with the exceptions of Czechoslovakia and East Germany, these countries' Christian Democratic *parties* survived only in exile, not in the homeland – their exclusion from these ongoing developments produced a total asymmetry in the domains of organization and ideology, not to mention an insurmountable gap in experiential understanding, between many of those parties and their Western European sister parties after 1989–1990.[40]

This book offers three sections followed by a conclusion linking all of the chapters. The *first section* deals with Christian Democracy in the international system, examining four international organizations that helped to

38 John Gimbel, *The Origins of the Marshall Plan* (Stanford, CA: Stanford University Press, 1976); Othmar Nikola Haberl and Lutz Niethammer, eds., *Der Marshall-Plan und die europäische Linke* (Frankfurt am Main: Lang, 1986); Michael J. Hogan, *The Marshall Plan: America, Britain, and the Reconstruction of Western Europe 1947–1952* (Cambridge: Cambridge University Press, 1987) (for Western European Christian Democrats, a study of the impact of the Marshall Plan is missing); Charles S. Maier and Günter Bischof, eds., *Deutschland und der Marshall-Plan* (Baden-Baden: Nomos, 1992).

39 For the US reactions and policies, see also László Borhi, *Dealing with Dictators: The United States, Hungary, and East Central Europe, 1942–1989* (Bloomington: Indiana University Press, 2016).

40 "Introduction," in *Christian Democracy in Europe since 1945*, ed. Gehler and Kaiser, 6; Anton Pelinka, "European Christian Democracy in Comparison," in *Christian Democracy in Europe since 1945*, ed. Gehler and Kaiser, 199.

create the framework for Christian Democratic action just before, during, and after 1989.

Kim Christiaens focuses on the World Confederation of Labor (WCL), the globalization of Poland's Solidarity trade-union movement during the 1980s, and the failure of the third way concept. He makes clear that dissidents' struggles in the CEE countries and their support from Western Europe were associated with a "return to Europe." And yet the WCL and the International Confederation of Free Trade Unions (ICFTU) concentrated their efforts on behalf of *Solidarność* not only on a European level. Christiaens notes that problems facing the Global South, rather than Europe, ran as dominant themes within the relationship between the WCL and *Solidarność*, but Christian trade unions tended to globalize the independent Polish trade union in real as well as imagined terms, and were especially interested in forging connections between the *Solidarność* program and "Third World" issues. These conversations came at a time in the 1970s and 1980s when Christian trade unionism faced a severe identity crisis in Western Europe, while Christian Democracy competed with Social Democracy and the Socialist International (SI) for influence in the transitions to democracy across the Global South, and especially in Latin America.

As far as the WCL's support for *Solidarność* is concerned, Christiaens identifies "a surprisingly awkward issue, especially due to their focus on détente and the Third World and their competition with Social Democracy and Cold War hawks à la Reagan and Thatcher." Building up connections with the "Third World" provided a means to position Solidarity within the vanguard of efforts at a "third way" that transcended the logic of the Cold War. According to Christiaens, this inspired the WCL to stress the connection with what were called "red dictatorships" in the Global South, such as Cuba and Sandinista Nicaragua, as well as with right-wing regimes, such as those in Chile and South Africa. The question of how to link support for *Solidarność* to campaigns for democracy and human rights in the "Third World" was one of the major conflicts between the Polish trade union and the WCL. Christiaens concludes: "Nevertheless, these connections in real and imagined terms with the Third World reveal how the end of the Cold War was not only forged by Eastern Europe integrating into the West, but also suggest how the 'opening of the East' in the 1980s was also related to an opening towards the Global South."

Andrea Brait and Michael Gehler detail the importance of the Third Follow-Up Conference on Security and Cooperation in Europe (CSCE) (after conferences in Belgrade and Madrid), which took place in Vienna in the waning years of the Cold War (from 1986 to 1989). They focus specifically on the role of Austria's foreign minister, the Christian Democrat Alois Mock, who announced the expansion of his country's role as a mediator between the two camps in Europe. At first, Mock was convinced of the significance of the Neutral and Non-Aligned (N+N) states and the relevance of the final document of the follow-up meeting in Vienna on 15 January 1989. When Mock met Hungarian foreign minister Gyula Horn on 27 June 1989 to cut down barbed wire along the iron curtain – a symbol of the Cold War – at the Hungarian-Austrian border – he stressed, in a conversation with his counterpart, the pragmatic role played by the N+N states within the framework of the CSCE process which would help to find a consensus in situations of crisis because they would act as mediators.[41] Mock was also very clear on the differentiated approach concerning the positive reforms in Poland, Hungary, and the USSR, as well as Austria's support for this course. Meanwhile, he reacted hesitantly and skeptically towards the political developments in Bulgaria, Czechoslovakia, the GDR, and Romania in 1989. In Mock's political assessment, the idea of a "common European house" proposed by Mikhail Gorbachev could be the future framework for peaceful and cooperative development in Europe, including the CSCE process. Mock, who was also convinced of the importance of cross-border cooperation, minority protection, and the right of self-determination in Europe consequently praised *glasnost* and *perestroika* and their role in inspiring historical developments in the CEE countries.

In the book's third chapter, Michael Gehler and Johannes Schönner present the designs of the European Democrat Union (EDU) to shape developments behind the Iron Curtain in the final years of communism's rule. The first Christian Democratic transnational party platform was the *Nouvelles Équipes Internationales* (NEI), which was formed in 1947, up through its renaming and transformation into the European Union of Christian Democrats (EUCD) in 1965.[42] The German parties, the *Christliche Demokratische Union* (CDU) and the *Christlich Soziale Union* (CSU), as well as the *Österreichische Volkspartei* (ÖVP), stood broadly for a pro-European conservative orientation. The goal of the EDU, founded in Salzburg in 1978, was to create a counterpart to the European People's Party (EPP)

41 Schmidt-Schweizer, "Die Öffnung der ungarischen Westgrenze für die DDR-Bürger im Sommer 1989"; Id., "Motive im Vorfeld der Demontage des 'Eisernen Vorhangs.'"

42 Michael Gehler and Wolfram Kaiser, eds., *Transnationale Parteienkooperation der europäischen Christdemokraten: Dokumente 1945–1965 / Coopération transnationale des partis démocrates-chrétiens en Europe: Documents 1945–1965 / Transnational Party Cooperation of European Christian Democrats: Documents 1945–1965* (Munich: Saur, 2004).

that had been brought into being as a faction of Christian Democrats in the European Parliament, that would nonetheless broaden the base beyond the European Parliament and beyond the Christian Democratic family, strictly understood.

The EDU combined many Christian Democratic parties from the European Communities as well as Christian Democratic and conservative parties from other European countries. This organization was therefore ideally placed to play a crucial role in brokering transnational ties among European non-governmental and non-state actors, which in turn laid the groundwork for the EDU to open a door for Western European Christian Democrats to exercise influence before, during, and after the revolutionary events of 1989. In the sense of political-network research and networking studies, a player such as the EDU needs to be considered, also to better understand the diplomatic and political decision-making processes of a range of European political actors during this crucial year. The transnational EPP federation of Christian Democratic member parties in the European Communities, founded in 1976, clearly differed from earlier forms of Christian Democratic cooperation because it became a faction of the European Parliament. Additionally, it was the intention of the CDU and the CSU to include British Conservatives and French civil groups in the EDU party alliance, but they ran into a categorical rejection by the Italian, Belgian, and Dutch parties. Unlike the EPP, the EDU embraced these parties as well.[43]

Before 1989, Christian Democratic and conservative parties united under the aegis of the EDU acted at the individual and bilateral levels vis-à-vis Central and Eastern Europe. In 1989, for the first time, the EDU was able to adopt a pan-European policy, which allowed freely-chosen Christian Democratic parties a previously unknown degree of freedom with parties and peoples of the CEE countries. Europeans were now able directly to make European party politics. The EDU spoke for Christian Democratic and conservative parties in Western, Central, and Eastern Europe. A stronger coordination started in the spring and summer of 1989. At the time of Hungary's transition to democracy, the EDU provided assistance

43 Thomas Jansen, *Die Entstehung einer Europäischen Partei: Vorgeschichte, Gründung und Entwicklung der EVP* (Bonn: Europa Union Verlag, 1996); see also Michael Gehler et al., eds., *Mitgestalter Europas: Transnationalismus und Parteiennetzwerke europäischer Christdemokraten und Konservativer in historischer Erfahrung* (St. Augustin-Berlin: KAS, 2013); Id., *Transnationale Parteienkooperation der europäischen Christdemokraten und Konservativen: Coopération transnationale des partis démocrates-chrétiens et conservateurs en Europe: Dokumente 1965–1979*, 2 vols. (Berlin-Boston: De Gruyter, 2018).

to its Hungarian supporters. In June 1989, the European Committee of the EDU met in Budapest.[44]

The EDU set up fact-finding missions to Hungary, Poland, and the Soviet Union; searched for candidates for EDU membership and the founding of future Christian and conservative political parties; looked for forms of institutionalized relations, coordinated future EDU members in the various European institutions, especially the Council of Europe, and also developed guidelines for economic and technical assistance programs for the CEE countries. The observations, perceptions, and judgments of the political developments in the CEE countries by EDU groups were dependent on the fast-paced revolutionary events, including incalculable and unpredictable outcomes.

The *second section* of this book focuses on movement-building efforts across the Iron Curtain. In the book's fourth chapter, Thomas Gronier focuses on the Community of Taizé. Despite the relatively modest role that his publications and speeches played in European public life before 1989, Brother Roger's impact on European cooperation was remarkable. The bonds formed by Taizé with Central and Eastern European bishops, as well as the trips of some of the brothers from Taizé behind the Iron Curtain in the 1960s, constituted elements for the movement's better knowledge of "the other Europe." Cold War or no, the Taizé community assured the creation of discreet and informal networks in almost every communist country in Eastern Europe. The revolutions of 1989 subsequently drove Brother Roger to become even more explicit about Europe. In May 1989, the Charlemagne Prize jury lauded Brother Roger on his community's pursuit of the "spiritual tradition of Europe as it was shaped by Benedict of Nursia and Francis of Assisi." In his response, Brother Roger paid homage to Robert Schuman, who "sought what could be the soul of Europe" and noted that, "in order to undergo a healing of its wounds, Europe needs to be built not from juxtaposed states but from ones that are closely united, one to the other."

In the next chapter, Helmut Wohnout focuses on contacts established by the Austrian People's Party (ÖVP) with political opposition groups in Central and Eastern Europe up to and including the revolutions of 1989. This process of forging contacts played out at various levels. Wohnout underlines that these attempts resulted more from single individuals in the party rather than as a result of a clearly-intended party-political strate-

44 Jenö Gergely, "Towards the One-party State: Nascent Christian Democracy in Hungary," in *Christian Democracy in Europe since 1945*, ed. Gehler and Kaiser, 155–172, here 168.

gy. Günther Engelmayer's activities via the Association of Christian Trade Unions (Fraktion Christlicher Gewerkschafter/FCG) and Erhard Busek's civil society initiatives operated separately from the EDU, as Johannes Schönner and I show in our contribution (see section I). Wohnout points out that these individuals also profited from a range of favorable circumstances. In contrast to EC and NATO member states, neutral Austria and "the spirit of Vienna" produced the climate necessary for international meetings in the physical vicinity of the Iron Curtain. Members of the ÖVP in Austria paved the way for establishing contact with dissidents and opposition groups in the Czechoslovak Socialist Republic as well as in the People's Republics of Poland and Hungary.

But the ÖVP's political influence was limited, especially in its years of opposition (1970–1986). In the years before 1989, this Austrian political party was not as financially and politically strong as the CDU in the FRG, and yet the Austrians found themselves in a much better geostrategic position with regard to prospects for penetrating behind the Iron Curtain. Austria and the ÖVP could offer humanitarian, ideological, and moral support to political activists in CEE. When Alois Mock became Minister of Foreign Affairs, he was able to strengthen his ambitions towards Central and Eastern Europe, but entry into the EC became the main goal of Austrian foreign policy when the country applied for membership on 17 July 1989. Mock was and remained a convinced Christian Democrat, strongly opposed to the illusion of "really existing socialism" because of its long-standing discrimination against free religious exercise by Christians in the communist world. Wohnout also stresses that Mock wanted to distance himself from the Austrian Socialists cooperating with the socialist regimes in Central and Eastern Europe. There appeared the new promise of a fallow field for the founding of Christian Democratic movements and political parties could be founded: in Hungary, Slovenia, and Slovakia. In Poland, contacts existed with the Solidarity opposition, but no links could be established at a party level. Wohnout makes clear that the 1989 euphoria did not last very long.

From the very start of his political career, the German CDU leader Helmut Kohl was opposed to communism, not only in the form taken within the GDR, but as a universal principle. He was convinced of the superiority of liberal democracy and the social market economy. As Alexander Brakel writes in the book's sixth chapter, Kohl did more than show sympathy towards the peaceful revolutionary events in Central and Eastern Europe and the existence of new political parties of similar ideological orientations. In fact, Kohl tried to support them financially and politically, and he achieved a great measure of success. The CDU was able to establish contact with almost all potential political allies, as Brakel shows. In some cases, a promising political partner could be started: this was notably true with regard to József Antall in Budapest. Kohl's CDU gave the Hungarian Christian Democrat full support; tragically, Antall died much too young in 1993 (aged 61 years).

Branches of the financially strong Konrad Adenauer Foundation (KAS) were opened in all of the CEE countries, yielding a transmission belt for incoming political and material support for new Christian Democratic parties. In that way, the Foundation was able to influence political development directly and substantially. Like the ÖVP, the CDU's activities – despite KAS's potential – could also not really change the unstable party political structures in Poland, Hungary, and Czechoslovakia. After a minor Christian Democratic spring in 1989–1990, no real Christian Democratic summer followed in the 1990s. Contrary to what Kohl thought in 1989–1990, these new Christian Democratic parties were "few and far between," as Brakel notes.

Giovanni Mario Ceci shows us in Chapter 7 that Italy's Democrazia Cristiana (DC) was aware of the effects of the fall of the Berlin Wall and its consequences for the Italian political system. The political changes were welcomed and viewed positively, but they also represented the end of the geopolitical era inaugurated by the Yalta Conference of February 1945. Leading Italian Christian Democrats were sure that these changes could be handled by preserving the continuity of the DC as an integral element of the Italian political-party system. They believed that, in contrast to the Italian Communists, they did not need to seek a new political identity or program in the face of communism's collapse in CEE. In reality, however, a new era had started. The Italian Christian Democratic Party came to an end.

The *third section* of this book covers homegrown Catholic politics and the rise and fall of Christian Democracy in the CEE countries across the 1989 divide. The Czechoslovak People's Party (ČSL) became a bloc party in the communist single-party system that followed the infamous Prague coup of February 1948. Its function was similar to that of the PAX group in Poland – to attempt to discipline the Catholic hierarchy while maintaining an allure of political Catholicism (in reality, coopted and compromised) in a communist system. Christian political movements – in the cases of the East German CDU and the ČSL actually rising to the level of political parties – helped to build up a facade of tolerance and pluralism behind which the communist dictatorship could hide its true workings. Yet this was only the first chapter, and not the final word, on the trajectory of Christian Democracy in Central and Eastern Europe after the Second World War. In the end, Christian Democratic parties would fail "fair and square" in the post-communist period, without constraint from Moscow.

In August 1989, Tadeusz Mazowiecki became the first non-communist prime minister in Central and Eastern Europe since the war. He was a long-standing and active member of Poland's Catholic Intelligentsia Club movement (KIK) in Warsaw and former long-time editor of the Catholic journal *Więź* (*Bond*). The new government did not have much maneuvering room because the USSR still existed, had stationed its troops in Poland, and Polish Communists retained national security posts within the government. Still, the Mazowiecki government had possibilities for improving the economy. Leszek Balcerowicz, deputy prime minister advised by American and Western European experts, designed an economic recovery plan, which was supposed to reduce Polish debts, control inflation and introduce a market economy.[45]

Neither the National Christian Union (ZChN) led by Wiesław Chrzanowski, who had been a member of the National Party both before and after the war, nor the Center Party (PC) really went in a recognizably Christian Democratic direction. The only "real" Christian Democrats appearing in Poland in the 1990s belonged to older generations, who had spent the Cold War in exile working in Christian Democratic movements representing a version of Central and Eastern Europe frozen in time from the late 1940s. Having joined the NEI and later the EUCD, the survivors from among the Christian Labor Party (SP) had then reimported themselves to Poland in 1989.[46]

Piotr H. Kosicki focuses on a Christian Democrat who ultimately chose to reject the label. This man is the aforementioned Tadeusz Mazowiecki, who also represents the horizon line of a distinctively Catholic politics in a democratic Poland. In the time of Gorbachev's loosening power over the

45 See also Piotr H. Kosicki, "After 1989: The Life and Death of the Catholic Third Way," *TLS - Times Literary Supplement*, 13 December 2013: 13–15.

46 Dealing with the fate of these exiles and their failure to re-enter Polish political life in the 1980s (paired with their substantial impact in the West and the Third World): Piotr H. Kosicki and Sławomir Łukasiewicz, eds., *Christian Democracy across the Iron Curtain: Europe Redefined* (London: Palgrave Macmillan, 2018) – important on this topic are the chapters by Paweł Ziętara ("Christian Democrats across the Iron Curtain," 177–220), Stanisław Gebhardt ("The Christian Democratic Union of Central Europe," 411–424) and Aleks Szczerbiak and Tim Bale ("Explaining the Absence of Christian Democracy in Contemporary Poland," 343–410).

CEE countries, Mazowiecki was at crossroads in his ideological and political thinking. The life-long Catholic socialist remained loyal to *Solidarność*, and when the Polish communists agreed to round-table discussions, Mazowiecki was Lech Wałęsa's first choice to negotiate with them. Although the round-table negotiations had included economists who shared Mazowiecki's "third way" sympathies, he chose another direction for his governmental policies. Lacking any economic training, he relied on the advice of close collaborators from *Solidarność*, who did not share his background in Catholic philosophy. Rather than looking to Emmanuel Mounier or Jacques Maritain, his economic advisor was Waldemar Kuczyński, who had spent most of the 1980s in Paris and who was in favor of a more controlled, liberal economic policy. When Mazowiecki was confronted with West German Christian Democrats' expectations, he replied, "I am a Christian and a democrat, but not a Christian Democrat." A former anti-communist dissident with a life-long commitment to "Catholic socialism," Mazowiecki broke with this aim when he became head of government, choosing neither Catholic socialism nor Christian Democracy, but instead a policy of reluctant, yet unrepentant, economic liberalism.

Chapter 9, written by Anton Pelinka, concerns Hungary and its political realignment in the era of the Christian Democratic statesman József Antall's ascent to head of government. In Hungary as in Poland, the peaceful establishment of a multi-party constitutional parliamentary democracy was achieved with round-table negotiations between reform communists and the democratically-oriented opposition.[47] Political parties in Hungary began to form in 1987. Jenö Gergely mentioned two new types that had developed out of the existing opposition movements: the League of Young Democrats (Fidesz), the Hungarian Democratic Forum (MDF), and the Alliance of Free Democrats (SZDSZ), on the one hand, and the re-established parties that had existed from 1945 to 1949, on the other. The latter included the Independent Smallholders' Party (FKgP), the Christian Democratic People's Party (KDNP), and the Hungarian Freedom Party (MSZP).

All of these "regime-change" parties held anti-communist programs. MDF, FKgP, and KDNP were situated at the center-right of the political spectrum. The social-liberal SZDSZ and the formerly radical-liberal Fidesz defined themselves as parties of the "political center." The left wing of the political landscape was occupied by the MSZP, which had been established by reform communists. Their goal was to become a social democratic party. The center-right parties were nationalist, although they wished

47 Schmidt-Schweizer, "Die politischen Auseinandersetzungen am 'Nationalen Runden Tisch.'"

for Hungary to become a member of the European Communities. These parties tended more towards conservative, traditional values and private ownership.

The first party to establish itself in September 1987 was the MDF of József Antall, as a democratic people's party encompassing populist, liberal, and Christian Democratic factions. As Gergely argues, the weakest of these wings within the party was Christian Democracy, "which made no attempt to define itself at an ideological level." The FKgP, re-established in November 1988 was a right-wing, anti-liberal party of special interests, focused on the defense of smallholding farmers. In spite of its slogan "God, Fatherland, and Family," the party had no links either to the churches or with post-1945 European Christian Democracy. In contrast, the KDNP, launched in September 1989 as the last of six new political parties, explicitly named itself a "Christian Democratic Party." Its ideology was based on modern European Christian Democracy, invoking conservative ideals and anchoring itself in firm opposition to communism and liberalism. The KDNP was committed to constitutional democracy, desiring the establishment of a social market economy. It had close links to the Catholic Church.[48]

The MDF won the first free elections held in 1990. In order to ensure governability, a pact was concluded with the second-largest party, the opposition social-liberal SZDSZ. The KDNP was the smallest parliamentary party, with just 22 seats. The government consisted of a coalition of the MDF, the FKgP, and the KDNP. Each of the coalition partners espoused Christian values, the establishment of national independence connected with the withdrawal of the occupying Soviet troops in June 1991, the creation of a democratic state based on the rule of law, and the reintroduction of a market economy. Nevertheless, the new center-right governing coalition failed to pursue Christian Democratic policies. In the MDF, the party's liberal wing determined policy, while the FKgP pursued conservative agrarian interests without any coherent ideology. For its part, while the KDNP stressed "pure" Christian Democratic principles and values, it was unable to translate them into the language of practical everyday politics and thus became the "grey party" of Hungarian politics.[49] According to Gergely, many reasons hindered the political success of Christian Democracy in Hungary:

48 Gergely, "Towards the One-Party State," 166–168.
49 Ibid., 168–169.

> Its politicians failed to account adequately for the effects of 50 years of atheistic, anti-ecclesiastical and anti-religious "education" and propaganda after 1945 – as a result of which the main body of Hungarian society had lost interest in religion. The Christian faithful had no knowledge of Christian Democracy and had grown accustomed to political passivity. A direct role of the churches was not necessarily helpful for the center-right parties as a whole, or for the KDNP. Prime Minister Antall and his supporters espoused a liberal Catholicism. The KDNP, on the other hand, was too much bound by its own traditions and unable to break away from its old habits. It was almost as if the party had shut itself away in the "ghetto" of rural Catholicism under the close control of the Church leadership. The voters gained the impression that the KDNP was a "clerical" rather than a modern Christian Democratic people's party.[50]

Unlike in Hungary, in Czechoslovakia the political transition played out in a mere matter of days in November 1989, and pluralistic structures arose in post-communist Czechoslovakia. The dominant civil movements until the first elections were the Czech "People's Forum" (OF) and the Slovak "Public against Violence" (VPN), whose success lay in not being political parties classically understood. The old bloc parties continued to exist in the form of the People's Party, which had succeeded in retaining a portion of its members and long-standing voters over four decades of socialism, but it did not have an image beyond a relatively small circle of Christian followers. It also had the reputation of being especially subservient to the communist regime.

The most serious conflicts within the People's Party were caused by the process of its transformation from a bloc party to an electoral party and the attendant distancing from policies and leading figures who had preceded November 1989. These conflicts led to factionalization among the deputies, with some compromising themselves by collaborating with the former state-security apparatus to form the "Christian-Social Union" in 1992. While political Catholicism again became an important factor in Slovak Politics, the Czechoslovak People's Party's (ČSL) election results have remained around four to six percent since 1990. The Party has joined with the Christian Democratic Union (KDU), a group that had evolved out of the Charter 77 wing, to form the ČSL-KDU, becoming part of all governmental coalitions up until the end of the conservative Václav Klaus's government in 1997. The party presented itself as conservative and a driving force in the transition to capitalism, but with a social conscience. As a

50 Gergely, "Towards the One-Party State", 169.

Christian party, it saw itself as especially committed to the Catholic Church and supported its claims in negotiations for restitution.[51]

Ladislav Cabada focuses on Christian Democratic political actors both in the late Czechoslovak Communist regime and during the Velvet Revolution of November 1989. He argues that, after the transition period, the history of Christian Democratic party politics in the Czech Republic was not a success story. The attempt to establish a new political party (KDS) after 1989 failed, although at least it was partially transformed into the Civic Democratic Party (ODS). The reasons for its limited success – according to Cabada – should be sought not only in the decades before 1989, but also before the Prague Coup of 1948. The Bohemian (Czech) experience was very distinct in comparison to the Moravian and Slovak ones. The Catholic Church in Bohemia did not succeed in carrying out any discernible grass-roots activism for larger cross-sections of society. Both the Catholic clergy and the Christians within Charter 77 failed to develop strategies that would address broader social groups. Meanwhile, the Catholic Church, which in any case was no strong supporter of Christian Democratic party-building, was never able to gain ground among the populations of Bohemia and Moravia.

In the book's eleventh chapter, Artūras Svarauskas analyzes the restoration of the Christian Democratic political tradition in Lithuania in 1989–1990 relative to what had existed prior to Lithuania's capture by the USSR in 1940. In the late 1980s, Lithuanian Christian Democrats acted in an unconventional way relative to their Christian Democratic counterparts across the continent. Namely, they did not participate in public political activities in the name of a party, but instead supported the Lithuanian national movement born in opposition to the USSR, the so-called *Sajūdis* (Lithuanian for 'movement'). No prominent political leaders came to the fore in the party. Instead, in a literal sense it became a people's party after the announcement of independence from the USSR via peaceful negotiation and compromise. This marked a clear difference from the acting and thinking of the interwar period, when Christian Democrats had been one of Lithuania's dominant political forces. After the declaration of independence in 1991, the Christian Democrats merged with the conservatives.

In the book's final chapter, Sławomir Łukasiewicz focuses on 1989 and the discontinuities of Cold War cooperation among Christian Democratic emigrés from CEE countries, who suffered from a lack of unified represen-

51 Christiane Brenner, "A Missed Opportunity to Oppose State Socialism? The People's Party in Czechoslovakia," in Gehler and Kaiser (eds.), *Christian Democracy in Europe since 1945*, 185–186.

tation. The exiles' disunity had long-lasting consequences when the EPP came looking at the turn of the 1980s and 1990s for trustworthy partners in the CEE countries. Very often they could not find real Christian Democrats or conservative politicians. As far as twenty-first-century Poland's Civic Platform was concerned, for example, only individuals could consider themselves Christian Democrats (not the party as a whole) and could thereby become a part of the EPP. Łukasiewicz shows that the EU's eastern enlargement in 2004 and the Europeanization of CEE parties also had a reciprocal impact on their Western European counterparts. The dividing lines between Western and Central or Eastern Christian Democrats were then reproduced within the European Union itself. Łukasiewicz speaks specifically about missed opportunities in the 1990s: "The heritage of specific Central European cleavages is still very powerful, and without understanding of this no real change can be made."

The analyses undertaken in this volume will shed light on the real prerequisites for Christian Democratic parties. Not Christianity and the Christian churches, but Roman Catholicism and the Catholic Church became the base from which Europe's Christian Democratic parties were able to develop after the Second World War. Christian Democratic parties were mainly a phenomenon of predominantly Catholic countries. In Western Europe, Italy, France, Belgium and Austria fulfilled these necessary conditions.[52]

The Christian Democratic potential of Poland, Czechoslovakia, and Hungary – likewise predominantly Catholic countries – is front and center in this book. Christian Democratic parties were, however, also a phenomenon of the Catholic protest against Leonid Brezhnev's vision of "really existing socialism." After the end of communism in CEE, Christian Democratic people's parties did not develop or play a major role in these countries. And yet, this book shows that Christian Democracy played an important, and heretofore unexamined, role in the fall of communism across Europe in 1989–1990, even though it had only minimal long-lasting impact on the party-political developments in the CEE countries.

52 Pelinka, "European Christian Democracy in Comparison," 204–205.

SECTION I

CHRISTIAN DEMOCRACY IN THE INTERNATIONAL SYSTEM: INTERNATIONAL INSTITUTIONS AND THE GROUNDWORK FOR 1989

1

THE FAILURE OF A THIRD WAY

The World Confederation of Labor and the Globalization of Solidarność during the 1980s

Kim Christiaens

Christian Democracy has not fared well in the history of East-West contacts during the Cold War, nor has it received much attention in accounts of solidarity campaigns on behalf of Eastern European dissidents.[1] Obviously, this can be related to the absence of a strong Christian Democratic tradition or successful party in post-communist Europe.[2] More generally, Christian Democratic internationalism has been regarded as relatively weakly developed in organizational and ideological terms, especially in comparison with its Social Democratic or communist counterparts.[3] By and large, mainstream accounts of international campaigns developed on behalf of dissidents have been dominated by the juxtaposition between right- and left-wing support. On the one hand, there was the public and covert support from the United States and its allied governments and

1 For key exceptions, see, e.g., Piotr H. Kosicki, *Catholics on the Barricades: Poland, France, and "Revolution," 1891–1956* (New Haven, CT: Yale University Press, 2018); Piotr H. Kosicki and Sławomir Łukasiewicz, eds., *Christian Democracy across the Iron Curtain: Europe Redefined* (London: Palgrave Macmillan, 2018); Wolfram Kaiser, *Christian Democracy and the Origins of European Union* (Cambridge: Cambridge University Press, 2007).

2 Tim Bale and Aleks Szczerbiak, "Why is there no Christian Democracy in Poland – and Why should We Care", *Party Politics* 14, no. 4 (2008): 479–500; Aleks Szczerbiak and Tim Bale, "Explaining the Absence of Christian Democracy in Contemporary Poland," in *Christian Democracy across the Iron Curtain*, ed. Kosicki and Łukasiewicz, 343–407.

3 Paolo Acanfora, "Christian Democratic Internationalism: The Nouvelles Équipes Internationales and the Geneva Circles between European Unification and Religious Identity, 1947–1954," *Contemporary European History* 24, no. 3 (2015): 375–391.

movements, which funded dissident activities.[4] On the other, there was the Western European left's support for human rights and democratization in Eastern Europe. The crushing of the Hungarian revolution in 1956 and the curtailing of the Prague Spring in 1968, for instance, have above all been remembered as turning points for the European left – communists and Social Democrats alike.[5] Their impact on Christian Democratic movements as well as the role the latter played in international support networks on behalf of Eastern European dissidents have been far less researched – beyond a number of studies on the role of Christian Democratic parties and party foundations in the transitions to democracy in post-communist Europe.[6]

Yet, in the 1980s, Christian Democratic parties and trade union movements presented themselves as active and even "unconditional" advocates of the independent Polish trade union *Solidarność* (Solidarity), which emerged in 1980, struggled against repression by the communist authorities, and became a model for transitions from communism in Central and Eastern Europe after its rise to power in 1989.[7] From the eruption of Polish workers' protest in the summer of 1980 onwards, Christian trade union movements supported what was to become the first mass opposition movement in Eastern Europe.

At the international level, the World Confederation of Labor (WCL) coordinated this support. Its origins stretch back to the International Federation of Christian Trade Unions (IFCTU), which was founded in 1920 and transformed itself into the World Confederation of Labor in 1968, mainly due to the influx of new members from Latin America, Africa, and Asia.[8] With the support of Christian trade union movements, parties and party foundations in Western Europe, such as the large Belgian trade union ACV/CSC, the French CFTC, and the Konrad Adenauer Foundation – the

4 Gregory F. Domber, *Empowering Revolution: America, Poland, and the End of the Cold War* (Chapel Hill: University of North Carolina Press, 2014). For a contemporary analysis of public perceptions in the early 1990s: "The Holy Alliance," *Time*, 24 February 1992, 14–21.

5 See for instance: Maud Bracke, *Which Socialism, Whose Détente? West European Communism and the Czechoslovak Crisis of 1968* (Budapest - New York: CEU Press, 2007).

6 Dorota Dakowska, "Les fondations politiques allemandes en Europe centrale," *Critique internationale* 3, no. 24 (2004): 139–154.

7 Idesbald Goddeeris, ed., *Solidarity with Solidarity: Western European Trade Unions and the Polish Crisis, 1980–1982* (Lanham, MD: Lexington, 2010); KADOC, Archives of the World Confederation of Labor (WCL), 325, Press Release, 8 March 1982.

8 Regarding the history of the IFCTU/WCL: Patrick Pasture, *Histoire du syndicalisme chrétien international: La difficile recherche d'une troisième voie* (Paris: L'Harmattan, 1999); Id., *Christian Trade Unionism in Europe since 1968: Tensions between Identity and Practice* (Aldershot et al.: Avebury, 1994), 85–136.

Brussels-headquartered WCL staged a series of global campaigns on behalf of *Solidarność*, supported its development in exile after the declaration of martial law in Poland in December 1981, and welcomed the banned Polish trade union as a member organization in November 1986.[9] Throughout the 1980s, public declarations by the WCL celebrated the independent Polish trade union as a model for the global "renovation of trade unionism."[10] This support has mostly been related to the explicitly Catholic profile of *Solidarność*, which identified with Christian social ethics and the Polish pope John Paul II.[11] Leading figures – including Lech Wałęsa – have celebrated in public declarations the support of the WCL as a crucial element in the legal recognition of *Solidarność* in April 1989 and the eventual collapse of the regime through negotiations and elections.[12]

Yet, this chapter will paint a more nuanced picture of that support: it reveals that public campaigns and solidarity declarations concealed a difficult and strained relation between the WCL and *Solidarność*. Strikingly, these conflicts were not only rooted in competition with Social Democracy, but also related to issues beyond Europe. Indeed, one of the main arguments of this article is that campaigns on behalf of *Solidarność* had often more to do with the Global South (also described here in the terms it was understood at the time, i.e. the "Third World") than with Eastern Europe, and were to a large extent inspired by the Polish trade union's potential at reconfiguring Christian trade unionism in a global context during the 1980s.

This chapter develops its arguments over three parts. The first section focuses on the relationship between the WCL and the fledging *Solidarność* movement from its inception in the summer of 1980 until the declaration of martial law in December 1981, which forced the independent trade union underground. It shows how *Solidarność* became a flashpoint for the internal identity crisis that marked the WCL. The second section focuses on the period during martial law, analyzing how the WCL aimed to globalize the Polish trade union by expanding its connections with international issues, most notably in Latin America, but lost much of its interest from

9 *Pourquoi Pas?*, 26 November 1987, 24; Kim Christiaens, "Podstawy do współpracy? Międzynarodowa Konfederacja Wolnych Związków Zawodowych i Światowa Konfederacja Pracy wobec powstania, zawieszenia i delegalizacji NSZZ 'Solidarność,'" in *Świat wobec "Solidarności" 1980–1989*, ed. Paweł Jaworski and Łukasz Kamiński (Warsaw: IPN, 2013), 210–224; Id., "The ICFTU and the WCL: The International Coordination of Solidarity," in *Solidarity with Solidarity*, ed. Goddeeris, 101–127.

10 *Intersocial* 47 (March 1979), 17.

11 *Solidarność News* 176 (July-August 1992), 1.

12 *Solidarność News* 134 (16–31 May 1989), 1.

1983 onwards. The third section delves into the relationship with *Solidarność* in the late 1980s and early 1990s, when the WCL and its affiliates tried to strengthen ties as part of their international policy in Eastern Europe, but failed in this endeavor.

From non-alignment to support?

Human rights violations in Eastern Europe were not high on the agenda of the international Christian trade union movement until the late 1970s. The International Federation of Christian Trade Unions (IFCTU) may well have condemned the crushing of the Hungarian Revolution and the Prague Spring in 1956 and 1968 respectively, as well as been harboring sections of exiled Christian trade unionists from countries such as Poland and Ukraine. Yet, from the late 1960s, anti-communism became increasingly overshadowed by competition with Social Democracy and a focus on the Third World. The transformation of the IFCTU into the World Confederation of Labor (WCL) in 1968 was mainly inspired by efforts to appeal to the Third World by adopting a pluralistic and "non-aligned" profile.

Through a focus on what its architect, the Belgian trade unionist August Vanistendael, dubbed a "spiritualist" and "emancipatory" trade unionism, the WCL tried to position itself as a "third way" between capitalism and communism.[13] Anti-capitalism allowed the organization to position itself especially vis-à-vis its much larger Social Democratic competitor, the International Confederation of Free Trade Unions (ICFTU), which was seen as a pawn of the American Cold War.[14] Anti-communism, however, was trumped by non-alignment and ambitions to free North-South relations from the burden of the East-West conflict, which underpinned rapprochement with the communist trade unions and their international confederation, the World Federation of Trade Unions (WFTU) on issues such as Third World development, East-West détente, and anti-apartheid over the 1970s.[15] The Third World also formed the major scope of the activities of the confederation: by the dawn of the 1980s, although it remained organizationally and financially dependent on Christian trade unions and parties

13 UCL, Archives Jan Kułakowski (AK), 6, CISL, 16th Congress, Luxembourg, 1–4 October 1968, August Vanistendael. Point V.

14 Magaly Rodríguez García, *Liberal Workers of the World, Unite? The ICFTU and the Defence of Labor Liberalism in Europe and Latin America (1949–1969)* (Bern: Peter Lang, 2010).

15 AK, 61, Quelques reflections sur les réalités, l'évolution et la direction de la CMT, 1984.

in Western Europe, about 60 of its 80 affiliated organizations came from Third World countries.[16]

Eastern European exile sections, for their part, moved on the margins of the organization. Attention to Eastern Europe only started to grow from 1976 onward, when the Polish-born trade unionist Jan Kułakowski became secretary-general of the WCL.[17] Kułakowski had many contacts with exiles from and dissident milieus active in countries such as Poland and Czechoslovakia.[18] He had a close relationship with the major *Solidarność* figure Tadeusz Mazowiecki and other former members of the Catholic group Znak, with whom he cooperated in the journal *Więź*. He geared the WCL to lodge complaints about trade union rights in Eastern European countries at the International Labor Organization (ILO), and he participated in campaigns on behalf of dissidents in Czechoslovakia and the Soviet Union.[19]

Yet, even under the leadership of a Polish exile and against the odds of the thawing East-West détente in the late 1970s, the WCL followed an ambivalent strategy towards Eastern Europe. It continued strategic cooperation with the WFTU against what Kułakowski called the "enemy number one," namely "any form of fascism or imperialism, which is imposed by international capitalism on the Third World."[20] The WCL maintained relations with the communist trade union movement in Poland, which invited Kułakowski and Christian trade union leaders from Belgium, the Netherlands and France on visits to Poland. Up until 1980, the reports of these visits – even those prepared by the deeply anti-communist and conservative Belgian trade union leader Jef Houthuys – stressed the need for contacts with the official trade union movement in the name of peace and détente, all the while paying little attention to dissident groups.[21] The latter regularly criticized the WCL for its selective focus on the Third World

16 "La confédération mondiale du travail," *Le Monde Diplomatique*, October 1980: 18.

17 Kułakowski lived beginning in 1946 in Belgium, was active in the Polish section of the ACV/CSC, and made a career in international trade unionism from the 1950s. Patrick Pasture, "Jan Kułakowski, from exile to international trade union leader and diplomat," in *Intégration ou représentation? Les exilés polonais en Belgique et la construction européenne*, ed. Michel Dumoulin and Idesbald Goddeeris (Louvain-la-Neuve: Academia-Bruylant, 2005), 99–120.

18 AK, 7, Contacts with Czechoslovakian Catholics, August 1969.

19 *Labor: Revue Mensuelle d'information et de formation syndicales* 56, no. 9 (September 1978); Jan Kułakowski and Leszek Jesień, *Spotkania na Bagateli: Polska Europa* Świat*: Z Janem Kułakowskim rozmawia Leszek Jesień* (Warsaw: Rhetos, 2004).

20 WCL, 100, "Quelques reflections à la suite d'un voyage privé en Tchécoslovaquie et en Pologne," Jan Kułakowski, 16 August 1978, 3.

21 WCL, 324, Conseil Central des Syndicats en Pologne, 23 April 1980.

and its low profile concerning the defense of human rights in Eastern Europe.[22]

In the summer of 1980, the WCL adopted, then, a notably ambivalent attitude with respect to the independent workers' movement that emerged out of the ongoing protests in Poland. After the confederation had issued a press communiqué in August 1980 declaring its solidarity with the Polish workers, the Polish developments came up for discussion during the Executive Committee's meeting in Brussels in September 1980.[23] The WCL congratulated the Polish workers on the results achieved in their struggle for independent trade unionism and democracy, and decided that, before meeting with the communist WFTU in Prague, a delegation should be sent to Poland for further investigation. However, this decision was not taken without underlining that the mission was only informational and exploratory.

The WCL, expressing solidarity with *all* Polish workers, made clear that it was averse to interfering with Polish workers' affairs and only aimed to gain insight into the situation. Emblematic for this prudent strategy were Jan Kułakowski's public declarations after his return from Poland in August 1980, where he had witnessed the social unrest and the strikers' movement during a holiday. The events and the struggle in Poland, he argued, were above all an internal matter that should be resolved by the Polish people.[24] The international trade union movement's task was only a matter of *moral* solidarity, without any political interference and "without Western trade union patterns making it difficult for them."[25]

Yet this position gradually tilted towards open support for *Solidarność* from the autumn of 1980 onward. In October 1980, the WCL Confederal Board realized the need to develop relations with *Solidarność*, since its plans for sending a mission to Poland had been thwarted by the Polish government. Nor was Tadeusz Mazowiecki allowed to travel to Belgium.[26] During visits to Poland in November and December 1980 and February 1981, Kułakowski was however able to develop contacts with Catholic intellectuals drawn from the Znak movement and the Catholic Intelligentsia Clubs (*Kluby Inteligencji Katolickiej*, KIK) who had joined *Solidarność* –

22 AK, 17, "Quelques reflections à la suite d'un voyage privé en Tchéchoslovaquie et en Pologne," 16 August 1976.

23 *Flash* no. 137 (1 September 1980): 1; WCL, 1161, Press Release, 4 September 1980.

24 See for instance: *La Cité*, 23–24 August 1980; *De Vakbondskrant*, 21 August 1980.

25 *Labor: Monthly Review on Trade Union Information and Training, Edited by the World Confederation of Labor* 8–9 (August–September 1980), 4.

26 WCL, 324, Jan Kułakowski to Jef Houthuys, 19 June 1981.

most notably, Mazowiecki and Andrzej Wielowieyski. These relations became instrumental in the establishment of a working relationship with the new trade union.[27]

Over the following months, the WCL launched material support campaigns among its affiliates in Western Europe. It provided assistance to help the Polish trade union to develop its organizational structures, including the acquisition of a study and research center and telephone equipment, and it established a Poland Solidarity Fund.[28] There were various reasons to explain this growing interest. Critically, there was the success and power of *Solidarność*. This had been uncertain in the summer of 1980, considering the previous unsuccessful protests of Polish workers in 1956, 1970, and 1976. However, after it gained legal recognition by the communist authorities in November 1980, the Polish protest movement and its pursuit of reforms turned out to be lasting. *Solidarność* was developing into a mass movement with millions of members and enjoyed considerable prestige, at home and abroad.

In consequence, supporting *Solidarność* became of great strategic advantage in terms of raising the profile of the WCL, especially because the confederation faced a deep identity crisis. French and Dutch members had left the organization, among others due to conflicts about the failed merger with the ICFTU. The internal crisis festered also beyond Europe: its regional organizations in Africa (FOPADESC) and Latin America (CLAT) regularly clashed with the policy in Brussels over issues such as the relation with communism and Social Democracy. By the late 1970s, it had become clear that "non-alignment" was difficult to maintain in a period in which Christian trade union movements were overshadowed by the "new labor internationalism" that had been reinvigorating Social Democracy in Western Europe and the Third World since the mid-1970s.[29]

The most striking dimension of the WCL's support was, indeed, its interest in using *Solidarność* to buttress its profile in the Third World. As early as October 1980, the Argentinean CLAT secretary-general Emilio Máspero insisted with the WCL leadership on a visit by *Solidarność* members to Latin America.[30] *Solidarność*, indeed, came into existence at an opportune moment for CLAT: its search for a third way suffered from the logics of the Cold War in Latin America. In the early 1970s, it had adopted a left-wing

27 WCL, 325, Poland, 24 February 1981.

28 WCL, 322, Project presented by the WCL in support of *Solidarność*, May 1981.

29 Peter Waterman, *Globalization, Social Movements, and the New Internationalisms* (London-Washington: Continuum, 1998), 45 and further.

30 WCL, 324, Invitation of Emilio Máspero to Solidarność Gdańsk, 9 October 1980.

profile and embraced a language of radical liberation, anti-capitalism, and socialism, especially to compete with its Social Democratic competitor, the Inter-American Regional Organization of Workers (ORIT), but it was at the same time discredited by its opponents as an anti-communist organization that was funded by the CIA and Western European Christian Democracy.[31] From the late 1970s, the organization re-discovered its Christian identity and strongly identified with the Polish Pope John Paul II, in order to give its smaller member organizations a clearer profile vis-à-vis Marxist-Leninist opposition movements and governments – Cuba, Grenada, and Nicaragua. From this perspective, the success of *Solidarność* was instrumental to present CLAT and Christian Democracy as a "third way" between capitalism and communism through an alliance between society, church, and labor.

With the intermediation of Tadeusz Mazowiecki, Jan Kułakowski arranged a Latin American tour for two *Solidarność* members in November 1980, shortly after the independent trade union was officially recognized by the Polish authorities.[32] The delegation consisted of Józef Przybylski and Zygmunt Zawalski. Przybylski was a welder at the Budimor steel factory near Gdańsk who had co-signed the Gdańsk Agreements on 31 August, and then became a board member of the Inter-Enterprise Founding Committee of *Solidarność*.[33] Zawalski was an electrical engineer at the Gdańsk Shipyard and a friend of Wałęsa's.[34]

The Polish delegation featured as prominent guests during the 18th Council of the CLAT in Lima, which professed solidarity with the Polish trade union and the launching of national support committees.[35] Afterwards, the two representatives went for seven days to the headquarters of CLAT in Caracas (Venezuela). Upon their arrival at the airport of Maiquetía, the Polish guests were welcomed by hundreds of trade unionists and members of the local Polish community.[36] Highly mediatized meetings

31 Gerhard Wahlers, *CLAT: Geschichte einer lateinamerikanischen Gewerkschaftsinternationale* (Bonn: Wehle, 1990).

32 Kim Christiaens and Idesbald Goddeeris, "Solidarność and Latin America. Encounters, Conflicts and Failures," *Archiv für Sozialgeschichte* 56 (2016): 445–461; Wahlers, *CLAT*.

33 Rafał Kalukin, "Zapluty karzeł z puszki. Rozmowa z Józefem Przybylskim," *Wyborcza.pl* (19 September 2009); WCL, 327, Letter from Jan Kułakowski to J.E. Humblet, 2 May 1984.

34 WCL, 327, Flor Bleux to W. Canini, 16 October 1984; Letter from Jan Kułakowski to Jesus Insausti, 19 September 1983.

35 WCL, 326, Posiciones y actuaciones de la CLAT en América Latina, s.d.

36 About the Polish diaspora in Venezuela, see: Feliks Żubr, "Wenezuela," in *Akcja niepodległościowa na terenie międzynarodowym 1945–1990*, ed. Tomasz Piesakowski (London: Polskie Towarzystwo Naukowe na Obczyźnie, 1999), 703–710.

took place with the leadership of the CLAT, the Venezuelan trade union CTV, the Christian Democratic president Luis Herrera Campíns, and the archbishop of Caracas. The Polish delegation also visited the University of Latin American Workers in San Antonio de los Altos (Caracas).[37] On their way back to Poland, the Polish delegation visited the Spanish Unión Sindical Obrera (USO) and the WCL headquarters in Brussels.

Yet these contacts soon ushered in the first major crisis between the WCL and *Solidarność*. The ICFTU fiercely criticized the tour across Latin America, and was soon joined by critical voices from within *Solidarność* itself. During Lech Wałęsa's visit to Rome in January 1981, founding members of *Solidarność* – including Karol Modzelewski and Anna Walentynowicz – denounced the efforts of the WCL to hijack *Solidarność*, to connect it to Christian Democracy, and to organize international contacts through Mazowiecki without the approval of *Solidarność*'s National Coordinating Commission.[38] *Solidarność* itself was indeed deeply divided in ideological terms: members or supporters with a Christian Democratic profile – such as Mazowiecki – had more in common with the WCL than members with a more Social Democratic or liberal profile. The latter advocated an alliance with the ICFTU and AFL-CIO and cooperated with them through a special liaison office in Stockholm.[39] The financial support resulting from this cooperation dwarfed that of the WCL, which was – not only by the ICFTU but also by members of the *Solidarność* leadership – belittled as an minoritarian offshoot of international trade unionism that continued to cooperate with communists "in the style of Neo-Znak."[40]

Polish criticism and doubts were also fueled by the internal conflicts that emerged within the WCL about support for *Solidarność*. Whereas the CLAT staged a bandwagon of international campaigns, and the WCL publicly embraced *Solidarność*,[41] Western European members showed little interest and some even kept their distance, with the Austrian FCG (*Fraktion Christlicher Gewerkschafter im ÖGB*) and the Spanish USO being the main exceptions. By March 1981, the FCG was the only member organization which had visited *Solidarność* in Poland. Belgian Christian Democrats trav-

37 *Informativo CLAT. Vocero del movimiento de los trabajadores comprometidos con la liberación de los pueblos de América Latina* 6, no. 53 (Diciembre 1980-Enero 1981), 12.

38 AK, 72, Letter from Jan Kułakowski to members of the WCL Executive Board and Lech Wałęsa, January 1981.

39 Andrzej Friszke, "The Znak Movement as the Moderate Wing of 'Solidarity,'" in *The Polish Solidarity Movement in Retrospect: A Story of Failure or a Success?*, ed. Dariusz Aleksandrowicz, Stefani Sonntag and Jan Wielgohs (Berlin: GSFP, 2009), 231.

40 WCL, 327, Solidarność en Pologne et à l'étranger en 1983, 2.

41 WCL, 325, 11 January 1982.

eled in 1980 to Poland, met with Polish state officials and with Poland's head bishop, Stefan Cardinal Wyszyński, but neglected *Solidarność*.[42] The Poland Solidarity Fund only received a limited number of contributions from the *Katholieke Onderwijsvereniging Nederland* (Catholic Education Union Netherlands), the Dutch CNV, the International Federation of Employees in Public Service/European Federation of Public Service Employees (INFEDOP/EUROFEDOP), and the Austrian FCG.[43] Furthermore, the WCL continued its contacts with the WFTU, which were only broken off in February 1982. Internally, Kułakowski admitted that *Solidarność* was not a priority. After the conflict about Latin America, he admitted that he did not want to "create the impression that the WCL will put Poland in the forefront of its pre-occupations (…) since the workers in most Third World countries are confronted with even more difficult situations and (…) their struggles are even harder."[44]

Relations with the *Solidarność* National Coordinating Commission resumed from May 1981, when the latter – after repeated pressure from Kułakowski – eventually accepted the invitation to visit Brussels and discuss the problems with the WCL leadership.[45] The delegation, consisting of the National Coordinating Commission's vice-president Ryszard Kalinowski and an international relations officer, expressed on the one hand *Solidarność*'s interest in establishing "a particularly close cooperation and mutual solidarity with trade unions in the Third World," but on the other hand stressed the distinctively Polish identity of *Solidarność*.[46] *Solidarność* refused to be guided in terms of international policy, stressed its apolitical profile by prioritizing contacts with trade union movements from the First, Second, and Third Worlds, and visited also the headquarters of the ICFTU and the Belgian socialist trade union in Brussels.[47] At the international level, *Solidarność* opted for a policy of non-affiliation.

Kułakowski continued to travel to Poland, and he attended conferences on human rights and trade unions, but was disillusioned by *Solidarność*, which in his opinion lacked an international orientation and was absorbed by its own internal elections. The connection with the Third World remained dominant in the WCL's understanding of the situation in Poland,

42 "Voyages dans l'autre Europe: Rencontre avec Charles-Ferdinand Nothomb et Hervé Hasquin," *Pourquoi Pas?*, 15 December 1988.

43 WCL, 322, Solidarity with Poland, s.d. See Helmut Wohnout's chapter in this volume.

44 WCL 327, Confidential to the members of the Orientation Committee 52/81, 16 March 1981.

45 WCL, 324, Telegram from Jan Kułakowski to Ryszard Kalinowski, 16 April 1981.

46 AK, 73, Suggestions pour un programme de politique internationale de NSZZ Solidarność, 1981.

47 *La Cité*, 2 May 1981.

though. When visiting the Christian Democratic opposition in Nicaragua in 1981, Kułakowski compared the repression by the Sandinista government with the communist take-over in Warsaw in 1945.[48] In June 1981, a WCL and CLAT delegation met with Lech Wałęsa under the aegis of the ILO conference in Geneva. WCL representatives from Latin America, Africa, and Asia joined Kułakowski and an ACV/CSC delegation during the First National Congress in September and October 1981. In their speeches, they focused more on the connections between *Solidarność* and the struggle for trade and human rights in the Third World than on issues in Eastern Europe.[49] In November 1981, the WCL invited vice-president Mirosław Krupiński to the WCL congress in Manila. In its analyses and campaigns, the WCL projected ideas and concepts about the Third World on *Solidarność* and, more broadly, on Eastern Europe. Kułakowski, for instance, flaunted Poland as a victim of "colonialism"[50] and treated *Solidarność* as a sort of projection screen for a new kind of trade union movement that went – or at least had to go – beyond the traditional models of the West and East, and in this way represented the WCL's policy of non-alignment.[51]

Such connections with the Third World were fueled by efforts to steer *Solidarność* away from Western models – most notably Social Democracy – and allowed the WCL to criticize the support of "rich trade unions squandering money for their own prestige."[52] *Solidarność* showed, however, little interest in an alliance with the Third World. The National Coordinating Commission of *Solidarność* refused, despite pressure from Kułakowski, to receive a CLAT delegation in Poland, and did not reply to invitations to join other campaigns.[53] From the spring of 1981 onwards, the National Coordinating Commission of *Solidarność* reduced the number of foreign visits in view of the internal elections during the First National Congress in the autumn of 1981.[54] During this congress, issues in the Third World remained outside the scope of discussion, with the exception of some references to the struggle against Pinochet in Chile and the murder of Sadat. Interest in the WCL was instrumental rather than ideological: the WCL was seen as a more acceptable partner than the ICFTU from the Polish authorities'

48 WCL, Interview with Kułakowski in *Spectator*, 19 December 1981.

49 WCL, 327, Rafael Léon Léon to Jerzy Milewski, 26 April 1983.

50 *Volksmacht*, 26 November 1976, 1, 4 and 5.

51 See also the published series of conversations with Kułakowski: *Spotkania na Bagateli*, 98–101 (about the WCL and Latin America) and 154 (about Máspero).

52 *De Volksmacht*, 18 September 1981, 6.

53 WCL, 325, Telegram from Bogdan Lis to Emilio Máspero, 2 July 1981.

54 WCL, 324, Letter from Jan Kułakowski to Alfred Gosselin, 2 June1981.

perspective, and cooperation was seen as a necessary element to protect *Solidarność*'s independent profile.[55]

The limits of globalizing Solidarność and dwindling support, 1981-1987

After the declaration of martial law on 13 December 1981 and the subsequent suspension and crushing of *Solidarność* under the Jaruzelski regime, international sympathy for the Polish opposition dramatically expanded.[56] The Polish crisis now became subject to a broadening mobilization. Trade unions were joined by groups that spanned the Left, churches, and human rights NGOs.[57] In Belgium, Italy, and France, Christian trade unionists and worshippers staged common campaigns with socialist trade unions, for instance by organizing work stoppages, lobbying their governments, and staging protest demonstrations and campaigns on behalf of imprisoned *Solidarność* members. The WCL lodged jointly with the ICFTU complaints at the level of the ILO, where they denounced the ban on *Solidarność* as a violation of human and trade union rights, demanded a commission of enquiry to investigate the situation, and submitted information to the ILO Freedom of Association Committee.[58] During the sixty-eighth session of the International Labor Conference, held in Geneva in June 1982, the WCL included, together with the ICFTU, exiled *Solidarność* members to represent the suspended trade union and to counter the official Polish delegation.

Indeed, not only the ILO, but also representatives of *Solidarność* who found themselves abroad at the moment of the declaration of martial law and started restructuring themselves in exile brought the WCL and ICFTU together. In July 1982, exiles established the *Solidarność* Coordinating Office Abroad, officially mandated by the Temporary Coordinating Office

55 WCL, 327, Confidential to the members of the Orientation Committee 52/81, 16 March 1981.

56 Helene Sjursen, *The United States, Western Europe and the Polish Crisis: International Relations in the Second Cold War* (Basingstoke-New York: Palgrave Macmillan, 2003); Patryk Pleskot, *Kłopotliwa panna "S": Postawy polityczne Zachodu wobec "Solidarności" na tle stosunków z PRL (1980–1989)* (Warsaw: IPN, 2013); Paweł Jaworski and Łukasz Kamiński, eds., *Świat wobec Solidarności 1980–1989* (Warsaw: IPN, 2013).

57 Natalie Bégin, "Kontakte zwischen Gewerkschaften in Ost und West: Die Auswirkungen von Solidarność in Deutschland und Frankreich. Ein Vergleich," *Archiv für Sozialgeschichte*, 45 (2005): 293–324.

58 WCL, 1164, Letter from Jan Kułakowski to Francis Blanchard, 8 January 1982; *Labor* 6–7 (June–July 1982), 3.

(TKK) to represent the Polish underground. Its headquarters in Brussels were hosted by the Belgian Christian trade union movement ACV/CSC, but the organization was accredited with both the WCL and ICFTU.[59] In the following years, the office cooperated with both internationals, which allowed it to be represented in international fora, for instance by financing worldwide travels and including members in their delegations to the ILO.[60] They relied on its networks to channel relief to and get information from the Polish underground. In 1982, in view of the second anniversary of the legal recognition of *Solidarność*, the WCL and ICFTU publicly merged their efforts in campaigns on behalf of the defense of "workers' fundamental rights," and agreed to confer regularly on the situation in Poland together with the European Trade Union Confederation (ETUC), which had united socialist and Christian trade unions at the European level since the 1970s.[61] In many respects, the ban on *Solidarność*, then, seemed to reduce the distance between the WCL and the ICFTU, as well as the WCL's troubled relationship with the Polish opposition prior to December 1981. The WCL broke off its relations with the communist WFTU after vice-secretary-general Dominique Aguessy openly reprimanded the latter's support for the Polish government in Havana in February 1982.[62]

Yet despite such common campaigns, the Polish crisis remained an awkward issue for the WCL. Caught between its interests in Europe and the Third World, as well as between anti-communism and anti-Americanism, the confederation was still divided about the ways to deal with *Solidarność*. Sectors close to Christian Democratic parties – most notably the leadership of the ACV/CSC – saw the Polish crisis in terms of a dichotomy between freedom and communism, whereas more progressive and left-wing sectors – including Kułakowski – stuck to the principles of "non-alignment" and "trade union pluralism."

After December 1981, the WCL's relationship with the Polish opposition continued to be inspired by interests beyond Europe. As early as Jan-

59 Idesbald Goddeeris, "Lobbying allies? The NSZZ Solidarność Coordinating Office Abroad, 1982–1989," *Journal of Cold War Studies* 13, no. 3 (2011): 83–125.

60 WCL, 327, Letter from Jan Kułakowski to Jef Houthuys, 27 January 1984.

61 WCL, 1163, Circular from Jan Kułakowski, 25 October 1982; ETUC Declaration on Poland (Press Release), 28 January 1981; Joint ICFTU-WCL-ETUC trade union action conference on solidarity with NSZZ Solidarność, 25 October 1982; *International Trade Union News* 17 (18 October 1982), 1; IISH, Archives ICFTU, 264, "Statement on Poland, 20 November 1982; Kristine Mitchell, "The European Trade Union Confederation at 40: integration and diversity in the European labor movement," *Labor History* 55, no. 4 (2014): 403–426.

62 Wereldverbond van de Arbeid, *5 jaren van strijd. Aktie en standpunten van het Wereldverbond van de Arbeid en zijn aangesloten organisaties ten overstaan van de evenementen in Polen.* Brussels: WCL, 1986, 29; *Labor* 2–3 (February–March 1982), 1–3.

uary and February 1982, Kułakowski sent a delegation of two *Solidarność* exiles to eight countries in Latin America, where they had to buttress campaigns by the CLAT in support of *Solidarność*, strengthen the connection with Christian Democratic parties and movements, and muster support for campaigns at the level of the ILO. In September 1982, Kułakowski accompanied a delegation of Coordinating Office members, including Jerzy Milewski, Tadeusz Konopka, Józef Przybylski, Bohdan Cywiński, Krzysztof Pomian, and the Polish editor-in-chief of the Vatican newspaper *Osservatore Romano* Rev. Adam Boniecki to Caracas, where they attended an international conference on "Poland-Latin America" organized by the CLAT.[63] The event was steeped in a spirit of anti-communism and was attended by bishops from Brazil and the US, as well as opposition trade unionists from Cuba and Nicaragua.[64] The CLAT celebrated the struggle of *Solidarność* as akin to its own struggle against totalitarian regimes of the right (such as in Argentina and Chile) and the Left (Nicaragua and Cuba), and drew analogies between the role of the Church and workers in fueling opposition in Poland and Latin America. It staged an international campaign against the de-legalization of *Solidarność*, and called upon its affiliates to demonstrate in front of Soviet embassies[65] and boycott trade and communication with Poland and the USSR.[66] Kułakowski accompanied Tadeusz Konopka and Krystyna Ruchniewicz to Argentina, where trade unions opposed the military junta.[67] In December 1982, after a stopover in Brazil, Ruchniewicz attended as a prominent guest the CLAT Congress in Bogota, where thousands of attendants, including a representative of the Afghan anti-Soviet resistance and the president of Colombia Belisario Betancur, proclaimed their support for *Solidarność*.[68]

At the beginning of 1983, the WCL supported the establishment of a Latin American branch of the *Solidarność* Coordinating Office Abroad in Caracas. At the initiative of the CLAT, Kułakowski sent Zygmunt Zawalski to Caracas to function as a permanent *Solidarność* representative in

63 Bohdan Cywiński, "El Catolicismo es la sangre de Polonia", *ABC* (Madrid), 21 January 1981, 7.

64 IISH, 49, Solidarność Nederland, CLAT. Boletín Prensa, Radio y Televisión, 1982; *CLAT Newsletter*, September 1982.

65 WCL, 326, Letter from Miguel Gazzera to Jorge Cuisana, 4 November 1982.

66 WCL, 326, Emilio Máspero to Solidarność Coordinating Office Abroad, 20 October 1982. More about this action in Idesbald Goddeeris, "Ministerstwo Spraw Zagranicznych 'Solidarności': Biuro Koordynacyjne NSZZ 'Solidarność', 1982–1989, część 1," *Pamięć i Sprawiedliwość* 10, no. 2 (2006): 345.

67 WCL, 328, Letter from Jan Kułakowski to José Mercedes Gonzalez, 6 August 1982.

68 IISH, 49, Solidarność Nederland, Conclusiones. Coloquio Movimiento de los Trabajadores Polonia-América Latina.

Latin America. Zawalski, who had been part of the first delegation to Latin America in 1980, was able to leave Poland with his wife and daughter through the intervention of the CLAT and the Venezuelan embassy in Warsaw in 1983. All of these initiatives were inspired by competition with the ICFTU, which supported – together with the AFL-CIO – the *Solidarność* Coordinating Office Abroad in Brussels with budgets that dwarfed those coming from the WCL. The WCL leadership and especially CLAT were skeptical about the relations between the ICFTU and the Coordinating Office Abroad. The latter's president Jerzy Milewski leaned more toward Social Democracy than toward Christian Democracy and had been involved in the founding of a rather left-wing political party, the PPP (Polish Labor Party), in 1981. In the first months after the declaration of martial law in December 1981, Milewski had lived in the United States, where he became acquainted with the AFL-CIO.[69] From Caracas, Zawalski had to buttress the legitimacy of the CLAT as most representative ally of *Solidarność* in Latin America, strengthen ties with Christian Democracy, and undermine the activities of solidarity groups that were set up by the Polish diaspora that leaned toward the AFL-CIO and Social Democracy.

However, things did not go as expected: Latin America once again became a source of conflict between *Solidarność* and the WCL. The *Solidarność* Coordinating Office Abroad only accepted the invitation to travel to the conference in Caracas in September 1982 on the condition that no common declarations would be made, and it refused to serve as co-organizer of the event. Its representatives stressed in public declarations that they were only guests of the CLAT, and scoffed at rumors that *Solidarność* would affiliate to the WCL or CLAT.[70] *Solidarność* delegation members refused invitations of the CLAT to travel to other Latin American countries, and Jerzy Milewski headed from Caracas to the headquarters of CLAT's regional competitor ORIT in Mexico. The Polish delegation's interests lay above all in strengthening the legitimacy of the *Solidarność* Coordinating Office in the eyes of the Polish diaspora in Latin America, collecting funds, and garnering support for international campaigns at the ILO.

The relationship reached rock bottom in 1983, when the *Solidarność* Coordinating Office in Brussels clashed with the WCL and CLAT about the activities of Zawalski in Caracas. Zawalski complained in letters to Milewski that the CLAT and Latin American trade unionists "are more con-

69 Goddeeris, "Ministerstwo," 317.

70 WCL, 326, Letter from Jerzy Milewski and Bohdan Cywiński to Jan Kułakowski, 13 September 1982; Letter from Jan Kułakowski to Emilo Máspero, 1 March 1982.

cerned about the Falklands and about how to stop American imperialism than about our issues."[71] The CLAT's criticism of the US was unwelcome for the *Solidarność* Coordinating Office Abroad, which received ample support from the US.[72] Similarly, the ways in which the CLAT connected campaigns on behalf of *Solidarność* to the Christian Democratic opposition against the Sandinistas in Nicaragua annoyed the *Solidarność* Office and other exiles in Western Europe, notably because the latter received much support among many allies in the West, such as Social Democrats and more left-wing groups, including progressive sectors within the Christian labor movement. These connections fueled unwelcome associations with the CIA, which funded the Contra-war in Nicaragua, and carried the risk of jeopardizing the international reputation of *Solidarność*.[73] To make things worse, the *Solidarność* Office found little concrete support among the CLAT, which did not dispose of the political and financial means to support the banned trade union in Poland. Eventually, Zawalski returned disillusioned to Belgium in November 1983 and was excluded from the Coordinating Office Abroad.[74]

Not only concerning Latin America, but also with respect to Africa and most notably the apartheid struggle, conflicts arose between *Solidarność* and the WCL. In the early 1970s, the WCL had cooperated with the WFTU and the South African Congress of Trade Unions (SACTU) in campaigns against apartheid.[75] Attention to South Africa dramatically expanded after the Soweto uprising in 1976, reaching its peak momentum in the 1980s. At the beginning of the 1980s, the WCL tried not only to find allies among the South African trade unions that started to embody the struggle against apartheid, but also considered support for the global anti-apartheid movement to be a critical means of strengthening its position in Africa.

Solidarność was deemed important to this strategy: it allowed the WCL to distance itself from its previous cooperation with communists and to appeal to non-communist trade unions inside South Africa. Kułakowski and other leading members of the WCL welded their support for *Solidar-*

71 Kim Christiaens and Idesbald Goddeeris, "Solidarność a Trzeci Świat. Część I. Chrześcijańsko-demokratyczna droga do Ameryki Łacińskiej," *Dzieje Najnowsze* 50, no. 1 (2018): 298.

72 Goddeeris, "Ministerstwo," 317.

73 Kim Christiaens, "Globalizing Nicaragua? An Entangled History of Sandinista Solidarity Campaigns in Western Europe," in *Making Sense of the Americas: How Protest Related to America in the 1980s and Beyond*, ed. Jan Hansen, Christian Helm and Frank Reichherzer (Frankfurt-New York: Campus, 2015), 155–177.

74 WCL, 327, Telegram from FEB to Jan Kułakowski, 3 November 1983.

75 Wouter Goedertier, "The Ambiguity of Solidarity: Belgium and the Global Struggle against Apartheid," DPhil thesis, Louvain, 2015, 288.

ność into campaigns against apartheid. In public declarations and at the level of international fora, the WCL stressed the view that the suppression of *Solidarność* was part of a worldwide decline of workers' rights, and that "the only credible voices are those protesting at the scandal of the internment of Wałęsa in Poland and at the same time denouncing the scandal of Mandela."[76] When the Botha government increased its repression in the 1980s, the WCL drew parallels between Poland and South Africa and discerned in the re-organizing trade union movements of South Africa a "new *Solidarność*."[77] Already in 1981, however, the cause of *Solidarność* had threatened to discredit rather than strengthen these efforts in South Africa. Indeed, the South African government initiated in September 1981 a recruitment plan for Polish refugees residing in Austria and transferred approximately 6,000 Polish citizens – including many *Solidarność* members – to South Africa in 1982.[78] This connection annoyed not only the black opposition, but also the WCL and the Catholic Church in South Africa, which strongly condemned this migration in a public letter.[79]

The WCL pressured the *Solidarność* Coordinating Office to distance itself from the apartheid regime, as it was "unfortunate that at a moment when *Solidarność* called upon the whole world's solidarity, it does not show at the same time its own solidarity with other oppressed people."[80] The Austrian trade union ÖGB, in response, staged information campaigns among Polish refugees outlining the true nature of apartheid and the fact that emigration to South Africa is "tantamount to the denial of livelihood to a black worker."[81] Eventually, in April 1982, the Coordinating Office's president Jerzy Milewski traveled to Kenya, Zambia, and Zimbabwe to profess solidarity with the anti-apartheid struggle and condemn Polish migration to South Africa, which he acknowledged as an approval of apartheid.[82] His statements were distributed among African trade unions during his mission.[83] Yet, anti-communist support for the apartheid regime among the Polish diaspora, along with the Warsaw commitment to anti-apartheid,

76 *Labor* 5 (May 1982), 1–5.

77 *Socialistisk Arbejderavis* no. 10 (June 1985), 8.

78 Kim Christiaens and Idesbald Goddeeris, "Solidarność i Trzeci Świat. Część II. Taktyczne sojusze z kluczowymi ruchami lat osiemdziesiątych XX wieku," *Dzieje Najnowsze* 50, no. 2 (2018): 262.

79 IISH Solidarność Nederland, 6, South Africa. The case against immigration: A letter to Polish Catholics from the Church in South Africa.

80 WCL, 326, Letter from Jan Kułakowski to Jerzy Milewski, 9 November 1982.

81 *Solidarność News* 1 (10 June 1983); IISH, Solidarność Nederland, 75, Apartheid.

82 WCL, 326, Letter from Jan Kułakowski to Jerzy Milewski, 9 November 1982.

83 WCL, 327, Letter from Jerzy Milewksi to Jan Kułakowski, 20 April 1983.

contributed to *Solidarność*'s low profile on this issue over the course of the 1980s.[84]

After 1983, relations between the *Solidarność* Coordinating Office Abroad and the WCL remained cool.[85] Kulakowski didn't trust the organization: he criticized the inclusion of new members into the organization and its development into what he called "*un appareil de coordination très étoffé*," saw Milewski as a "Polish governor," and tried to circumvent the office through direct contacts with the Coordinating Commission inside Poland.[86] In December 1983, the Austrian Christian trade unionist Günther Engelmayer traveled to Gdańsk to discuss with Wałęsa, Lech Kaczyński, Arkadiusz Rybicki, and Piotr Nowina-Konopka the possibilities for strengthening the position of Christian Democratic trade unions in international campaigns on behalf of *Solidarność*.[87]

The WCL focused its campaigns at the level of the ILO, including Polish representatives in its delegations and publishing information on the situation inside the country.[88] In January 1984, Kułakowski testified to the ILO Commission of Enquiry about the continuation of repression in Poland that had forced an authentic trade union into illegality, but he linked it to a global decline of worker's rights in other countries. The CLAT continued to profess its moral solidarity with *Solidarność* in a number of campaigns that mainly proceeded through the Catholic intellectuals Bohdan Cywiński and Tadeusz Konopka, who were both close to the Vatican. With the financial support of 25,000 DM provided by the Konrad Adenauer Foundation, CLAT translated Cywiński's book *The Polish Experience* into Spanish and circulated several thousand copies among its members to publicize the Polish struggle.[89] For the WCL, the support for and of what was dubbed a "famous Polish historian" like Bohdan Cywiński and translations of his book into other languages were deemed important to enhance "the prestige of the WCL, notably in Poland."[90] The CLAT also invited him to visit

84 *Kultura* 429, no. 6 (1983): 170–171 and a copy of *Słowo* in IISH, Solidarność Nederland, 75.
85 WCL, 327, Letter from Jan Kułakowski and Flor Bleux to Tymczasowa Komisja Koordynacyjna NSZZ Solidarność, May 1984.
86 WCL, 327, Solidarność à l'étranger en 1983, 2.
87 WCL, 328, Mission of Günther Engelmayer to Poland, December 1983.
88 Idesbald Goddeeris, "The limits of lobbying: ILO and Solidarność," in *ILO Histories: Essays on the International Labor Organization and its Impact on the World during the Twentieth Century*, ed. Jasmien Van Daele et al. (Bern et al.: Peter Lang, 2011), 423–441.
89 WCL, 327, Jan Kułakowski to Emilio Máspero, 10 December 1984; Letter from Georg Ziegler to Hans Werner Dahl, 27 September 1984.
90 WCL, 327, Letter from Jan Kułakowski to Jef Houthuys, 27 January 1984.

its members in Caracas, Bogota, Buenos Aires, Montevideo, and Brazil.[91] Yet the *Solidarność* Coordinating Office Abroad in Brussels expanded its cooperation with the CLAT's regional competitor affiliated to the ICFTU: ORIT had more political weight, grouping the largest Latin American trade unions and having a seat in the Governing Body of the ILO.

By contrast with the disinterest in the CLAT and its anti-communist struggles in Cuba and Nicaragua, solidarity with the Chilean labor opposition against the right-wing Pinochet regime became the principal international issue embraced by *Solidarność* in the 1980s.[92] This connection was deemed to be instrumental for protecting its trade union profile, making clear that *Solidarność* was not a right-wing or clerical movement, and securing support among Social Democratic trade union movements in the West, for which the association with the Church and the Right remained a difficult issue. Indeed, the connection between the struggle against Pinochet in Chile and Jaruzelski in Poland was successfully orchestrated by the ICFTU.[93] The latter tied the trade union opposition movements in both countries together, and used its support for *Solidarność* as a toehold to make inroads to Christian leaders within the labor opposition in Chile, which opted for affiliation to the ICFTU after the end of the Pinochet regime.

In the mid-1980s, material support from the WCL mainly proceeded through its respective Belgian, Dutch, and French affiliates ACV/CSC, CNV, and CFTC.[94] The Belgian trade union financed the salaries of some members of the Coordinating Office Abroad, such as those of Ruchniewicz, Henryk Jagiełło, and Przybylski.[95] The WCL lobbied with Christian Democratic organizations for a monthly support of 100 USD to Tadeusz Mazowiecki.[96] Direct support was however limited, also in the quarters of international Christian Democratic organizations, such as the World Union of Christian Democrats and the Christian Democrat International, which

91 WCL, 327, Emilio Máspero to Jan Kułakowski, 29 May 1985.

92 Robert Brier, "Poland's Solidarity as a Contested Symbol of the Cold War: Transatlantic Debates After the Polish Crisis," in *European Integration and the Atlantic Community in the 1980s*, ed. Kiran Klaus Patel and Kenneth Weisbrode (New York: Cambridge University Press, 2013), 99–100.

93 Kim Christiaens, "The Difficult Quest for Chilean Allies. International Labor Solidarity Campaigns for Chile in the 1970s and 1980s," in *European Solidarity with Chile, 1970s–1980s*, ed. Kim Christiaens, Idesbald Goddeeris and Magaly Rodríguez García (Bern et al.: Peter Lang, 2014), 97–129.

94 *Labor. Edition Interprofessionelle* no. 1 (January 1985), 3.

95 WCL, 327, Letter from A. Lievens to R. De Schryver, 8 July 1983.

96 WCL, 327, Letter from Jan Kułakowski to Jef Houthuys, 8 November 1983.

saw the Church as only possible ally given the continued repression of *Solidarność*.[97] Kułakowski was disillusioned by *Solidarność* and the ways in which it was used as an instrument of the Cold War instead of a symbol of trade union pluralism.[98] The image of *Solidarność* – backed by Thatcher and Reagan – needed international contextualization against the backdrop of economic crisis, neoliberalism, and a groundswell of peace campaigns on behalf of East-West détente and disarmament in the mid-1980s.[99] Solidarity declarations from *Solidarność* in support of the British miners or connections with resistance against the right-wing Pinochet regime had to make clear that support for *Solidarność* was a struggle over human rights that transcended the Cold War.[100]

In 1986, *Solidarność* officially affiliated to the WCL by virtue of a special procedure due to the common affiliation with the ICFTU. *Solidarność* may well have celebrated this symbolic gesture important to the worldwide acknowledgement of the "'*Solidarność* fact' at a moment when our own [Polish] government [was] leaving no stone unturned to make the world forget us." Yet it did not provoke much enthusiasm in the ranks of the WCL, which only ratified the affiliation in 1987.[101]

The confederation was absorbed by internal problems. Financial deficits and troubles crippled its functioning, while conflicts over ideology and strategy continued to divide regional sections. Other issues became more central in the policy of the WCL in the mid-1980s, notably its policy in Africa due to anti-apartheid, the negotiations about the Lomé agreements, and efforts to extend its presence in Africa.[102] The lack of interest in Poland also became apparent to *Solidarność*. The *Solidarność* Coordinating Office regularly complained about the dwindling interest of the WCL and other trade union movements in Poland, and the predominance of normalization policies with the Jaruzelski regime. In 1985, Milewski regretted that the UN Human Rights Commission had not approved a resolution on Poland for two consecutive years, and that other global hot spots such as Afghanistan, Chile, and South Africa diverted attention from Poland.[103] Campaigns on behalf of *Solidarność* would revive only from 1988 onward.

97 WCL, 327, Letter from Angelo Bernassola, 31 August 1984.
98 AK, 61, Reflections Kułakowski, January 1984.
99 Christie Miedema, "Struggling Against the Bomb or Against the Bloc Divide? The Dutch Peace Movement and Eastern Europe," *Dutch Crossing: Journal of Low Countries Studies* 39, no. 3 (2015): 261–274.
100 *Flash, Bulletin d'Information de la section polonaise – CSC*. Tadek Oruba, no. 8 (1984), 8.
101 *Labor* 7–8 (July-August 1987), 4.
102 AK, 37, Letter from Kułakowski, 28 June 1983 and Note à l'attention d'Eugène Akpemado, s.d.
103 Christiaens and Goddeeris, "Solidarność i Trzeci Świat. Część II," 256.

Solidarność and the future of trade unionism in Eastern Europe after 1989

After a wave of strikes beginning in March 1988, the Polish regime started to crumble. It was forced to accept *Solidarność* as a full partner in the round-table negotiations that paved the way for democratization and the relegalization of the independent trade union. As these changes start to unfold in Poland from spring 1988 onward, the WCL and its affiliates rediscovered the role of *Solidarność* as a means of helping to fill the vacuum that emerged in Poland and in other Eastern European countries. From 1988 onward, the leadership of the WCL – which was headed by the Argentinean trade unionist Carlos Custer from late 1989 onward – traveled regularly to Poland to attend public conferences and meet with high-ranking *Solidarność* members. In August 1988, for instance, Kułakowski traveled together with ICFTU secretary-general John Vanderveken to Poland, where they attended an international conference on human rights in Kraków staged by Freedom and Peace and *Solidarność* for the implementation of the Helsinki Agreements.[104]

The WCL strengthened its relations most notably with regional *Solidarność* sections with whom the French CFTC and the Belgian ACV/CSC maintained bilateral relations, in Małopolska and Lublin respectively. Covert financial support – mainly coming from these Belgian and French members – was funneled inside Poland, especially to fund media and journals, such as *Tygodnik Gdański* and *Tygodnik Małopolska*.[105] In May 1989, Bolesław Mikołajczak – a member of the ACV/CSC Polish section – traveled at the request of Kułakowski to Berlin to transfer 14,090 DM to Jan Dworak – secretary of the weekly *Solidarność*.[106] The next month, a WCL delegation visited Wałęsa, Mazowiecki, and Bogdan Lis, offering the post of vice-president to *Solidarność*.[107] Support was fueled by requests from *Solidarność*, competition with the ICFTU, and the goal of strengthening tendencies sympathetic to the WCL and Christian Democracy.[108] In May 1990, the WCL held its confederal board in Gdańsk and launched a program of new exchanges, as well as a campaign to celebrate the 10th anniversary of *Solidarność* and the 70th of the WCL.

104 WCL, 329, Mission to Poland in August 1988.
105 WCL, 322, Mission to Poland by Johan Verstraete, May 1991.
106 AK, 78, Rapport de mission syndicale, 9 May 1989.
107 WCL, 325, Letter from Jan Kułakowski to Lech Wałęsa, 12 July 1989.
108 AK, 78, Rapport de Mission syndicale, 9 May 1989.

This turn to *Solidarność* was part of a broader interest in the establishment of Christian Democratic trade unions and parties in the transitional countries of Eastern and Central Europe. Being the only affiliate in a "socialist" country, *Solidarność* had to open the way for bilateral relations with trade unions in other countries.[109] Krzysztof Dowgiałło – a *Solidarność* activist from Gdańsk who had been elected to the Polish Parliament in June 1989 was – strategically – appointed vice-president for Europe in November 1989. Together with Teresa Zabża – a close collaborator of Lech Wałęsa who was responsible for relations with the WCL – he was sent out for missions to countries such as Hungary, Ukraine, Czechoslovakia, Belorussia, and Latvia.[110] The WCL financed publications that had to counter rather negative perceptions that had existed among many dissidents across Eastern Europe since its détente policies in the 1970s, notably by stressing and duly magnifying its support for *Solidarność* in the course of the 1980s. In 1990, the WCL opened an office in Vienna with the support of Austrian Christian Trade Unions to coordinate efforts to establish new trade unions, in cooperation with a central WCL coordinating committee for Eastern and Central Europe.[111] These activities were linked to a broader mobilization by Christian social movements and church groups – such as CIDSE, the international umbrella association of Catholic social justice organizations, and Pax Christi – which developed a plethora of initiatives to access the transitional societies of Central and Eastern Europe.[112] Rather than enthusiasm, however, it was anxiety that inspired much of this interest: next to the question of how the Catholic Church could re-position itself in the new political context and the competition with Social Democrats and other political tendencies, the relations between post-communist Europe and the Third World were a key issue.

Indeed, in the late 1980s and early 1990s, the Third World continued to inspire, color and motivate to a large extent the relations of the WCL with Central and Eastern Europe. The WCL's interest in internationalizing *Solidarność* remained primarily focused on the connection with Latin America. In November 1989, Lech Wałęsa attended as its most iconic guest the 22nd Congress of the WCL in Caracas,[113] and met with different unionists and dignitaries, including the Venezuelan president Carlos

109 WCL, 328, Letter from Kułakowski to Lech Wałęsa, 17 January 1989.

110 WCL, 330, Letter from Carlos Custer to Krzysztof Dowgiałło, 28 June 1990.

111 WCL, 1566, Letter from Carlos Custer to Stefan Jurczak, 12 December 1991.

112 See for instance: KDC, Pax Christi International, 610, "Bevrijding van onderaf in Latijns-Amerika en Midden- en Oost-Europa," 1992.

113 *Flash* no. 347 (1 June 1989), 1.

Andrés Pérez.[114] During the meeting, Kułakowski dwelt extensively on the recent developments in Eastern Europe, and the need for a dialogue between the Third World and Eastern Europe to form a new, authentic trade union movement after the close of the Cold War.[115] At the end of 1989, Bohdan Cywiński traveled as a representative of *Solidarność* to Venezuela, Colombia, Chile, and Paraguay.[116] When delegations of the WCL attended the iconic festivities that marked *Solidarność*'s rise to power – such as its Second Congress in April 1990 or the inauguration of Lech Wałęsa as president of Poland in December 1990 – they above all reveled in connections that buttressed a shared identity between Eastern Europe and the Third World, stressing concerns such as "underdevelopment," "colonialism," or the need of an "holistic" trade union movement that contrasted with the bureaucracy of Western trade unionism.[117]

The WCL confederal board in Gdańsk in May 1990 discussed *Solidarność*'s potential to inspire campaigns over South Africa and Cuba with Tadeusz Mazowiecki, Polish Prime Minister since September 1989 and the first non-communist government leader in the Eastern Bloc.[118] The next month, in June 1990, Mazowiecki was together with Nelson Mandela – who had been released from prison in February of that year – welcomed as guest of honor during the 77th General Session of the ILO. For *Solidarność*, their presence "symbolised the common achievements of the ILO in ending communism and apartheid."[119] CLAT enlisted – in vain – Wałęsa's support for the candidacy of the Cuban opposition leader Gustavo Arcos Bergnes for the 1991 Nobel Peace Prize.[120] The connection with the Third World continued throughout the 1990s, when Christian trade union NGOs – such as Sotermun in Spain and Wereldsolidariteit / Solidarité Mondiale in Belgium – turned their projects of solidarity with the Third World into humanitarian projects in Eastern Europe – "Europe's Third World."[121] Many of these campaigns were driven by concerns about tensions between the "East" and the "South," due to growing currents of xenophobia and the critical sentiment towards the "colored comrades" of

114 José Ignacio Urquijo, *El movimiento obrero de Venezuela* (Lima: OIT/UCAB/INAESIN, 2004), 52.
115 WCL, 1656, Speech by Jan Kułakowski, 1988 (and 1989).
116 Christiaens and Goddeeris, "Solidarność and Latin America."
117 WCL, 322, Speech by Carlos Custer to the Solidarność Congress in April 1990.
118 WCL, 330, Solidarność, 1 June 1990.
119 *Solidarność News,* 154 (July 1990). In 1981, Bronisław Geremek, one of *Solidarność*'s most famous advisers, had also participated in an ILO anti-apartheid commission.
120 WCL, 330, Letter from Teresa Zabża, 24 October 1990.
121 WCL, 2239, Letter from Solidaridad con les Trabajadores del Tercer Mundo, 17 October 1996.

the defunct communist regimes in post-communist Europe, but also due to the fear that channeling aid flows towards Eastern Europe would be to the detriment of the South.[122]

Policies of expansion into post-communist Europe were, however, difficult to achieve. By late 1991, the WCL had been able to include – next to *Solidarność* – new members in Romania, Hungary, and Slovakia.[123] These affiliates were nonetheless small in terms of memberships and political clout, with Cartel Alfa in Romania as the main exception. The Eastern European policy of the WCL had already been crippled in Poland, where its relationship with *Solidarność* remained troubled. *Solidarność* became increasingly fragmented, due to splits into and across newly formed political parties that were established in view of elections as well as due to ideological discussions about the post-communist transition. By November 1989, it had already become clear to Kułakowski that the WCL had not been able "to prevent the leaders of *Solidarność* from stressing their preferential option for the ICFTU."[124] The WCL leadership attributed this to the latter's financial power, but also to a broader fascination with the "American way of living and Marlboro" in post-communist Poland.[125] However, this was only one part of the story: it also hinged on a crippled and ambivalent relationship with *Solidarność* ever since it was founded in 1980.

Conclusions

The struggle of *Solidarność* and other dissidents in Eastern Europe, as well as the support they received in Western Europe, has mostly been understood in terms of a "return to Europe."[126] Admittedly, something can be said for such a view when taking stock of the campaigns of the WCL on behalf of *Solidarność*. From its emergence in Gdańsk in the summer of

122 See for instance: KDC, Archives Vincentius Vereniging Nederland (VVN), 2314, Comprehensive Report on ICT Study Tour of Eastern Europe in 1991, including meeting with Halina Bortnowska (Pax Christi Poland).

123 WCL, 1566, Letter from Carlos Custer to Stefan Jurczak, 12 December 1991.

124 AK, Report on Poland, 1989.

125 WCL, 1656, Mission in Poland by Johan Verstraete, 5–12 May 1991.

126 Jacques Rupnik, "The legacies of dissent: Charter 77, the Helsinki effect, and the emergence of a European public space," in *Samizdat, Tamizdat, and Beyond: Transnational Media During and After Socialism*, ed. Friederike Kind-Kovacs and Jessie Labov (New York: Berghahn, 2013), 324; Joanna Bar, "From Communism to Democracy: the Concept of Europe in Cracow's Press in the Years 1975–1995," in *Europa im Ostblock: Vorstellungen und Diskurse (1945–1991)*, ed. Christian Domnitz, José M. Faraldo and Paulina Gulińska-Jurgiel (Cologne et al.: Böhlau, 2008).

1980 onward, the independent Polish trade union searched for models in terms of labor organization and legislation in Western Europe, while the WCL and the ICFTU united their efforts on behalf of *Solidarność* at the European level. During the 1990s, former WCL secretary-general Jan Kułakowski served as ambassador of the Polish government to the European Communities and as chief negotiator and one of the principal architects of Poland's membership of the European Union.

Still, it is striking how themes in the Third World rather than in Europe ran as a dominant theme through the relationship between the WCL and *Solidarność* during the 1980s. Christian trade union movements aimed to globalize *Solidarność* in real and imagined terms, and were especially interested in forging connections between the independent Polish trade union and issues in the Third World. There were many reasons for this. Christian trade unionism in Western Europe faced a deep identity crisis in the 1970s and 1980s, while Christian Democracy competed with Social Democracy in the transitions to democracy in the Third World, most notably in Latin America. Consequently, the policy of the WCL towards *Solidarność* was to a large extent outlined by its regional confederation in Latin America, which connected the plight of Poland with Nicaragua, Cuba, and Chile. Yet the connection with the Third World should also be viewed in a broader perspective.

There was above all the novelty of the phenomenon of *Solidarność*. Whereas international solidarity and human rights campaigns had hitherto mainly been focused on the Third World, *Solidarność* developed into the first sustained opposition movement in Eastern Europe and the first dissident movement that could not be ignored in the West. Recipes and networks which had previously been deployed in campaigns on behalf of the Third World became now models for supporting *Solidarność*. The link with the Third World helped make sense of *Solidarność*, and to adjust its ideological profile. It was indeed a movement that could mean different things to different people, and its profile remained subject to debate over the course of the 1980s – partly due to internal diversity but also because it offered a projection screen for competing and divergent ideas in the West emerging both from the right and left sides of the political spectrum.[127] All in all, support for *Solidarność* was for the WCL and its allied Christian Democratic labor movements a surprisingly awkward issue, especially due to their focus on détente and the Third World and their competition with

127 Stefan Berger, "Solidarność, Western Solidarity, and Détente: A Transnational Approach," *European Review* 16, no. 1 (2008): 75–84.

Social Democracy and Cold War hawks à la Reagan and Thatcher. Forging connections with the Third World offered a means to position *Solidarność* squarely at the center of efforts at building a "third way" that surpassed the logics of the Cold War. This inspired the WCL to stress the connection with the struggle against what were called "red dictatorships" in the Third World, such as Cuba and Sandinista Nicaragua, and right-wing regimes, such as those in Chile and South Africa. These connections were also believed to enhance its appeal to *Solidarność*, which showed however little interest in cooperation and leant more to the ICFTU.

Yet *Solidarność* also contributed to this global identity.[128] Already in 1981, the leadership of *Solidarność* had aligned itself – at least rhetorically – with the Third World – as Poland was itself struggling for independence and sovereignty.[129] In 1986, Bohdan Cywiński and an anonymous *Solidarność* militant from Poland professed in an interview with Jan Kułakowski and the Beninese trade unionist Dominique Aguessy their deep sympathy with trade unionists from Africa and Latin America, juxtaposing their openness and holistic vision on trade unionism with the dullness and bureaucracy of their Western counterparts.[130] Latin America – where transitions to democracy were being completed during the 1980s – influenced strategies of the Polish opposition.[131] Not only ideology but also strategy played indeed its part. When the *Solidarność* Coordinating Office Abroad noticed how support from *Solidarność* had dwindled in the wake of normalization policies towards the Jaruzelski regime after the crisis of December 1981, it strategically connected to issues such as apartheid and Chile to dramatize the mission of *Solidarność*.

In the end, however, *Solidarność* faced many hurdles in internationalizing its cause. Its foreign policy was crippled by Cold War alliances – such as the support of the Polish government for anti-apartheid and Sandinista Nicaragua – but also by the competing interests of its international allies and by the lack of a clear international policy. The connections with the Third World may well have been glamorized in the 1990s, when the end of colonialism and communism were celebrated as one common victory of human rights and Polish historians started to cherish the global dimen-

128 Patryk Pleskot, *Solidarność, Zachód i węże: Służba Bezpieczeństwa wobec emigracyjnych struktur Solidarności 1981–1989* (Warsaw: IPN, 2011), 23.

129 AK, 73, Suggestions pour un programme de politique internationale de NSZZ Solidarność, 1981.

130 "Solidarność i Trzeci Świat," *Widnokrąg* 1 (1986): 25–36.

131 See for instance: Jadwiga Staniszkis, *Self-Limiting Revolution*, ed. Jan T. Gross (Princeton, NJ: Princeton University Press, 1984).

sions of *Solidarność*,[132] they were however deeply contested prior to and after 1989. The question of how to weld support for *Solidarność* to campaigns for democracy and human rights in the Third World was indeed one of the major sources of conflict between the Polish trade union and the WCL throughout the 1980s. Nevertheless, these connections in real and imagined terms with the Third World reveal how the end of the Cold War was not only forged by Eastern Europe integrating into the West, but also suggest how the "opening of the East" in the 1980s was also related to an opening towards the Global South.[133]

132 See for instance "From Solidarność to Freedom: International Conference. Warsaw-Gdańsk, 29–31 August 2005," www.girodivite.it/IMG/pdf/raport_25-en.pdf.

133 Galia Chimiak, "From Solidarność to Global Solidarity? The Engagement of Polish Civil Society in Development Cooperation," *Studia Socjologiczne* 222, no. 3 (2016): 165–198.

2

THE CSCE VIENNA FOLLOW-UP MEETING AND ALOIS MOCK, 1986–1989

Andrea Brait and Michael Gehler

The Cold War, and in particular its end, has received much attention in recent years in contemporary historical research.[1] The role of Austria has also been studied in detail.[2] The CSCE Vienna Follow-up Meeting (1986–1989), however, which ended shortly before the dramatic developments in the summer and fall of 1989, has hardly been analyzed at all.[3] This meeting undoubtedly brought about a clear further development in the effort to reduce tensions between East and West, which was shown, among other things, by the fact that talks on the conventional European Armed Forces were now part of the CSCE process, as the Austrian Foreign Ministry emphasized in a review in 1992. In addition, the so-called Human Dimension Mechanism was established to allow permanent monitoring of the implementation of agreements.[4] The former Austrian Foreign Minister Alois Mock, who was the Christian Democratic leader involved in steering these meetings, made clear their significance after a quarter century when he described this as a "second major breakthrough" in the relationship

1 See Ulf Engel, Frank Hadler and Matthias Middell, eds., *1989 in a Global Perspective* (Leipzig: Leipzig University Press, 2015); Wolfgang Mueller, Michael Gehler, and Arnold Suppan, eds., *The Revolutions of 1989: A Handbook* (Vienna: Verlag der Österreichischen Akademie der Wissenschaften, 2015); Mary Elise Sarotte, *1989: The Struggle to Create Post-Cold War Europe* (Princeton, NJ: Princeton University Press, 2009); Svetlana Savranskaya, "The Logic of 1989: The Soviet Peaceful Withdrawal from Eastern Europe," in *Masterpieces of History*, ed. Svetlana Savranskaya, Thomas S. Blanton and Vladislav Zubok (Budapest-New York: Central European University Press, 2010), 1–47; Vladimir Tismaneanu and Bogdan C. Iacob, eds., *The End and the Beginning: The Revolutions of 1989 and the Resurgence of History* (Budapest-New York: Central European University Press, 2012).

2 See Andrea Brait and Michael Gehler, eds., *Grenzöffnung 1989. Innen- und Außenperspektiven und die Folgen für Österreich* (Vienna-Cologne-Weimar: Böhlau, 2014).

3 See Sarah B. Snyder, "The foundation for Vienna: A reassessment of the CSCE in the mid-1980s," *Cold War History* 10, no. 4 (2010): 493–512.

4 See BMAA, *Die Konferenz für Sicherheit und Zusammenarbeit in Europa (KSZE) (Rückblick und Ausblick), Stenographische Protokolle des Nationalrats*, XVIII. GP, III-71 der Beilagen.

between East and West, after the treaty on the global reductions of Intermediate Nuclear Forces (INF).[5]

Austria's Christian Democratic party, the People's Party (ÖVP), had supported the CSCE course from the beginning, while the Vienna-based international coalition of Christian Democratic and conservative parties, the European Democrat Union (EDU), had been rather skeptical about the CSCE process in the 1970s and the first half of the 1980s.[6] However, this all changed in the course of the Vienna negotiations as Moscow's efforts to achieve political change created possibilities for concrete agreements within the CSCE. Austrian Foreign Minister Mock played a decisive role here in his capacity as chairman of the ÖVP from 1979 to 1989 and Austrian foreign minister from 1987 to 1995. From 1979 to 1998, he was also President of the EDU and thus played a central role in shaping the orientation of numerous Christian Democratic, liberal-conservative, and conservative political parties in Europe in the decade before and after 1989.

In the course of exercising his duties, Mock worked to encourage Austria to make an active contribution to the easing of tensions between East and West, as he emphasized in parliament shortly after his election as chairman of the ÖVP.[7] As early as 1972, the ÖVP had laid down its program of principles (Salzburg Program): "Peace as the highest goal of our foreign policy can only be permanently secured by the establishment of universal justice. We reject the arms race, which endangers humanity, and welcome any initiative for genuine détente in the world."[8]

Much attention was paid to the CSCE in the Government Declaration of 28 January 1987:

> The Conference on Security and Cooperation in Europe is the central forum for progress towards a pan-European peace order. The federal government will therefore endeavor to provide impetus for strengthening this

5 See Marilena Gala, "From INF to SDI. How Helsinki reshaped the transatlantic dimension of European security," in *The Crisis of Détente in Europe*, ed. Leopoldo Nuti (London: Routledge, 2009), 111–123; "Ein Schritt Richtung Mensch," www.kleinezeitung.at/k/politik/4117520/KSZE_Ein-Schritt-Richtung-Mensch (19 March 2016).

6 See Document 122: "Bericht über ein KSZE-Vorbereitungstreffen in Genf," 20 December 1974; Document 139: "Entwurf einer Entschließung der EUCD zur KSZE," 4 July 1975; and especially Document 223: "Entschließung des Exekutivkomitees der EVP zur Konferenz von Belgrad," 2 March 1977, in *Transnationale Parteienkooperation der europäischen Christdemokraten und Konservativen 1965–1979. Coopération transnationale des partis démocrates-chrétiens et conservateurs en Europe. Dokumente 1965–1979*, 2 vols., ed. Michael Gehler et al. (Berlin: De Gruyter, 2018), 810–811, 871, and 1134–1135.

7 See Michael Gehler, *Österreichs Außenpolitik der Zweiten Republik. Von der alliierten Besatzung bis zum Europa des 21. Jahrhunderts* (Innsbruck-Vienna-Bozen: StudienVerlag, 2005), 583f.

8 See Salzburger Programm der Österreichischen Volkspartei, 1972, Pkt. 4,11,2.

> pan-European cooperation through initiatives in all areas. At the Vienna Follow-up Meeting, it will make every effort to dismantle barriers between people in Eastern and Western Europe, to strengthen economic cooperation between all European states and to seek ways of increasing common security, including in the military field, through disarmament measures. The federal government assumes that only the full implementation of the standards of conduct laid down in the Helsinki Final Act will generate the intergovernmental confidence which is one of the prerequisites for long-term peaceful development.[9]

The ÖVP thus clearly showed its support for Austria's earlier CSCE course and its engagement within the neutral and non-aligned (N+N) states. The focus of Mock's foreign policy was clearly marked by the fact that before 1987 he had already been particularly involved with developments in Central and Eastern Europe, including as Head of Cabinet for the former Federal Chancellor Josef Klaus. Since the early 1980s, his party had fostered close contacts with dissidents and opponents of regimes behind the Iron Curtain. From 1979, his party colleague Erhard Busek regularly traveled to meet with dissidents throughout Central and Eastern Europe. Since taking office as Foreign Minister, Mock had advocated changes in the political and human rights situations of Austria's eastern neighbors. He openly questioned the position of the communist states that the discussion of domestic human rights issues meant interference in internal affairs. While traveling to these states, he met prominent dissidents such as Václav Havel and Andrei Sakharov.[10] More than his predecessors Rudolf Kirchschläger, Erich Bielka-Karltreu, Willibald Pahr, Erwin Lanc, Leopold Gratz, and Peter Jankowitsch, who were either non-partisans or members of the Austrian Socialist Party (SPÖ), Mock focused on so-called "silent diplomacy."[11] He not only wanted to negotiate problems such as humanitarian cases at the sidelines of political meetings without publicity, but in fact also saw the CSCE process as an opportunity for fundamental regulations.

The following analysis takes a closer look at the CSCE Vienna Follow-up Meeting and focuses in particular on the assessments of Mock. Due to the lack of basic historical research on the Vienna Follow-up Meeting, its fun-

9 Stenographisches Protokoll, 2. Sitzung NR XVII. GP, 45.

10 See Helmut Wohnout, "Vom Durchschneiden des Eisernen Vorhangs bis zur Anerkennung Sloweniens und Kroatiens. Österreichs Außenminister Alois Mock und die europäischen Umbrüche 1989–1992," in *Grenzöffnung 1989*, ed. Brait and Gehler, 185–187.

11 Maximilian Graf, "European Détente and the CSCE. Austria and the East-Central European Theatre in the 1970s and 1980s," in *The CSCE and the End of the Cold War*, ed. Nicolas Badalassi and Sarah B. Snyder (New York, NY: Berghahn Books Incorporated, 2019), 249–274, here 252.

damental significance must be established in order to make clear its significance for Christian Democratic designs for Central and Eastern Europe before, during, and after the revolutions of 1989.[12] The aim of this chapter is therefore to highlight the broader trajectory and contemporary assessments of the CSCE process in the last decade of the Cold War, while the specific implications for Christian Democracy will be more extensively addressed later in this volume, in Helmut Wohnout's contribution.

The CSCE follow-up process and the state of the art

In the 1950s, the Soviet Union proposed a collective security system for Europe in order to head off prospects for deeper integration of the Federal Republic of Germany (FRG) into the West. In the middle of the 1960s, these Soviet initiatives were renewed, but the West – represented by the member states of the European Communities and by NATO – reacted with restraint. North American and Western European powers declared the need for a simultaneous treatment of all relevant questions concerning civil and human rights.

In July 1966, the member states of the Warsaw Pact proposed a conference to discuss the preservation of peace and political cooperation. This suggestion was repeated in 1969. In 1970, the NATO Council agreed, on the condition of advancing the negotiations regarding the question of Germany. This was achieved with the so-called East Treaties of 1970, the Four-Power Agreement with regard to the status of Berlin, and the German-German Basic Treaty of 1972.[13]

In July 1973, the Conference on Security and Cooperation in Europe (CSCE) started with a Foreign Ministers' meeting. The negotiations ended with the signing of the Helsinki Final Act on 1 August 1975 by heads of state and governments. Thirty-three member states from across Europe, plus Canada and the United States, were the signatories. Three relevant issues were the focus of the CSCE. Basket 1 especially embraced questions of security in Europe. Basket 2 focused on cooperation in terms of economy, science, technology, and environment, while basket 3 included questions of civil and human rights, especially exchanges in the domains

12 Regarding Mock's specific contacts and projects behind the Iron Curtain, see Helmut Wohnout's chapter in this volume.

13 See Thomas Fischer, "Die Sowjetunion, Österreich und die finnische KSZE-Initiative vom 5. Mai 1969," in *Osteuropa vom Weltkrieg zur Wende*, ed. Wolfgang Mueller and Michael Portmann (Vienna: Verl. der Österr. Akad. der Wiss, 2007), 313–339.

of information and culture.[14] Baskets 1 and 3 were highly controversial, but the so-called neutral and non-aligned countries acted successfully as mediators.[15] Both sides considered the Final Act a success. The member states of the Warsaw Pact now had confirmation of the inviolability of their borders, and the West was expecting progress regarding human and civil rights within the Eastern Bloc states. The Final Act from August 1975 forced all CSCE member states to cooperate, and it also strengthened the Western influence in the Eastern societies for the purpose of providing support to civil right groups. Finally, it also facilitated the transformation process of the post-Stalinist regimes in Central and Eastern Europe.[16]

In parallel with the CSCE process, international tensions dissipated in the 1970s. The policy of détente was supported not only by the so-called *Ostpolitik* pursued by the German Chancellor Willy Brandt and Foreign Minister Walter Scheel, but later on also by the long-term Foreign Minister Hans-Dietrich Genscher.[17] The policy of active neutrality practiced by Austria's Chancellor Bruno Kreisky together with the Swedish Prime Minister Olof Palme also strengthened the process of détente in Europe.

14 See Michael Cotey Morgan, *The Final Act: The Helsinki Accords and the Transformation of the Cold War* (Princeton-Oxford: Princeton University Press, 2018); Carla Meneguzzi Rostagni, ed., *The Helsinki Process: A Historical Reappraisal* (Padova: CEDAM, 2005).

15 See Sandra Bott et al., eds., *Neutrality and Neutralism in the Global Cold War: Between or within the Blocs?* (Abingdon, Oxon-New York, NY: Routledge, 2016); Thomas Fischer, *Neutral Power in the CSCE: The N+N States and the Making of the Helsinki Accords 1975* (Baden-Baden: Nomos, 2009); Jürgen Dinkel, *Die Bewegung Bündnisfreier Staaten: Genese, Organisation und Politik (1927–1992)* (Berlin: De Gruyter Oldenbourg, 2015); Benjamin Gilde, "Hüter des Dritten Korbes. Die humanitäre KSZE-Politik Österreichs in Belgrad und Madrid zwischen Bundeskanzler, Diplomaten und internationalen Spannungen," in *Die KSZE im Ost-West-Konflikt*, ed. Matthias Peter and Hermann Wentker (Berlin-Boston: De Gruyter, 2013), 155–172; Jussi M. Hanhimäki, "Non-Aligned to What? European Neutrals and the Cold War," in *Neutrality and Neutralism in the Global Cold War*, ed. Sandra Bott et al., 17–32; Hanspeter Neuhold, ed., *CSCE: N+N Perspectives: The Process of the Conference on Security and Cooperation in Europe from the Viewpoint of the Neutral and Non-aligned Participating States* (Vienna: Braumüller, 1987); Hanspeter Neuhold and Stefan Lehne, "The Role of the Neutral and Non-Aligned Countries at the Vienna Meeting," in *The Human Dimension of the Helsinki Process*, ed. Arie Bloed and Pieter van Dijk (Dordrecht-Boston-Norwell: Nijhoff; sold and distributed in the USA and Canada by Kluwer Academic Publishers, 1991), 30–53.

16 See Michael Gehler, "Konferenzen über Sicherheit und Zusammenarbeit in Europa (KSZE)," in *Lexikon der deutschen Geschichte 1945–1990*, ed. Michael Behnen (Stuttgart: Kröner, 2002), 365–366.

17 See Angela Romano, *From détente in Europe to European détente: How the West shaped the Helsinki CSCE* (Brussels-New York: Peter Lang, 2009); Pouland Villaume and Odd Arne Westad, eds., *Perforating the Iron Curtain: European Détente, Transatlantic Relations, and the Cold War, 1965–1985* (Copenhagen: Museum Tusculanum Press, University of Copenhagen, 2010).

However, the first follow-up meetings in Belgrade (1977–1979) and Madrid (1981–1983) were not success stories.[18] The Russian intervention in Afghanistan in 1979, the NATO Double-Track Decision taken in the same year, the boycott of the 1980 Summer Olympics in Moscow, as well as the implementation of martial law 1981 in Poland, produced new confrontation between East and West. The danger of a breakdown of the whole CSCE process grew.[19] This serious threat could be avoided thanks to mediations by the neutrals.[20]

Despite these setbacks, in the end the CSCE process played a decisive role in facilitating détente and cooperation in Europe. Starting in the mid-1980s, the CSCE follow-up process also served to support the Secretary General of the Communist Party of the Soviet Union Mikhail Gorbachev and his reform policy.[21] In this domain, too, the CSCE Vienna Follow-up Meeting from 1986 to 1989 made an important contribution. Starting in 1991, the CSCE also tried to develop a kind of rescue mechanism with regard to the dissolution of the Warsaw Pact.

Historical research has long neglected almost anything regarding the CSCE. This was revealed in 2009 and 2014 when multiple "anniversary" studies about the revolutions of 1989 were published.[22] In overviews about the Cold War, the CSCE often seems like a tangent to the policy of détente in the power conflict between East and West, as Matthias Peter

18 See Vladimir Bilandžić, Dittmar Dahlmann and Milan Kosanović, eds., *From Helsinki to Belgrade: The First CSCE Follow-up Meeting and the Crisis of Détente* (Göttingen-Bonn: V & R Unipress, 2012).

19 See Leopoldo Nuti, ed., *The Crisis of Détente in Europe: From Helsinki to Gorbachev, 1975–1985* (London: Routledge, 2009).

20 See Thomas Fischer, *Keeping the Process Alive: The N+N and the CSCE Follow-Up from Helsinki to Vienna (1975–1986)* (Zurich: Center for Security Studies, ETH Zürich, 2012).

21 See Anatoly Adamishin and Richard Schifter, *Human Rights, Perestroika, and the End of the Cold War* (Washington DC: United States Institute of Peace, 2009); Vojtech Mastny, "Did Gorbachev Liberate Eastern Europe?" in *The last Decade of the Cold War*, ed. Olav Njølstad (London-New York: Cass, 2004), 402–423; Marie-Pierre Rey, "Gorbachev's New Thinking and Europe, 1985–1989," in *Europe and the End of the Cold War*, ed. Frédéric Bozo et al. (London-New York: Routledge, 2008), 23–35; Yuliya von Saal, *KSZE-Prozess und Perestroika in der Sowjetunion. Demokratisierung, Werteumbruch und Auflösung 1985–1991* (Munich: Oldenbourg, 2014); Andrei Grachev, "Gorbachev and the 'New Political Thinking,'" in *The Revolutions*, ed. Mueller, Gehler and Suppan, 33–46.

22 See for a summary: Wolfgang Mueller, "The Revolutions of 1989: An Introduction," in *The Revolutions*, ed. Mueller, Gehler and Suppan, 3–30.

points out.[23] However, political science became interested in the contribution of the CSCE process and its effect on Central and Eastern Europe early on. The first studies mainly produced general assessments of the negotiation results.[24]

The extent to which the CSCE process made a contribution to the end of the Cold War is still a matter of debate.[25] Research regarding the revolutions of 1989 primarily claimed the so-called "Gorbachev effect" in addition to economic changes during this time.[26] Tensions at the military level clearly also underwent massive reduction. Thus the CSCE process is surely not the only factor, yet still must not be overlooked. According to Philipp Ther, the CSCE created an international social community, thereby initiating a social dynamic underestimated by Eastern Bloc regimes. This created an unprecedented opportunity for new dissident movements, like Poland's Workers' Defense Committee and Czechoslovakia's Charter 77, which explicitly justified their activities in reference to the CSCE resolutions.[27]

Since 2010, some historical studies have been conducted that explicitly deal with the CSCE process. The research project "Der KSZE-

23 See Matthias Peter, *Die Bundesrepublik im KSZE-Prozess 1975–1983. Die Umkehrung der Diplomatie* (Berlin: De Gruyter Oldenbourg, 2015), 10. This is especially noticeable in the three-part series *The Cambridge History of the Cold War*, where not one of 72 articles mentions the CSCE in detail. The CSCE-process is primarily mentioned in publications regarding human rights during the Cold War: Rosemarie Foot, "The Cold War and human rights," in *The Cambridge History of the Cold War*, ed. Melvyn P. Leffler and Odd Arne Westad (Cambridge: Cambridge University Press, 2010), 445–465. See also Olav Njølstad, ed., *The Last Decade of the Cold War: From Conflict Escalation to Conflict Transformation* (London-New York: Cass, 2004); Kevin McDermott and Matthew Stibbe, eds., *The 1989 Revolutions in Central and Eastern Europe: From Communism to Pluralism* (Manchester-New York: Manchester University Press, distributed in the United States exclusively by Palgrave Macmillan, 2013); Mark Kramer and Vít Smetana, eds., *Imposing, Maintaining, and Tearing Open the Iron Curtain: The Cold War and East-Central Europe, 1945–1989* (Lanham-Boulder-New York et al.: Lexington Books, 2014).

24 See Michael Zielinski, *Die neutralen und blockfreien Staaten und ihre Rolle im KSZE-Prozeß* (Baden-Baden: Nomos Verlagsgesellschaft, 1990); Wilfried von Bredow, *Der KSZE-Prozess. Von der Zähmung zur Auflösung des Ost-West-Konflikts* (Darmstadt: Wissenschaftliche Buchgesellschaft, 1992).

25 For a summary see Matthias Peter and Hermann Wentker, "'Helsinki-Mythos' oder 'Helsinki-Effekt'? Der KSZE-Prozess zwischen internationaler Politik und gesellschaftlicher Transformation. Zur Einleitung," in *Die KSZE im Ost-West-Konflikt*, ed. Peter and Wentker, 1–14.

26 See Mastny, "Did Gorbachev Liberate Eastern Europe?"; Rey, "Gorbachev's New Thinking and Europe"; Helmut Altrichter, *Russland 1989. Der Untergang des sowjetischen Imperiums* (Munich: Beck, 2009), 318–330; Archie Brown, *Seven Years that Changed the World: Perestroika in Perspective* (Oxford: Oxford University Press, 2009); Savranskaya, "The Logic of 1989"; Grachev, "Gorbachev and the 'New Political Thinking'"; Christoph Boyer, "1989 und die Wege dorthin," *Vierteljahrshefte* für *Zeitgeschichte* 59, no. 1 (2011): 101–118.

27 See Philipp Ther, *Europe since 1989: A History*, trans. Charlotte Kreuzmuller (Princeton, NJ: Princeton University Press, 2018), 35.

Prozess: Multilaterale Konferenzdiplomatie und ihre Folgen 1975–1989/90" ("The CSCE process: Multilateral conference diplomacy and its results 1975–1989/90"), which was initiated by the Munich-Berlin Institute of Contemporary History in cooperation with the University of Paris IV and the University of Erlangen-Nuremberg, under the sponsorship of the Leibniz Association, has made a decisive contribution to the research, resulting in a series of monographs. Anja Hanisch focused on the GDR and the CSCE process from 1972–1985: "Between East-dependency and the right to travel."[28] Benjamin Gilde published on "Austria and the CSCE process from 1969–1983 focusing on neutrals' mediation in a humanitarian mission."[29] Philip Rosin published on Switzerland and the CSCE process, trying to analyze the impact of Swiss neutrality on Gorbachev's reform policy.[30] Yuliya von Saal analyzed the relationship between the CSCE process and the program of *perestroika* within the Soviet Union.[31] Finally, Matthias Peter analyzed the role played by the FRG within the CSCE process from 1975 to 1983.[32] He stressed the important role played by Foreign Minister Genscher, who realized the relevance of the CSCE follow-up process, in contrast to Chancellor Helmut Schmidt who nonetheless gave the Foreign Ministry free rein and let him go on the CSCE trip completely alone because Schmidt was much more focused on issues of economy, currency and hard power of security. Volumes on the CSCE follow-up have also been published, especially by Matthias Peter and Hermann Wentker on the CSCE in the context of the East-West conflict, international policy and social transformation through 1990.[33]

Both editors concluded that there was much more a Helsinki effect than a Helsinki myth, which had been posited by famous scholars and politicians since the late 1970s. This negative image within the historiography has been substantially revised by monographs published in the last years. The outcome of the CSCE Vienna Follow-up Meeting from 1986 to 1989 underlined that the effects were decisive and much more influential than the belief in a Helsinki myth.

28 Anja Hanisch, *Die DDR im KSZE-Prozess 1972–1985. Zwischen Ostabhängigkeit, Westabgrenzung und Ausreisebewegung* (Munich: De Gruyter, 2012).
29 Benjamin Gilde, *Österreich im KSZE-Prozess 1969–1983. Neutraler Vermittler in humanitärer Mission* (Munich: Oldenbourg Verlag, 2013).
30 Philip Rosin, *Die Schweiz im KSZE-Prozess 1972–1983. Einfluss durch Neutralität* (Munich: Oldenbourg, 2014).
31 Saal, *KSZE-Prozess und Perestroika in der Sowjetunion.*
32 Peter, *Die Bundesrepublik im KSZE-Prozess.*
33 Matthias Peter and Hermann Wentker, eds., *Die KSZE im Ost-West-Konflikt. Internationale Politik und gesellschaftliche Transformation 1975–1990* (Berlin-Boston: De Gruyter, 2013).

However, there is still a dearth of studies on the role played by the CSCE at the end of the Cold War and the effects of the negotiations at the CSCE Vienna Follow-up Meeting in particular.[34] The most detailed descriptions of the CSCE Vienna Follow-up Meeting are from Stefan Lehne, a member of the Austrian delegation,[35] and from Hans-Heinrich Wrede, a member of the delegation of the Federal Republic of Germany.[36] Both texts offer detailed insights into the development of the negotiations, but are more primary sources than scholarly literature.[37] Two years after the conclusion of the final document of Vienna a volume was published which presented a range of analyses of that document from the perspectives international law and political science.[38] The results of the negotiations on security policy have already been evaluated very precisely.[39] However, the general effects of the CSCE Vienna Follow-up Meeting remain largely unresearched.

The remaining pages of this chapter do not, of course, suffice to completely close the research gap. On the basis of Austrian media coverage, however, the way in which the results of the CSCE Vienna Follow-up Meet-

34 See Victor-Yves Ghebali, *La diplomatie de la Détente: La CSCE, d'Helsinki à Vienne (1973–1989)* (Brussels: Bruylant, 1989); Michael Groth, "Fortschritte im KSZE-Prozeß. Das dritte Folgetreffen in Wien," *Europa Archiv* (1989): 95–102; Daniel C. Thomas, *The Helsinki Effect: International Norms, Human Rights, and the Demise of Communism* (Princeton, NJ: Princeton University Press, 2001), 236–247; Floribert Baudet, "'It was Cold War and we wanted to win': human rights, 'détente,' and the CSCE," in *Origins of the European Security System*, ed. Andreas Wenger, Vojtech Mastny and Christian Nuenlist (London-New York: Routledge, 2008), 183–198; Helmut Altrichter and Hermann Wentker, eds., *Der KSZE-Prozess. Vom Kalten Krieg zu einem neuen Europa 1975 bis 1990* (Munich: Oldenbourg Wissenschaftsverlag, 2011); Sarah B. Snyder, *Human Rights Activism and the End of the Cold War: A Transnational History of the Helsinki Network* (New York: Cambridge University Press, 2011); Oliver Bange, "Der KSZE-Prozess und die sicherheitspolitische Dynamik des Ost-West-Konflikts 1970–1990," in *Wege zur Wiedervereinigung*, ed. Oliver Bange and Bernd Lemke (Munich: Oldenbourg Verlag, 2013), 87–104; Walter Süß, "Die Wiener KSZE-Folgekonferenz und der Handlungsspielraum des DDR-Sicherheitsapparates 1989," in *Die KSZE im Ost-West-Konflikt*, ed. Peter and Wentker, 219–231; Saal, *KSZE-Prozess und Perestroika in der Sowjetunion.*

35 Stefan Lehne, *The Vienna Meeting of the Conference on Security and Cooperation in Europe, 1986–1989: A Turning Point in East-West Relations* (Boulder-San Francisco-Oxford: Westview Press, 1991).

36 Hans-Heinrich Wrede, *KSZE in Wien. Kursbestimmung für Europas Zukunft* (Cologne: Verlag Wissenschaft und Politik, 1990).

37 The same is true for the analysis of Ambassador Liedermann regarding Austria's role during the CSCE: Helmut Liedermann, "Österreichs Rolle beim Zustandekommen der KSZE," in *Mit anderen Augen gesehen*, ed. Oliver Rathkolb, Otto M. Maschke and Stefan August Lütgenau (Vienna-Cologne-Weimar: Böhlau, 2002), 491–521.

38 Arie Bloed and Pieter van Dijk, eds., *The Human Dimension of the Helsinki Process: The Vienna Follow-up Meeting and its Aftermath* (Dordrecht-Boston-Norwell: Nijhoff; sold and distributed in the USA and Canada by Kluwer Academic Publishers, 1991).

39 Stephan Martini, *Die sicherheitspolitische Funktion der KSZE im entspannungspolitischen Konzept der Bundesrepublik Deutschland 1975–1990* (Berlin: Mensch & Buch, 2006), 298–390.

ing were presented in public is analyzed. This is where the role of Christian Democracy proved decisive – in particular, the leadership of Austrian Foreign Minister Alois Mock. To what extent these correspond to the actual course and results of the negotiations should be examined in a larger study, which should also include governmental documents and oral history.

The outcome of the CSCE Vienna Follow-up Meeting

The CSCE Vienna Follow-up Meeting started on 4 November 1986 and finished with the 162nd plenary session on 15 January 1989. Two years of negotiations by 35 CSCE member states brought a balanced and substantial final document.[40] This was a rather surprising result. A few months earlier, in March 1988, the German head of delegation Ekkehard Eickhoff had stated that the Vienna Conference "is far away from making big progress."[41] What did Eickhoff mean by "progress," and what was so controversial? The US delegation made progress contingent on Soviet concessions with regard to human rights, while the Warsaw Pact member states defined progress with respect to a conference on conventional disarmament in Europe. Additionally, there was also fundamental dissent in the West. While the FRG wanted a catch-all approach embracing all elements of political, military, economic and humanitarian components, the US, France, and Great Britain were mainly interested in the inviolable protection of human rights. There was also a fundamental conflict between Hungary and Romania regarding the treatment of minorities. As Wrede reports, Mock repeatedly moved the CSCE process along in critical phases with high-level personal telephone conversations with counterparts and colleagues.[42]

Concerning Basket 2 on economic East-West cooperation in the field of science, technology and environment there were no concrete proposals made or substantial results reached in Vienna.[43] The breakthrough concerning regulations in basket 3 was finally reached in the last months of negotiations. There is no doubt that the N+N states were active coordinators in special working groups and made a decisive contribution to the success of the CSCE Vienna Follow-up Meeting. On 18 December 1988,

40 See Wrede, *KSZE in Wien*; Lehne, *The Vienna Meeting*.

41 Wilhelm Bruns, "Mehr Substanz in Ost-West-Beziehungen. Zur dritten KSZE-Folgekonferenz in Wien," *Aus Politik und Zeitgeschichte* B12 (1989): 3.

42 Wrede, *KSZE in Wien*, 126.

43 Lehne, *The Vienna Meeting*, 173.

they presented a new draft for the final document, which had been prepared in May 1988 and was then accepted by all CSCE participants. None of the 35, with the exception of Romania, had serious objections to the draft.

Strangely enough, the disagreements did not follow East-West lines. When looking at the issue of disarmament and the proposed East-West conference on the economy, there were clear differences within the Western group of states. Concerning disarmament, there were differences between the US and France, for example, and with regard to economic issues between the US and EC member states more broadly.

Both of the German states played a constructive role. The FRG as well as the GDR was ready to compromise. This is also a reason why Vienna could be the site of progress and success.

Remarkably, the most difficult subjects saw the greatest advances. A balanced and substantial outcome was the result of, first, a mandate for a new conference on conventional disarmament in Europe and, second, a mixture of mutual concessions and the economic weakness of the Communist world. Optimism that East-West relations were on the right track seemed to be justified.[44]

With the CSCE Vienna Follow-up Meeting a new quality of cooperation and coordination could be observed because conventional disarmament, which did not play a big role in the Helsinki Final Act, was now reserved for a special negotiation forum. Negotiations on the conventional European Armed Forces were now part of the CSCE process and a conference on confidence- and security-building measures was also scheduled.

At the beginning of the CSCE Vienna Follow-up Meeting, there was no expectation that the 35 CSCE states would agree to a final document laying out precise arrangements concerning future cooperation in the field of humanitarian issues. The agreements reached in Vienna included the right to free movement, freedom of choice of residence within the borders of each state, the right to travel from one district to another, and the possibility of returning to one's own country. Any imposition of restrictions upon these rights was to be a matter solely of exceptional circumstance. These measures were particularly important for family meetings and the reunification of family members. In a further CSCE document, the West's demand for freedom of movement was described in detail for the first time. This contributed to the cross-border traffic of visitors, including also the possible gradual reduction of limitations in order to facilitate travel

44 See Bruns, "Mehr Substanz in Ost-West-Beziehungen."

and exchange and to make family reunification possible. This aspect was very important for the West German policy pursued by Helmut Kohl and Hans-Dietrich Genscher. Another improvement made by the CSCE Vienna Follow-up Meeting final document was a three-step consultation process and verification mechanism concerning the safeguarding of human rights. Agreements were reached that included the right of each CSCE state to submit unresolved cases. Three follow-up conferences on human rights were also planned: a first one for 1989 in Paris, a second for 1990 in Copenhagen, and a third for 1991 in Moscow.[45]

In the area of human rights, issues such as religious freedom, the rights of religious communities, and the rights of national minorities were also described in detail. The practice was to be controlled and improved by all means in order to prevent abuses and violations of human rights.[46]

Assessment by Austrian Foreign Minister Alois Mock

In 1987, the Christian Democrat Alois Mock succeeded Peter Jankowitsch, a Social Democrat, at the helm of the Austrian Foreign Ministry. This did not change Austria's fundamental foreign policy line, for example with regard to demands in the field of human rights. However, Mock showed a strong personal interest in achieving positive results at the CSCE Vienna Follow-up Meeting.

In April 1987, shortly after taking charge of the ministry, Mock pushed the idea of getting new and better results in Vienna than the CSCE community had seen in Belgrade or Madrid. He made it very clear that Austria's position at the literal center of Europe should help achieve good results, especially on conventional disarmament. Mock was very much in favor of this issue being part of the whole CSCE process because the negotiations on the Mutual and Balanced Force Reductions (MBFR) had proven a complete failure. He also underlined the productive impact of the N+N states, in order to contribute to progress on the issue of conventional disarmament. But the Austrian head of the delegation at the conference, Rudolf Torovsky, made it very clear at a press conference that the neutrals were entering into the Vienna conference with no common position on disar-

45 See "Die Moskauer Konferenz über die Menschliche Dimension der KSZE," *Europa Archiv* 46, no. 23 (1991): D579-D593.

46 Bruns, "Mehr Substanz in Ost-West-Beziehungen," 7; Stefan Lehne, "Vom Prozeß zur Institution. Zur aktuellen Debatte über die Weiterentwicklung des KSZE-Prozesses," *Europa Archiv* 45, no. 16 (1990): 499–506.

mament and security issues. There were slight differences between the Swiss, Swedish, and Finnish and the Yugoslav delegations. Other questions seemed to be of greater importance to them. Austria then took the lead in order to push the idea of conventional disarmament.[47]

More broadly, Mock saw new horizons opening for the neutral states of Europe. The signing of the treaty on the global reduction of Intermediate Nuclear Forces (INF) in Washington also strengthened the development of the negotiations in Vienna.[48] In May 1988, Mock also considered the withdrawal of Soviet troops in Afghanistan and the rapprochement between the EC and COMECON as an important contribution to the development of the negotiations. According to him, these developments signaled new flexibility for the neutral and non-aligned states, which allowed new space for maneuver. He meant that, for the first time since 1945, there was a new chance to overcome the ideological, political and economic barriers dividing Europe in two. The N+N states therefore had a vital interest in not interrupting the ongoing process of détente, but consolidating and strengthening it.[49]

At the end of 1988, Mock was finally convinced that a compromise could be found on the remaining controversial issues, and he invited the foreign ministers of the CSCE states to Vienna for a final meeting in mid-January 1989. British Foreign Secretary Geoffrey Howe later thanked Mock for taking this risk.[50]

Most of the participating politicians were very satisfied with the results.[51] The United States Secretary of State George P. Shultz considered the CSCE Vienna Follow-Up Meeting to be a new beginning of the CSCE process. Compared to the final results from Helsinki and the beginning of negotiations in Vienna, a great amount of progress was made.[52] Gorbachev also argued that the final document of the Vienna Follow-up Meeting was a great success in terms of results, goals, and foreseeable consequences.[53]

In his closing speech, Mock himself stressed that the outcome of the Vienna Meeting was a result of positive developments in international relations. In particular, the INF agreement was decisive in this regard. Mock

47 "Mock fordert neue Impulse bei KSZE," *Die Presse*, 11 April 1987.

48 See Gala, "From INF to SDI."

49 "Mock sieht neue Chancen für neutrale Staaten," *Die Presse*, 13 May 1988.

50 See "Zwischen EG und Menschenrechten," *Die Presse*, 18 January 1989.

51 See "Das abschließende Dokument des KSZE-Folgetreffens in Wien vom 15. Januar 1989," *Europa Archiv* 44, no. 5 (1989): D133-D164; "Der Abschluß des Wiener KSZE-Folgetreffens. Erklärungen der Außenminister," *Europa Archiv* 44, no. 6 (1989): D165-D194.

52 See "Allgemeine Zufriedenheit mit Wiener Konferenz," *Die Presse*, 18 January 1989.

53 See "Goratschow: Großer Erfolg," *Der Standard*, 18 January 1989.

declared, "The time that has passed since then has probably been the most dynamic of the last four decades in East-West relations. For us, here and now, this means a new quality of the East-West relationship and the opportunity for further positive development."[54]

The Austrian Foreign Minister emphasized in particular the agreements on human contacts and described the final document as a "document of open minds." In his view, it was also a "document of change" and showed the changed attitude of some states regarding human rights. In addition, the mutual responsibility that was set out in the final document was also central.

The Vienna Meeting established a system of mutual monitoring in the humanitarian dimension, which became a first step towards a more permanent infrastructure for the protection of human rights in all of Europe. No one could continue to claim that human rights were a purely internal matter for any given state. Further cooperation regarding trade and industry was also planned. Mock also suggested the creation of a Europe-wide system that would help in case of catastrophes like the earthquake in Armenia.[55] The Foreign Minister of Austria concluded his speech with a note that only political practice would show how seriously the states (he obviously meant the communist states of Central and Eastern Europe) would take the regulations set out in the Vienna Follow-up Meeting. Despite earlier CSCE agreements, there are still "countries where religious freedom is violated, dissidents are pursued and national minorities are discriminated. Let us close this Vienna Follow-up Meeting with a sign of hope: may those countries also recognize that progress and the future can only be achieved to the extent that the individual person pays due respect to him or her (…)."[56]

54 "Viel Lob in den Bestandaufnahmen," *Die Presse*, 18 January 1989: "Die Zeit, die seither verstrichen ist, war in den Ost-West-Beziehungen die wohl dynamischste der letzten vier Jahrzehnte. Dies bedeutet für uns, hier und heute: eine neue Qualität des Ost-West-Verhältnisses sowie die Perspektive einer weiteren positiven Entwicklung."

55 See "Viel Lob in den Bestandaufnahmen," *Die Presse*, 18 January 1989; "Allgemeine Zufriedenheit mit Wiener Konferenz," *Die Presse*, 18 January 1989; "Für ein europaweites Katatrophenhilfesystem," *Der Standard*, 18 January 1989.

56 "Viel Lob in den Bestandaufnahmen," *Die Presse*, 18 January 1989: "Länder, die weiterhin die Religionsfreiheit mißachten, Dissidenten verfolgen, nationale Minderheiten diskriminieren und in ihrem Bestand gefährden. Lassen wir dieses Folgetreffen mit einem Zeichen der Hoffnung ausklingen: mögen auch diese Länder erkennen, daß es Fortschritt und Zukunft nur in dem Maße gibt, in dem der Einzelmensch den ihm gebührenden Respekt erführt (…)."

Open questions remain

At the end of the Vienna Follow-up Meeting, Mock was very optimistic, announcing an expansion of Austria's role as a mediator between the blocs.[57] Even half a year later, Mock was convinced of the future importance of the N+N states and the significance of the final document of the CSCE Vienna Follow-up Meeting. When Mock met the Hungarian Foreign Minister Gyula Horn on 27 June 1989 to cut down the last remaining parts of the iron curtain – the symbol of the Cold War – he underlined in a conversation with his Hungarian counterpart the role played by the non-aligned and neutral states within the framework of the CSCE process, who would help to strike a consensus in situations of crisis by acting as mediators. Mock pointed out that the Viennese final document would be a step forward and that the CSCE meeting in Paris regarding the human dimension would be unlikely to go much beyond Vienna. He also made very clear statements regarding the ongoing, positive reforms within communist Poland, Hungary and the USSR, which Austria supported.[58]

In contrast, Austria viewed the political developments in Bulgaria, Czechoslovakia, the GDR, and Romania more critically. Mock thus referred to the different pace of reforms and was skeptical about the overall progress of the Soviet Bloc. In his view, the idea of a "common European house" proposed by Gorbachev could become the future framework for peaceful and cooperative development in Europe, including the process of CSCE. Finally, Mock praised again *glasnost* and *perestroika* and the historical developments in Central and Eastern Europe.[59]

Apart from such statements, however, research has not yet sufficed to document in detail the role of the N+N states at the Vienna Follow-up Meeting. Thomas Fischer contends that "the role of neutral mediators was no longer needed in the CSCE at the Vienna meeting to the same degree as before."[60] Neuhold and Lehne even believe that a consensus could have

57 See "Für ein europaweites Katastrophenhilfesystem," *Der Standard*, 18 January 1989.

58 See Wohnout, "Vom Durchschneiden des Eisernen Vorhangs bis zur Anerkennung Sloweniens und Kroatiens"; Martin Eichtinger, "Österreichs Außenpolitik in Zentral- und Osteuropa nach dem Annus mirabilis 1989. Das Engagement des österreichischen Vizekanzlers und Außenministers Alois Mock nach dem Zusammenbruch des Kommunismus," in *Viribus unitis*, ed. Ilona Slawinski and Joseph P. Strelka (Bern-Berlin-Frankfurt am Main et al.: Peter Lang, 1996), 103–122.

59 Amtsvermerk "Offizieller Besuch des ungarischen AM Horn; Gespräche mit HBM, 26. 6. 1989; Internationale Themen," BMEIA, GZ 222.18.23/25-II.SL/89, Zl. 187-Res/89.

60 Fischer, *Keeping the Process Alive*, 148.

been reached without the N+N states' mediation,[61] and the daily newspaper *Der Standard* wrote that "where the big players agree, the small ones are no longer needed."[62] This is in direct contradiction with the statement of the United States Secretary of State Shultz, who not only thanked Mock personally for his commitment to a good conclusion of the Vienna Follow-up Meeting, but also rated the role of the N+N states as positive in general.[63]

Another desideratum of research concerns the effects of the Vienna CSCE Follow-up on the further developments of the years 1989–1991, in particular the revolutions and the collapse of the Soviet Union. Wilfried Loth assumes that there was "no direct path from the CSCE process to the revolutions of autumn 1989 and the break-up of the Soviet empire."[64] However, based on earlier studies, a certain effect on the development of civil rights movements can be identified, although there is no consensus regarding its intensity. As an example, in his analysis concerning the impact of the CSCE process on actors in the Warsaw Pact states, Peter Schlotter noted that Western values became increasingly important in the politics of the Soviet Union.[65] Yuliya von Saal emphasized that, because of the mediation in Vienna, the domestic political possibilities of Central and Eastern European countries grew significantly.[66]

The Foreign Ministers' statements at the end of the Vienna Follow-Up Meeting suggest that Austria was perceived as a good host. FRG Foreign Minister Hans-Dietrich Genscher stated during his talks with Austrian Federal Chancellor Franz Vranitzky that Austria had significantly advanced the negotiation process.[67] Still, the end of the Cold War was marked by the CSCE in Paris, not in Vienna. In 1990, "merely" the Conference on Security and Confidence Building Measures and the Conference on Conventional Disarmament were held here.[68] One theory as to why Vienna was not cho-

61 See Neuhold and Lehne, "The Role of the Neutral and Non-Aligned Countries at the Vienna Meeting," 50.

62 See "Nüchternes Kagraner Kongreßende," *Der Standard*, 18 January 1989: "Wo sich die Großen einig sind, werden die Kleinen nicht mehr gebraucht."

63 See "Gesprächsreigen am Rande der KSZE," *Die Presse*, 17 January 1989.

64 See Wilfried Loth, "Der KSZE-Prozess 1975–1990: eine Bilanz," in *Die KSZE im Ost-West-Konflikt*, ed. Peter and Wentker, 323–331.

65 See Peter Schlotter, "Das Ende der Systemkonfrontation 1989/1990: Der Beitrag des KSZE-Prozesses," in *Deeskalation von Gewaltkonflikten seit 1945*, ed. Corinna Hauswedell (Essen: Klartext Medienwerkstatt, 2006), 115–128.

66 See Saal, *KSZE-Prozess und Perestroika in der Sowjetunion*, 363.

67 See "Genscher bei Vranitzky," *Die Presse*, 19 January 1989.

68 See Heinz Magenheimer, "Konventionelle Stabilität und Sicherheit in Europa. Truppenreduktionen, Umrüstungen und Wiener VKSE-Konferenz," *Aus Politik und Zeitgeschichte*, B 36 (1990): 3–12.

sen as the venue for the special summit is the so-called "Waldheim Affair."[69] In the period of the Vienna Follow-Up Meeting from 1986 to the very beginning of 1989, the Austrian Federal President Kurt Waldheim was a highly controversial figure. He was accused of being a war criminal during the Second World War, when he served in the German Wehrmacht under General Löhr. Despite the fact that no proof of this was found, Waldheim was completely isolated. No one from the EC-12 and the 23 NATO member states wanted to make a visit to Vienna and shake hands with Waldheim at this time in his term.[70]

The conclusion of the Vienna Follow-up Meeting was accompanied by multiple ceremonial occasions in Austria. President Waldheim did not play any significant role during these; instead, the mayor of Vienna Helmut Zilk, Federal Chancellor Vranitzky, and Foreign Minister Mock acted as hosts. The Austrian diplomats stated at home and abroad that foreign government members who wanted to have meetings would be welcomed, but they would not force any unwanted meetings.[71] Consequently, the "Waldheim Affair" is not the only reason why there was no Charter of Vienna in 1990, but rather a Charter of Paris produced later in the same year. In that respect, the Austrians could not expect to earn laurels for that solemnly published declaration ending the Cold War that was signed in Paris.

69 This was argued by former Austrian diplomats acting in the 1980s (Peter Jankowitsch, Albert Graf von Rohan and others) interviewed by the author when he was preparing his monograph on Austria's foreign policy, see also: Gehler, *Österreichs Außenpolitik der Zweiten Republik*, 560.

70 See Michael Gehler, "Die Affäre Waldheim. Eine Fallstudie zur Instrumentalisierung der NS-Vergangenheit zur politischen Vorteilsverschaffung 1986–1988," *Geschichte in Wissenschaft und Unterricht* 69, no. 1/2 (2018): 67–85; Cornelius Lehnguth, *Waldheim und die Folgen. Der parteipolitische Umgang mit dem Nationalsozialismus in Österreich* (Frankfurt am Main - New York: Campus Verlag, 2013); Michael Gehler, "'...eine grotesk überzogene Dämonisierung eines Mannes...'. Die Waldheim-Affäre 1986–1992," in *Politische Affären und Skandale in Österreich*, ed. Michael Gehler (Innsbruck: Studien-Verl., 2007), 614–665.

71 See "35 Außenminister in Wien: Der Kongreß tagt und tanzt," *Kleine Zeitung*, 17 January 1989; "Nach dem KSZE-Marathon lädt Wien nun zum Tanz," *Der Standard*, 17 January 1989; "Jetzt darf der Kongreß tanzen," *Die Presse*, 18 January 1989.

3

"HELPING HANDS" ACROSS THE FENCE

The Stance of the European Democrat Union toward Developments behind the Iron Curtain*

Michael Gehler and Johannes Schönner

The European Democrat Union (EDU) is at once one of Europe's most important and least understood transnational political networks of the late twentieth century. Conceived as a means of integrating Christian Democrats above all, but also reaching across the proverbial aisle to the Conservative political family, the EDU was explicitly intended to seek members and partners beyond the European Communities, and even behind the Iron Curtain.

This chapter represents a systematic historical study of the ramifications of the EDU's activities for the Soviet-controlled countries of Central and Eastern Europe, and for their transition out of communism. First, the chapter will explain the role of the EDU within the framework of European Christian Democrats and Conservatives and its importance for the revolutionary year of 1989. Second, it will define the most significant *dramatis personae* in the EDU's cross-Iron Curtain activities. The promising contacts in the late 1980s between the EDU and the Communist Party of the USSR will then be explored. Fourth and finally, we will turn to the countries which by the time of the 1989 revolutions had become the EDU's top priorities, Poland and Hungary, making the case that the EDU both succeeded and failed in its attempt to shape these countries' political transitions. In particular, this chapter makes the case that the development of the Democratic Forum in Hungary was decisively shaped by the multi-layered support of the EDU, which in turn conditioned developments in the German Democratic Republic (GDR) related to the question of German unification.

* This is a revised and updated version of a text published in earlier form as Michael Gehler and Hannes Schönner, "The European Democrat Union and the Revolutionary Events in Central Europe in 1989," in *Europa und die deutsche Einheit: Beobachtungen, Entscheidungen und Folgen*, ed. Michael Gehler and Maximilian Graf (Göttingen: Vandenhoeck & Ruprecht, 2017), 739–766.

The origins of the European Christian Democrats and Conservatives

After 1945, conservative Catholic and Christian Democratic parties gained a historically unprecedented influence over the political life of Western Europe. There was no lack of new incentives, nor at the same time of obstacles on the road to transnational contacts and organized party cooperation. Nevertheless, the secret meetings of the "Geneva Circle" (1947–1955) as well as cooperation within the *Nouvelles Équipes Internationales* (NEI), which were formed in 1947,[1] up through their renaming and transformation into the European Union of Christian Democrats (EUCD) in 1965, were characterized by continuous debates about how far coordination should go in both political and ideological matters.[2]

The transnational European People's Party, founded on 29 April 1976, clearly differed from earlier forms of Christian Democratic cooperation. It assumed the form of federation of Christian Democratic parties, but was restricted to the member states in the European Community. The official inaugural assembly took place on 8 July 1976, in Luxembourg. For the EPP's founders, the aim was to create a parliamentary faction.[3]

It was the intention of the German Christian Democratic Union (CDU) and the Bavarian Christian Social Union (CSU) to include British Conservatives and French civil groups in the EPP alliance, but they ran into categorical opposition from the Italian, Belgian, and Dutch parties. Against this backdrop, the Austrian People's Party (ÖVP) under the leadership of Josef Taus and Alois Mock, with the support of the German union parties of the CDU (Helmut Kohl), the CSU (Franz Josef Strauss), and the British Con-

1 Michael Gehler, "Der 'Genfer Kreis': Christdemokratische Parteienkooperation und Vertrauensbildung im Zeichen der deutsch-französischen Annäherung 1947–1955," *Zeitschrift für Geschichtswissenschaft* 49, no. 7 (2001): 599–625; Id., "The Geneva Circle of West European Christian Democrats," in Michael Gehler and Wolfram Kaiser, *Christian Democracy in Europe since 1945*, vol. 2 (London-New York: Routledge, 2004), 207–220; Michael Gehler and Wolfram Kaiser, eds., *Transnationale Parteienkooperation der europäischen Christdemokraten: Dokumente 1945–1965* (Munich: Saur, 2004); Michael Gehler et al., eds., *Transnationale Parteienkooperation der europäischen Christdemokraten und Konservativen. Dokumente 1965–1979* (Berlin: De Gruyter Oldenbourg, 2018).

2 Thomas Jansen and Steven Van Hecke, *At Europe's Service: The Origins and Evolution of the European People's Party* (Berlin: Springer, 2011), 21–28; Beata Kosowska-Gąstoł, "A Truly 'European' Christian Democracy? The European People's Party," in *Christian Democracy across the Iron Curtain: Europe Redefined*, ed. Piotr H. Kosicki and Sławomir Łukasiewicz (London: Palgrave Macmillan, 2018), 127–152.

3 Thomas Jansen, *Die Entstehung einer Europäischen Partei: Vorgeschichte, Gründung und Entwicklung der EVP* (Bonn: Europa-Union-Verlag, 1996); Id., *Die Europäische Volkspartei. Entstehung und Entwicklung* (Brussels: EDP, 2006).

servatives, made efforts to expand the narrow ideological framework of "Christian Democracy" and to create a broader spectrum for cooperation among European parties occupying the center of the political spectrum, both within and outside the EC. The CDU/CSU and the ÖVP stood for an increased European-conservative orientation that, with the EDU that was founded in 1978, attempted to create an counterpart to the EPP, but with a broader base of support and participation.[4]

The EDU, Christian Democrats & Conservative framework, and the revolutions of 1989

Starting in 1978, Conservative and Christian Democratic parties joined together for common work in the EDU. This new organization did not, however, lead to a consensus with respect to a binding goal of integration. The term "European integration" was hardly used; rather, the discussion was of "European cooperation." Nevertheless, in the view of the EDU, the Europe of that time was not to be limited by its existing borders. The goal was for a greater Europe in the sense of an ideological and geopolitical alliance of civil, democratic parties with an intended influence on opposition groupings in the communist sphere.[5]

The EDU was intended not only as a catch-all for the center-right parties, especially as a counterweight to the Socialist International (SI), but also as a substitute for those Christian Democratic and Conservative parties that had not been accepted into the EPP either for programmatic reasons or due to non-membership in the EC. The ideological rifts between Christian Democrats and other center-right parties, especially the British Conservatives and French neo-Gaullists, were in no way reconciled with the two-track (EUCD-EDU) arrangement. The relationships between the EDU and the EUCD or the EPP – which, since the founding of the EDU, had been from time to time also designated as dualist – continued to evolve.

More and more European parties attempted to overcome this dilemma within the framework of the EPP as a faction in the European Parliament. The EDU acted more as a working group or working community of Conservatives and Christian Democrats than as a European party. Those who

4 See Andreas Khol, Lars Tobisson and Alexis Wintoniak, eds., *Twenty Years European Democrat Union 1978–1998* (Vienna: EDU, 1998).

5 "Das Europakonzept der EDU, Dokumente zur ÖVP-Außenpolitik," Archive of the Karl von Vogelsang Institute (AKVI, Vienna), Sign. 2358.

are involved in evaluating the importance of EDU policy in the years and months preceding the beginning of the so-called *annus mirabilis* of 1989 have to consider the changes in the broadly understood European center-right's East-West policy in light of the new Soviet policy. The chronology of the "year of change" – stretched to include the period 1987–1988 – represents an adequate longitudinal cross-section describing the work of the EDU, its focus, its contacts, and its expectations. After all, in 1989 the EDU was already able to look back on a decade's worth of progress in the course of its trial period as Europe's "Christian Democratic party family."

And in contrast to the European People's Party, founded two years before the EDU, in 1976, the EDU saw itself from the beginning neither as the extended arm of a military alliance nor as a strictly defined economic area. Rather, mutual cooperation and collaboration with sometimes divergent political parties were at the center of its political work. This distinction would prove crucial in 1989.

Only the hegemony of Christian Democratic and Conservative parties in Western Europe made possible the increased importance of the EDU, as well as the EDU member parties. If *glasnost* and *perestroika* had been initiated ten years earlier, socialist parties would have prevailed in the governments of most Western European countries. It was only national governmental responsibility that enabled the EDU to act as a meaningful partner against both the Soviet Union and the governments of countries belonging to the Council for Mutual Economic Assistance (COMECON).

Party visits by the EDU and/or EPP delegations to the same partners in communist-run Central and Eastern European countries often followed one after the other. This "race to the east" was also reflected in the fact that, in the meantime, the party foundation of the US Republicans had established a political office in Poland (Warsaw), even before the Konrad Adenauer Foundation did so in 1989.[6]

6 See the memoirs of Dieter A. Schmidt, head of the CSU Foreign Policy Department: "After the historic turnaround in 1989–90, a great number of parties from CEE pushed into the European political parties' associations. In the case of the socialists, as well as the case of the EPP, liberals, conservatives, greens, and communists. The motives for this were clear. It was expected that this membership would provide support and benefits in bringing the respective countries closer to the EU and their subsequent membership. The national party programs were adapted to the requirements and wishes of the EPP accordingly. If the EPP was an important and solid basis for the joint work of EP members and the EPP Group, the EDU had always seen more than the EC and the EU. That was extremely important prior to the decisive expansion moves." Michael Gehler et al., eds., *Mitgestalter Europas: Transnationalismus und Parteiennetzwerke europäischer Christdemokraten und Konservativer in historischer Erfahrung* (St. Augustin-Berlin: Konrad-Adenauer-Stiftung, 2013), 436.

Leading figures of the EDU

Who were the key players in the EDU? Founded in 1978, the EDU was administered and represented by two Austrians, EDU President Alois Mock and Executive Secretary Andreas Khol, from Vienna's central office.[7] Thus, the Austrian Christian Democratic People's Party (ÖVP) played a defining role within the EDU. The actual influence of Christian Democratic and Conservative parties, however, came from across the parties' spectrum within the European Community. The two German parties, the CDU and CSU, the British Conservatives, and the French Rassemblement pour la République (RPR), as well as the Scandinavian parties Hoyres Hovedorganissasjon (Norway) and the Moderata Samlingspartiet (Sweden), formed the gravitational center of the EDU.

It is no secret that the defining figure of Christian Democratic party cooperation from the early 1980s onwards, especially within the EPP, was German Chancellor Helmut Kohl.[8] How he was received and perceived in the EPP, whether there were critics of his assertive manner and dominant role, and in what respects he differed from his predecessors like Mariano Rumor or Leo Tindemans and successors like Jacques Santer, are questions that must still be resolved through further research. Next to Kohl, the other leading Christian Democratic representative was Alois Mock. In 1979, Mock became President of the EDU (1979-1998) and from 1983 to 1987 also of the International Christian Democratic Union (IDU). Following the 1986 elections in Austria, Alois Mock was Austrian Vice Chancellor in the government of Franz Vranitzky (SPÖ) from 1987 to 1989. He held the position of foreign minister from 1987 to 1995, leading Austria into

7 Michael Gehler and Johannes Schönner, "Transnationale christdemokratische Parteienkooperationen in Europa 1965–1989: Der Beitrag österreichischer Ideen und Initiativen," in *Demokratie und Geschichte: Jahrbuch des Karl von Vogelsang-Instituts zur Erforschung der Geschichte der christlichen Demokratie in Österreich*, 11/12 (2007/2008), ed. Helmut Wohnout (Vienna-Cologne-Weimar: Böhlau, 2009), 271–318. In total, the following parties were members of the EDU during the period under investigation: Austrian People's Party (Austria), *Dimokratikos Synagermos* (Cyprus), *Det Conservative Folkeparti* (Denmark), *Kansallinen Kokoomus* (Finland), *Rassemblement pour la République* (France), Christian Democratic Union/Christian Social Union (Germany), *Nea Demokratia* (Greece), Progressive Citizenship/Patriotic Union (Liechtenstein), Høyres Hovedorganisasjon (Norway), *Partido del Centro Democratico e Social* (Portugal), *Alianza Popular* (Spain), *Moderata Samlingspartiet* (Sweden), *Anavatan Partisi* (Turkey), and the Conservative and Unionist Party (United Kingdom).

8 Martin Eichtinger and Helmut Wohnout, *Alois Mock: Ein Politiker schreibt Geschichte* (Vienna-Graz-Klagenfurt: Styria, 2008), 148–152, here 155.

the European Union.[9] Kohl and Mock took the decisive steps of bringing the EPP and EDU into a close working relationship. It is not too far-fetched to argue that Mock acted very loyally toward Kohl, who felt himself to be not only a patriarch but also a protector of Austria's European policy ambitions and interests.[10] Mock established also close contacts with Jacques Chirac and Margaret Thatcher, who joined the EDU meetings in the 1980s.

The promising contacts between the EDU and the Communist Party of the USSR

In order to properly classify the revolutionary events of 1989, it is also necessary to work out the shift from 1987–1988 to 1989 in Western European political actors' agendas toward the Soviet Bloc. Without a doubt, the policies of the EDU member parties and the whole organization have been reweighted in many areas, irrespective of all of the continuities evoked. Official political contacts with the leaders of the Warsaw Pact and socialist state parties were unimportant – in contrast to the Western European parties of the Socialist International. It was even considered practically immoral to maintain contacts with the Eastern European heads of state if there were no simultaneous contacts with civil society groups and dissidents. Likewise, "party foreign policy" before 1989 was consistently defined in the face of tense East-West relations, and in particular on issues of disarmament and security. Only with CPSU General Secretary Mikhail Gorbachev's arrival in power in 1985 did this diplomatic taboo change. The Kremlin suddenly became "sexy."

In 1988, German policy was still basically identical to "security and disarmament policy." When, in June, the Intermediate-Range Nuclear Forces (INF) Treaty for the reduction and destruction of the mid-range missiles went into force through the signing of the ratification treaties in Moscow, the EDU also welcomed this step as contribution to confidence building

9 On this topic, see Hans-Peter Schwarz, *Helmut Kohl: Eine politische Biographie* (Munich: DVA, 2012).

10 "Mock's Discussions with Helmut Kohl and Hans-Dietrich Genscher, 6–7 October 1987," Information, Johann Plattner, Vienna, 12 October 1987, ÖStA, AdR, BMaA, II-Pol 1987, GZ. 518.02.42/18-II.1/87.

and stabilizing the political situation in Europe.[11] Already in 1987, the negotiations had largely moved forward – not least on the personal initiative of Gorbachev. The two German states had a special role when the treaty came into effect, since the GDR and the Federal Republic of Germany (FRG) were both potential target areas for a first strike and therefore particularly felt the threat from the rockets. Bonn and East Berlin therefore urged their respective coalition partners to give up their weapons.[12]

But what was a feint, and what was honest diplomacy? The economically disastrous situation of the Soviet Union was in essence a creation of the West. Thus, Soviet economic growth was supposed to be eight percent to meet the current five-year plan. In 1988, it was only two percent, which was described as "Stalinist cosmetics" by EDU founding member Franz Josef Strauss at the meeting of the EDU Steering Committee in Madrid on 15 April 1988, just as the dominant mood oscillated between cautious curiosity and pessimism, based on the experiences of the past. Most of the EDU leaders saw in Gorbachev someone who was only aiming at an improvement of the communist system, not at fundamental change. The fact that the Soviet economy not only stagnated but also fell into ruin, that civilian research was not taking place, and that the life expectancy of Soviet citizens fell significantly from the mid-1980s onward was only worked out in detail later by analysts and historians.[13]

Nevertheless, within the framework of its own analyses, the EDU tried to at least pose questions about the possible economic and political alternatives for the Soviet Union under Gorbachev. This was the purpose of the intensive cross-Iron Curtain contacts. The EDU's strategic arm for all "European ideological" questions was the so-called Committee No. 1 for European Structures and European Policy, chaired by the Prime Minister of Rhineland-Palatinate, Bernhard Vogel. This committee met every

11 See Curt Gasteyger, "Europa nach dem INF-Abkommen," *Aus Politik und Zeitgeschichte* 10 (1988): 3–10. The question of incorporating British and French missile systems had paralyzed US-Soviet negotiations on disarmament since the beginning of the 1980s. The Soviets always demanded that English and French warheads to be attributed to the American arsenals. This was also one of the reasons why, from 1983 onwards, US medium-range Pershing missiles were stationed in the FRG. As a direct consequence of the failure of the INF negotiations, the Conference on Security and Cooperation in Europe (CSCE) was also affected by these tensions until 1987.

12 On the deeper German background of the negotiations, see Jeffrey Herf, *War by Other Means: Soviet Power, West German Resistance, and the Battle of the Euromissiles* (New York: Free Press, 1991).

13 For the most recent literature on this subject, see Stefan Karner, "Von der Stagnation zum Verfall: Kennzeichen der sowjetischen Wirtschaft der 1980er Jahre," in *Der Zerfall des Sowjetimperiums und Deutschlands Wiedervereinigung*, ed. Hanns Jürgen Küsters (Cologne-Weimar-Vienna: Böhlau, 2016), 15–18.

three months. In 1988, the main focus was on European agricultural policy, EC-EFTA (European Free Trade Association) negotiations, as well as the upcoming 1989 European elections. Although the changes underway in the Soviet Union and (parts of) Central and Eastern Europe were carefully registered in 1988, EDU representatives did not expect any serious shifts in power. A focus on the military balance and the "transparency of the military activities" continued to drive East-West dialogue talks against a common threat well into the year 1989.[14]

On the occasion of the eleventh Party Leaders' Conference in Rhodes on 23 September 1988, EDU representatives discussed the domestic developments in the Communist countries of Central and Eastern Europe. The Steering Committee was asked to observe and analyze the development of democratization and the formation of new political groups in these countries. At its 36th Meeting (General Meeting), which was held in Vienna in November 1988, the Steering Committee discussed the most recent developments behind the Iron Curtain. There was a first exchange of opinion with representatives of emerging democratic movements from Poland, Hungary, and Yugoslavia. As a result of its discussions, the Steering Committee decided to take the following course of action: since a clear distinction had to be drawn between the different countries, pursuing a distinct course of action toward each country was recommended. The two EDU Committees (Steering Committee and Committee on Europe) were to harmonize their further procedures and expected to reach their decisions on the basis of information gathered on site, in an open dialogue with both government bodies and social organizations belonging to a nascent civil society.[15]

Personal contacts with Mikhail Gorbachev had been a central aspect of the EDU's strategic work and planning since 1987–1988. The contacts of the EDU leadership with the Soviet Union under Gorbachev shaped the agenda for several visits, the most important of which were those in May

14 See for example, the EDU Strategy Paper for the 10th IDU Party Leaders' Conference, Berlin, 24 September 1987: "The party leaders call for verifiable and comprehensive agreements to establish a stable ratio between the conventional forces of NATO and the Warsaw Pact throughout Europe by means of the elimination of existing imbalances in favor of the Soviet Union. Such agreements must not lead to increased pressure from conventional forces in other directions or parts of the world (...). The Party Leaders also call for militarily significant and politically binding agreements on further confidence and security building measures in Europe based on those agreed upon in Stockholm in 1986, to increase the transparency of military activities." AKVI, EDU Collection, Sign. EDU/1987/1434, 4.

15 See the protocol for the 36th General Meeting in Vienna, 26 November 1988, AKVI, EDU Collection, Sign. EDU/1988/1583, 5.

and September 1989. Under Gorbachev, the Communist Party of the Soviet Union (CPSU) was very interested in establishing contacts with Conservative parties in Western Europe. For their part, among Conservatives and Christian Democrats alike, at the outset of glasnost and perestroika, there were particularly strong doubts about the sincerity of the reformist will of the Soviet leadership.

The EDU held internal discussions within its Steering Committee on several occasions concerning relations between EDU member parties and the communist parties of Warsaw Pact countries. In general, such relations were subject to criticism, particularly in view of the fact that the victims of human rights violations in these countries might interpret such contacts as a kind of legitimization of the communist single-party system. In the meantime, no decisions were taken regarding an official EDU policy vis-à-vis communist parties.

In 1989, the situation had changed in that relations between the EDU member parties and communist parties could no longer be considered strictly in reference to the question of legitimization. This argument could now clearly be refuted by stating from the very beginning and in public that the issues to be discussed were democracy and human rights, and that contacts were also to be established with opposition groups. From this point of view, there were no basic objections to informative talks and non-institutionalized contacts with the Communist Party of the Soviet Union. Apart from a few exceptions among the EDU member parties, this was a fundamentally new state of affairs across the EDU. A joint approach of all EDU member parties appeared to be more meaningful than bilateral party-to-party talks. A joint approach was coordinated properly from the outset, and thus, the risk of misunderstandings in bilateral contacts could be eliminated.[16]

Any new contacts were to demonstrate the implementation of the principle of free movement, as laid out by the Vienna Follow-up Meeting of the Conference on Security and Cooperation in Europe in its Vienna Conclud-

16 See the protocol of the EDU Steering Committee on 7 December 1989 in Munich (the Munich Statement): "The EDU Steering Committee notes with satisfaction that also in the GDR and in Czechoslovakia reforms of really existing socialism have now been initiated. The EDU will support these developments, and has instructed its committee on 'European Structures and European Policy' under the chairmanship of Dr. Bernhard Vogel, to undertake a Fact Finding Mission to Czechoslovakia and to hold the next meeting of the Committee in Berlin." AKVI, EDU Collection, Sign. EDU/1989/1083, 1–4.

ing Document.[17] The EDU could not pursue contacts in the Soviet Union, unless EDU member parties were guaranteed the right to meet any individual and any group anywhere and at any point in time. On the one hand, in the EDU meetings with Soviet representatives in May and September 1989, a strong downward trend and changing expectations were documented. As early as the spring, many conservative observers questioned the irreversibility of the Soviet reform course. On the other hand, at the beginning of 1989, the Soviet leadership felt that it was enough to convince conservative circles in the West of the seriousness of Gorbachev's course in order to win over the entire political spectrum of the West, including the critics and doubters who remained on the fringes.[18]

Regarding the Soviet attitude towards maintaining these contacts with EDU bodies, conservative circles in the West were often also the key to economic, scientific, and technical cooperation. Gorbachev had attempted to establish a good relationship with Christian Democrats and Conservatives in Western Europe, as well as conservative politicians in the United States, including US President Ronald Reagan, Britain's Prime Minister Margaret Thatcher, and Franz Josef Strauss, the Bavarian Prime Minister until his death in 1988.[19] Thatcher, as is well known, was the first Western top politician to spontaneously declare in December 1984 on the occasion of a London visit of the then-second man in the Kremlin: "I can do business with him."[20]

Rightly, the Austrian EDU representatives recognized the opportunity to promote an understanding of Austrian EC policy during these talks. At

17 Matthias Peter and Hermann Wentker, eds., *Die KSZE im Ost-West-Konflikt: Internationale Politik und gesellschaftliche Transformation 1975–1990* (Munich: De Gruyter Oldenbourg, 2012); Benjamin Gilde, *Österreich im KSZE-Prozess 1969–1983: Neutraler Vermittler in humanitärer Mission* (Munich: Oldenbourg, 2013); Wilhelm Bruns, "Mehr Substanz in den Ost-West-Beziehungen: Zur dritten KSZE-Folgekonferenz in Wien," *Aus Politik und Zeitgeschichte* 12 (1989): 3–9; Stefan Lehne, *The Vienna Meeting of the Conference on Security and Cooperation in Europe, 1986–1989: A Turning Point in East-West Relations* (Boulder, CO: Westview Press, 1991); Hans-Heinrich Wrede, *KSZE in Wien: Kursbestimmung für Europas Zukunft* (Cologne: Verlag Wissenschaft und Politik, 1990).

18 Stefan Karner et al., eds., *Der Kreml und die deutsche Wiedervereinigung 1990: Interne sowjetische Analysen* (Berlin: Metropol Verlag, 2015), 13–16.

19 See the protocol of the Statement of the EDU Party Leaders on the EDU Conference in Rhodes, 22–24 September 1988: "Since the last meeting of EDU party leaders on the occasion of the EDU and IDU Party Leaders' Conference in Berlin in September 1987, there have been decisive changes concerning relations between the West and the Soviet Union. The arms race cannot be won and requires sacrifices that the Eastern European countries, with their less efficient economies, are unable to make. The superiority of market economic models has been proven a hundred times." AKVI, EDU Collection, Sign. EDU/1988/1141, 2–5.

20 See the autobiography of Margaret Thatcher, *The Downing Street Years* (London: Harper Collins, 1993).

the same time, Austrians remained some of the most vocal (external) critics of the slow-moving plan for an Internal Market within the framework of the EDU. From the perspective of 1988, the finalization of the Internal Market and the simultaneous creation of a larger European Economic Space (EES) merely remained a vision. On the one hand, it should be taken into account that the EDU included not only EC member parties, but also parties that belonged to the EFTA and not the EC. Thus, the development of East-West contacts was also subject to the negotiation of these internal western tensions. As a result, the individual EFTA countries and parties that were represented in the EDU, such as Austria and Sweden, began to push for full membership in the European Communities.

This fundamental consideration of further EC membership led Brussels itself to make additional bilateral concessions to reduce pressure on the Community. The European Union's market position was deliberately emphasized. As a result, all rapprochements within the framework of EDU integration negotiations and conferences were to be viewed exclusively from a market-economic perspective. Discussions on market integration clearly capture the heart of the issue within the EDU on the eve of 1989. In 1988, the realization of a Western European single market was still being sought along a timetable that envisioned realization by 1992.[21]

The importance of a confluence between market-economic considerations (EC-EFTA negotiations) and the new foreign policy developments behind the Iron Curtain becomes clear in the person of Bernhard Vogel. The former CDU Minister-President of Rhineland-Palatinate was Vice President of the EDU in 1988–1989 and as such responsible for foreign policy negotiations alongside Alois Mock. Vogel was already warning persistently against a painful division of (Western) Europe that could result from competition between the EC and the EFTA, when foreign policy conditions in crucial areas began to change at the same time. As a German,

21 From this point of view, this was also not a contradiction. For example, in the context of the "Debate on Questions of European Integration," Fritz König (ÖVP) asked for the achievement of the four freedoms (with the inclusion of Austria), while at the same meeting, Elmar Brok (CDU) formulated, "Different social services in Community countries become competitive factors on the internal market. If it is not possible to approach by evolutionary means the different social levels of the countries by means of minimum standards at a high level, the internal market cannot be created without social conflict. The aim is to increase the economic performance of the less developed countries. (...) If we do not see this context, there is a great risk that national social systems could be harmonized in such a way that they could be regarded as social dumping by trade unions and large parts of the population, as a reduction in acquired workers' rights and the like." Both of these findings were, as far as Western Europe was concerned, prophetic and accurate; after the year 1989, however, they were invalidated. AKVI, EDU Collection, EDU Protocol, Party Steering Committee, Rhodes, September 1988, Sign. JB 1988.

Vogel also knew that German "unification" was conceivable only through pan-European integration. As always, the key to East Berlin was in Moscow. From January to May 1989, relations between Bonn and Moscow underwent a further intensification. The shift from global geopolitics to an intensely regional focus – most impressively manifested by Helmut Kohl and Mikhail Gorbachev – put the GDR under pressure, especially in the east at the Oder-Neisse border shared with Poland, but never fully and formally resolved under international law. Even in Hungary and the Soviet Union, the signals of democracy could not to be ignored.

On 8 May 1989, a revolutionary meeting between Bernhard Vogel and the foreign policy adviser of Soviet General Secretary Gorbachev, Valentin Falin, was held in Vienna. In their discussions, the Soviet side made clear that the EDU was preferred to the Socialist International as a dialogue partner since EDU member parties had shown more skill in governing Western Europe. The EDU assessed this as "new, hitherto unknown realism in the communist countries."[22]

Already at this meeting in May 1989, it was agreed that the EDU would continue this talk under the leadership of EDU Executive Secretary Andreas Khol in Moscow in September 1989. In fact, in September 1989, Khol, at the head of the EDU delegation, did not meet with Mikhail Gorbachev, but with Falin and other senior members of the Politburo, as well as representatives of dissident groups and representatives of the Russian Orthodox Church. It was a fundamentally different attitude from that which still prevailed in 1988. In other words, there was nothing more that could be conceived in 1988, not even that a year later there would no longer be any "ideological fear of contact."[23]

At the cusp of 1988–1989, EDU policy on the Soviet Bloc still primarily boiled down to information policy. At its 37th meeting, held on 10 March 1989 in Lisbon, the EDU Steering Committee decided with regard to Po-

22 See the Lisbon Statement, EDU Steering Committee, 10 March 1989/Lisbon. AKVI, EDU Collection, Protocol Lisbon 1631.

23 After the EDU meeting with Valentin Falin, head of the International Section of the Central Committee of the CPSU and a full member of the Central Committee, on 10 May 1989 in Vienna, Bernhard Vogel answered journalists' questions: "After years of no contact, the time is now ripe to hold talks with this important part of Europe. In any case, there is no longer any fear of ideological contact at all within the EDU." Valentin Falin said at the same press conference that "the conversation is not only a positive beginning to a hopefully productive collaboration but also a symbolic sign of the profound changes in the political landscape of Europe. I emphasize the importance of human contact for the solution of common European problems, even if it is likely to take longer to understand each other beyond ideological boundaries. How does the Chinese proverb go? 'A long journey begins with the first step.'" AKVI, EDU Collection, press releases and press conferences, Sign. JB 1988.

land that an EDU delegation was to visit Warsaw in May 1989, in order to analyze the political and constitutional changes in the wake of the round-table talks between the communist government and representatives of the still-illegal Solidarity trade-union movement. The EDU delegation was to meet with representatives of both the government and this new political opposition in order to discuss future political, economic, and cultural relations.[24]

But still, the negative voices had not declined, especially among the Scandinavian member parties, which warned against excessively ambitious strategies of democratization and reform in individual CEE states. The fear was that the fate of the 1968 Prague Spring might be repeated, and the result was to inveigh against what was perceived as risky diplomacy.

Poland and Hungary as priorities

Seen from this perspective, the meeting of the EDU European Committee in Budapest from 19 to 21 June 1989 was a turning point in the entire history of the EDU. During these June days, the EDU, as an organization, began to realize that the political upheavals behind the Iron Curtain were not a singular event. The fact that Alois Mock and Andreas Khol had taken key positions underlines the scope of action of the president and his executive secretary. While Hungary and Poland had been at the center of the observations up to then, the decision was made to send observation missions to as many Eastern and Central European countries as possible. The focus of the EDU's new *Ostpolitik* was to explore the extent to which reforms were occurring in the individual countries and in what ways these reforms could be supported by the EDU.[25]

It was the aim of the EDU missions to investigate how far the democratic reforms and transformations had already progressed, and moreover, how to support further reform steps. The Budapest meeting was organized completely by the Austrians and the ÖVP foreign policy expert Rainer

24 Report on the 37th Meeting of the EDU Steering Committee in Lisbon, 9–10 March 1989. AKVI, EDU Collection, Sign. EDU/1989/1820, 4–7.

25 See the correspondence and protocols concerning the contacts between the EDU and the representatives of political parties in Poland, in Hungary, and others in summer 1989. AKVI, EDU Collection, (for example) Sign. EDU/1989, 1937, 2–12; Sign. EDU/1989, 1838, 1–10, or Sign. EDU/1989, 1902, 6–8.

Stepan (see his function further below). Thanks to Stepan's personal contacts, the EDU was able to get in touch instantly with opposition groups.

When, in July 1989, the Hungarian opposition groups forced elections, EDU contacts provided by the Austrians and especially Rainer Stepan were suitable "keys" to electing later non-communist parliamentarians. It was evident now that a large number of partners had previously failed due to the lack of both suitable candidates and contacts in Western Europe. The EDU was able to achieve a rich political harvest in 1989.[26]

The EDU understood how to predict the key economic indicators as far as they were available from Eastern Europe. The true drama of the Soviet economy, which was close to insolvency, however, was not yet known in the summer of 1989. State and party leaders in the West knew very well that political reforms in the COMECON countries had been forced by those countries' economic weaknesses. Consequently, Budapest's economic problems were also discussed with the leading economists and economic journalists. In order to keep pace with political developments, the EDU increased the number and frequency of its meetings. All information and assessments were supposed to be communicated quickly within the party platform.

But even at the 38th meeting of the EDU Steering Committee in Stockholm on 30 June 1989, the "Stockholm Declaration," published afterwards, did not reveal any prospects for an impending overthrow of the communist system in Central and Eastern Europe. Under the leadership of Mock, the Christian Democrats expressed their support for the reductions and restructuring of Western troop deployments in Europe, initiated at the last NATO summit with US President George H.W. Bush, as "these would be part of the ongoing East-West talks on Security and trust building." In the summer of 1989, the aim of the EDU's East-West policy was "to achieve a stable and secure balance in Europe, with lower troop levels (...)."[27]

As far as contacts with the Soviet Union were concerned, future decisions were made in Stockholm. The EDU Steering Committee agreed to accept the invitation of the EDU Executive Secretary to Moscow in the

26 Beyond all its contacts to Czechoslovak, Polish, and Hungarian oppositions, the EDU had partners also in the Soviet Union. For example, in Ukraine, there was very close contact to the *Ruch* Movement. Founded in the Austro-Hungarian Monarchy, the *Ruch* was banned after 1918. Illegal throughout all the intervening decades, *Ruch* took over responsibility for Ukrainian self-government in 1990–1991. Cornelia Göls, *Die politischen Parteien in der Ukraine* (Frankfurt am Main: Peter Lang, 2008).

27 Stockholm Declaration, Protocol of the 38th Meeting of the EDU Steering Committee, 30 June 1989 in Stockholm. AKVI, EDU Collection, Sign. EDU/1989/1668.

autumn to discuss political reforms in Europe, cooperation between East and West in the domains of commerce and of environmental protection. The EDU, through this offensive commitment to maintaining contacts, stood out from other Western European party networks, which had not advanced their contacts into the lion's den.

Still, caution and skepticism – perhaps even a fear of taking on the impossible – constrained far-reaching changes in Eastern and Central Europe. A few days before the Stockholm Declaration, on 27 June 1989, a memorable event occurred. Mock cut through the border fence with his Hungarian colleague Gyula Horn at the Burgenland-Hungarian border. These memorable media images of cutting through the border fence made it clear to the European public on both sides of the Iron Curtain that the erosion of the existing power division had become unstoppable.[28] Mock was acknowledged in the international media for his personal courage and farsightedness. However, the general symbolism of the role played by Austria, the neutral country at Europe's center, remained little recognized in many places.[29]

In this historic phase, the European party leaders were urgently looking for guidance, which at least enabled a policy-based view in the medium term. In the summer of 1989, from 24 to 26 August, an EDU parliamentary conference took place in Antalya, Turkey. In a total of eight resolutions, the EDU parliamentarians attempted to give a direction to their own interests.[30]

A few days before the EDU conference in Prague, a peaceful demonstration memorialized the suppression of the Prague Spring by Warsaw Pact troops on the twenty-first anniversary. Through this demonstration – blended with the ongoing demands of the burgeoning opposition forces of 1989, such as human rights and freedom of speech and expression – the Czechoslovak single-party state saw itself challenged in all of its own certainty. Numerous Czechoslovak and foreign demonstrators were beaten

28 Maximilian Graf, "Die Welt blickt auf das Burgenland. 1989 – die Grenze wird zum Abbild der Veränderung," in *Das Burgenland als internationale Grenzregion im 20. und 21. Jahrhundert*, ed. Maximilian Graf, Alexander Lass and Karlo Ruzicic-Kessler (Vienna: Neue-Welt-Verlag, 2012), 135–179; Maximilian Graf, "Ein Musterbeispiel der europäischen Entspannung? Die österreichisch-ungarischen Beziehungen von 1964 bis 1989," in *Österreich und Ungarn im 20. Jahrhundert*, ed. Csaba Szabó (Vienna: Institut für Ungarische Geschichtsforschung, 2014), 261–280.

29 Eichtinger and Wohnout, *Alois Mock*, 145–166.

30 The first three resolutions can be described as politically relevant in the context of the revolutions of 1989; the remaining resolutions concern specific topics that were destined for the West as well.

and imprisoned. In a sharp resolution, the EDU Parliamentary Conference condemned this demonstration of power in Prague. Importantly, the Polish parliament and individual Hungarian opposition politicians also criticized this approach.[31]

Any long-term strategic planning was evidently made difficult – perhaps even impossible – at this stage of development. The external political situation, and the drama within the communist world, which was deepening from week to week, blurred the boundaries between action and reaction. This also applied to an intergovernmental grouping like the EDU. From 21 to 23 September 1989, the IDU party leadership conference took place in Tokyo. Within the framework of this meeting – and so as not to waste any time – the IDU hosted discussions on further courses of action within the EDU. The IDU chairmanship commissioned the EDU Steering Committee to draw up an aid program for newly-formed democratic parties in the countries of Central and Eastern Europe. The Steering Committee was also called upon to "seek ways of making contacts to such parties, including the possibility of membership or other institutional links. (...)." In Tokyo, EDU President Alois Mock presented the results of recent analyses of Soviet domestic affairs.[32]

The EDU office in Vienna had added four states of the Soviet Bloc to its political agenda. Rapid contacts were to be established – in the following sequence – with the Soviet Union, Poland, Hungary, and finally Slovenia, where the political changes had progressed at incredible speed. The fact that the EDU wanted to cooperate directly with opposition forces in the Soviet Union and also explicitly mentioned Slovenia – instead of Yugoslavia – still appears remarkable even decades later.[33]

The fact that the EDU wanted to go directly to the Soviet Union, and thus to Gorbachev, reflected not so much the degree of agreement on an agenda for negotiations as the mutual trust that had been expressed. The interactions between the Vogel Commission, which had already begun its work in the spring of 1989, with the official Soviet state and party apparatus as well as public groups, continued seamlessly. In the EDU's analysis

31 See the "Resolution No. 1 of the Plenary Meeting on the 2nd EDU Parliamentary Conference, Antalya, 24–26 August 1989 (Call for the Release of Demonstrators by Czech Authorities)," *EDU Yearbook 1989*, 75.

32 "How can the Soviet Union and its allies in Eastern Europe be persuaded to implement the necessary political, economic, and humanitarian reforms, which must necessarily precede fundamental agreements on arms control?" Protocol Party Leaders' Conference, 21–23 September 1989/Tokyo, AKVI, EDU Collection, Sign. EDU/1672–1674.

33 EDU Basic Report, Soviet Union, AKVI, EDU Collection, Sign. EDU/1639–1650.

of possible Christian-oriented Russian partners, there were obvious uncertainties and fundamental difficulties in transposing Western European definitions to Russian conditions. However, these EDU assessments had produced a list of names, consisting of figures who would intervene actively in later historical events. Despite the establishment of an explicitly named Christian Democratic Party of Russia in the summer of 1989, the EDU leadership considered it unlikely that a real party system would develop in the near future.[34]

The EDU, especially Mock, paid more attention to an interregional group led collectively by Andrei Sakharov, Yuri Afanassiev, Victor Palm, former chess master Anatoly Karpov, and Boris Yeltsin. In the view of the EDU, this group fulfilled the function of an opposition group, although its members could not be categorized by specific political parties or ideologies. Some of them, according to EDU analyses, were described as "communists," who were not reformable. Some from this interregional group still believed in a "kind of reform communism," others were "liberal," and finally a few were considered "conservative."[35]

The EDU mission to Moscow in early September 1989 is therefore not easy to judge in historical terms. Neither can this trip be seen as generally successful or failed. From 5 to 9 September, Secretary General Khol, Antti Peltomäki, and Bernd Fischer visited the capital of the Soviet Union, not least in the hope of meeting Gorbachev. This hope finally crumbled. There was no meeting. Nevertheless, this second mission was important for the EDU Executive Secretariat in reaffirming the seriousness of the Christian Democratic commitment to the Soviet side, led once again by Falin.

In the cases of Poland and Hungary, it was very clear that it would be difficult to distinguish between fully committed Christian Democratic groups from among the multitude of supposed opposition movements that would fit the content and structure of the Western European Christian Democrats. It was above all here that the German Chancellor and CDU chairman Helmut Kohl, who throughout the 1980s had long argued for a pragmatic approach, sought to promote all relevant groups even-handedly. Accordingly, the attempt was made to address the entire democratic party system

34 "Background Paper for the Negotiations with the Communist Party of the Soviet Union: Meeting of the EDU Delegation with the Soviet Representatives Valentin Falin and Gennadij Schikin on 5 May 1989 in Vienna": "the EDU cannot pursue contacts in the Soviet Union, unless EDU member parties are guaranteed that they will be able to meet any individual and any group anywhere and at any point in time." *EDU Yearbook 1989*, 135.

35 EDU Aid Program for newly founded Democratic Parties in the Soviet Union, Poland, Hungary, and Slovenia, 30 October 1989, AKVI, EDU Collection, Sign. EDU/1989/1706.

equally and from the same level on the part of the Western European parties. A departure from this support policy would only take place through clear internal political shifts in these countries themselves, but there was a distinction between contacts on the one hand and financial support on the other. From the point of view of the leading EDU member parties, one condition had not yet sufficed to assure the other.[36]

In Poland, from the summer of 1989 onwards, the lack of unity within the recently relegalized Solidarity trade-union movement had become more and more pronounced. The separation between Solidarity as an electoral bloc and the group of functionaries identifying with a plethora of new and different political parties on Solidarity's margins had also been highlighted at the EDU office in Vienna.

As a result, political parties were only able to develop slowly in the autumn of 1989. Even in the middle of October, the fog had not yet lifted for the EDU because – as the Union's analysts wrote cryptically – at the time there were

> two Christian Democratic groups (...) currently in Poland. (...) In the spring of 1990, an EDU mission to Poland is to be carried out in order to analyze the development of the party system more closely. The Konrad Adenauer Foundation will open an office in Warsaw in the near future, and the CDU will be asked to explore ways of cooperation between the EDU and the Konrad Adenauer Foundation in this area.[37]

The example of Poland points to a western struggle for influence underway already in the summer of 1989. Namely, the Adenauer Foundation was not the only western party foundation that was looking to establish roots in the disintegrating communist world. The National Republican

36 See the correspondence and protocols concerning the contacts between the EDU and the political parties in Poland, in Hungary, and others in summer 1989, AKVI, EDU Collection, (for example) Sign. EDU/1989, 1836, 2–4; or Sign. EDU/1989, 1902, 6–8. In particular, see the recommendations for action, Meeting of the Committee No. 1 in Budapest, 19–21 June 1989: "these general recommendations for action apply in particular to Hungary and Poland where there is a need to give spiritual, material, and structural aid to the democratic movements in these countries. Special training and similar assistance ought to be primarily confined to followers of an EDU-oriented ideology. The EDU should recommend that, on a governmental level, all-out efforts be made so that Hungary may be in a better position to institute economic reforms." *EDU Yearbook 1989*, 181–182.

37 See Alexander Brakel's chapter in this volume. The note refers to a group outside the Parliament led by Siła-Nowicki, while the other group refers to *Sejm* deputy Marek Jurek. In the end, the EDU Office in October 1989 recommended inviting Marek Jurek to sit on the next EDU Steering Committee, and it decided to provide financial support for his party, whatever its outcome. See the basic paper of the EDU office in Vienna. AKVI, EDU Collection, Sign. EDU/1989/1706.

Institute for International Affairs from the United States also produced a Polish program, as did the Socialist International. The EDU Office in Vienna was careful not to support parties that had already been funded by other Western party organizations. Since the Budapest meeting, the EDU coordinators surrounding Mock and Khol urged that mutual exchanges of information between EDU members be established and institutionalized after numerous EDU and IDU parties and party detachments had dealt with the issue of Soviet Bloc contacts on a bilateral basis.[38]

On 17 December 1989, Mock repeated the demonstrative gesture of cutting the previously insurmountable border fence, this time on the Czechoslovak border near Laa/Thaya. Now Mock's counterpart was the Czechoslovak Foreign Minister Jiří Dienstbier, who, for his part, had urged him, like Hungary, to put an end to the deadly border in a symbolic act undertaken jointly with Austria.[39]

The EDU was the only Christian Democratic force to maintain contacts with dissident groups, especially in Hungary, Czechoslovakia, and Poland, as early as the beginning of the 1980s. Beginning with the birth of *Solidarność* (Solidarity) in Poland in 1980, EDU was in close contact with Polish Christians.[40] When, in Czechoslovakia, a sign-up campaign was organized for the Prague Cardinal František Tomášek in Czechoslovakia in 1986 – also with the support of Charter 77 – the EDU tried to provide logistical and political assistance under Mock and Stepan. After all, this democratic petition was signed by 600,000 people, all well aware that it could be associated with personal reprisals.[41]

The third emphasis in the policy of the EDU – besides the Soviet Union and Poland – was Hungary. In comparison to the other two countries the disruption of the ruling communist system was advanced comparatively well in 1988–1989 in Hungary. The party system was evolving toward

38 See also the recommendations for action, Meeting of the Committee No 1 in Budapest, 19–21 June 1989: "Also, as a matter of principle, any reform movement ought to be given general support. However, some caution is needed when offering help to communist reformers. This may ultimately nourish a dominating role of the Social Democrats, a process greatly encouraged by the Socialist International." *EDU Yearbook 1989*, 182.

39 Helmut Wohnout, "Vom Durchschneiden des Eisernen Vorhangs bis zur Anerkennung Sloweniens und Kroatiens: Österreichs Außenminister Alois Mock und die europäischen Umbrüche 1989–1992," in *Grenzöffnung 1989: Innen- und Außenperspektiven und die Folgen für Österreich*, ed. Andrea Brait and Michael Gehler (Vienna: Böhlau, 2014), 185–220, 196.

40 Regarding the contacts that Western European Christian Democracy had with *Solidarność* before and after 1989, see the Digital Archive of the European Center for Solidarity, www.ecs.gda.pl/title,Jezyk,pid,1032,lang,1.html.

41 See the protocol of the 31st EDU Steering Committee on 13 November 1987 in Paris, AKVI, EDU Collection, Sign. EDU/1987/1460, 1–15.

pluralism. The Austrian Minister of Science and later Chairman of the ÖVP, Erhard Busek, together with Rainer Stepan, Director of the Karl von Vogelsang Institute (located in the Vienna-based Political Academy of the ÖVP), were early pioneers and "scouts" of transnational exchange with emerging civil society groups in the communist system. In the course of 1989, these contacts became politically meaningful for the EDU. Stepan, a close political adviser of Mock, offered his support to dissident groups often under personal risk, provided mentorship and guidance to young democratic movements, and began to educate students in Budapest and in Vienna.

The Hungarian Democratic Forum under the leadership of József Antall saw itself as an EDU-like party, which had similarities to the CDU/CSU and ÖVP. From the standpoint of the EDU, this basic attitude was expressed as a desire to join the Christian Democratic party family as soon as possible. At the joint initiative of Alois Mock and Helmut Kohl, the Democratic Forum of the EDU Steering Committee was held from 6 to 7 December 1989. With financial support from the Hungarian parties, the EDU leadership established the Hungarian Democratic Forum. The Independent Smallholders' Party, the Christian Democratic People's Party, and Fidesz – which ultimately proved to be the lasting influence among middle-class parties in Hungary – were to be supported with small financial sums.[42]

The overall situation in Hungary cannot be judged solely on the basis of the ideological orientation of the individual parties and movements. Contacts with the EDU had far-reaching consequences, extending beyond the realm of economics. An important secondary political aspect was Hungary's ethnic policy and the protection of national minorities in Hungary itself and in neighboring countries (especially ethnic Hungarians in Romania and Czechoslovakia, later Slovakia). From the outset, the Antall government paid tribute to the rights of national minorities, as far as they could be historically argued. The fact that the Hungarian side received support from very few Western partners was often lamented by Budapest. Also in this area, the EDU was an exception. Last but not least, Alois Mock drew upon Austrian experiences with South Tyrol to establish a foundation for

42 See the recommendations for action, Meeting of the Committee No. 1 in Budapest, 19–21 June 1989 again: "With respect to Hungary, the EDU support would relate to the groups and/or parties listed below: Hungarian Forum, Free Democrats, Fidesz, Smallholders' Party, Christian Democratic People's Party. In this connection a party caucus of the respective members of parliament as well as scholarships for a selected group of journalists might be envisaged." *EDU Yearbook 1989*, 181–182.

bilateral cooperation. The EDU's initiative of strengthening Hungarian minority rights in Romania and Slovakia bore Mock's signature.[43]

It needs to be reiterated that existing bilateral contacts had already existed before the start of the revolutions of 1989. These partnerships in the fields of economics and culture were expressly recognized and promoted by the EDU. If there were any concerns within the EDU that intra-regional relations between the individual states of Central and Eastern Europe would run counter to the overall objective of European integration, then these voices would not prevail within the EDU. In particular, EDU President Alois Mock welcomed, not least for historical reasons, the mutual assistance and coordinated approach. On 15 February 1991, representatives of Czechoslovakia, Poland, and Hungary met in Visegrád (Hungary) and agreed on mutual support and cooperation to achieve common goals and values. Conceived as a free trade agreement, the Visegrád Group was predicated on the assumption that, after the collapse of the Soviet Bloc, the most urgent shared problems had to be solved as cooperatively as possible. In this regard, the group saw itself as complementary to the *Pentagonale* or to the Central European Initiative, which was politically too heterogeneous due to the membership of Western nations (Austria and Italy).

In addition to the common goals regarding EU and NATO accession and increased cooperation in the fields of the economy and culture, the Visegrád Group was above all concerned with technical cooperation and issues regarding national minorities. A reciprocal political vote of the Visegrád-3 (V3, later V4, following the Velvet Divorce of Czechoslovakia) states was placed in the foreground, without previous Western consultation. The alliance between the three, later four, Central and Eastern European states had been initiated and decided by Christian Democratic or at least decidedly Christian politicians (Václav Havel, Lech Wałęsa, and József Antall). In its essence, the initiative also bore the foundations of Christian Democratic economic and social policy. Three days after signing of the Visegrád Agreement, EDU President Alois Mock addressed the press, stressing the Western orientation of the Visegrad Alliance and its Western values:

> Foreign Minister and EDU President Alois Mock welcomes the results of the Tripartite Hungary-CSFR-Poland Summit.
> Reform efforts must continue to be consistently supported. Foreign Minister Alois Mock welcomed the results of the Tripartite Summits of Budapest

43 See Anton Pelinka's chapter in this volume.

> and Visegrád, where on Friday the heads of state of Hungary, Poland, and the CSFR agreed to closer cooperation between their three countries, rejected totalitarianism, and emphasized their full affiliation with the Western community of values. The closer cooperation of these countries, Alois Mock emphasized, is also a natural result of the transition from totalitarian communist regimes to democracy and a social market economy.[44]

Shortly thereafter, Mock also stressed the strategic importance of the Visegrád Alliance. The close cooperation between the transitioning states not only ensured mutual recognition of a shared tradition of Western values, but also ensured to a high degree that no new Russian claims could be made on the sovereignty of these countries. Alois Mock's comments would have rung hollow, if the Visegrád initiative had been followed by a failure of Western policy:

> on the recent coordination of the policies of Hungary, Poland, and the CSFR, the Austrian Foreign Minister and EDU President Alois Mock said he welcomed this initiative as it is a clear sign that the new democracies are breaking away from the system of real socialism. Dr. Alois Mock will work on behalf of the Council of Europe to continue supporting the Eastern European countries, as it would be a "disgrace" for the West not to be able to secure change in the East.[45]

The creation of the V3 (V4) of course involved a balancing act between East and West. What was possible with a direct neighborhood policy? And did the "mighty" European states of the West really need to be involved? After its founding in 1991, influential EC states welcomed the Visegrád Group without delay, which meant that it was also viewed this way in the West more broadly.[46] This historical reasoning explains the strong popu-

44 Austria Presse Agentur (APA)/ÖVP-Pressedienst vom 16. Februar 1991.

45 APA/Austrian People's Party Press Service, 18 February 1991.

46 The 14th Party Leaders' Conference of the EDU, 12-13 September 1991 in Paris, underscored the importance of the Visegrád Free Trade Agreement with a position paper on the development of the EC (Rapporteur Elmar Brok, CDU): "Point 2, Expansion: The European Economic Area should guarantee that the EC Common Market does not create new barriers. Although countries that are not EC members cannot participate in EC decision-making, close cooperation with them is sought. (...) The planned association agreements with the reform countries in Central, Eastern, and Southeastern Europe, in particular with the ČSFR, Poland, and Hungary, must be pushed forward quickly, not least for political reasons. They must serve to stabilize the economy and the social and economic situation in these young democracies. (...) Investing in Central Europe is equivalent to investing in European security." AKVI, EDU Collection, EDU Committee for European Structures, 14th Party Leader Conference, Paris, September 1991.

larity of the "Spirit of Visegrád" among the populations of the four represented states. Since 1991, no government of the V4 – whether belonging to the political left or right – has questioned the legitimacy and necessity of the Alliance.

The upcoming German question

In the meantime, in the autumn of 1989, political developments in the GDR had become unpredictable, changing radically from one day to the next. Within the EDU, too, the revolutions of 1989 unleashed an unprecedented dynamic, and again this played itself out principally within the framework of the integration process. However, the coming of the year's end made clear that even the strongest euphoria could only cover a few expectations in the long run. By the close of 1989, the EDU had established itself as a stage for transnational contacts, which were quite comparable with those of the institutionalized meetings within the EC.

The big migration from the GDR to the FRG was only possible in view of the opening of the Hungarian border to Austria in September 1989. This had been achieved with the help of the EDU's Chairman Mock. Kohl expressed the Germans' gratitude to the Austrians for their assistance. West Germany's Social Democrats were now trying to profit from the developments and attempting to show that these changes had all been due to their policies, Kohl argued. They were trying to make the public forget that they and the East German Socialist Unity Party (SED) had only recently signed papers of cooperation. Social Democrats now wanted to jump on the running train and get themselves into the driver's seat of the locomotive.

Nevertheless, the CDU's policy would have been decisive anyway. The EDU deliberately set up initiatives and statements within the scope of its meetings to present German unification as a legitimate wish of the entire German people and, thus, also as a democratic demand for European Christian Democracy.[47] After all, from the very moment of its founding

47 Bonn Statement 1990, adopted by the EDU Steering Committee on 25 October 1990. The Steering Committee of the EDU held its 43rd meeting in Bonn, on 25 October 1990: "Under the chairmanship of the Austrian Foreign Minister and EDU Chairman, Dr. Alois Mock, the representatives of eighteen Christian Democratic, conservative, and other like-minded parties from across Europe deliberated on matters of European policy. The Steering Committee expresses its satisfaction to hold the first meeting after the German unification on October 3, 1990, in Bonn, at the seat of the Federal Government of the unified Germany. Since its founding in 1978, the EDU had always supported German unification in word and deed. Thanks to the firmness of the free Western democracies, Atlantic solidarity, and the success of the social market economy,

in 1978, the EDU had raised German unification to a political postulate. Having remained an abstract goal until 1989, the project of unification was nonetheless unreservedly supported by all EDU member parties. It is therefore all the more surprising that German historiography has virtually stifled this EDU achievement and this pan-European, Christian Democratic contribution. At the same time, this dimension of the German story also transcends its own federal initiatives and Christian Democratic commitment.[48]

The year 1989, however, cannot be viewed in isolation from developments in Western Europe, just as it cannot be reduced to only a story of events in the East. The outcome of the elections to the European Parliament in 1989 was important.[49] Notable was the low electoral participation, which was basically a disgrace for all of the participating and "European" parties. EDU member parties were not in the least exempted. The fact that the euphoria of the Central and Eastern European reform initiatives and upheavals had played out simultaneously with this lack of democratic legitimacy was quietly regretted, but without any other kind of self-reflection, this was dismissed as a very early "system error" by both the EDU and the EC.

This did not alter the fact that the CDU and the CSU, as well as the Democrazia Cristiana (DC), had won these elections with their candidates. However, from the point of view of the "*annus mirabilis*," the European elections showed no special thematic features. On the contrary, it was pointed out in June that questions of nuclear disarmament and foreign-policy stability, maintaining the status quo in the sense of a balance of power, had priority over the support of post-communist reform efforts.

especially in the Federal Republic of Germany, the smooth and unexpected unification of Germany had now come about. The mandate of the Bonn Basic Law is herewith fulfilled. Germany is now in the position to pursue at full strength its political aims, which are the continuing European integration within the framework of a new pan-European architecture determined by the plans for building the European Community and a global European peace order." AKVI, EDU Collection, Sign. JB 1990/22.

48 Even in the most recent publications of the Konrad Adenauer Foundation on "The Fall of the Berlin Wall" and "German Reunification" from 2016, one does not find discussion of the role of the EDU. See Hanns Jürgen Küsters, ed., *Der Zerfall des Sowjetimperiums und Deutschlands Wiedervereinigung. The Decline of the Soviet Empire and Germany's Reunification* (Cologne-Weimar-Vienna: Böhlau, 2016).

49 The European Parliamentary election took place on 18 June 1989.

The main political theme of these elections to the European Parliament in 1989 was the development of the internal market and the further convergence of the EC and COMECON. The fact that the Joint Declaration, adopted on 25 June 1988, included the EFTA states as well as Malta and Turkey had been the result of EDU pre-planning.[50]

Conclusions

The year 1989 was a new beginning in many respects. This also included the fact that for the first time the EDU was able to adopt a pan-European policy, a policy which for the first time allowed freely chosen Christian Democratic parties to partner to a previously unknown degree of freedom with the societies and emerging new political parties of a Europe in transition from communist rule. For the first time since 1945, Europeans were able to directly make European party politics. The ties to Moscow and Washington had been either set at arm's length or completely cut.

From then on, the EDU spoke for Christian Democratic and Conservative parties in Western and Eastern Europe. That the EDU, under the organizational leadership of the ÖVP, became the "stage" for the European Round Table on the Danube ship *Mozart* in January 1990, underscores the pioneering Austrian leadership of Western European efforts to accelerate the emergence of like-minded partners to the East. For the first time since the end of World War II, Western and Eastern European Christian Democratic party representatives, along with the participation of Americans and Russians, gathered here and discussed their future together. Freedom of speech and freedom of movement as well as the emotional uptick of parties from Eastern and Western Europe were never again achieved in this form within the framework of a common party network.[51]

50 Since its founding, but especially since 1987–1988, the EDU had argued for including Turkey in the EC. The rationale was the mutual bilateral ability for economic profit for Turkey, but above all for the Western European states, under the leadership of the Federal Republic of Germany. This became the mantra for the promises of expansion made to Ankara. See Madrid Meeting, adopted by the EDU Steering Committee on 15 April 1988, AKVI, EDU Collection, Sign. JB 1988/280.

51 The EDU Executive Secretary informed the EDU Committee that Austrian Deputy Prime Minister Josef Riegler had invited Eastern Europeans and Western Europeans alike to attend the "Round Table on Europe," to be held on 11–12 January 1990, on a ship on the Danube. EDU party leaders would get the respective invitations in the course of a week, and they were invited to nominate four parliamentarians for the conference. The Austrian People's Party organized this Round Table together with the International Cooperation Fund (London) and bore all costs. See the invitation, program, and protocol of the first Round Table Europe Meeting in Vienna, AKVI, Material related to the ÖVP at the federal level, Sign. 2836.

It is well known that representatives from all Yugoslav national groups and national states participated in this meeting. The tensions within the Yugoslav ethnic groups represented at this conference were also apparent to the EDU. Although it took place before other party mergers, this EDU initiative could still not alter the political and human disaster of Yugoslavia in the following year, 1991.

Now, within the framework of the EDU, two sets of Central and Eastern European parties, namely those from the Czech and Slovak Federal Republics and Hungary, were formally invited, and their leaders were equally represented. At the same time, the three Baltic States had already been invited to send representatives as observers.

Regarding security policy in 1990, there was the deceptive opinion that the economically defeated Soviet Union would henceforth only appear as a regional power, whether under the aegis of Russia or as a Commonwealth of Independent States. The permanent advancement of European political politics was regarded as the ultimate maxim, but the EDU was not able to clearly define the boundaries of Europe, unlike the clearly defined political boundaries of the EC. In the euphoria of the almost weekly dramatic developments in the collapsing Soviet Bloc, the EDU saw the geographical boundaries of Europe and future political space as identical.

At the Helsinki conference in August 1990, there was confidence that the integration of the European states would surely succeed in overcoming the economic heritage of "really existing socialism." Little attention was paid to cultural and psychological differences. The assessment of the future of the Soviet Union in the summer of 1990 was also important. The EDU conference clearly highlighted the USSR's emerging economic inequalities, nationality struggles, and political unrest. Even in 1990, however, the political imagination within the EDU was insufficient to recognize an impending complete disintegration of the Soviet Union in 1991. On the contrary, a fundamental economic policy reform of the giant empire was anticipated, and no more than a democratic "change within the Soviet Union" was expected.[52]

Before 1989, the Christian Democratic and conservative parties acted at the individual and bilateral levels vis-à-vis Central and Eastern Europe. A stronger coordination started in the spring and summer of 1989. When looking at the agenda, goals and priorities of the EDU, the discussion of various topics shows that Central and Eastern Europe took priority, especially Poland, Hungary, and the USSR. The Baltic states, the GDR, and

52 Ibid., 14–15.

Czechoslovakia were only secondary or tertiary in importance. Then, there were also EC-EFTA relations, which were of interest to the EDU, as was European security (Arms Control and Measures of Confidence Building between NATO and the Warsaw Pact). In sum, then, what were the EDU's achievements with regard to Central and Eastern Europe?

1. Discussion of and decisions on a range of crucial topics: supporting and strengthening of the ongoing reform processes in Poland, Hungary, and the GDR; welcoming the opening of borders; underscoring a policy of durable stability of peace and freedom in Europe; underlining Germany's unity as a precondition for stability and peace in Europe; the acceptance of the right of self-determination of the Germans.
2. Fact-finding missions to Hungary, Poland, and the Soviet Union.
3. Searching for candidates for EDU membership and the founding of future conservative Christian political parties.
4. Looking for forms of institutionalized relations, including coordination of future EDU members in the various European assemblies and institutions, especially the Council of Europe.
5. Developing guidelines for economic and technical assistance programs for Central and Eastern Europe – in this field, the EDU served as a predecessor of the European Bank for Reconstruction and Development.

Did this work at all levels? The observations, perceptions, and judgments of the political developments in Central and Eastern Europe by EDU groups were a function of fast-occurring revolutionary events, with incalculable and unpredictable outcomes. From a Christian Democratic or a Conservative point of view, contacts established with political personalities were often misleading und unsuccessful. In Poland, the EDU could be of help in the preparations for the Round Table before the elections, but the political system remained insecure and unstable. The political development was in flux and the political party system remained fragile and splintered. The coalition partners in the government changed. Tadeusz Mazowiecki could not be won over to the EDU working group. In the end, Poland in 1988–1989 was more oriented toward the US than toward Europe. The US Republicans dominated the scene and opened a foreign office in Warsaw earlier than the Adenauer Foundation. For reasons of stability, the US Republicans first set their priorities on the old party system. Therefore, Republican goals differed from EDU intentions. The case of Hungary was judged as too optimistic by EDU representatives. Fidesz was more or less neglected, while József Antáll was supported. He became prime minister of the first freely elected Hungarian government but died of cancer in

1993; his party's electoral strength did not long survive him. With regard to Croatia and Slovenia, the EDU judged the centrifugal tendencies in Yugoslavia correctly.

The story of the EDU's involvement in the transition from communism in Central and Eastern Europe stresses the necessity of focusing on non-governmental and non-state actors and the role they played during the revolutionary events of 1989. In the sense of research into the formation, expansion, and impact of political networks, a player such as the EDU must be considered, also to better understand the diplomatic and political decision-making processes during that crucial year.

SECTION II

FROM WEST TO EAST: CROSS-IRON CURTAIN MOVEMENT-BUILDING EFFORTS

4

THE COMMUNITY OF TAIZÉ AND THE REVOLUTIONS IN EUROPE IN 1989*

Thomas Gronier

For all the attention devoted to Christian politics, the ground-up formation of cross-Iron Curtain networks of transmitting ideas, practices, and beliefs constituted a crucial long-term precondition for the kind of institution-building efforts pursued in Central and Eastern Europe in the 1980s and 1990s by Christian-affiliated public organizations ranging from the European Democrat Union to the World Confederation of Labor. For this reason, a study of Christian Democracy's role in the fall of communism in Europe must also consider the social, political, and intellectual influence of contacts forged through the uniquely impactful faith community of Taizé. The goal of this chapter is therefore two-fold: to offer the first historical sketch of Taizé's contribution to the reintegration of a divided Europe over decades in the second half of the twentieth century; and to document Taizé's role as a crucial transnational network preparing the groundwork for subsequent political initiatives of the sort under discussion in the remaining chapters of this volume.

Until recently, the history of Taizé had not yet been written. The considerable influence that Taizé left on generations of Europeans makes its serious historical study necessary. This gap was filled in 2018 with the publication of the first documented history of the Taizé Community by Silvia Scatena (Bologne, Il Mulino, 2018) not yet translated from Italian. However, this study, which goes back to the origins, stops in 1974, the year of the Youth Council. Subsequent developments in the community, compared with developments on the European continent (1989), are therefore not addressed. Silvia Scatena's book is nevertheless a major contribution to a historiography that has long remained rather limited. However, this historiography included a number of interesting documents on which we have relied here: the books of the founder himself, Brother Roger

* Translated from the French by Cole Stangler.

Schutz; his own statements and letters from Taizé addressed to the youth of Europe and around the world, and translated into multiple languages; and, finally, a significant number of works written by those close to the community or by Christian journalists.[1] Though often of high quality, many such works do not lend themselves well to a historical analysis of the Taizé phenomenon.[2] Most of them offer an apologetic narrative on the life and actions of Taizé's founder and do not provide the critical and distanced lens that is required of historians. Nevertheless, the absence of Taizé in bibliographies should be filled in the coming years.[3]

Brother Roger Schutz (1915-2005)

The son of a Calvinist pastor, he was born in French-speaking Switzerland, in a village in the Jura region not far from the French border. In contrast to the three so-called founding fathers of Europe – Italy's Alcide De Gasperi, Germany's Konrad Adenauer, and France's Robert Schuman, all Christian Democrats by political affiliation – Schutz was not Catholic by birth. He was, nevertheless, like them, a man from a border region. Another point he had in common with these great men was that Schutz had been fundamentally shaken by the experience of World War II and its aftermath. Early on, he felt a calling that never left him: a drive to realize the unity of Christians or, at the very least, to aid in their coming together.

Schutz thus decided to form a community with other young Protestants with the goal of working toward this unity. In 1940, he settled in the village of Taizé in Burgundy with this goal in mind. In leaving his native Switzerland, he also hoped to live in solidarity with war victims. From 1941 to 1942, he hosted and protected Jews in addition to making contact with the French Resistance. After the German invasion of France's *zone libre*, Schutz became increasingly worried about the Gestapo and decided to stay in Switzerland before returning for the Liberation of France. In 1945,

1 It is in his journal that one finds most of the news commentary. That includes six works edited by Presses de Taizé, also in English: *Ta fête soit sans fin* (*Festival without end*, 1971), *Lutte et contemplation* (*Struggle and contemplation*, 1973), *Vivre l'inespéré* (*A life we never dared hope for*, 1976), *Étonnement d'un amour* (*The wonder of a love*, 1979), *Fleurissent tes déserts* (*And your desert shall flower*, 1982), *Passion d'une attente* (*A heart that trusts*, 1985).

2 Among these works, one should note the most recent: a very detailed biography by Sabine Laplane, *Frère Roger de Taizé – Avec presque rien* (Paris: Éditions Cerf, 2015); Jean-Claude Escaffit and Moïz Rasiwala, *Histoire de Taizé* (Paris: Éditions du Seuil, 2008); Yves Chiron, *Frère Roger, le fondateur de Taizé* (Paris: Éditions Perrin, 2008).

3 Silvia Scatena, *Taizé: le origini della comunità e l'attesa del concilio* (Zurich: LIT, 2011).

he hosted German prisoners, many of whom had been poorly treated in France.

Without a doubt, the images of Europe at war left a lasting impression on Schutz, as they did for many of his contemporaries. Moreover, the decision to build the community in the village of Taizé was not an accident: it was located close to Cluny, whose abbey had become known across Europe in the Middle Ages as a symbol of monastic renewal and a first-rate intellectual center. One can draw parallels between Cluny's European influence and that of Taizé in more recent times, even if this sort of longitudinal comparison between distant periods remains delicate. Drawing a parallel between the involvement of Brother Roger, as he came to be called, and the post-World War II Christian Democratic political renaissance across Western Europe is less obvious, yet Schutz shared with Schuman and his fellow Christian Democrats a common ideological framework that drove them almost simultaneously into effective transnational activism intended to reshape the world around them. The key ingredients of their shared ideological framework included a commitment to (non-Marxist understandings of) social justice, solidarity with developing countries, an open and welcoming stance toward migrants, and a prioritization of family and human economy. We can find declarations of these values in the social teaching of the Catholic Church from at least the 1890s onward, but at least in Brother Roger's case the immediate textual references for ideas were the Gospels and the writings of early Doctors of the Christian Church, from Anselm to Aquinas.

Taizé and Europe before 1989: the conversion story

Brother Roger and Europe: a modest place in his writings

What place did Europe occupy in the thought of Brother Roger? Without a doubt, it held a significant place in the general ethos of the movement that he created, albeit a more modest one in his actual writings and declarations. He was far more loquacious on other major contemporary matters of global social concern, such as poverty in the Global South.[4]

His interest in questions related to the southern hemisphere was more significant than in Europe-related questions. He seemed to have a gener-

4 Solidarity actions would be led by the community in Latin America as well, notably through *Opération Espérance* (*Hope*).

al vision of the world in which Europe was simply one continent among others. As a result, Europe was not a major focus in the early years of the community. This stood in contrast, for example, with the pontiff at the helm of the Catholic Church when Schutz was building his community, Pope Pius XII, who rarely missed an opportunity to encourage European unity and made no effort to conceal his support for Christian Democracy as a blueprint for postwar society.[5] Brother Roger did not have a particular yearning for a Christian Europe or for Christian Democracy. His calls for justice were based largely on his interpretation of the Gospel.[6]

In reality, Europe became a part of Taizé

Slowly but surely, the renowned community of Taizé took on a European dimension that it had not initially chosen. Across Europe, young people and adults alike were attracted by the unique experience of a Protestant community of monastic character that sought to become ecumenical. The first brothers were Swiss, but soon the community took on a European – and ultimately global – character.[7] The liturgy of Taizé appealed across borders: simple and open, accompanied by beautiful songs in every language, including Latin. It had a kind of universal character, "a liturgy that incorporated both Eastern and Western legacies," according to the philosopher Marguerite Léna.[8]

Then came another sign of Europe's entry into Taizé: in 1961, the brothers decided to build a church, since the small Roman church in the village that dated from the twelft century had become too cramped. The large new Church of Reconciliation, as it became known, was built by a team of young Germans under the banner of the *Aktion Sühnezeichen Friedensdienste* (ASF) reconciliation movement, a group that sought to promote an alternative image of Germany after the Second World War, in the spirit of penance for Germany's recent Nazi past.[9] Although the community was founded during World War II, it seemed scarcely affected by the war's international consequences during its first few years of existence, in particular the division of Europe.

5 See, e.g., Philippe Chenaux, *Une Europe vaticane? Entre le Plan Marshall et les Traités de Rome* (Brussels: Ed. CIACO, 1990).

6 Interview by the author with Brother Charles-Eugène, 12 September 2016. (He served as secretary to Brother Roger.)

7 At the beginning, all the brothers were Protestant. The first Catholic brother joined the community in 1969.

8 Marguerite Léna, "Taizé et l'Europe," *Le Monde*, 25 December 1992.

9 This movement was founded in 1958 by Lothar Kreyssig following the synod of the Evangelical Church in Germany. Kreyssig resisted against the elimination of the disabled in Nazi Germany.

The early 1960s: Brother Roger confronts a divided Europe

In 1958, Brother Roger was officially received by Pope John XXIII. This encounter would prove to be one of the most significant of his life.[10] John XXIII asked Roger to serve, along with Brother Max Thurian, as one of the 101 non-Catholic observers at the Second Vatican Council.[11] Roger went on to attend every session of the council and had the opportunity to meet several Eastern European bishops, including Karol Wojtyła (the future Pope John Paul II), František Tomášek, and Franjo Šeper. It was also during this time that Jerzy Turowicz, editor-in-chief of the Polish Catholic weekly *Tygodnik Powszechny*, became close to the Taizé community, which he later helped to publicize in communist Poland.[12]

In 1960, German Brother Christoph joined the community. He had been a young soldier in the Wehrmacht before he was taken captive in the Soviet Union. Deeply affected by the construction of the Berlin Wall in 1961, Christoph informed Brother Roger of his desire to travel to East Germany (the German Democratic Republic, GDR), driven by a desire not to abandon his compatriots on the other side of the Iron Curtain. Brother Roger encouraged him on this path, and Christoph traveled to the GDR several times, later joined by another German brother.

The presence of Taizé in the so-called Popular Democracies thus began in East Germany for linguistic reasons – the two brothers being German – before extending to Poland, Hungary, and Czechoslovakia. In the GDR, the Lutheran Church represented a certain social force that communist authorities could not ignore, not unlike the Catholic Church in Poland.[13] In both cases, state religious policies were not as brutal as those in Czechoslovakia or Hungary. Moreover, personal stories concerning the consequences of the Second World War affected the community. The family of Brother Alois, hailing from the Sudetenland, was expelled from Czechoslovakia in 1945.[14] In keeping with events in Europe, one can say that the Cold War

10 When Angelo Giuseppe Roncalli, future Pope John XXIII, was nuncio to France, he granted authorization for Protestants to pray in the Roman Catholic church in Taizé. See Escaffit and Rasiwala, *Histoire de Taizé*, 42.

11 Max Thurian (1921–1996) was one of the first brothers to join the community and a frequent traveling companion of Brother Roger.

12 Escaffit and Rasiwala, *Histoire de Taizé*, 140.

13 Compare, e.g., Robert F. Goeckel, *The Lutheran Church and the East German State: Political Conflict and Change under Ulbricht and Honecker* (Ithaca, NY: Cornell University Press, 1990); Piotr H. Kosicki, *Catholics on the Barricades: Poland, France, and "Revolution," 1891–1956* (New Haven, CT: Yale University Press, 2018), chs. 3–8.

14 See *Étonnement d'un amour*, 68.

became part of Taizé. The interest of the community and its founder in European affairs began, in earnest, with this consciousness-raising moment of the 1960s.

The 1980s: the first meetings in East Germany and Poland

Poland and East Germany occupied a special place in the community's activities behind the Iron Curtain. Brother Roger made his first voyages to Eastern Europe at the beginning of the 1970s. He often visited Poland and took part in the pilgrimage of Piekary, starting in 1973.[15] By the same token, each year, a small group sent by the community took part in the pilgrimage of Częstochowa, to pray before the venerated icon of the Black Madonna.

Taizé meanwhile exerted a certain influence over Polish Christians, even though generally they were not inclined toward ecumenism.[16] In reality, while Catholicism was nearly hegemonic in Poland, it was not monolithic. It was influenced by French social Catholicism, as the more self-styled "progressive" current of Catholic socialism.[17] Two important publications, *Znak* and *Więź,* testified to the intellectual vitality of this Catholicism. The PAX publishing house, a Catholic group (though not recognized as such by the Polish episcopate) that collaborated with the communist regime, had translated and edited certain works about Taizé.[18]

Taizé came from the Free World and offered Poles a kind of Christianity that broke with the image of a crucified country. In this respect, its reception dovetailed nicely with attempts by more progressive and liberal currents within the Church in Poland to important the lessons of Vatican II into the Polish mainstream under the auspices of "open Catholicism."[19] Taizé offered a simple and open liturgy. It brought fresh air. In 1977, the first Polish brother entered the community. A group of Poles was able to participate in the 1980 European meeting in Rome. However, a larger Pol-

15 Escaffit and Rasiwala, *Histoire de Taizé*, 140.

16 In 1986, Brother Roger was awarded an honorary doctorate from the Catholic Theological Academy of Warsaw despite his lack of desire for the academic world.

17 On this subject, see the excellent work by Piotr H. Kosicki, *Catholics on the Barricades.*

18 Jean-Marie Paupert, *Taizé i Kościół jutra* (Warsaw: Instytut Wydawniczy PAX, 1969) (a translation of *Taizé et l'Église de demain*). This publishing house later released the journals of Brother Roger (1969–1974) under the title *Niech twoje święto trwa bez końca* (Warsaw: Instytut Wydawniczy PAX, 1972) (translation of *Que ta fête soit sans fin*), re-released in 1982.

19 Piotr H. Kosicki, "Vatican II and Poland," in *Vatican II behind the Iron Curtain*, ed. Piotr H. Kosicki (Washington, DC: Catholic University of America Press, 2016), 127–198.

ish group was barred from attending the following year's meeting in London due to the imposition of martial law on 13 December 1981.[20]

During the Piekary pilgrimage of 1979, Brother Roger left quite an impression on Polish workers in a speech that proved prophetic. He said that great social changes are accomplished not only by men who are heads of state, but also that such changes are often accomplished by regular people like Polish workers. Brother Roger knew that the Virgin Mary was an important figure for Polish Catholicism and Polish national identity. As such, he compared the simple mineworkers with the Virgin Mary, the mother of Jesus, who also came from humble origins according to the Gospel.

Following in the footsteps of the two pioneering German brothers, Brother Roger traveled to the GDR a number of times, notably to Dresden in 1980, where he was welcomed by the Lutheran bishop Monsignor Johannes Hempel. The Dresden meeting also had the effect of bringing together youth from other countries under communist rule. Taizé thus permitted the development of relationships between young Christians hailing from Eastern Europe. Meetings took place in Erfurt, Leipzig, Magdeburg, and Schwerin. The 1986 meeting in East Berlin assumed a special significance because it brought together thousands of young East Berliners, taking place as it did at two different sites, Saint Hedwig's Cathedral (Roman Catholic) and St. Mary's Church (Protestant). This meeting also served as an opportunity for a number of smaller, local churches to organize themselves on a community-wide basis and bring themselves together in Taizé-style prayer. In so doing, it created a lasting network in East Berlin. The 1986 Berlin meeting succeeded a starting point because it began social mobilization under ecumenical auspices, bringing together energies that one would later identify in the revolutionary events of October 1989 in the GDR, notably at the Gethsemane Church.[21]

In other so-called "people's republics," the penetration of Taizé was more discreet but no less effective. A few meetings were organized, but with less visibility than those that took place in Poland and East Germany. Authorities tightly controlled religious activities. In Prague in 1981, Brother Roger was refused authorization to speak. While addressing Czech seminarians, Brother Roger confided in them, "If I cannot speak with you, I will keep silent with you."[22] Václav Havel, for his part, recalls

20 In spite of the situation, trucks with food were sent from Taizé to Poland in December 1981.

21 See the video available online *Wege des Vertrauens ... Zur DDR-Zeiten*, https://vimeo.com/317448924, 19 min (Ateliers et Presses de Taizé (A&PT) Production, 2011).

22 Laplane, *Frère Roger de Taizé*, 427.

attending a Taizé meeting in Prague and meeting Brother Roger when he was a spokesperson for the dissident movement Charter 77.[23] As had been the case in Prague, while visiting in Budapest in 1983, Brother Roger was unable to obtain authorization to speak.

The "discreet" development of a vast network of friends in the East

The development of this transnational network of friends behind the Iron Curtain proved significant well beyond the parameters of Taizé itself. Many Taizé brothers traveled to communist Central and Eastern Europe starting in the 1970s. These were informal visits that relied on local churches. Brothers visited families in apartments, where priests and other Christians joined them. These visits centered around a fraternal meal and time for prayer. Taizé brothers who experienced them recall: "We did nothing other than pay a visit."[24]

In their telling, the meetings were in no way about defying the communist regime or holding political activities.

The key for Taizé brothers was to provide a basic presence that allowed contacts to be made. Those who were visited understood they would receive subsequent visits from brothers, in fidelity and continuity. The house of the Kaplan family in Prague was one such site of welcoming and prayer.[25] Young Westerners were later sent by the Taizé community to the East. They were typically young women, less likely to be stopped and held at border crossings. These young people visited families or other students. They sometimes needed to memorize addresses so as not to have any compromising documents in case of a search by authorities. These young Westerners also joined other youth in summer camps or during winters in the mountains, officially known as sport or entertainment camps. These camps took place far from police surveillance and were organized, as weeks were at Taizé, around a schedule of three prayers a day. They were held annually for several years.

Thus, in the course of two decades, the 1970s and 1980s, vast networks of friends took root, and a flow of information was established across the Iron Curtain to each visited country. This self-driven system did not have

23 Escaffit and Rasiwala, *Histoire de Taizé*, 143.

24 Interview with Brother Charles-Eugène, 12 September 2016.

25 See the video available online with the spouses Maria and Jiří Kaplan, entitled *The History Between Taizé and Prague*, https://vimeo.com/109302099, 32 min., A&PT Productions, 2014.

a direct link with the Vatican's *Ostpolitik*, understood as a matter of diplomatic normalization. Indeed, the Taizé community had no diplomatic activity at the governmental level, nor did it seek any information from episcopates on either side of the Iron Curtain. Still, it maintained relationships with local churches. Although Taizé brothers insist that these actions were neither clandestine nor secret but "discreet," they were nevertheless a form of opposition that one might describe as passive. At any rate, this form of action revealed itself to be effective, judging by the success of the subsequent European meetings held in Central and Eastern Europe once the revolutionary transition out of communism was underway: in Wrocław in 1989 (50,000 participants), Prague in 1990 (80,000 participants), and Budapest in 1991 (75,000 participants).

The time of transition, 1989-1991: an affirmation of Taizé's European calling

The origins of the European meetings

At the end of the 1970s, Taizé organized European meetings that took place at the end of the year in capitals or large cities.[26] These meetings were thus a continuation of the Youth Council started by Brother Roger in 1974 and one of the forms taken by the "Pilgrimage of confidence on Earth," initiated in 1985.[27] Until 1989, these meetings can be described as "European" because they took place in Europe, and the participants were mostly Europeans. However, the speeches were not exclusively European; aimed at youth, they took on a more universalist, pastoral character.

And yet, once again Europe was present in the sense that the meetings connected thousands of youth from across the continent and helped them to build and expand a transnational network. They certainly contributed to the construction of a European spirit and conviction among many of the youth who participated. Taizé community trips to Eastern Europe led brothers to become aware of another Europe – and with it, of the hopes, dreams, and spiritual needs that youth on the other side of the Iron Curtain evidently could not receive from Leonid Brezhnev's cynically term "really existing socialism."

26 The first European meeting was held in Paris in 1978. Nevertheless, these meetings were not exclusively European. For example, international meetings in Madras took place in 1985 and 1988.

27 *Préparer le concile des jeunes, audacieuse aventure* (English edition: *Dare to live*) (Les Presses de Taizé, 1973).

One particular journalist seems to have played an important role in Brother Roger's evolution with respect to Europe: Hubert Beuve-Méry (1902–1989), founder of the *Le Monde* daily in 1944. He was agnostic, but became friends with Roger Schutz and visited Taizé from 1958 onward. After the editor's death, Roger wrote, "If we've been able to successfully organize annual intercontinental meetings of youth in Taizé, as well as youth meetings in Eastern and Western Europe, it is safe to say that [Beuve-Méry's] broad vision of Europe and talents played a part." [28]

Between 1980 and 1987, a certain number of meetings initiated by the Taizé community took place on the other side of the Iron Curtain. For the first time, in May 1987, Western European youth participated in the meeting in Ljubljana, then, in May 1989, in the meeting held at Pecs.

The beginnings of the Taizé community as an actor in the transition

The May 1989 Pecs meeting served as a prelude to the three great meetings held in Wrocław, Prague, and Budapest. At the time, Hungary was still under the monopolistic control of Hungarian communists, although the regime had recently made concessions and seemed increasingly disorganized in the wake of the 1988 resignation of long-time Party leader János Kádár. Taizé's May 1989 European meeting in Pecs took place at almost the same time as the dismantling of the barbed wire installations on the Austrian-Hungarian border on 2 May 1989 had begun. In Pecs, there were certain signs of change: young participants at the Taizé meeting who could not be hosted by families stayed in state-run schools. State-run television broadcast much of the event. One can say that this was authentically European with the exception of Romania, which remained outside of the scope of the reformist spirit ushered into the European communist world by Gorbachev's *perestroika*. The French daily *La Croix* led with the headline "Taizé leaves the Iron Curtain Ajar," and on the front page: "Young Easterners and Westerners Meet, Respond to Taizé's Call."

In Pecs, one can already identify some of the main themes of the three great future European meetings. In his talks and discussions, Brother Roger highlighted the necessity of reconciliation, of making the earth a habitable place and of leaving behind the era of international suspicion in order to enter an "era of confidence." He recalled the words of Pope John XXIII: "We

28 Roger Schutz, "Sa dernière visite à Taizé," *Le Monde*, 9 August 1989.

aren't interested in making historical judgments; we're not trying to find out who was right and who was wrong. We say: Let's reconcile!"[29]

A few months later, at the beginning of October 1989, the GDR was approaching the 40th anniversary of its foundation in unfavorable conditions. Growing social discontent had been perceptible across the country. Regular "Monday Protests" had begun on 4 September in Leipzig at the St. Nicholas Church and spread to other cities in the GDR. Police began arresting protesters in September 1989. At the beginning of October, religious vigils were organized in Berlin for the liberation of those held by the security services, including non-believers. As the presence of tanks in the main streets showed, tension was mounting. Meanwhile, many Germans were attempting to leave East Germany via Hungary and Czechoslovakia. The Gethsemane Church became one of the rallying points of protest in East Berlin. In it, demonstrators fleeing the police could find refuge.

Participants in the Taizé meeting in 1986 arrived in the church and took part in prayer and fasting. The slogan of the day was *Wachet und betet*, or "Watch and pray," a line that served as the second sentence of the Taizé song *Bleibet hier und Wachet mit mir* sung during the vigils.[30] On 9 October, the church found itself surrounded by tanks as the entryway was filled with candles. According to those close to the Taizé community, this lighting of the entryway was an invocation of the Saturday night prayers at Taizé, during which the church was progressively lit up with candles held by each participant.

Through their presence in the Gethsemane Church, participants close to the Taizé community felt as if they had contributed to the peaceful character of the revolution even though they had not directly taken part.[31] Events intensified noticeably the following month. Some weeks later, Taizé held its next European meeting, this time in Wrocław, Poland.

Taizé and the formation of a common European youth

Between 1989 and 1991, Central and Eastern Europe was transformed, the Iron Curtain eradicated. At the same time, great nights of rediscovered liberty were followed by modest mornings of confrontation with reality. But at the end of 1989, celebration was the order of the day.

29 John XXIII, speech to the priests of Rome, 29 January 1959.
30 Matthew 26:38: "Stay here and hold vigil with me: Hold vigil and pray."
31 *Wege des Vertrauens ... Zur DDR-Zeiten.*

Taizé's Wrocław meeting took place in December 1989. A non-communist government had been put in place in Poland under the leadership of the prominent Catholic writer Tadeusz Mazowiecki, following the "semi-free" elections of the previous June 4. The organization of the Wrocław meeting took place without serious difficulty, thanks to the support of the bishop of Wroclaw, Cardinal Henryk Gulbinowicz. The Berlin Wall had just fallen, and Europe was experiencing a taste of happiness mixed with astonishment.

One year later, the Prague meeting arrived in a different context. The Romanian dictatorship had fallen, and Germany had been unified, but post-communist countries struggled in the face of a kind of economic backwardness, which ran the risk of creating a new kind of East-West division. The local context was not favorable: the Czechoslovak Catholic Church had in large part been destroyed by the communist secret police, and the Czech part of the country, with the exception of certain regions of Moravia, was not particularly religious. Still, this did not seem to dissuade the Taizé brothers, who managed to attract 80,000 youth.

Slightly fewer attended the meeting in Budapest 1991 than at the Prague meeting. The Budapest version also opened in a new context: the euphoria that accompanied the end of communist dictatorships was beginning to evaporate. This was the same year and the same city where the European Democrat Union was sponsoring a gathering of prospective self-declared Christian Democrats from across the transitioning countries of Central and Eastern Europe. In other words, this was a time of fluid identifications, a time ripe for Western Europeans to travel eastward in an attempt to shape a Europe united and integrated in their own image. Europe was not yet fully at peace, and the war in Yugoslavia served as a painful reminder. Moreover, the countries that had rediscovered liberty needed to confront their pasts. The Hungarian Church needed to be rebuilt. It had been badly weakened by decades of communist rule, as if the clergy and faithful had internalized communist domination and struggled to turn the page. This domination had a lasting influence on the life of the Church.[32]

32 See the dissertation by Nicolas Bauquet, "Pouvoir, Église et société en Hongrie communiste, 1944–1964. Histoire intérieure d'une domination" (PhD diss., Institut d'études politiques de Paris, 2013).

The speeches of Brother Roger[33]

In his short speeches given to young people during the three big meetings, Brother Roger tackled several themes, whose formulations varied depending on historical and local contexts. The themes included the liberty of peoples, the construction of Europe, reconciliation, and European relations with the countries of the Global South.

In his 29 December address at Hala Ludowa in Wroclaw, Brother Roger invoked the freedom of peoples: "This year, several peoples have seen iron curtains fall and at the same time, walls of fear and humiliation. These last weeks, many have begun to pray during the day, and sometimes at night, seeking the liberty of peoples." He continued by referencing "the youth of the West who were able to join here the youth of the East who are inspiring and will continue to inspire such a beautiful hope across Europe." On 2 January, he finished his address with the sentence: "And it's through you, yes through you, that there will be light across all of Europe." Brother Roger focused particularly on Romania, which witnessed terrible days of bloodshed at the end of 1989. The following year, in Prague, he expressed his joy at the presence of Romanian youth. In Budapest in 1991, he again employed the term "liberty of peoples," but in a different context, that of overcoming discouragement so as not to give up "taking risks for the liberty of peoples." One does not find the enthusiasm of Wrocław in the two subsequent meetings, without a doubt due to the difficulties of the transition that had become apparent by that point. The Polish meeting was the first large gathering in a former Soviet-dominated state. It also took place shortly after the fall of the Berlin Wall. These historical conditions account for the joy that permeated Brother Roger's speeches.

The second important theme that Schutz tackled is that of the construction of Europe. On 1 January in Wrocław, he invited young people not to "miss this stunning moment in history," to take responsibility, wherever possible, and to "construct the human family, and in particular, the European family." He echoed the theme he had invoked in front of workers during the Piekary pilgrimage of 1979: "Like the mother of God, you are the humble of this world that prepare the paths of the future for many others across the world." One year later, Brother Roger began his December 28 address with a question: "Why get on the road in the middle of winter and meet in Prague from all across Europe? We've come to prepare

33 Brother Roger's addresses at the meetings in Pecs, Wrocław, Prague, and Budapest were not published, but were generously made available to me by Brother Charles-Eugène.

ourselves to take great responsibilities in order to participate in the construction of a Europe that is peaceful, free, and reconciled." Here he is addressing young people, inviting them to become engaged and to harness their talents in pursuit of this goal. In Budapest in 1991, in the context of difficult economic and social transitions, the tone was even more serious, almost taking the form of a warning: "Europe currently needs to be built. All of Europe must become a large and common family. It's a vital question for all of our futures."

The third theme tackled by the founder of Taizé and the one on which he would linger the most was that of reconciliation. In effect, the community of Taizé was built on the fundamental idea of the reconciliation of the Christian family. On 31 December in Wrocław, Brother Roger was more specific about Europe: "I would now like to speak to you about Europe. In Europe there have been wounds. In the East, many were affected by fear, humiliation, violence, prison. Those from the East may not know that, in the West, many were affected deeply by giving the impression of being passive." He recalled the visits of the Taizé community in the East, since 1962, initiated by Brother Christoph, before returning to present challenges: "And today, to continue, to build a European family, everyone, from East to West, we need to heal. We know that it's in interior life that we find this healing."

He did not forget to recall the words of John XXIII on reconciliation, a veritable leitmotif of these meetings. Speaking on 1 January 1990 in Prague before young people, Schutz said, "To reconcile among Christians, not to be stronger than others, but with the idea of rebuilding Europe, this is certainly one of the main priorities." He insisted heavily on reconciliation because he feared the possibilities of a spirit of vengeance taking over in this time of transition from autocracy. He evidently had in mind the sad settling of scores that had taken place in France during the Liberation.[34] In effect, forgiveness has been an especially important Christian virtue in the theology of Taizé. Brother Roger continued, "If the 80,000 youth who came from across Europe to Prague did everything they could to become creators of reconciliation, they would open [up] priceless prospects for the future of the European family. Europe needs to undergo a deep reconciliation." He also cited the Gospel of Matthew: "Leave everything, and first go and be reconciled to your brother and sister" (5:24). He invited the audience to make the coming year one of reconciliation. The following day,

34 See Brother Roger on this question in *Étonnement d'un amour*, 17–19.

1 January, he noted that prayer unleashes creative and inventive energies for the construction of this Europe.

In Budapest in 1991, having in mind no doubt the difficulties of post-communism, Brother Roger warned the audience with a touch of concern: "We will search for how to build Europe through love, a love of Christ, the source of freedom. (...) Today, for those of us who seek to build Europe, peace of the heart is extremely vital. Peace between human beings begins with one's peace of the heart." On 1 January, he returned to the idea of reconciliation: "Coming from all across Europe, are we conscious enough that there is, for all of us, a necessity that carries the name of reconciliation? We need to reconcile ourselves at our core, that is to say where we live." He continued, "In these final years of the 20th century, there exists another need. It is reconciliation within nations and between peoples. And for Europe, like never before, the time has come to do everything so that it is reconciled and peaceful." Brother Roger then commented on John XXIII's sentences on reconciliation: "Without forgiveness, there is no future for a people. A people cannot exist in plenitude if it tears itself apart in political struggles. Without forgiveness, there is no future for freedom in the great European family." On 3 January, in a televised prayer, Roger began his address as follows: "These days, we celebrate liberty. In order to reach this day where so many youth from East and West met and discovered each other, many men, women, youth, and even children, because of Christ and the Gospel, had to undergo long periods of perseverance and suffer from torment, fear, and arrests."

For the first time in these three meetings, Brother Roger had made a direct reference to the persecutions of the communist period. He then ended his speech, "It so happens that the memory of wounds and humiliations transmits itself from generation to generation." Here, he warned young people that the process of forgiveness is no brief matter.

Beyond a spiritual and social reunification of Europe, we have seen also the importance that Brother Roger attached to the countries of the Global South. At Vatican II, he had made a number of connections with bishops from Latin America. Two decades later, with the first European meeting in Wrocław, he issued a kind of warning that reflected his general conception of the world – especially relevant today in the face of the global refugee crisis: "Around me there are youth from the southern continents. Why are they here? It's because building Europe shouldn't make us forget other continents. We don't want to build the human family by isolating ourselves, but rather by together constructing a complete human family spanning the whole world."

The Taizé community did not lose sight of the southern countries following the collapse of the Iron Curtain in Europe. From 22 to 25 February 1991, shortly after the Prague meeting, the community held a youth meeting in the Philippines. The globally minded Brother Roger could not grasp the notion of a Europe detached from other continents. He distanced himself from any sort of Eurocentrism by recalling during the Prague meeting, "Across the world there are millions of children who know the struggle of deprivation, in particular in Ethiopia." He continued, "Let's see what we can do for them." On 31 January, he asked both halves of Europe to consider a more global approach to solidarity: "With modest means, we want to accomplish some humble moves between East and West. One of them will be to express a concrete solidarity with the children of certain regions of Eastern Europe."[35] And, he insisted on the point that remained deeply important to him: "Taking on the responsibility of rebuilding a united Europe should not cause us to forget the other continents."

During the Wrocław meeting, therefore, Brother Roger spoke of Europe with warmth and emotion, sometimes with an element of lyricism when he employed the term "liberty of peoples" or the phrase "light on Europe." His message was ethical, not confessional, as he spoke not of refounding Europe "on Christian values," but instead of building a "European family." He evoked "a very bright hope for Europe." He was conscious of the fact that the end of the division of Europe was a historic event. Without a doubt, the images of youth from both sides of the Iron Curtain finally reunited had the effect of impressing and moving him. He had expected, like many of his contemporaries, that perhaps the process would not go so quickly. For a man whose lifelong battle was for the unity of Christians, Schutz witnessed a powerful movement of unity of another kind that captured the focus of his own commitment. Did the end of the continent's division convert him to the idea of Europe?

35 Taizé's solidarity with Eastern Europe assumed concrete form with the publication of the New Testament in the relevant languages and the delivery of these copies by the tens of thousands as part of Operation Hope (which began in the 1960s with Latin America). The goal was to help make up for the lack of religious references in countries experiencing through the control of atheistic materialism.

The newspaper *La Croix*: broadcasting Taizé's European calling

La Croix (The Cross) was founded in 1883 by the congregation of the Assumptionists. With very conservative roots and anti-Dreyfusard, even anti-Semitic, stances, the newspaper criticized Pope Leo XIII's call for French Catholics to rally behind the French Republic and was verbally sanctioned by Rome. In the early twentieth century, however, the newspaper rebounded and established itself as a mainstream voice. In the 1930s, it had turned away from the group *Action Française* (without entirely abandoning certain anti-Semitic tendencies), helped to found Catholic Action, and favored keeping the JOC (Young Christian Workers) within the French Church.[36] It became more impartial, but consistently defended the positions of the Papacy. Although *La Croix* fell subject to censorship under the Vichy regime, a number of its journalists became involved in the Resistance. After 1945, the newspaper confirmed its progressive orientation, all the while maintaining its Catholic identity. It was favorable to the worker-priest movement before the Vatican effectively put an end to that experiment. *La Croix* was one of the first newspapers to condemn the torture practiced by the French Army during the Algerian War. It approved of the progressive positions taken at Vatican II. It seemed to follow the position of the French episcopate in support of European unification. It is recognized today as a high-quality source within the French press, even among those far from the Church. In contrast to a section of the French clergy, who have long remained indifferent, if not suspicious, of Taizé, the newspaper showed itself to be favorable to the community. *La Croix* cheered Taizé's impact on youth and its ecumenical vocation, which went in the same direction as Vatican II. Articles devoted to Taizé were thus relatively frequent in *La Croix* from the moment of the movement's founding.[37]

Taizé's Wrocław meeting had attracted 700 young people from the Soviet Union, a fact highlighted in the pages of *La Croix* as "Faith, from beyond the Urals." The reference to the Ural Mountains recalled General De Gaulle's formulation, "Europe from the Atlantic to the Urals." Just a few days earlier, *La Croix*'s 30 December 1989 headline had read "*Solidarność* welcomes Taizé," borrowing the words of a banner deployed on the entrance way of a Polish train station. On 4 January, *La Croix*'s headline read

36 *Jeunesse ouvrière chrétienne* (Young Christian Workers) was founded in 1925 by the Belgian priest Joseph Cardijn and imported to France in 1927 by Rev. Georges Guérin.

37 Émile Poulat and René Rémond, *Cent ans d'histoire de La Croix* (Paris: Éditions du Centurion, 1988); Yves Pitette, *Biographie d'un journal* (Paris: Éditions Perrin, 2011).

"Taizé, a breath of fresh air for Europe" and its second page, "This year, the gathering was marked by the joy of liberty. Solidarity, reconciliation, and world peace: such was the theme – oh how wise – of this especially fervent ecumenical meeting."

An article announcing the Prague meeting in the 21 December edition of *La Croix* began with these words: "This time, nobody should be missing. Except maybe the Albanians."[38] The day following the meeting, *La Croix*'s headline read: "Youth Momentum for Europe."[39] In the same edition, Brother Roger gave an interview declaring, "I often ask myself about the hierarchy of priorities. To make up with each other in order to build Europe is certainly one of our most pressing needs." In a *La Croix* article from 15 January 1992, one can then read about the Budapest meeting:

> Eastern societies have to live side by side with their recent past: martyrs and traitors, the courageous and the cowards, the tortured and the tyrants, everyone needs to begin walking this excessively difficult path of reconciliation, not to remain prisoners of the past, but to get to work on a new life. (…) Europe, after so much evil caused by hate, is ready for the challenge of declaring itself in favor of reconciliation.[40]

La Croix undeniably underlined the support offered by the European meetings to the European idea among young people. After forty years of being closed off, it is true that a thirst for Europe existed in the countries of the former Soviet Bloc, right alongside ambiguity and anxiety over the precise path for re-entry into Europe. One can observe the same evolution in the speeches of Brother Roger: the joy of Wrocław, the more realist enthusiasm of Prague, and the anxiety of Budapest.

The host countries

The heads of state of the countries that hosted the European meetings followed the custom of delivering messages to Brother Roger and the participants. Though at first blush, they might appear fairly conventional, the messages clearly outlined the contours of those statesmen's supranational visions for their countries' European futures.

38 "Taizé: 80,000 youth expected in Prague," *La Croix*, 21 December 1990.

39 *La Croix*, 3 January 1991.

40 Title of the article: "The Option of Reconciliation," Headline: "The relevance of Taizé's Message," signed by László Lukács, Hungarian priest, president of the UCIP (*Union Catholique Internationale de Presse*, or International Catholic Press Union) for Europe.

Polish Prime Minister Tadeusz Mazowiecki – one of his country's leading Catholic thinkers, founding editor of the journal *Więź* (Bond), and a long-time friend of Taizé – concluded his written message to participants with this phrase: "At the beginning of 1990, I hope for you and for the good of us all that Europeans are able to elevate themselves above artificial divisions so that we can move closer to a common Europe founded on Christian values." One can already foresee the Polish approach to Europe with Christianity as a marker of identity.[41]

At the end of December 1990, Czechoslovak President Václav Havel conveyed in his message his emotion to see 80,000 European youth assembled in Prague. He put it thus:

> our capital, after Paris, Rome, London, Barcelona, Wrocław, and other cities, finds its place in the spiritual thread sown by cities with their cathedrals, their inhabitants and the common faith that connects them. This thread, fine and strong at the same time, makes up Europe. (...) the pilgrimage of confidence on Earth comes to help us seek and find sources of faith and new spiritual values, lost in the course of decades of totalitarian rule.

The legendary dissident invoked "the long path of reconciliation that should bring us one day to this desired Europe, bringing together men and women united with each other, in happiness and fraternity."[42]

Havel did not speak of Christian values, but of a spiritual thread and spiritual values. Unlike Mazowiecki, for example, he was not religious, yet he saw himself as having "faith" in life and in the existence of a meaning to the universe.[43] The message of the Czech president takes us back to Milan Kundera's internationally renowned 1984 essay "The Tragedy of Central Europe."[44] In it, the novelist contended that the countries of "Central" Europe in reality are part of the West, since they are as deeply rooted in Roman Christianity. He is angry that, in the course of the Cold War, Western Europe had increasingly come to consider Sovietized Central Europe as no longer part of the West. Kundera, in fact, identified the "West" with Europe: "the word Europe does not represent for them (central European countries) a geographical phenomenon but a spiritual idea equaling the

41 See Piotr H. Kosicki's chapter in this volume.

42 He would say at the death of Taizé's founder: "Brother Roger was for me one of the spiritual pillars of a Europe in the process of unifying itself."

43 In *Letters to Olga*, written in prison, Havel expresses himself on the subject of belief and faith. Václav Havel, *Letters to Olga* (New York: Knopf, 1988).

44 Milan Kundera, "The Tragedy of Central Europe," *The New York Review of Books*, 26 April 1984, translated from the French by Edmund White.

word West." Dying in Budapest in 1956 in front of Soviet tanks was dying for one's country but also for Europe.

In the spirit of Kundera's influential essay, Havel's message to the Taizé meeting seemed to say that Central Europe has politically rejoined the West, meaning Europe, and that the despoliation of Europe's center by the Soviets was now over. Wrocław and Prague were thus in the process of rediscovering their place in Europe alongside Paris, Rome, and Barcelona.

In the words of the Hungarian President, Árpád Göncz, one could feel the difficulties facing nations confronted with regime change: "Taizé is like a flame of faith that burns for everyone in a cold and dark world. Taizé is a yeast of love in a world that is like poorly leavened bread." Prime Minister József Antall was more specific on the subject of Europe.[45] He mentioned Taizé as a starting point for the participants' pilgrimage to Budapest, noting the Taizé village's proximity to the old Cluny Abbey, the site of "pre-medieval monastic sources of European spirit and culture." Antall believed that Taizé could contribute to the refounding of the European family, and he drew attention to the role that youth could play in the future of Europe: "I hope that the spirituality of Taizé, the engagement and concrete initiatives of young people also contribute in such a way that Europe can be rebuilt without upheaval."

Conclusions

Despite its relatively modest role in his writings and speeches until 1989, Brother Roger's contributions to the construction of Europe were considerable. The bonds formed with the Eastern bishops when the Council was taking place, as well as the trips taken by some of the Taizé community members to the GDR in the 1960s, played a crucial role in shaping Brother Roger's understanding of "the other Europe." The founder of Taizé willingly established a parallel between religious division – the schisms that had led to Christianity's separation into Roman Catholicism, Eastern Orthodoxy, and Protestant churches – and the geopolitical division of Europe into East and West.

As for the contributions of the Taizé community to the events of 1989, they were real and long-lasting, yet at the same time more difficult to evaluate. They consisted of assuring a regular and faithful presence to the discreet yet relentless construction of a vast informal network encompassing

45 József Antall received the Robert Schuman Prize in 1991, preceding Brother Roger by one year.

almost every communist country in Central and Eastern Europe. Taizé was not a political institution, yet it assembled a social community across the collapsing Iron Curtain. The revolutions of 1989 drove Brother Roger to be even more explicit about Europe – and especially in reference to the role that the continent should play in assuring the development of the Global South. On this last point, Brother Roger was in dialogue with his old acquaintance from Vatican II, the Polish-born Pope John Paul II. In his message to Taizé's 1991 European meeting in Budapest, the pope encouraged "youth to discover together what Christian sources bring in terms of inspiration, strength and hope (...) in order to develop solidarity between European nations without forgetting the necessary mutual aid between peoples of the North and South." This exhortation explicitly echoed Brother Roger.

The fact of his having been awarded the Charlemagne and Robert Schuman Prizes speaks to Schutz's engagement on behalf of a united Europe – an agenda that was not immediately evident from the start of his activities during the Second World War. In May 1989, the jury for the Charlemagne Prize congratulated Brother Roger's and his community's pursuits of the "spiritual tradition of Europe as it was shaped by Benedict of Nursia and Francis of Assisi."[46] The panel of the Schuman Prize, awarded in 1992, justified its decision as follows: "In his exemplary way of overcoming political and religious difficulties, Brother Roger strengthened the hope that antagonisms that exist in Europe can be healed. The laureate maintains great confidence in the future of a united Europe and in so doing walks the path blazed by Robert Schuman."[47]

In her speech, Catherine Lalumière, general secretary of the Council of Europe, added, "Europe needs you! The youth of Eastern Europe absolutely need these meetings and this extended hand. In return, they bring and will continue to bring limitless richness to the youth of Western Europe." In his response, Brother Roger paid homage to the French Christian Democratic founding father of an integrated Europe, Robert Schuman, who "sought what could be the soul of Europe" and noted that "in order to undergo a healing of its wounds, Europe needs to be built not from juxtaposed states but from ones that are closely united, one to the other."[48] Unlike Schuman, Brother Roger Schutz was no politician, yet like Schuman, he created a transnational network that laid the groundwork for Christian Democratic projects intended to reimagine and rebuild Europe in fundamental ways.

46 These texts were generously made available to me by Brother Charles-Eugène.
47 Ibid.
48 Ibid.

5

"TO RESTORE DIGNITY TO THE PEOPLE IN THE COMMUNIST DICTATORSHIPS"

ÖVP Contacts with the Political Opposition in Central and Eastern Europe until 1989-1990

Helmut Wohnout

This chapter examines the connecting strands from representatives of the Austrian People's Party (ÖVP) to political opposition groups, dissident circles, and dissident intellectuals behind the Iron Curtain in the 1980s. This concerns first and foremost the contacts of the Group of Christian Trade Unionists to *Solidarność* in Poland and the network that the Viennese ÖVP Chairman Erhard Busek developed for individuals and groups in multiple countries. This played out against the backdrop of the Austrian Socialist Party's (SPÖ) single-party government under Chancellor Bruno Kreisky and a coalition of the SPÖ with the FPÖ after 1983. Only after 1987 did the People's Party again bear any governmental responsibility. As the junior partner in a government with the SPÖ, it was responsible for foreign policy in the person of Alois Mock during the upheavals in Central and Eastern Europe in 1989. Finally, the ÖVP pursued party-level contacts with the emerging parties in Central and Eastern Europe that were ideologically close to its views.

Contacts of the Christian trade unions in Austria with Solidarność in Poland

From the founding of the Second Republic, the trade union movement in Austria has been represented by the Austrian Trade Union Federation (ÖGB), which sees itself as a unified trade union. The individual sub-unions are united under its auspices. From a political point of view, Social Democratic trade unionists have always been the dominant majority party in the federation and have held the office of the ÖGB president. By contrast, from the outset, the Association of Christian Trade Unions (*Fraktion Christlicher Gewerkschafter*, FCG) formed only a minority.[1] From the 1970s onward, the ÖGB had good contacts with the communist state unions in some of the countries of the Eastern Bloc.[2] After the first oil crisis, Federal Chancellor Bruno Kreisky made considerable efforts to boost exports from Austrian nationalized industries to communist Central and Eastern Europe. Despite Poland's already considerable foreign trade deficit at that time, Austria's exports to Poland rose sharply. Loans in the incredible amount of approximately 30 billion schillings were granted by the 1980s.[3]

Therefore, the socialist trade union leadership was taken aback, if not embarrassed, when in August 1980 the Polish strikers in Gdańsk and Szczecin placed the admission of free and independent unions at the top of their list of demands to the communist leaders of Poland.[4] From the first moment, however, Austrian Christian trade unionists showed sympathy with the new Polish movement. Their chairman, Johann Gassner, demanded effective solidarity action in the presidium of the ÖGB, combined with financial support for the workers striking under the leadership of Lech Wałęsa in the Gdańsk Lenin Shipyard. However, the ÖGB leadership found itself prepared only for a verbal solidarity statement on 26 August 1980, and wanted to await further developments. As a result, the Christian trade unionists decided to go it alone. Led by the new Federal Secretary of the

1 The Christian Trade Union faction was nominally separate from the Austrian People's Party. *De facto*, however, there were close links, all the more so as numerous leading FCG officials were also representatives of the ÖVP. This also applied to Günther Engelmayer, who from 1983 was an ÖVP local councilman and from 1987 onward city councilman in Vienna. Therefore, the FCG was always publicly perceived as being – in line with its party color – a "black" union.

2 "Austria was one of the very few members of the International Confederation of Free Trade Unions (ICFTU) who developed relations with official communist trade unions in Czechoslovakia, Hungary, and Poland in the late 1960s and, more importantly, in the 1970s, including close personal relations. These contacts started after ILO meetings and ended sometimes in hunting expeditions into the Eastern Bloc." Oliver Rathkolb, "An Ambivalent Attitude of Trade Unions und Political Parties," in *Solidarity with Solidarity: Western European Trade Unions and the Polish Crisis, 1980–1982*, ed. Idesbald Goddeeris (Lanham, MD: Lexington, 2010), 280–281.

3 Maximilian Graf, "Kreisky und Polen: Schlaglichter auf einen vernachlässigten Aspekt der österreichischen 'Ostpolitik,'" in *Bananen, Cola, Zeitgeschichte: Oliver Rathkolb und das lange 20. Jahrhundert*, vol. 2, ed. Lucile Dreidemy et al. (Vienna-Cologne-Weimar: Böhlau Verlag, 2015), 702–703.

4 Andrzej Paczkowski and Malcolm Byrne. "The Polish Crisis: Internal and International Dimensions," in *From Solidarity to Martial Law: The Polish Crisis of 1980–1981*, ed. Andrzej Paczkowski and Malcolm Byrne (Budapest: CEU Press, 2007), 5–6.

FCG, 39-year-old Günther Engelmayer, a three-member delegation flew to Warsaw on 27 August 1980, and traveled from there on to Gdańsk.[5] At that time, the outcome of the strike was still uncertain. It was not until the historic agreement of 31 August 1980 that the creation of an independent trade union was approved in principle (formal legalization followed in November) and the right to strike was granted. But signs of consensus were already appearing as Engelmayer arrived. That is probably why the Austrian delegation was able to reach the Lenin Shipyard relatively unhindered and was led past the international journalists to Lech Wałęsa. That same evening, Engelmayer had a first conversation with Wałęsa about the future prospects of the strike movement.

The next morning, Engelmayer witnessed Lech Wałęsa climbing onto the factory gate and praying and singing Polish religious hymns with thousands of sympathizers outside of the Lenin Shipyard before informing them of the current state of the negotiations.[6] Later, Engelmayer gave a solidarity address to approximately 1,000 strikers and on the open stage presented Lech Wałęsa with 150,000 Austrian schillings (about 10,000 US dollars) from the strike fund of the FCG. The photo in which Lech Wałęsa held up the bundle of bills went out around the world the following day and found itself, for example, on the front page of *The New York Times*.[7] In his statement to the strikers, Engelmayer emphasized that, for him as a Christian trade unionist, the principles of Catholic social teaching and the realization of human rights were decisive. He declared his solidarity with all workers who work for free and independent unions. He emphasized to international media representatives that this was not a political activity, but rather "an act of international trade union solidarity." He saw it as a moral duty to "uphold the legitimate demands of Polish workers in the interest of human rights and to give support."[8] Engelmayer was impressed not only by Lech Wałęsa's personality and by the prudence of the strikers but also by the cooperation of intellectuals and workers, as manifested in Lech Wałęsa's advisory group.[9]

5 FCG Archives (Vienna), B4 01.02, "Solidarität mit den Arbeitern in Polen: FCG-Vertreter in Danzig" (Solidarity with the workers in Poland: FCG representatives in Gdańsk), FCG Presse- und Informationsdienst, 27 August 1980; Manuscript Engelmayer "Polen – eine Lektion für Ost und West" (Poland: a lesson for East and West) (no date).

6 FCG Archives, B4 01.01, Speech manuscript, Günther Engelmayer, "Solidarität mit den Menschen in Osteuropa" (Solidarity with the Peoples of Eastern Europe) EKV-Conference, 4 October 1980.

7 *New York Times*, 29 August 1980.

8 FCG Archives, B4 01.02, Letter Engelmayer to Kułakowski, 1 September 1980.

9 FCG Archives, B4 01.01, Speech manuscript, Günther Engelmayer, "Solidarität mit den Menschen in Osteuropa" (Solidarity with the Peoples of Eastern Europe) EKV-Conference, 4 October 1980.

The Austrian trade unionists' gesture of solidarity would, therefore, not remain a one-time action. On 1 September, FCG Chairman Johann Gassner announced the establishment of a Solidarity Committee for Polish Workers. Its members were the FCG, the Austrian People's Party (ÖVP), the Catholic Workers' Movement, and the Working Group of Catholic Associations. Thus, a platform was created which had been established not only by Christian trade unionists and the Austrian People's Party, but also by two ecclesiastical lay organizations.[10]

In hindsight, Engelmayer emphasized that his spectacular action was not just about encouraging the Polish workers through a gesture of solidarity, but also about achieving a model effect.[11] As a result, according to him, the American Metalworkers' Union, as well as numerous Western trade union federations, would have provided financial aid. Through the involvement of the World Confederation of Labor, a sort of umbrella organization of Christian trade union movements, he subsequently succeeded in buying printing presses, copy machines, and the like, and in making them available to the new Polish trade union movement.[12] This was founded under the name of *Solidarność* on 17 September in Gdańsk. By the end of 1980, it had nearly nine million members. Almost all dissident groups in communist Poland had joined it.[13]

Between the fall of 1980 and the imposition of martial law in Poland on 13 December 1981, the Austrian Christian trade unionists were able to intensify their contacts with the new trade union movement. Johann Gassner established contact with key Solidarity advisor Bronisław Geremek (a professor of medieval French history), whom he met in Geneva. Günther Engelmayer participated, now as an official representative of the ÖGB and together with a Social Democratic colleague, as a guest delegate at the Congress of Solidarity from 5–9 September 1981 in Gdańsk. On this occasion, he also became acquainted with the other intellectual advisers of *Solidarność*, including Tadeusz Mazowiecki, Jacek Kuroń, Adam Michnik, and Rev. Józef Tischner. After the Congress, Engelmayer made a first, cautious political assessment of the Solidarity Union. He rejected a comparison with the political spectrum in the free countries of Europe, to the west of the Iron Curtain. He also acknowledged that the leaders of Solidarity could not be called Christian Democrats. But by their commitment to

10 ÖVP-Press Service, 1 September 1980.

11 FCG Archives, B4 01.01, Manuscript Paul Lendvai/Günther Engelmayer, Poland 1980.

12 FCG Archives, B4 01.02, ÖGB Activity Report 1980. Günther Engelmayer, The Founding of the KGZE, in 25. KGZE Conference on Trade Union Cooperation in Europe, Vienna, 18–21 April 2013.

13 Paczkowski and Byrne, "The Polish Crisis," 11.

the guiding principles of Catholic social teaching, personhood, subsidiarity, and solidarity, they were much closer to the Christian Democratic camp than to its Social Democratic counterpart. This would find expression not least in the decidedly anti-Marxist attitude of *Solidarność*.[14] Indeed, the program adopted at the Congress was something of an attempt to find a "third way" between communist-style socialism and capitalism.[15]

The extent to which this solidarity was shaped by Austrian domestic politics became clear in September 1981. At an election event in the run-up to the works council elections at the flagship plant of Austrian nationalized industry, the VOEST steel mill in Linz, Socialist Chancellor Kreisky commented on Poland. The second oil crisis had also left its mark on Austria. In addition to rising unemployment and a growing national debt, nationalized industry was showing the first signs of crisis. The VOEST steel works in Linz acted as one of the main buyers for Polish coal deliveries. However, Polish coal imports based on government loans remained below the contractually fixed quotas.[16] Kreisky had been cautiously positive about the formation of an independent trade union movement in Poland after the agreement that had been reached in Gdańsk in late 1980.[17] Now, he effectively blamed Solidarity, linking a decline in coal deliveries to the "events" in Poland. However, he did not blame the Polish government for this, but instead the Polish coal miners. In view of the Austrian loans granted to Poland, they also had obligations to Austria, according to the federal chancellor.[18]

The remarks came at a time when pressure from the USSR on the Polish leadership was increasing. Kreisky's comments were immediately appropriated by the state-run Polish media in the spirit of anti-union official government propaganda. In the West, however, the reaction was the opposite. The reputable Swiss *Neue Zürcher Zeitung* spoke of a "*faux pas* by Kreisky" if he implicitly blamed *Solidarność* for failing to respect the treaties.[19] Günther Engelmayer immediately organized a meeting with *Solidarność* officials from the Silesian mining areas, which took place on 26 September in Gdańsk. In it, the miners indignantly rejected Kreisky's statements. The miners could not be blamed for contracts concluded with

14 FCG Archives, B4 01.01, Manuscript, "Polens Christ-Gewerkschafter" (Poland's Christian Trade Unionists), September 1981.

15 Paczkowski and Byrne, "The Polish Crisis," 23.

16 Graf, "Kreisky und Polen," 703.

17 Rathkolb, "An Ambivalent Attitude of Trade Unions and Politcal Parties," 269.

18 *Arbeiter Zeitung*, 19 September 1981; *Die Presse*, 19–20 September 1981.

19 *Neue Zürcher Zeitung*, 20–21 September 1981.

the Polish government, whose fulfillment would be totally unrealistic given the state of the coal mines.[20] The complaints of the miners, combined with attacks on Chancellor Kreisky, soon found themselves in Austrian media, leaked by Engelmayer.[21]

While money and material donations to the new movement were in the foreground in the first period, from mid-1981 onwards, it became apparent that more was now needed in terms of providing know-how, training, and similar soft skills.[22] An initial ten-day training session was scheduled for a group led by Bronisław Geremek during a visit to Vienna planned for January 1982.[23] With the imposition of martial law on 13 December 1981, however, all plans to intensify cooperation came to nothing.

But the Austrian Christian trade unionists did not let the contacts break off completely once established. At the end of May 1982, Günther Engelmayer again undertook a mission to Poland. It was coordinated with the World Confederation of Labor and the *Solidarność* office in Brussels. It was a private trip, and Engelmayer was accompanied by his wife. In Kraków he met with senior Catholic Church representatives and the closest confidants of the interned Lech Wałęsa. Among them were his wife, Danuta Wałęsa, the priest for the Gdańsk Lenin Shipyard, Rev. Henryk Jankowski, and the renowned philosopher and Solidarity chaplain Rev. Józef Tischner. Engelmayer got the impression that the underground *Solidarność* was already consolidated and coordinated. He received complete lists of political prisoners and internees, which he forwarded to Amnesty International and the World Confederation of Labor.[24] At this point in time, concrete assistance was only possible on a smaller scale for humanitarian work. With funds received from Christian trade unionists in the Netherlands, Engelmayer supported a holiday campaign initiated by Rev. Jankowski for the children of the interned.[25] Through the *Pax Christi* organization, it was possible to bring to Poland the tents for the summer camp together with a shipment of medicines and baby food.

20 FCG Archives, B4 01.02, 2 October 1981, "Bericht über eine Aussprache mit Funktionären der Solidarność aus den schlesischen Bergbaugebieten am 26.9.1981 in Danzig" (Report on the meeting with functionaries of *Solidarność* from the Silesian mountain mining areas on 26 September 1981).

21 *Wochenpresse*, 30 September 1981.

22 FCG Archives, B4 01.01, Protocol of the second Meeting of the Solidarity Committee on 31 August 1981.

23 FCG Archives, B4 01.01, Letter from Werner Hinterauer to Bronisław Geremek, 5 August 1981; B4 01.02, Letter from Werner Hinterauer, 29 October 1981.

24 FCG Archives, B4 01.02, Trip report, Poland trip from 26 May to 29 May 1982.

25 FCG Archives, B4 01.02, File note Engelmayer, 29 June 1982; Letters from Engelmayer to Arie Hordijk, 29 June 1982, 16 July 1982.

At the end of March 1983, Engelmayer again met personally with Lech Wałęsa in Gdańsk. It was, according to Engelmayer's account following his return, the first meeting of a Western union official with Wałęsa after the imposition of martial law. Engelmayer was able to establish that Wałęsa, although largely isolated by the authorities, was in close contact with the *Solidarność* underground.[26] He discussed an initiative with Wałęsa that he subsequently carried out at the 69th Session of the International Labor Conference in Geneva. There it was possible with the support of many Western member states to establish an inquiry committee to take action against Poland for the violation of international conventions on freedom of association by virtue of Article 26 of the ILO (International Labor Organization) statutes. He himself was nominated by the WCL as a witness for this procedure. He was able to give testimony for this process in January 1984 based on a recent meeting with Wałęsa just before Christmas 1983. Wałęsa had in the meantime been awarded the Nobel Peace Prize and requested a "very tough course." In addition to the legal issues, it seemed important to Wałęsa to emphasize above all "the moral situation." On this occasion, Engelmayer also reported to Wałęsa on a personal conversation with the German Minister of Labor, Norbert Blüm, and his offer of support for Solidarity, and recommended that Wałęsa contact him directly.[27]

Regarding the procedure itself, the ILO considered the ban on *Solidarność* to be a breach of the international convention on trade union freedom. It did not recognize the state-run new unions. By suspending its membership, Poland was able to avoid being formally condemned by the ILO.[28] Within Austria, the ÖGB leadership still distrusted *Solidarność*. Above all, the powerful longtime ÖGB President Anton Benya refused to recognize *Solidarność*. He saw it as a political movement directed against the regime and denounced its character as a union, with the Catholic primacy of *Solidarność* further increasing his skepticism.[29] For a long time, the FCG Group tried in vain to persuade the Socialist majority in the ÖGB to change its attitude towards the trade union situation in Poland. In particular, the Christian trade unionists blamed the ÖGB leadership for having become the first western union federation to establish contact with

26 FCG Archives, B4 01.03, Summary of the results of a meeting with Lech Wałęsa on 28 March 1983 in Gdańsk, by Günther Engelmayer. Compare this with Engelmayer's guest column in *Wochenpresse*, 12 April 1983.

27 FCG Archives, B4 01.03, Memorandum of a conversation with Lech Wałęsa from 3:00 to 6:00 p.m. (St. Brigitta).

28 FCG Archives, B4 01.05, Presse- und Informationsdienst der FCG Nr. 143/86.

29 Rathkolb, "An Ambivalent Attitude of Trade Unions and Political Parties," 269.

the new union created by the government after the imposition of martial law.[30] The regime-friendly behavior of the ÖGB leadership culminated in an invitation to the chairman of the Central Council of Polish Trade Unions in October 1986 in Vienna, which was sharply criticized by Engelmayer.[31]

When, beginning with Hungary, the first signs of the formation of autonomous trade union groups also began to appear in other countries behind the Iron Curtain, the Austrian idea of providing a platform for contact with and between the trade union-oriented dissident groups in Central and Eastern Europe and the Christian trade unionists in Western Europe arose again. It was no coincidence that the naming process was inspired by an analogy with the Conference for Security and Cooperation in Europe (CSCE), and in the spring of 1989, it established the "Conference of Trade Union Cooperation in Europe – KGZE." Its first conference took place on 28 April in Vienna. Under the general programmatic theme "Trade Union Freedom and Pluralism," a total of 82 participants from eleven countries met, including a Polish delegation led by Tadeusz Mazowiecki and Rev. Józef Tischner. Hungary was represented by Pál Forgács, president of the Union of Scientific Employees of Hungary and member of the National Council of the League of Hungarian Democratic Trade Unions, as well as representatives of all seven new Hungarian trade unions. From Belgium came Jan Kułakowski, secretary general of the World Confederation of Labor. Representatives from Yugoslavia, Czechoslovakia, Germany, the Netherlands, Switzerland, Luxembourg, and South Tyrol were also present. In the same year, on 3 and 4 November 1989, just a week before the Berlin Wall came down, the second KGZE conference was held in Budapest.[32] Austrian Foreign Minister Mock and Minister of Science Busek had served as opening speakers in Vienna, while in Hungary Foreign Minister Gyula Horn opened the session.[33]

The first KGZE conference in Vienna also ushered in other important developments. Initiated by Engelmayer, it was possible for the first time to bring together the *Solidarność* delegation with the newly elected ÖGB

30 Klaus Bachmann, "Poland and Austria," in *"Peaceful Coexistence" or "Iron Curtain": Austria, Neutrality, and Eastern Europe in the Cold War and Détente, 1955–1989*, ed. Arnold Suppan and Wolfgang Mueller (Vienna-Berlin: LIT Verlag, 2009), 388.

31 FCG Archives, B4 01.05, Referat für internationale Verbindungen (Referat for International Relations) Karl Heinz Nachtnebel, "Delegation des Zentralrates der polnischen Gewerkschaften" (Delegation of the Central Council of Polish Unions), 25 September 1986; Presse- und Informationsdienst der FCG: "Engelmayer: ÖGB fällt Lech Wałęsa in den Rücken" (Engelmayer: ÖGB backstabs Lech Wałęsa), 1 October 1986.

32 *Austria Presse Agentur* (*APA*), *0143 5 AI*, 28 April 1989.

33 25. KGZE Conference on Trade Union Cooperation in Europe, Vienna, 18-21 April 2013.

President Fritz Verzetnitsch. But even at a time when the talks at the Round Table were already in full swing (February-April 1989), the ÖGB had been hesitant. The conversation with Verzetnitsch was deeply disappointing for Mazowiecki.[34] When Engelmayer was in Warsaw at the time of Tadeusz Mazowiecki's nomination as Prime Minister of Poland in late August, Bronisław Geremek, now leader of the *Solidarność* representation in the Polish *Sejm*, again asked him to apply for the rapid recognition of the ÖGB.[35] It would take until 1990 for the ÖGB to recognize *Solidarność*.[36]

The "Central European" Erhard Busek

Beginning in the late 1970s and early 1980s Erhard Busek was the first Austrian politician to build a network of opposition in Poland, Hungary, the then Czechoslovakia, and (partly) Yugoslavia. Busek was then considered a rising star within the ÖVP. In his mid-thirties, he was already secretary general of the party in 1975–1976, and in 1976 he took over the local ÖVP party group in Vienna – in view of the SPÖ's domination of Vienna a difficult undertaking to say the least. In this role, Busek developed a modern concept for urban policy, gained significant votes in the municipal elections in Vienna in 1978 and 1983, and became deputy mayor. Part of his program centered on the development of an independent "urban foreign policy" with a focus on Austria's immediate neighbors in the Danube region. Vienna in the mid-1970s was something of a terminus for the free West; north and east of it was more or less "no man's land."

During his activities as a youth functionary in Catholic lay organizations and as chairman of the Austrian Federal Youth Council in the course of the 1960s, Busek had already made contacts with dissident Christian circles in Czechoslovakia and in the GDR. From 1967 onward, he established a permanent connection to Catholic academic circles in Prague; a year later he met for the first time with the then Auxiliary Bishop, and later Cardinal, František Tomášek. From there, Busek remained in contact with him, providing him with theological literature, later also with medicine.[37] Busek experienced up close how the hopes of the Prague Spring had faded and how the repressive Husák years of so-called "normalization" had provoked

34 Erhard Busek, *Mitteleuropa: Eine Spurensicherung* (Vienna: Kremayr & Scheriau, 1997), 50.
35 FCG Archives, B4 01.05, Travelogue of the trip to Warsaw on 21 August 1989.
36 Rathkolb, "An Ambivalent Attitude of Trade Unions and Political Parties," 284.
37 Busek, *Mitteleuropa*, 17.

disappointment and resignation. From this point on, he felt a moral obligation to maintain contacts with opposition parties close to him behind the Iron Curtain. He wanted to teach people that they were not disregarded by the West.[38] In retrospect, he wrote, "The key phrase for me was that a friend from the dissident scene, when asked what I should do for him, said to me, 'Thou shalt not forget us.' That was an invitation for me. This ultimately led to my systematic engagement on behalf of the dissidents."[39]

With intellectual curiosity he began to develop a "neighborhood strategy."[40] Above all, he had in mind those Central and Eastern European countries that, although historically and culturally diverse, had become, because of the Iron Curtain, a blind spot in the minds of their compatriots. Erhard Busek's aim was to "acknowledge that we have neighbors with whom we have not only lived in a lively and close, though sometimes difficult, relationship, but with whom we have much in common today."[41] He wanted them, through the political realities created by Yalta, not to permit a hermetic separation between East and West. He appealed to Europe, underlining its spiritual roots, and found himself in line with the newly elected Polish-born pope in the autumn of 1978.

In the beginning, Busek's activism was often predicated on initiatives and ideas that were not necessarily political and even less partisan in nature. His activities were often firmly rooted in the realm of ideas, avoiding the ostentatious in favor instead of consistent and thoughtful principle. A significant example can be mentioned here: in 1979, as part of the Austrian Research Community that he headed together with the historian Gerald Stourzh, Busek created the Anton Gindely Prize for the History of the Danube Monarchy, to be awarded to outstanding scholars on both sides of the Iron Curtain who wrote their works based on sources in several languages (including Yiddish) from the old Austrian monarchy, something that was the exception, and not the rule, at least in Austria at that time. The key criterion for the award was that an intellectual contribution should be made documenting the linguistic and cultural diversity of the post-Habsburg space. The awards provided Busek with welcome opportunities to bring intellectuals from countries behind the Iron Curtain to Vienna as "keynote speakers," among them Stanisław Stomma in 1981 or

38 Busek, *Ein Porträt aus der Nähe: Im Gespräch mit Jelka Kušar* (Klagenfurt-Vienna-Ljublijana et al.: Wieser, 2006), 157–165; Id., *Mitteleuropa*, 13–19.

39 Id., *Ein Portrait aus der Nähe*, 165.

40 Id., *Lebensbilder* (Vienna: Kremayr & Scheriau, 2014), 145.

41 See Erhard Busek and Gerald Stourzh, eds., *Nationale Vielfalt und gemeinsames Erbe in Mitteleuropa* (Vienna-Munich: Verlag für Geschichte und Politik, 1990), 10 (Busek, zum Geleit).

Władysław Bartoszewski, arrested in Poland after the proclamation of martial law in 1983, often overcoming considerable logistical difficulties and harassment.[42]

From the late 1970s onward, Busek, often accompanied by journalists, undertook his legendary visits to opposition and regime opponents and Church representatives in countries behind the Iron Curtain. For the most part, he avoided official appointments with communist officials, the goal being to avoid unintentionally legitimating those regimes with his travels to communist countries. The writer Jörg Mauthe, perhaps Busek's closest political companion in those years, interpreted his journeys as "an attempt to expose half-forgotten traces and leave new ones, to tie one or the other thread to the gossamer web, that perhaps could one day be condensed into a carpet called Central Europe."[43]

Starting in 1980–1981, Busek began to develop intensive ties to Poland.[44] The prerequisites for these were given insofar as the communist state authorities had long granted Poland's Catholic intelligentsia certain freedoms in having contacts with the West. This began after the 1956 "thaw" with an agreement between then Party leader Władysław Gomułka and Cardinal Stefan Wyszyński and was therefore vehemently defended by the Church.[45] Many of Busek's interlocutors came from the intelligentsia circles whose activities were made possible by those agreements. Some of the best-known – like Poland's future prime minister Tadeusz Mazowiecki – had played a crucial role in the founding of the *Solidarność* trade union movement.

Among them was also one of Busek's earliest confidants in Poland, Rev. Józef Tischner.[46] With his book *Spirit of Solidarity*, Tischner became the programmatic thinker for the trade union movement.[47] The cosmopolitan priest was professor of philosophy at the Pontifical Academy in Kraków. He stayed in close contact with his former metropolitan archbishop, Karol Wojtyła (who had also been one of Tischner's academic advisors for the PhD), even after Wojtyła was elected pope. Tischner acted as an emissary of the pope when he asked Busek to support the creation of a center for scientific meetings in Vienna.

42 See Busek and Stourzh, eds., *Nationale Vielfalt und gemeinsames Erbe in Mitteleuropa.*

43 Jörg Mauthe, *Demnächst oder Der Stein des Sisyphos* (Vienna: Edition Atelier, 1986), 107.

44 Władysław Bartoszewski, "Der Ostreisende," in *Erhard Busek: Ein Porträt*, ed. Elisabeth Welzig (Vienna-Cologne-Weimar: Böhlau, 1992), 263–267.

45 Paczkowski and Byrne, "The Polish Crisis," 4–5.

46 Busek, *Mitteleuropa*, 21–22.

47 Józef Tischner, *The Spirit of Solidarity*, trans. Marek B. Zaleski and Benjamin Fiore (San Francisco: Harper & Row, 1984).

The first considerations on the basis of which this idea began to mature had already come to light during Busek's Poland trip in April 1981.[48] Busek succeeded in winning the Socialist Mayor of Vienna, Leopold Gratz, over to the idea. Thus, the Institute for Human Sciences was created, with Krzysztof Michalski and Józef Tischner at its helm.[49] It became one of the main pioneers of the idea of civil society and was to play an important role as a think tank in the transformation processes in Central and Eastern Europe. Starting in 1983, the Institute for Human Sciences organized the so-called Castelgandolfo Talks every two years, in which the Polish pope always participated as an interested listener. For Busek as well as for the polyglot Viennese Cardinal Franz König, the Castelgandolfo Talks were always a fixture in their calendars.

In addition to Tischner, Tadeusz Mazowiecki and Bronisław Geremek soon numbered among Busek's regular discussion partners. He became acquainted with Mazowiecki as a central figure in the Catholic Intelligentsia Clubs (*Kluby Inteligencji Katolickiej*) when Mazowiecki began to temper the overly optimistic views of many of his Solidarity compatriots in the summer of 1981. Later, Busek also came to understand that Mazowiecki and Bronislaw Geremek were close confidants of Lech Wałęsa.

On his first visit to Austria in September 1983, John Paul II, with a view beyond the borders of the Iron Curtain, delivered his *Europavesper* sermon on Vienna's historic Heldenplatz, appealing to the "cultural commonality on the European continent," representing "a common heritage." As in his visits to Poland, the pope spoke of "the dignity of the human person" and "respect for the right to free development in compassionate solidarity."[50] To underscore the cross-border dimension of European freedoms, the cardinals of Kraków, divided Berlin, Zagreb, and Paris were invited to speak after John Paul II. The pope had not spoken exclusively to Catholics at the event. It was a message to all the inhabitants of Europe, especially to those who lived behind the Iron Curtain. Already during his first visit to Poland in 1979, he had handled this in a similar fashion.[51]

In the year of John Paul II's first visit to Austria, Busek had once again been able to meet with prominent representatives of the Polish opposi-

48 Gerhard Wilflinger, "Der Mitteleuropäer," in *Erhard Busek. Ein Porträt*, ed. Welzig, 250.

49 Busek, *Mitteleuropa*, 66–67.

50 *Europavesper* on the Heldenplatz, sermon by John Paul II, 10 September 1983, at http://w2.vatican.va/content/john-paul-ii/de/homilies/1983/documents/hf_jp-ii_hom_19830910_celebrazione-vespri.html (accessed 6 January 2019).

51 Mikołaj Kunicki, "Between Accommodation, Resistance, and Dialogue: Church-State Relations in Communist Poland, 1945–1989," in *"Peaceful Coexistence" or "Iron Curtain,* ed. Suppan and Mueller, 405.

tion and the delegalized *Solidarność* movement. The journeys now also had the purpose of informing a broad public in the West about the conditions in Poland. For this purpose, Busek included journalists in his small tour groups for whom he arranged special interview appointments with his interlocutors. Back in Vienna, he invited journalists to press briefings and background discussions. This was so that they could obtain authentic information about the conditions in the communist states: beyond Western clichés about the alleged reformability of the communist states within existing social conditions. This was an essential corrective to the Western idea of détente politics, where dissidents were often seen as annoying nuisances on the way to détente and economic cooperation. Especially after his trips to Poland, Busek repeatedly succeeded in placing reports not only in the Austrian media but also in the large German newspapers like *Die Welt* or the *Frankfurter Allgemeine Zeitung*, thereby raising general public awareness of the conditions in Poland.

All in all, Austria had become something like a window on Poland. Reporters from neutral Austria enjoyed more freedom of movement in Poland than those of other Western countries, for example those from West Germany.[52]

In the second half of the 1980s there was some relaxation of tensions in Poland. In 1986, all political prisoners were released.[53] At that time, Busek, with the help of the then Austrian ambassador in Warsaw, Richard Wotawa, who was politically close to him, managed to obtain an exit visa for Mazowiecki for the first time since the imposition of martial law, enabling him to travel to Vienna and then on to see the pope in Rome.[54] Finally, Busek witnessed Mazowiecki, Geremek, and Tischner participating all together in the Castelgandolfo Talks in 1989, in parallel with the critical days of political negotiations at Poland's Round Table, as Mazowiecki and Geremek remained permanently connected with Warsaw by telephone, on the one hand, while in direct contact with Pope John Paul II, on the other.[55]

To create a platform for discussion with artists, scientists, and intellectuals from other countries, a goal also pursued by Busek, the Vienna

52 Bachmann, "Poland and Austria," 391.

53 Id., "Poland 1989: The Constrained Revolution," in *The Revolutions of 1989: A Handbook*, ed. Wolfgang Mueller, Michael Gehler and Arnold Suppan (Vienna: Verlag der Österreichischen Akademie der Wissenschaften, 2015), 50.

54 Archive of the Karl von Vogelsang Institute (AKVI, Vienna), Sign. 2819 (Erhard Busek Papers), Folder for Poland Trip, Letter Ambassador Wotava to Busek, 6 June 1986; Telegram Austrian Embassy Warsaw to Ministry of Foreign Affairs, Vienna, 24 June 1986.

55 Busek, *Mitteleuropa*, 48–50.

ÖVP established "Club Pro Vienna." Among the speakers between 1981 and 1989 were numerous oppositionists and critical spirits, some having emigrated from the communist states, including Władysław Bartoszewski, Józef Tischner, Alexander Zinoviev, Leszek Kołakowski, the archbishop of Ljubljana Alojzij Šuštar, Stefan Kisielewski, Stanislaw Lem, György Konrád, Peter Hanák, Ljuba Tadić, and Tadeusz Mazowiecki.

The term "Central Europe" as used by Busek, in contrast to the term "East," was intended to debunk the notion of a uniform, Soviet-dominated cultural space, starting in Bratislava and ending in Vladivostok. Returning from one of his trips to Poland, he wrote – in a line evocative of iconic Czech emigré novelist Milan Kundera's celebrated 1984 essay "The Tragedy of Central Europe" – "Speaking of the East: We have to change our terminology because the people in Poland, Hungary, Czechoslovakia, etc., do not see themselves as the East, but as Central Europe. Can we not at least give them this help in recognizing them as Central Europe?"[56]

In the book *Projekt Mitteleuropa,* written in 1986 together with the historian Emil Brix, Busek clearly distinguished himself from Friedrich Naumann's old concepts of Central Europe formulated at the beginning of the twentieth century.[57] It was also not about a nostalgic reminiscence or even plans for a re-establishment of the old multi-ethnic state of the Habsburgs. In the face of the Iron Curtain and a hermetic border only 50 kilometers east of Vienna, Busek wanted to make a contribution to rediscovering the intellectual and cultural commonalities defining Central Europe, based on the principle of the European neighborhood. Certainly, much of his *Mitteleuropa* concept remained, perhaps quite deliberately, fragmentary.

From the second half of the 1980s, accession to the European Community became the declared goal of the ÖVP. From this point forward, Busek, even in his own party, struggled with the prejudice that he wanted to build an alternative to entry into the European Community with his vision of Central Europe. This was incorrect, as Busek himself was one of the vehement advocates for EC membership within his party. For him, these were complementary goals. In a speech in the fall of 1987, for example, Busek argued that "Austria should pursue an active European policy in both directions: on the one hand, it is right and important to seek accession to the EC (...). But at the same time we must realize the opportunity Austria has to approach our eastern neighbors and enable the population in these countries to extend their freedoms." Austria should, according to Busek,

56 Erhard Busek, "Eine geballte Kraft," *Wochenpresse*, 10 September 1985.

57 See Erhard Busek and Emil Brix, *Projekt Mitteleuropa* (Vienna: Ueberreuter, 1986).

be the advocate for those Europeans "who upheld Europe as a house of common origin as well as a goal of future community."[58]

Busek had not expected a rapid collapse of the communist system in the 1980s. Of course, he had not been blind to the erosion of the power of communist hardliners in some countries. Since the second half of the 1980s, he had repeatedly said that the Iron Curtain had "rusty spots," which could be used to drill small holes and create "viable bonds of understanding, shared hope, and human solidarity."[59] His intention was to provide support to dissident groups and members of the emerging opposition, morally as well as, as far as possible, through smaller material relief operations. Busek found himself in agreement on this point with the Viennese Cardinal Franz König. Asked what he could do with his intensive contacts to aid Catholic opposition circles in the communist countries, the cardinal had once said in the mid-1980s that he was concerned "with existence, with breathing room, with relieving pressure." Even König did not reckon with the imminent collapse of the system at that time, but he spoke of the "further development of an already existing discrepancy between theory and practice, between doctrine and life in these countries."[60] Busek had felt like this already at that time, albeit with his picture formulated more pointedly and politically by the "rusty spots."

Promoted by Busek's travels, a successful cooperation developed between the Styrian Farmers' Union of the ÖVP and the Styrian Chamber of Agriculture and *Solidarność*.[61] At the initiative of his friend from the days of the Catholic youth movement, Styrian Member of Parliament and State Councilman Hermann Schaller sent to Poland agricultural machinery and equipment that was no longer being used. Agricultural cooperatives were then founded there. In addition, there was a great need to catch up on agricultural training for farmers in southern Poland. On this occasion, training and scholarship programs in Styrian agricultural schools were agreed with representatives of the farmers' branch of *Solidarność*. In 1989–1990, these actions were extended at the instigation of the entire Austrian Farmers' Union, with the support of the other federal states.[62]

58 Wilflinger, "Der Mitteleuropäer," 238.

59 Ibid, 239. Even today, Busek speaks of "rust holes" so large that one could pass things through them. Busek makes similar statements in many of his books, e.g., Busek, *Lebensbilder*, 185.

60 Andreas Unterberger, "Auf der Suche nach Mitteleuropa. Eine Idee gewinnt Gestalt, entzieht sich aber jeder Planung," *Die Presse*, 1–2 February 1986.

61 AKVI, Sign. 2819 (Erhard Busek Papers), Protocol of the Poland Trip from 20–25 November, 1982.

62 AKVI, Sign. 2536, File 1989, Correspondence Rainer Stepan, "Polenhilfe – Stand der Aktion in den Bundesländern" (Aid to Poland – State of Activity in the Federal States), 13 February 1990.

From the mid-1980s, Busek also intensified his contacts in the direction of Hungary. Already at the Viennese ÖVP Congress in October 1986, Busek had used the title "Danube Metropolis Vienna" for his political speech.[63] Hungary was considered to be a special case within the Soviet hemisphere. Apart from economic joint ventures, the first common political projects emerged, such as the joint World Expo between Vienna and Budapest envisaged for 1995. In this context, the image of the common bridging function of the two cities between East and West was repeatedly conjured up. When non-communist political groups began to emerge in Hungary, Busek was at the forefront of Western support for them. This was especially true of the Magyar Democratic Forum (MDF), founded in September 1987 in Lakitelek, a village east of Kecskemét.[64] On 10 September 1988, Busek participated in an ecology symposium held by the emerging Democratic Forum in Esztergom.[65] The immediate reason for this was the planned joint Czechoslovak-Hungarian Danube power plant project at Gabčíkovo-Nagymaros. There, Busek met for the first time József Antall, who appeared to him from the beginning to be the appropriate leader of the developing party.[66] Shortly thereafter, Busek organized an open day in Vienna under the motto "Independent Voices from Hungary" to provide a platform for representatives of the new group in the West as well. Wherever he could, he promoted and accompanied the MDF in its transformation into a political party.[67]

Alois Mock – Party Chairman of the ÖVP and Foreign Minister, 1989

Alois Mock took office as party chairman of the ÖVP in early summer 1979. The change of leadership in the ÖVP was a consequence of the recent electoral defeat of the ÖVP by the SPÖ of Chancellor Bruno Kreisky, who had been in office since 1970. With Mock, foreign policy gained in importance in the opposition work of the ÖVP. Alois Mock, fluent in several foreign

63 AKVI, Sign. 2819 (Erhard Busek Papers), Invitation: "23. Ordentlicher Landesparteitag der Wiener Volkspartei" (Twenty-Third Regular State Party Convention of the Vienna People's Party), 6 October 1986.

64 Arnold Suppan, "Austria and its Neighbors in Eastern Europe, 1955–89," in *The Revolutions*, ed. Mueller, Gehler and Suppan, 430.

65 ÖVP-Press Service, 10 September 1988.

66 Busek, *Mitteleuropa*, 94–97.

67 AKVI, Sign. 2819 (Erhard Busek Papers), Program of the Open House, Day of Open Borders, Vienna – Budapest, 17 September 1988.

languages, had a personal affinity for foreign affairs. In the 1960s, he had been cabinet chief of then Chancellor Josef Klaus before he became minister of education in 1969 for almost a year. In particular, Klaus' *Ostpolitik* remained exemplary for Mock. As early as 1965, Josef Klaus had urged the Council of Europe to make sure that the eastern part of Europe was not forgotten.[68]

Alois Mock, as opposition leader, pursued a strictly anti-communist and pro-American course. He saw it as a way to distinguish himself from Kreisky. Since the election of Ronald Reagan as American president, however, Kreisky had become more and more distanced from US foreign policy and found himself in a sense within the Socialist International with Willy Brandt and Olaf Palme.

That Mock took over not only the chairmanship of the ÖVP but also the function of president of the EDU from his predecessor Josef Taus was advantageous because the EDU offered Mock an international platform on which he was able to distinguish himself from Kreisky.[69] One of those occasions when he clearly opposed Kreisky's foreign policy concerned the imposition of martial law in Poland. Kreisky responded with "surprising understanding."[70] Austria did not join in the sanctions of the US and its allies against Poland. Kreisky pointed out that Jaruzelski had pre-empted what was worse, a Soviet military intervention.[71] Mock, on the other hand, demanded the withdrawal of the visa requirement for Polish refugees introduced the week before the imposition of martial law and called for material help for the Polish people.[72] For him, the events in Poland were evi-

68 Concerning Josef Klaus' Ostpolitik, see Helmut Wohnout, "The Klaus Era, " in *The Republic of Austria 1918–2018. Milestones and Turning Points*, ed. Heinz Fischer (Vienna: Czernin, 2018), 143–145.

69 See Michael Gehler and Johannes Schönner's chapter in this volume.

70 Benjamin Gilde, *Österreich im KSZE-Prozess 1969–1983: Neutraler Vermittler in humanitärer Mission* (Munich: Oldenbourg Verlag, 2013), 405.

71 On the fundamental question to what extent Jaruzelski had chosen "the lesser evil" with the imposition of martial law, see Anton Pelinka, *Jaruzelski oder die Politik des kleineren Übels: Zur Vereinbarkeit von Demokratie und Leadership* (Frankfurt am Main: Lang, 1996).

72 In 1981, the flow of Polish refugees to Austria had swelled to around 30,000, with the solidarity of the Austrian population at this time posing a stark contrast to previous waves of refugees in 1956 and 1968 that had been kept within strict limits. However, traditional host states such as the United States, Canada, or Australia did not signal readiness to accept large numbers of refugees. Gilde, *Österreich im KSZE-Prozess,* 405; Michael Gehler, *Österreichs Außenpolitik der Zweiten Republik: Von der alliierten Besatzung bis zum Europa des 21. Jahrhunderts* (Innsbruck-Vienna-Bozen: StudienVerlag, 2005), 485.

dence that "the principles of communism are incompatible with the values of freedom, democracy, and social justice."[73]

The conflict over Poland escalated further when Chancellor Kreisky made a polemical allusion regarding the role of the Catholic Church in Austria during the Dollfuss-Schuschnigg dictatorship in the 1930s, saying that in Poland it had once again become clear that the Catholic Church was not suited to leading the working class. Once again, it was shown that, while the Church was a great moral authority, it could not give people political advice. The ÖVP and Mock spoke of an "enormous derailment."[74] Even with Cardinal König, who wanted a frictionless working relationship with the Social Democrats, Kreisky's explanation led to a temporary rupture.[75] Again and again, ÖVP officials, based on their Christian orientation, accused the SPÖ of rejecting *Solidarność*.[76] Even the mainstream *Frankfurter Allgemeine Zeitung* speculated that the close connection between the working class and the Church in Poland "did not fit the political-ideological world view of the Socialist and agnostic Kreisky."[77]

The ÖVP had the majority in the second chamber of the Austrian Parliament, the *Bundesrat*, at that time. This made it possible to adopt a motion for a resolution in the spring of 1982 in which it sharply condemned the imposition of martial law in Poland. The resolution called for the "termination of martial law, the release of prisoners, and freedom of action for the democratically elected functionaries of the popular movement *Solidarność*." At the same time, the Austrian government was accused of rendering aid to the military regime in Poland through its statements.[78]

Thereafter, too, Mock showed himself to have an open ear for opponents of the regime and dissidents. Decisive for him was his social Catholic worldview, combined with a clear Western orientation and a strictly anti-communist attitude. Intellectuals with good contacts to the dissident

73 AKVI, Sign. 2413, Manuscript of a commentary for the news magazine *Profil* on 15 January 1982. Also, Mock sharply criticized the processes in Poland in an EDU resolution. The text of the declaration of 30 January 1982 has been published in: Esther Schollum, "Die Osteuropa-Aktivitäten der Politischen Akademie," in *Österreichisches Jahrbuch für Politik 1991*, ed. Andreas Khol, Günther Ofner and Alfred Stirnemann (Vienna-Munich: Verlag für Geschichte und Politik/Oldenbourg Verlag, 1992), 495–496.

74 *Die Presse*, 15 January 1982.

75 Wolfgang Petritsch, *Bruno Kreisky: Die Biographie* (St. Pölten-Salzburg: Residenz Verlag, 2010), 303–304; Rathkolb, "An Ambivalent Attitude of Trade Unions and Politcal Parties," 281–283.

76 *Die Presse*, 16 January 1982.

77 *Frankfurter Allgemeine Zeitung*, 16 January 1982.

78 Number 2491 of the annexes to the stenographic protocols of the Federal Council (Report of the Foreign Affairs Committee on application 30/A-BR/82 of the Federal Councilors Dr. Schambeck and comrades concerning development in Poland [II-404 of the supplements]).

scene, such as the founder and long-time director of the Austrian Society for Literature, Wolfgang Kraus, or the writer György Sebestyén, were among his circle of conversation partners and advisers.

Mock narrowly missed winning the majority in the National Council elections in 1986. After all, he had led the ÖVP back into government after a long opposition period of 16 years, albeit only as a junior partner in a coalition with the SPÖ under Chancellor Franz Vranitzky. Until the spring of 1989, he was chairman of the ÖVP, vice-chancellor and minister of Foreign Affairs. After that, he occupied only the position of foreign minister until 1995. In his function as foreign minister, he held that the position taken by the communist states, according to which the discussion of land-based human rights issues meant interference in internal affairs, was unacceptable. This was reflected in Mock's emphasis on meeting with prominent dissidents when traveling to their respective countries.

This was the case, for example, when he first traveled to Prague in July 1987 to pay a visit to his Czechoslovak counterpart Bohuslav Chňoupek. Mock insisted on meeting Václav Havel during his visit to Prague. No such request had ever been made by his predecessors, and the Czechoslovak Foreign Ministry agreed only on the condition that the meeting was not allowed to appear in the official program of the visit.[79] Mock already knew Havel. In his time as minister of education in 1969–1970, he had awarded Havel the Austrian State Prize for European Literature. This had been launched a few years earlier with the intention of facilitating contact with Eastern and Central European writers. Accordingly, the winners in the 1960s had always come from countries on the other side of the Iron Curtain.

Alois Mock was aware that Europe was about to change, but he had not foreseen or even anticipated the dimensions of the impending upheavals. However, he noted attentively how Mikhail Gorbachev's reforms on the other side of the Iron Curtain had started: "A wind of change is blowing in Eastern Europe," as he put it then.[80] He saw Europe on the cusp of a transition from a "period of mere coexistence" to a "phase of broadest cooperation." For Austria, this meant basing its European policy on two pillars: economic participation in the internal market and "our neighborhood and *Ostpolitik* (...). The Danube Region, a replica of the greater Europe, is a hot

79 Martin Eichtinger and Helmut Wohnout, *Alois Mock: Ein Politiker schreibt Geschichte* (Vienna-Graz-Klagenfurt: Styria Verlag, 2008), 191.

80 This was the opinion that Mock expressed at the EDU Party Leader Conference in Rhodes, in September 1988; Eichtinger and Wohnout, *Alois Mock*, 191.

topic: while cultural ties embody the heritage of the past, tariff reductions, joint ventures, and cross-border pollution are the challenges of the present day."[81]

When one reads these lines, one can speculate whether Mock had a premonition; maybe it was just the expression of a philosophically based hope. But one thing is clear: Mock expected no imminent system break. For example, the joint ventures he had named had become successful examples of bilateral cooperation between Austria and Hungary on the basis of the differing status quo for economics and ideology in the respective countries.

In January 1989, the follow-up conference of the Conference for Security and Cooperation in Europe took place in Vienna.[82] In the East, the progress made on disarmament was viewed positively, while in the West, the "human dimension mechanism" adopted at the conference was highly valued.[83] In the course of the year 1989, Foreign Minister Mock called this monitoring mechanism into effect three times: on human rights violations in Czechoslovakia, Romania, and Bulgaria.[84] In the case of Czechoslovakia, the CSCE mechanism contributed to its success. Václav Havel, arrested on 21 February 1989, and sentenced to nine months' imprisonment, was released by the Prague authorities following worldwide protest in May.

As Central and Eastern European reform efforts began to soften the communist monopoly on power in the spring of 1989 as a result of developments in Hungary and the Round Table in Poland, Mock defined the Austrian attitude as follows: these were sovereign decisions by the respective states, but which Austria supported within its means. An opening to the world by countries to the east of Austria's borders would enhance the country's options. This was particularly the case with regard to the special quality of the bilateral relations with Hungary that already existed in the sense of the traditional Austrian neighborhood policy. In addition, with regard to Hungary, Mock already had the perspective of European integration in view.[85] He therefore paid special attention to developments in Hungary as well as those in Poland. Still, he remained cautious with re-

81 Alois Mock, "Europa – Realitäten und Visionen," *Europäische Rundschau*: *Vierteljahreszeitschrift für Politik, Wirtschaft und Zeitgeschichte* 3, no. 16 (1988): 3–7, 7.

82 See Andrea Brait and Michael Gehler's chapter in this volume.

83 "The final document (...) was a breakthrough in various respects. This was particularly true with regard to the human dimension of the Helsinki process." Thomas Fischer, "Austria and the Helsinki Process," in *"Peaceful Coexistence" or "Iron Curtain"*, ed. Suppan and Mueller, 200.

84 *Außenpolitischer Bericht 1989*, 87.

85 Michael Gehler, *Deutschland von der Teilung zur Einigung. 1945 bis heute* (Vienna-Cologne-Weimar: Böhlau Verlag, 2010), 307–309.

gard to Bulgaria, the Czechoslovak Republic, the GDR, and Romania, where there was little sign of reform potential.[86] Mock repeatedly made proposals aimed at assisting the transitioning countries, such as when in May 1989, he spoke out in favor of giving Poland and Hungary observer status in the Council of Europe.[87] In June, at the EFTA Ministers' Conference in Kristiansund, he launched a massive six billion dollar joint economic aid package from the EC, EFTA, and US. Although he had been encouraged by France's Foreign Minister Roland Dumas to take this initiative, it met with little support.[88]

In retrospect, the central event of the first half of 1989 came on 27 June, when Alois Mock and his Hungarian counterpart Gyula Horn cut through the Iron Curtain at the common border in an ostentatious political gesture. For a brief time, the Austrian Foreign Minister had intervened in the course of world political events. The de facto dismantling of the border installations was already in progress at this time.[89] The joint performance, which was initiated at Mock's request, was thus nothing more than the symbolic reconstruction of an ongoing process. At the crucial point, there was a perfect mass media staging. It had far-reaching consequences, especially in the GDR. For on 27 June the East Germans were given irrefutable proof in the form of television pictures in their living rooms via ARD Tagesschau, after which the Iron Curtain between Hungary and Austria had become brittle. Ever since the picture of the cutting of barbed wire at the border, which has become one of the iconic photographs of 1989, everyone knew that there was an unsecured border in the East without alarm systems, mines, or electric fences. Accordingly, Helmut Kohl also saw in the pictures the "departure signal" for GDR citizens willing to leave the country.[90] Michael Gehler's statement aptly describes the impact of Mock's and Horn's action: "Without the influence of the media, the events of the sum-

86 Id., "Austria, the Revolutions, and the Unification of Germany," in *The Revolutions*, ed. Mueller, Gehler and Suppan, 443–445; Id., "Austria: The Revolutions in Central and South Eastern Europe: Austrian Perceptions and International Reactions 1989–90," in *Disintegration and Integration in East-Central Europe 1919 – post-1989*, ed. Wilfried Loth and Nicolae Păun (Baden-Baden: Nomos, 2014), 189–191.

87 *Die Presse*, 5 May 1989.

88 *Die Presse*, 31 August 1989.

89 Andreas Oplatka, *Der erste Riss in der Mauer: September 1989 – Ungarn öffnet die Grenze* (Vienna: Zsolnay Verlag, 2009), 42–48, 87–88.

90 Helmut Kohl, *Erinnerungen 1982–1990* (Munich: Droemer Knaur Verlag, 2005), 910.

mer of 1989 would have been unimaginable."[91] This was also significant for the further course of events in 1989.

Austrian foreign policy no longer played the role of an actor in the narrowest sense during the developments in late summer and early autumn. The transit of East German refugees via Hungary and Austria to the Federal Republic was agreed between the Hungarian and German governments. Mock was contacted by the German side only after the secret summit between Miklós Németh and Helmut Kohl at Schloss Gymnich on 25 August 1989 regarding the expected refugee flows. On the Austrian side, tens of thousands of visas were issued outside of standard bureaucratic procedure, and the care of the refugees was transferred to the Austrian Red Cross, whereby the country's neutrality was preserved when viewed from the outside.[92]

Mock played an independent role after the fall of the Berlin Wall on 9 November 1989. For Mock, the topic of German unity was not a taboo from the start. For a long time, he did not react in as restrained a way as many other Austrian politicians, diplomats, and intellectuals. The Germans had to be given the right of self-determination just like everyone else, Mock explained the day after the fall of the Berlin Wall. Therefore it was easier for him than for many other politicians inside and outside of his party to support without reservation Helmut Kohl's policy of merging the two German states under the auspices of a far-reaching integration in the West. Especially with regard to Austria's EC accession aspirations, this attitude proved to be wise insofar as Kohl in turn supported Mock's efforts at political integration with great verve.

At the ÖVP Federal Party Congress in Graz on 24–25 November 1989, the party leadership led by the new Party Chairman and Vice Chancellor Riegler, Mock, and Busek held a panel discussion on the future of Europe. Rev. Józef Tischner and the chairman of the Slovenian Peasant Union, Ivan Oman, sat with them on the podium. Notwithstanding the fact that as Foreign Minister Mock cooperated closely with the reform communists in Hungary, like Foreign Minister Horn or Deputy Prime Minister Péter

91 Gehler, "Austria: The Revolutions in Central and South Eastern Europe," 197. In contrast, Kiss emphasizes the character of the political gesture, failing to mention the media impact on the developments in Germany. László J. Kiss,"Politik und Wahrnehmung. Ungarns (Außen-) Politik im Übergang – Österreichs Außenpolitik im Zuge der Umbruchsjahre (1988–*1991)," in Grenzöffnung 1989: Innen- und Außenperspektiven und die Folgen für Österreich,* ed. Andrea Brait and Michael Gehler (Vienna-Cologne-Weimar: Böhlau, 2014), 421.

92 Helmut Wohnout, "Vom Durchschneiden des Eisernen Vorhangs bis zur Anerkennung Sloweniens und Kroatiens. Österreichs Außenminister Alois Mock und die europäischen Umbrüche 1989–1992," in *Grenzöffnung 1989*, ed. Brait and Gehler, 198–202.

Medgyessy, Mock made it clear that it was no longer about a reform process within communism but "about replacing this regime." One would now experience "how the second shame of Europe is breaking up" after "the first shame of our century, National Socialism," had already long ago been broken.[93] The relatively harsh language was characteristic of Mock's thinking, marked by the Cold War, a transatlantic orientation, and uncompromising anti-communism.

This was also reflected in his behavior when, at the end of November 1989, the Czechoslovak government announced the dismantling of the border fortifications and, shortly thereafter, immediate freedom of travel. Mock responded reservedly. He did not want to give any political support to the communist Prime Minister, Ladislav Adamec, in view of the Velvet Revolution that had started unfolding. On 10 December, the new government of national unity was already in place in Prague. The first deputy prime minister was Ján Čarnogurský on the Slovak side. As late as 25 October, Mock had intervened with the communist government for his release from prison.[94]

Mock took a particularly consistent stance in the end toward the final bloody act during the 1989 upheaval in Romania. Earlier, like other ÖVP politicians, he had repeatedly criticized systematic violations of human rights, in particular the program of settlement systematization. Among other things, he had initiated the CSCE mechanism of the human dimension. After the deportation of Pastor László Tőkés from Timişoara in mid-December 1989, spontaneous demonstrations were answered by the regime with an order to shoot to kill. They triggered a first bloodbath.[95] Immediately, Mock took the side of the demonstrators, abandoning the diplomatic restraint otherwise customary for a foreign minister.[96] After the demonstrations spread to Bucharest, he requested that an emergency meeting of the UN Security Council be convened, an initiative that was immediately joined by the (West) German government.[97] Even if they ultimately failed there because of vetoes by China and the USSR, it was an unmistakable gesture.

93 *Österreichische Monatshefte* 8 (1989), 22.

94 Gehler, "Austria: The Revolutions in Central and South Eastern Europe," 199.

95 Concerning the events in Romania, see Peter Siani-Davis, *The Romanian Revolution of December 1989* (Ithaca, NY: Cornell University Press, 2005).

96 In an emotional appearance on Austrian television after the first deaths, he spoke of an "evil communist regime" that would not be forgotten after everything that had happened, abandoning the otherwise diplomatic demeanor of a foreign minister. *APA 0399 5 AI*, 18 December 1989.

97 *APA, 0445 3 AA*, 20 December 1989.

Cooperation with Central and Eastern European neighbors in the wake of the system change in 1989–1990

"Our ideas overcome all boundaries. Freedom, property, justice for the new Europe." It was a self-confident poster text that the ÖVP had publicized throughout Austria at the turn of the years 1989–1990.[98] The party at this time felt it had history on its side – a supposed inevitability, which otherwise happens more often in left-wing and progressive parties and turns out to be mostly deceptive.

In the course of 1989, the representatives of the ÖVP in the government had always vehemently sided with the reform movements in the Central and Eastern European states. Besides Mock, Erhard Busek, who had been a member of the government as minister of science since April 1989, also played a role. When Tadeusz Mazowiecki was appointed prime minister in Poland on 24 August 1989, Busek paid him a visit the next day, together with the new party chairman of the ÖVP and Vice Chancellor Josef Riegler as the first foreign guests as a demonstratively friendly gesture. Conversely, the new Polish Foreign Minister Krzysztof Skubiszewski made his first visit abroad to his Austrian counterpart Mock in Vienna.

The party-level activities were coordinated by the Political Academy of the ÖVP.[99] In many cases, they were synchronized with those of the EDU, especially as Andreas Khol held the posts of both executive secretary of the EDU and director of the Political Academy. In many cases, the EDU delegation's trips to the reform countries were conceived by the Austrian side and implemented with Austrian participation.[100] The support of the ÖVP included both training programs and material assistance for technical equipment, etc., as well as specific assistance in election campaigns in individual countries.

There were many obstacles and problems in the Central and Eastern European countries. There was a shortage of qualified staff because many opponents of the regime had been denied access to higher education institutions. The countries also had no relevant political experience in dealing with a pluralistic party democracy and lacked the infrastructure for effective political work. In all these points, "reformed" party cadres of commu-

98 AKVI, Poster Archive, 1989.

99 The Political Academy is the party academy of the ÖVP, similar to the Konrad Adenauer Foundation of the CDU, albeit with much more limited resources.

100 See the contribution of Michael Gehler and Johannes Schönner in this volume.

nist origin were ahead of their new, democratic counterparts. Wherever contacts did not already exist, be it through Erhard Busek's travels, the FCG's Polish connections or the ÖVP Farmers' League's initiatives, finding the right contacts was not always easy. Therefore, it was initially based on a broad approach. This was also due to the fact that, from the point of view of the ÖVP, the ideological orientation of numerous nascent groups was not quite foreseeable. It was also found that the labels chosen by individual groups did not always agree with their own ideological self-images.[101]

With regard to Poland, two close associates of Andreas Khol's undertook a three-day trip to Warsaw in February 1989. It was to serve both to prepare for the EDU mission and to probe contacts for bilateral cooperation at the party level, beyond *Solidarność*. It offered them a very uneven picture of numerous divided groups.[102] Austrian observers with some knowledge of Poland noted that the situation was not to be judged according to a superficial left-right scheme. It was obvious that after the elections of 4 June 1989 the initial differences between the original *Solidarność* movement and the grassroots Citizens' Committee were beginning to appear in more radical form in some areas.[103] At the beginning of the new decade, the Citizens' Committee would then fragment into a multitude of parties.[104] In an internal analysis at the beginning of February 1990 it was argued that the ÖVP had found promising and close-knit groups in Poland's Christian Labor Party and in the Christian National Union.[105]

In comparison, the situation in Hungary was clearer. On the one side were the newly emerging political parties, on the other the reform communists. They emancipated themselves more and more from the old apparatus in the hope that they would be able to salvage themselves in the democratic age, whose success they regarded as inevitable. In view of the fact that some exponents of the reform communists such as Imre Pozsgay enjoyed a certain popularity in the West, the director of the Political Academy of the ÖVP, Andreas Khol, strongly reminded everyone of the

101 Esther Schollum, "Die Osteuropa-Aktivitäten der Politischen Akademie," *Österreichische Monatshefte* 7 (1989), 32–33.

102 AKVI, EDU-Collection, File Poland 1989–1991, Travelogue for Warsaw, 8–10 February 1989, Mag. Esther Schollum, Mag. Rainer Stepan.

103 This was also the opinion of Günther Engelmayer during his visit to Poland. FCG Archives, B4 01.05, Travelogue of the trip to Warsaw on 21 August 1989. The EDU reached similar conclusions at the EDU. See the contribution of Michael Gehler and Johannes Schönner in this volume.

104 Bachmann, "Poland 1989," 68–69.

105 AKVI, Sign. 2536, File 1989, Correspondence Rainer Stepan, "Brief information on the main parties and promising parties in Poland, Hungary, and Czechoslovakia regarding the upcoming elections," 2 February 1990. See also Piotr H. Kosicki's chapter in this volume.

long-standing policy of the ÖVP not to cooperate at the party level with block parties or reform communists. The partners of the ÖVP were the forces of the opposition: from the Small Farmers to Antall's Democratic Forum to the Free Democrats and the Social Democrats. They all preferred Antall "over those communist politicians who are now trying to build a life raft in the form of reform communism as a bridge to democratic times."[106]

In truth, after the EDU's fact-finding missions, it was already clear which parties were really supported by the EDU and thus by the ÖVP in the forthcoming elections in Hungary. These were the Democratic Forum, the Small Farmers' Party and the Christian Democratic People's Party. There were, however, important gradations. The first point of contact was József Antall's Democratic Forum, which was assessed to be the most professional and the best prepared for the forthcoming elections.[107] The MDF seemed to correspond to the ÖVP's hope for a "genuine social integration party of the Western type."[108] Accordingly, Andreas Khol was also present at the congress of the Democratic Forum in October 1989 in Budapest.[109] As early as August 1989, the first freely elected Hungarian MP, Gábor Roszik, stated in an interview on Austrian radio that the Democratic Forum intended to adopt a political course modeled on the Austrian People's Party and the Christian Democrats in Germany.[110] Cooperation with the Free Democrats was not pursued any further. There had been contacts with Fidesz in 1988–1989, but they were also not pursued. Within the EDU, the CSU in particular had argued against Fidesz on the grounds that Viktor Orbán's party was close to the German FDP and was already being supported by the Friedrich Naumann Foundation.[111]

106 Andreas Khol, "Internationale Splitter," *Österreichische Monatshefte* 5 (1989), 37.

107 This is also reflected in the ledger of material and financial assistance provided to the three Hungarian parties until February. The most significant donations went to the Democratic Forum, followed by the Smallholders' Party and the Christian Democratic People's Party. This prioritization also continued with the planned support payments for the spring 1990 election campaign. AKVI, Sign. 2536, File 1989, Correspondence Rainer Stepan, compilation from 22 February 1990; Organizational Program for Commodities, 9 February 1990.

108 AKVI, Sign. 2536, File 1989, Correspondence Rainer Stepan, "Brief information on the most important and, in the coming elections, promising parties in Poland, Hungary, and Czechoslovakia," 2 February 1990; Schollum, "Die Osteuropa-Aktivitäten der Politischen Akademie," 502–509.

109 Schollum, "Die Osteuropa-Aktivitäten der Politischen Akademie," 502–509.

110 AKVI, EDU Collection, File Hungary, No. 1989/1683, 18 August 1989, Interview with Mr. Gabor Roszik, Member of the Hungarian Parliament.

111 AKVI, EDU Collection, File Hungary, No. 1989/1687, List of democratic groups in Eastern Europe, 6 October 1988; Telefaxes from Dieter A. Schmidt, head of the Office of Foreign Relations of the CSU, to Andreas Khol, 9 October 1989 and 12 October 1989. See also Helmut Wohnout, "Die Umbrüche 1989 aus der Perspektive der österreichischen Außenpolitik unter besonderer Berücksichtigung des bilateralen Verhältnisses zu Ungarn," in *Österreich und Ungarn im 20. Jahrhundert*, ed. Csaba Szabó (Vienna: Publikationen der ungarischen Geschichtsforschung in Wien, 2014), 335–336.

Regarding Czechoslovakia, the situation in the Slovak part of the country was clear. Here, there was a close connection to the Christian Democratic Movement of the acting deputy prime minister of the ČSSR appointed in December 1989, Ján Čarnogurský. A few weeks before the formation of the government, several ÖVP politicians had vehemently campaigned for the release of the detained regime critic. When the Velvet Revolution spread to the Slovak part of the country, Erhard Busek appeared at the mass rallies of the Public against Violence movement in Bratislava. With regard to the Christian Democratic Movement, observers were aware that they enjoyed popular support in Slovakia. It was organized on-site by Ivan Čarnogurský, the brother of Ján Čarnogurský. Since mid-1989, there had been contacts with the Political Academy of the ÖVP, and a group of leading cadres had already attended seminars in Vienna. In return, Andreas Khol participated in the founding congress in Nitra on 17 February 1990.[112]

From the point of view of the ÖVP, the situation in the Czech part of the country was considerably more difficult. It cooperated with the Christian Democratic Party of the Catholic dissident Václav Benda, who had been arrested by the communists and was a Charter 77 signatory, but it was aware that Benda's party lacked a broad base of support among the population. In addition, there was the Czech People's Party, but in the eyes of the ÖVP it had the flaw of being the successor to a concessioned party that had continued to function throughout the communist era.[113] In the elections of June 1990, these two parties ran together as the Christian Democratic Union.

In Yugoslavia, contacts were established with the relevant movements developing in Slovenia. The longest-standing contacts here also traced themselves back to Erhard Busek's travels. In 1982, he had visited Archbishop Alojzij Šuštar in Ljubljana for the first time. Šuštar was not a politically minded bishop, but rather a supporter and motivator of the intellectual heritage of the Slovene nation in the communist period. He gathered Slovene intellectuals around him, and so during his visits to the bishop's court Busek met the later party founder of the Christian Democrats, Lojze Peterle, as well as the later Prime Minister and Foreign Minister Dimitrij

112 AKVI, EDU-Collection, File CSFR, "Establishment of the Christian Democratic Movement in Nitra on February 17, 1990," 19 February 1990.

113 AKVI, Collection of Protocols of the Federal Executive Board (BPV), 13 March 1990 (Report Khol); AKVI, Sign. 2536, File 1989, Correspondence Rainer Stepan, "Brief information about the most important and, in the coming elections, most promising parties in Poland, Hungary and Czechoslovakia," 2 February 1990; Letter Rainer Stepan to Gustav Vetter, 26 February 1990. See also Ladislav Cabada's chapter in this volume.

Rupel.[114] Ties were now closest with the Christian Democratic Party of Slovenia under Lojze Peterle. But the ÖVP also had good connections with the Farmers' Union of Ivan Oman, which was renamed the Slovenian People's Party at the beginning of the 1990s.

These partnerships reached a high point with the "Round Table Europe," organized by the ÖVP on 11 and 12 January 1990 in Vienna. It was a unique event in the European revolutions of 1989–1990, with no fewer than 28 delegations in attendance. Representatives from democratic organizations from all countries of the imploded Eastern Bloc, with whom the ÖVP had developed a basis for discussion, took part in it.[115]

Compared to the neighboring countries mentioned, contacts with other Central and Eastern European countries remained loose, although there was no lack of effort here. These included, for example, the links with the nascent groupings in the Croatian Republic of Yugoslavia. Especially noteworthy in retrospect (if not entirely flattering) is that among the participants from Croatia at the January 1990 Round Table Europe in addition to representatives of the Croatian Peasants' Party and the Croatian Democratic Alliance, Franjo Tuđjman was there as chairman of the Croatian Democratic Union (HDZ).[116]

However, the ÖVP cooperated with no other party so closely and successfully – if only temporarily – as with Antall's Democratic Forum in Hungary. In the spring of 1990, he won 43 percent of the votes and was able to form a coalition with the Small Farmers' Party and the Christian Democrats, the three parties supported by the ÖVP in the election campaign.[117] At the EDU Party Leadership Conference in Helsinki, his party and his two coalition partners were admitted to the EDU, as were three parties from the ČSSR.[118] Antall himself became vice-chairman and thus one of Mock's deputies in the EDU. At the closing rally of the ÖVP before the National Council elections in October 1990, Antall participated as a foreign guest of Vice Chancellor Riegler. In his speech, he thanked Austria for its support

114 Busek, *Mitteleuropa*, 117–118.

115 The conference is documented in Josef Riegler, ed., *1st Round Table Europe: Vienna MS Mozart. 11-12. January 1990* (Vienna: Politische Akademie, 1990).

116 Riegler, ed., *1st Round Table Europe*, 80.

117 The ÖVP provided substantial material assistance, for example by printing posters, etc. The CDU also provided a lot of support, as the ÖVP and CDU sought to coordinate with each other here. AKVI, Sign. 2536, File 1989, Correspondence Rainer Stepan, "Supporting the electoral battle of related Hungarian parties," 15 January 1990.

118 From the ČSSR the Czechoslovak People's Party, Václav Benda's Christian Democratic Party, and Ján Čarnogurský's Christian Democratic Movement of Slovakia were admitted. *EDU Yearbook 1990*, 42–44.

on the path to freedom. He noted specifically that the ÖVP had made a notable contribution through its solidarity with and support for the Democratic Forum.[119]

Conclusions

In the 1980s, the ÖVP had established contacts with dissidents behind the Iron Curtain at various levels. These sprang up through 1988–1989 more out of the personal initiatives of individual protagonists in the party rather than as a systematic strategy. The turn to a calculated strategy occurred only on the eve of the *annus mirabilis*, partly in conjunction with the activities of the European Democrat Union. The fact that some contacts were established on the Austrian side was due to many favorable factors. Worth mentioning are the historical horizon of experience as well as the geopolitical situation of the country located directly on the Iron Curtain. Austrian neutrality also played a role because it opened up greater negotiating room in cooperation with the opposition that NATO or the EC states could not offer.

Finally, the ÖVP, so long as it was an opposition party, had greater leeway. On the other hand, it could offer only moral support. Its effective political power remained limited. The fact is that opportunities were created at times to great effect: Günther Engelmayer's FCG activities and Erhard Busek's initiatives are striking proof. As of 1987, Minister Alois Mock, responsible for foreign affairs, succeeded in remaining steadfast for long stretches in his position as an opposition leader. If one asks about motivation, there are a number of motives. The fundamental Christian Democratic conviction that led to natural opposition to the historical materialism of the communist regimes, including their hostility towards religion, deserves mention here. In addition, however, the desired demarcation of SPÖ policy and its cooperation with the communist governments behind the Iron Curtain, which corresponded to the attitude of several left-wing parties in Europe, also played a role as a domestic political motive.

With the emerging upheavals in 1988–1989, the first systematic contacts took place at the party level. It was possible to establish closer contacts, especially in the immediate vicinity of the protests. There too, parties emerged which, in terms of their orientation, corresponded to the social integration party model, based on programs combining Christian

119 *APA*, 29 September, 1990; *APA 0094 5 II*.

Democratic values with a liberal character. This was especially true of the MDF and its coalition partners in Hungary, the parties in the Slovenian part of Yugoslavia, and the Christian Democratic Movement in Slovakia. Difficulties were already being encountered in the Czech part of Czechoslovakia. In Poland, on the other hand, there was a relatively close network of contacts with those former opponents of the regime, such as Mazowiecki, Geremek, or Bartoszewski, who were to hold important posts in the years following 1989, but it was not possible to establish close ties at the party level.

Amidst the euphoria of the 1989–1990 upheaval, there were ambitious expectations that could not be fulfilled. ÖVP Chairman Josef Riegler, for example, saw in Round Table Europe an attempt to establish a lasting platform of encounter and dialogue between Western Europe and the new democratic movements.[120] It would be repeated only once more, with a geographical focus on Southeastern Europe. Alois Mock, on the other hand, confidently stated at the EDU Party Leader Conference in Helsinki in August 1990, "la fin de l'ordre de Yalta est avant tout notre victoire, celle de nos démocraties, de nos valeurs, de nos idées. Il faut faire tout pour que la nouvelle Europe soit façonnée selon nos valeurs au service des citoyens européens."[121]

At the very latest with the Austrian elections in October 1990 the ÖVP was brought back to reality. It had suffered a painful loss of votes. Financial problems and internal leadership discussions prevented it from acting as patron of related movements in the transitioning states to the same extent as before.

But in the end cooperation was also limited by the Central and Eastern European parties themselves. In addition, in some cases there were also language barriers and cultural differences, sometimes even historical prejudices. In the long run, the first generation of Christian democratically oriented politicians, often former dissidents, could not succeed. Among other things, this was due to the fact that the former underground activists were not as proficient in day-to-day politics as the politicians trained under communism, who returned to power relatively quickly under other party names. Where it seemed most promising, in Hungary, the charismatic Prime Minister Antall died early without any leader of comparable stature waiting in the wings.

120 Riegler, ed., *1st Round Table Europe*, 6.
121 "The end of the rule of Yalta is above all our victory, that of our democracies, of our values, of our ideas. It must be made absolutely clear that the new Europe will be shaped according to our values in the service of European citizens." *EDU Yearbook 1990*, 47.

Nevertheless, the achievements of these figures, who played a key role in overcoming communism in Central and Eastern Europe out of a self-professed sense of Christian responsibility, are historical fact. According to the slogan of Polish *Solidarność*, they helped to restore dignity to people living in the communist dictatorships.

6

FINDING PARTNERS IN THE EAST

Helmut Kohl and the Fledgling Center-Right in Central and Eastern Europe

Alexander Brakel

"Fifty to sixty percent of my working time as chancellor I dedicated to my job as party chairman," Helmut Kohl once confessed.[1] Given a complex system with more than half a million members, this is not astonishing. But to Kohl the Christian Democratic Union (CDU) represented more than a vehicle to power. Unlike other federal chancellors such as, for example, Konrad Adenauer, Gerhard Schröder, or Angela Merkel, Kohl was a dyed-in-the-wool party politician.[2]

Therefore, it was not astonishing that he also gave great weight to parties on an international scale, for example the cooperation with other Christian Democratic parties, as well as parties of the political center, across the world, but especially in Europe. This cooperation took place first and foremost in the respective federations, the European People's Party (EPP), the European Union of Christian Democracy (EUCD), and Christian Democrat International.

At the same time, Kohl had been chancellor of the Federal Republic of Germany since 1982, and in this position he depended on working constructively with heads of states who belonged to other political factions. From time to time the interest in cooperation at the state level was, therefore, in tension with collaboration at the party level. To Kohl, the state-political dimension of his actions was always of higher priority. Both elements – the great attention to party politics and its simultaneous subordination to the political interests of the Federal Republic (as well as the personal factor) – were likewise revealed in his emerging relationships

1 Heribert Schwan and Tilman Jens, *Das Vermächtnis: Die Kohl-Protokolle* (Munich: Random House, 2014), 65.

2 Hans Peter Schwarz, *Helmut Kohl: Eine politische Biographie* (Munich: Dt. Verl.-Anst., 2012), 125–132.

with the political opposition parties in soon-to-be-post-communist Central and Eastern Europe from 1989 to 1990. The CDU's involvement across the region, led personally by Kohl, both drove and exposed the limitations of Christian Democracy's potential in countries transitioning out of the collapsing Soviet Bloc.

The endless search for an ally: the Polish case

The question of how to deal with the tremendous political changes on the other side of the Iron Curtain arose soon after the Polish Solidarity movement (*Solidarność*) had loosened the first brick in the wall. In its meeting in March 1989, the European Democrat Union had approved a concept paper about how to deal with the situation in Poland and Hungary.[3] The organization recommended cautiously establishing contacts with the emerging political forces there, while at the same time building bridges to the communist governments.[4] A month later, Christian Democrat International went one step further, describing the fostering of Christian Democratic movements in the Eastern Bloc as a priority.[5] Kohl was not present at either of these meetings but was kept informed by the head of the CDU office for external relations (*Büro für Auswärtige Beziehungen*, BAB). He clearly supported this approach, and the next month saw a huge upswing of meetings with representatives from Central and Eastern European countries.

The first to contact the CDU was Zygmunt Drozdek, a long-time Catholic activist in the People's Republic of Poland and the deputy chairman of the newly re-established Polish Christian Labor Party (*Stronnictwo Pracy*, SP). He met with a staffer from the BAB and requested financial support.[6] The German side was interested and started to look more deeply into the party. The results of this inquiry were sobering, so instead of laying the groundwork for a successful collaboration, the meeting marked the beginning of a series of failures to identify a suitable partner party for the

3 See Michael Gehler and Johannes Schönner's chapter in this volume.

4 Note on the EDU Board meeting, 13 March 1989, Archiv für Christlich-Demokratische Politik (ACDP, Konrad-Adenauer-Stiftung) 07-001-10307. On SP's exile in the 1940s and re-establishment in the 1980s, see Jarosław Rabiński, "The Elimination of Christian Democracy in Poland after World War II," in *Christian Democracy across the Iron Curtain: Europe Redefined*, ed. Piotr H. Kosicki and Sławomir Łukasiewicz (London: Palgrave Macmillan, 2018), 153–176; Jan Majchrowski, "Chadecja w III Rzeczypospolitej," *Znaki Nowych Czasów* nos. 5-6 (2003): 103–120.

5 Note on the CDI Political Office meeting, 6-7 April 1989, ACDP 07-001-10307.

6 Note on the meeting with Zygmunt Drozdek, 12 April 1989, ACDP 07-001-10307.

CDU in Warsaw. Despite its socialist-sounding name, the SP proved to be a real Christian Democratic party with a long history dating back to the 1930s, and its platform showed a significant overlap with that of its German counterpart. However, the German Embassy in Warsaw did not see much future for them: "Wrong approach, wrong time, wrong people" was the lapidary verdict. The Konrad Adenauer Foundation (*Konrad-Adenauer-Stiftung*, KAS), the CDU-associated think-tank with a vast network of international offices, was less categorical in its assessment of SP, but advised likewise against a strong engagement.

In general, the political situation in Poland proved to be too confusing for German Christian Democrats to decide on a partnership. KAS recommended waiting for the dust to settle and collecting further information. The imminent opening of a KAS office in Warsaw was intended to facilitate this.[7] The party passed the information on to Klaus Francke, a CDU member of the German Federal Parliament who traveled frequently to Central and Eastern Europe to establish political contacts there.[8] In general, the CDU closely monitored the political and party developments in Poland, and the BAB informed Kohl about the findings on a regular basis.[9]

The first semi-free elections in Poland on 4 June 1989 proved the CDU's skepticism right. Of the 261 constituencies that were contested, the Solidarity candidates won all but one. Probably no party would have been able to seriously compete with the shining heroes of the peaceful revolution, but the constant infighting among minor Christian Democratic parties and their weak platform diminished their chances even further.[10]

Pundits, including representatives of the Polish Catholic Church, still saw huge potential for Christian Democracy in a country that not only had a long-standing Catholic tradition but also was seeing an upswing in Church attendance after the slow end of communist rule. However, a combination of more appealing candidates and a modernized platform would be needed. So would be a consolidation of the multiple small par-

7 Note regarding the relationship between the CDU and the SP, 25 April 1989, ACDP 07-001-10307.

8 Confidential note on the SP in Poland, 27 April 1989, ACDP 08-009-093-1.

9 E.g. Report on the situation in Poland, 9 May 1989, Report about the trip of the "Eastern Europe" subcommittee of the North Atlantic Council to Warsaw, 9 May 1989; Report about the visit of a Polish delegation to Bonn, 17 May 1989, ACDP 08-009-093-1.

10 Report about the trip of the EDU Europe committee to Poland, 2 June 1989, Letter by Heiner Geißler to Member of Parliament Umland, 22 June 1989, ACDP 08-009-093-1. On the weakness of Polish Christian Democracy in 1989, see Aleks Szczerbiak and Tim Bale, "Explaining the Absence of Christian Democracy in Contemporary Poland," in *Christian Democracy across the Iron Curtain*, ed. Kosicki and Łukasiewicz, 343–410, esp. 348–349.

ties claiming Christian Democratic ideology. CDU emissaries kept pushing their Polish colleagues on these three issues.[11] And the Germans continued to look for potential Polish partners, both outside and inside the Solidarity movement. They won the approval of the Communist Party, which still held the majority of the seats in the *Sejm* after the June 1989 elections, to open the Warsaw branch of the Adenauer Foundation in order to have their own representatives on the ground.[12]

In spite of the overwhelming victory of *Solidarność*, which appreciated the CDU for its strong anti-communist stance, the Germans were reluctant to throw their lot in with the labor union-cum-party.[13] Because he did not want to jeopardize his relations with the Polish government and because of the chaotic structure of *Solidarność*, Kohl preferred not to send a message of congratulations, but asked Bernhard Vogel, the then head of KAS to do so on behalf of the foundation and the party alike.[14]

Over the course of the next few months, Poland saw its peaceful transformation from a communist into a democratic country. *Solidarność* remained the dominant power. In August and September, Tadeusz Mazowiecki formed the first non-communist government. A new constitution was introduced in December. Finally, a year later the country went to the polls to elect its president. Both Mazowiecki and Lech Wałęsa were running, and both tried to garner support by building parties, thus opening a new window for the CDU to find a long-term partner. In March 1990, the Center Agreement (*Porozumienie Centrum*, PC) was formed as a self-proclaimed Christian Democratic party led by Jarosław Kaczyński to support Wałęsa's presidential ambitions. Early on, PC reached out to the CDU for support, asking in particular for technical support and assistance in putting together the party's platform. On the one hand, Kohl remained skeptical and conditioned material support on further positive developments, in the meantime supporting ties with other parties. On the other hand, he

11 Report about the trip of the EDU Europe committee to Poland, 2 June 1989, Letter by Heiner Geißler to Member of Parliament Umland, 22 June 1989, ACDP 08-009-093-1. See also Piotr H. Kosicki's chapter in this volume.

12 Ibid.

13 Ibid.

14 Letter by Fischer to Kohl, 6 June 1989, ACDP 08-009-093-1. See also "Es war für Polen schwer verständlich, dass es für uns immer einen Zusammenhang zwischen der Grenzfrage und der Wiedervereinigung gab. Gespräch mit Bernhard Vogel," in *"Wir vergeben und bitten um Vergebung": Der Briefwechsel der polnischen und deutschen Bischöfe von 1965 und seine Wirkung*, ed. Basil Kerski, Thomas Kycia and Robert Żurek (Osnabrück: Fibre, 2006).

did not reject an invitation to the PC party conference and asked KAS to invite their leadership to Bonn.[15]

At the same time, the CDU did not burn all of its bridges with the SP, but it became more and more obvious that the party was failing to attract voters.[16] Its miserable performance in the local elections in May 1990 proved that point once more.[17] However, the German assessment was not shared at the European level. The European Democrat Union (EDU), an umbrella organization of center-right parties in the European Community, threw in its lot with the SP and warned against *Solidarność*.[18] The EUCD, another umbrella organization, suggested concentrating its support for Polish parties on the SP, a suggestion with which Kohl deeply disagreed.[19]

Already in October 1989, the chancellor had complained to the CDU steering committee:

> We should have as many contacts as possible, but we should realize that this is a thing that is still in motion. I, for example, am quite unhappy that the Christian Democrat International [...] at this moment already knows how relations with the partners of tomorrow or the day after tomorrow will be. I do not know yet. I think it is complete nonsense because none of us knows which groups will appear. I do not know what the parliament in Hungary will look like after the elections; I do not know it of Poland [either].[20]

A month after the local elections, the CDU pulled its weight and issued a memorandum on how to proceed with party cooperation in Central and Eastern Europe. The paper named the consolidation of the party landscape right of center as the main objective of Western support. Only parties that showed good results at the ballot box should be supported; therefore, any support before elections should be limited and preliminary, and a one-sided commitment to individual parties should be avoided. The paper then cited a whole list of potential partner parties in different Central and Eastern European countries. In Poland, no party was positively singled

15 Report about the BAB trip to Warsaw, 29 March 1990, ACDP 08-009-135-2. On Kaczyński's attempts to reach out also to the EDU, see Piotr H. Kosicki's chapter in this volume.

16 Report on the current state of the SP, 6 April 1990, ACDP 08-009-135-2; Report about the SP party convention, 30 April 1990, ACDP 08-009-135-2.

17 Note on the local elections in Poland on 27 May 1990, 6 June 1990, ACDP 08-009-135-2.

18 Letter by EPP Secretary General Thomas Jansen to Bernd Fischer, Head of BAB, 6 June 1989, ACDP 08-009-093-1.

19 Note on the invitation to the SP party convention, 19 April 1990, ACDP 08-009-135-2.

20 Helmut Kohl, *Berichte zur Lage, 1989–1998*, ed. Günter Buchstab and Hans Otto Kleinmann (Düsseldorf: Droste, 2012), 21.

out, but the CDU explicitly named the Christian Labor Party as outdated and unsuccessful. The memorandum was sent to both the EPP and its parliamentary group.[21]

In the meantime, the Germans deepened their contacts with the PC without embracing them as their main Polish partner. Although the party seemed to be more relevant and energetic than the SP, it remained to be seen whether it could turn from a mere vehicle of Wałęsa's presidential campaign into a successful party.[22] Delegations were invited to Germany, and the CDU youth organization *Junge Union* was encouraged to reach out to the PC youth; the party publicly showed its support by sending official emissaries to PC conventions.[23]

At the same time, given the unclear future political landscape, the CDU established ties with other parties too, including a tiny, fledgling Christian Democratic movement under the leadership of Senator Pawłowski as well as the Polish Peasants' Party (*Polskie Stronictwo Ludowe*) that had only recently cut ties with the communist party, which it had served as a loyal concessioned partner party since 1949.[24] Although clearly aware of its Social Democratic leanings, the CDU even lent an ear to Mazowiecki's Citizens' Movement for Democratic Action (*Ruch Obywatelski Akcja Demokratyczna*, ROAD).

ROAD openly confessed to being interested in links with both the CDU and its Social Democratic rival, the SPD. But Mazowiecki was far too important a player to be dismissed, especially as the SPD in the eyes of many Poles seemed to be compromised because of its close relations with the communist party. So Kohl asked his Minister of Social Affairs, Norbert Blüm, to reach out to this party. As an exponent of the CDU's labor union wing and a prominent member of the left-leaning Christian Democratic Employees' Association (CDA), Kohl deemed him to be able to build bridges into the Polish moderate left-wing camp.[25] Politicians from a variety of parties were invited by KAS for a workshop on political transformation in

21 Position paper on collaboration with Christian Democratic parties in Central, Eastern, and Southeastern Europe, 22 June 1990, ACDP 08-001-624/3.

22 Report about meeting with 66 Polish parliamentarians, 28 September 1990, ACDP 08-009-135-2.

23 Francke, Report about trip to Poland, 23 August 1990, ACDP 08-009-135-2; Report on Bonn visit by Zdzisław Najder, 23/20/1990, ACDP 08-009-135-2.

24 Francke, Report about trip to Poland, 23 August 1990, ACDP 08-009-135-2.

25 Ibid; Exchange of letters between Blüm, Francke and CDA chairman Fink, 25 October 1990, ACDP 08-009-135-2.

Germany,[26] and KAS was ordered not to concentrate its work on a single party.[27]

In March 1991, the Liberal Democratic Congress (*Kongres Liberalno-Demokratyczny*, KLD) under its chairman Donald Tusk left *Solidarność* and started to act as an independent party. Although the split was partly ideological – Tusk objected to the Christian Democratic platform that Jarosław Kaczyński wanted to give the PC – the CDU tried to win the KLD over.[28] This was of special importance as Jan Krzysztof Bielecki, who had become Prime Minister in January, was a KLD member. He himself had long-standing contacts with European liberal parties and was, therefore, reluctant to follow Kohl's proposal to join the EDU, but open to bilateral relations with the German Christian Democrats. Kohl offered support via KAS and encouraged other center-right parties like the British Tories and the US Republicans to support the KLD.[29] Tusk was invited to Bonn, and Kohl urged his fellow party members at the EDU to pave the way for KLD's quick accession to the organization.[30] At the same time, the membership request from the PC was also accepted.[31] In general, the CDU adhered to the line not to commit to one single party as long as it had not proved its sustainability in elections. The PC, the Peasants' Party, and KLD were equally supported with seminars and advice,[32] but frustration with Kaczyński was growing. He had three times rejected an invitation to visit Germany and openly declared his willingness to accept one only if Kohl would receive him personally.[33] And during his successful election campaign he played the anti-German card, resorted to populist slogans, and criticized Bielecki's market-oriented reforms.[34]

The outcome of the elections to the *Sejm* in October 1991 was disappointing from a CDU perspective. No party had received more than 12.5 percent of the vote, and among the potential CDU partners none garnered even nine percent. With around seven and a half percent KLD did not live up to the Germans' expectations.[35] Kohl suggested providing fur-

26 Agenda and list of participants, Workshop on transformation with Polish politicians, 23 September 1990, ACDP 08-009-135-2.

27 Survey on the domestic situation in Poland, 7 November 1991, ACDP 08-009-172-1.

28 Francke, Report about trip to Poland, 4 March 1991, ACDP 08-009-172-1.

29 Note on contacts with the KLD and Prime Minister Bielecki, 2 August 1991, ACDP 08-009-171-2.

30 Report about the trip to Poland, 18 July 1991, ACDP 08-009-171-2.

31 Note on contacts with the KLD and Prime Minister Bielecki, 6 September 1991, ACDP 08-009-171-2.

32 Report about the trip to Poland, 18 July 1991, ACDP 08-009-171-2.

33 Ibid.

34 Detailed analysis of the election results in Poland, 5 November 1991, ACDP 08-009-172-1.

35 Results of the Sejm elections, 7 November 1991, ACDP 08009172-1.

ther training for KLD staffers and support for the building of stable party structures. The CDU would further try to influence its Polish partners to form a joint parliamentary group of center-right parties, which might later evolve into a united party.[36] The Adenauer Foundation was ordered to deepen its support and strengthen its work in the regions, especially in Opole and Wrocław.[37] However, the party had to admit that, more than three years after the revolutions of 1989, it still lacked a reliable partner party in the largest country in Central and Eastern Europe.

The successful case: Hungary

In Hungary, the CDU found a different environment that was both more difficult and easier at the same time. Although the Iron Curtain had gotten its first cracks owing to the events in Poland in 1980, the reform process in Hungary in 1989 was more important for German politics. Already here, the basic dilemma of Kohl's dealings with the states of Eastern and Central Europe revealed itself: the chancellor – deeply entrenched in Catholicism and politically socialized in Christian Democracy from youth onward – felt a deep dislike towards socialism, and especially towards the communist dictatorships of the Eastern Bloc. But now he had to deal with the fact that the reform process in some of these countries had been launched by communists. While he had been wary of the Soviet leader Mikhail Gorbachev for a long time, he seemed to accept the wholeheartedness of the Hungarian reform endeavors very quickly.[38] Moreover, the government of Miklós Németh had enabled thousands of East Germans to escape from the GDR by opening the borders, thereby setting East-West German relations in motion. Kohl knew exactly that he could not do without the reformers in the communist ranks. As they were not undisputed in their own parties, he had to sidestep everything that could weaken their position. This characterized his attitude towards the reform-oriented wing of the Hungarian Socialist Workers' Party.[39] Furthermore, the Hungarian communist reformers enjoyed greater support within the country than their Polish comrades.

36 Detailed analysis of the election results in Poland, 5 November 1991, ACDP 08-009-172-1.

37 Preparations for conversation between Kohl and Bielecki, 13 November 1991, ACDP 08-009-172-1; Francke, Report about trip to Opole, 4 December 1991, ACDP 08-009-172-1.

38 Hermann Wentker, "Vom Gegner zum Partner: Gorbatschow und seine Politik im Urteil Helmut Kohls," *Historisch-Politische Mitteilungen* 22 (2015): 1–34.

39 Helmut Kohl, *Erinnerungen: 1982–1990* (Munich: Droemer Knaur Verlag, 2005), 920–923.

No one in the Hungarian opposition wielded influence remotely comparable to that of Lech Wałęsa, nor was there anybody with his charisma. What might be seen as a disadvantage for the opposition proved to be a blessing in disguise, as it allowed several oppositional parties to emerge and prosper. But in the beginning it was a burden.[40]

When, in April 1989, the Hungarian Socialist Workers' Party staged a conference on the subject of East-West relations and invited the CDU, Kohl sent two members of the Bundestag (Francke and Volker Rühe) to demonstrate the CDU's participation. At the same time, it was important for him to make it clear that an official party cooperation which would have given precedence to the MSzMP ahead of the democratic opposition did not exist.[41] Two months later, the newly established Europe Committee of the EDU held its first meeting, symbolically, in Budapest. Chairman Vogel made certain to meet with representatives from both the communist and opposition parties as well as with clergymen, researchers, and journalists. He stressed support for democratization while abiding by strict non-interference. At the same time, he suggested opening a KAS office to identify and support promising politicians and parties close to the CDU.[42] The most probable candidate for such a partnership was the Hungarian Democratic Forum (*Magyar Demokrata Fórum*, MDF). Established in 1987, still under the communist regime, as a conservative party, it had approached the CDU early on. In October 1989, its members invited Kohl to their party convention, an offer that he declined. To show his sympathy without arousing the ire of the ruling communist party, he sent a member of parliament, who would address the convention on behalf of the CDU without even delivering a personal message from Kohl.[43]

At the same convention, József Antall was elected chairman, and he soon turned out to be the most important politician for Hungary's transition to democracy and a market economy. In January of the following year, he met with Francke, who once more served as Kohl's emissary to Central and Eastern Europe. Antall thanked Francke for the CDU's support and asked for material support, which Francke politely declined.[44] However, his par-

40 Note on the meeting of the EDU Europe committee in Budapest, 19-21 June 1989, ACDP 07-001-10308.

41 Memorandum concerning the participation of the CDU at the MSzMP "East-West Conference," 19 April 1989, ACDP.

42 Note on the meeting of the EDU Europe committee in Budapest, 19-21 June 1989, ACDP 07-001-10308.

43 Note regarding MDF convention, 19 October 1989, ACDP 07-001-10308.

44 Francke, Report about trip to Budapest, 30 January 1990, ACDP 08-009-138-1.

ty did receive a computer, a rental car with a loudspeaker and paper for the campaign trail. In February, Antall visited Bonn, and Kohl received him personally. As a token of his support, the chancellor granted him a joint photo opportunity and stressed in front of journalists that Antall's policy would eventually lead the country into the European Community. In private, he stressed the importance of a broad electoral coalition.[45]

Unlike in Poland, in Hungary the CDU had bet on the right horse. Not only did Antall win the elections with almost a quarter of all valid votes, but he also formed a center-right coalition with the Independent Smallholders', Agrarian Workers' and Civic Party (*Független Kisgazda-, Földmunkás- és Polgári Párt*, FKgP), and the Christian Democratic People's Party (*Kereszténydemokrata Néppárt*, KDNP).[46] This was exactly what Kohl and his party had hoped to see. And they were ready to provide the necessary material and moral support, as well as extensive training. Antall was given a car for the time before he entered office; the KAS offered seminars for all three parties, and the head of the CDU/CSU parliamentary group made a public speech at an MDF event. Kohl supported the three parties in their efforts for EDU membership and recommended joining the EUCD, too.[47] The parties received training for campaigning, parliamentary work, party structures, and municipal politics.[48] A group of experts from the parliamentary group in the German Federal Parliament was sent to Budapest to assist the MDF parliamentary group in questions of organization, strategic communication, PR, management, and the like.[49] During the campaign for local elections, the CDU offered material support (although Kohl, who had an election to win himself, cautioned against too much generosity).[50]

Altogether, the Hungarian case showed that the German chancellor was more than willing to help moderate right-wing parties in the former communist bloc as long as they managed to garner a significant number of votes and offered an appealing, pro-European platform.

45 Note on the visit of MDF chairman Antall, 21 February 1990, ACDP 07-001-10310.

46 See Anton Pelinka's chapter in this volume.

47 Dregger, Speech, 5 April 1990, ACDP 08-009-138-1; Note on visit to the coalition parties in Budapest, 6 June 1990, ACDP 08-009-138-1.

48 MDF secretary general's visit to Bonn, 18 June 1990, ACDP 08009-138-1.

49 Note on potential support for the MDF parliamentary group, 13 July 1990, ACDP 08-009-138-1.

50 Note on material support for Hungarian partner parties, 9 August 1990, ACDP 08-009-138-1.

The trouble with geopolitics: Czechoslovakia, the Baltic States, and Yugoslavia

The winds of change reached Czechoslovakia later than they did Poland and Hungary, but the ensuing Velvet Revolution happened much faster. The first negotiations between the government and the opposition started only in late November 1989, but only a month later leading dissident Václav Havel was elected president. Although the CDU decided to leave direct support of Czechoslovak parties mainly to the Hanns Seidel Foundation, closely associated with the CDU's Bavarian sister party, the Christian Social Union, it still established contacts with newly founded parties.[51] In February 1990, two CDU members of the Federal Parliament traveled to the founding party convention of the Slovak Christian Democratic Movement (*Kresťanskodemokratické hnutie*, KDH).[52] A week later, an exploratory group consisting of Vogel, Francke, and Fischer was sent to Prague to get an overview of the emerging party landscape. Apart from the Slovak Christian Democratic Movement, they met with representatives of the Czech Christian Democratic Party (*Křesťanskodemokratická strana*, KDS), and the Czechoslovak People's Party (*Československá strana lidová*, ČSL), extended invitations to Bonn and asked the Adenauer Foundation to investigate further.[53]

During the election campaign, all three parties received support in the form of consulting and visiting German politicians, who came as guest speakers for public rallies.[54] The CDU continued its support despite the parties' relatively meager results in the parliamentary elections in June and urged them to join the government in order to survive.[55] The Germans kept giving advice, sending experts to their partners and helping financially.[56] Soon, however, the CDU and CSU had to accept that it was probably the Civic Forum (*Občanské forum*, OF) of Václav Klaus and not one of their part-

51 Report on the current state of parties in Czechoslovakia, 28 March 1990, ACDP 08-009-137-2.

52 Report about the trip to the founding congress of the Slovak Christian Democratic Movement, 19 February 1990, ACDP 07-001-10310.

53 Report about the trip to Prague, 27 February 1990, ACDP 08-009-137-2. See also Ladislav Cabada's chapter in this volume.

54 Note on the KDH international secretary's visit to Bonn, 17 May 1990, ACDP 07-001-10310; Note of the ČSL to the CDU, 25 May 1990, ACDP 07-001-10310; Note on the visit to Prague, 31 May 1990, ACDP 07-001-10310.

55 Note on the election victory of the Civic Forum, 11 June 1990, ACDP 07-001-10310.

56 Note on conversation with KDH chairman Ján Čarnogurský, 11 September 1990, ACDP 08-009-137-2. See also Ján Čarnogurský, "Christian Democracy in Slovakia," in *Christian Democracy across the Iron Curtain*, ed. Kosicki and Łukasiewicz, 425–438.

ners who would become the decisive political power right of center.[57] But from an early stage onward, the question was not only about how to pick a partner party that could come up with a suitable platform and electoral success. Of equal, if not higher, importance was the geopolitical question. Kohl tried to uphold the territorial integrity of Czechoslovakia and did not support a "divorce" into separate Czech and Slovak states. He therefore tried to influence the emerging partner parties in this direction.[58]

The geopolitical aspect was even more important in the two other cases of dissolving states in post-communist Europe: The Soviet Union and Yugoslavia. The chancellor was of the opinion that the territorial integrity of the USSR should be preserved. He showed little sympathy for the national ambitions of the Baltic Soviet republics to regain their independence, fearing that the collapse of the empire might result in major geopolitical instability. And he did not want anything to jeopardize the imminent German unification.[59] If he had already exercised restraint towards Polish and Hungarian opposition leaders, he did so even more in the case of the Soviet Union. At an EDU meeting in November 1989, the Germans suggested acting with reserve towards new political parties from the Warsaw Pact countries and Yugoslavia.[60] When the first Christian Democratic parties from the Baltics knocked on the CDU's doors, Kohl did not openly reject them and was prepared for party officials to meet with them, but he did not commit to anything.[61] In June 1990, the CDU actively opposed an invitation for Baltic parties to the EDU conference in Helsinki.[62] Two month later, Kohl stuck to that line but showed a general openness for their EUCD and EDU membership in a mid-range perspective.[63]

In the case of Yugoslavia, Kohl took a similar line. Although the potential collapse of the multi-ethnic state in the south of Europe was very unlikely to pose any risk to Germany's reunification, the geopolitical ramifications could be dire. The CDU chairman, therefore, refrained from gestures that

57 Note on conversation with KDH chairman Ján Čarnogurský, 11 September 1990, ACDP 08-009-137-2. See also Ján Čarnogurský, "Christian Democracy in Slovakia," in *Christian Democracy across the Iron Curtain*, ed. Kosicki and Łukasiewicz, 425–438.

58 Note on KDH international secretary's visit to Bonn, 17 May 1990, ACDP 07-001-10310; Note on conversation with KDH chairman Ján Čarnogurský, 11 September 1990, ACDP 08-009-137-2; Francke, Report about the trip to Prague, 20 September 1990, ACDP 08-009-137-2.

59 Kohl, *Berichte*, 228, 243, and 247.

60 28th session of the EDU Europe commission, 13 November 1989, ACDP 07-001-10308.

61 Position paper on collaboration with Christian Democratic parties in Central, Eastern, and Southeastern Europe, 22 June 1990, ACDP 08-001-624/3.

62 Note on the session of the EDU steering committee, 26 June 1990, ACDP 07-001-10310.

63 Note on the party convention of the Estonian National Independence Party, 27 August 1990, ACDP 07-001-10310.

could encourage secession. After the first free Croatian parliamentary elections in spring 1990, the CDU decided to make all contacts to Croatian parties contingent on their acceptance of the Helsinki Accords, i.e. endorsement of regional minority rights with simultaneous preservation of Yugoslavia's national integrity.[64] The party recommended this cautious approach to the other EDU parties and explicitly warned against Franjo Tuđman because of his radical nationalist views.[65] Although Kohl did not change his position, already in the fall of the same year the CDU had to cave in to reality, and did not veto the fact-finding mission which the EDU wanted to send to Yugoslavia in search of potential partners.[66]

Eventually, the desire for national independence trumped all other considerations. Both the Soviet Empire and Yugoslavia failed to survive the year 1991. Kohl's ambitions to influence his new partners in a different direction, failed. Nonetheless, he achieved another goal that he had already set for himself at an early stage: the reunification of Europe. With the fall of the Iron Curtain, Kohl saw the chance to overcome the division of the continent caused by World War II and the ensuing Cold War. He therefore expected all potential partner parties to be pro-European, with the ambition to join the EC. At the party level, he actively advocated for the Christian Democratic Union of Central Europe (CDUCE), an exile association of Christian Democratic organizations from communist countries, to be dissolved.[67] Founded at the height of the confrontation between the Eastern and the Western blocs, it now seemed obsolete to him.[68] The goal of all future cooperation, he declared, should be the establishment of a United States of Europe.[69]

64 Note on the parliamentary elections in Croatia, 14 May 1990, ACDP 07-001-10310.

65 Position paper on collaboration with Christian Democratic parties in Central, Eastern, and Southeastern Europe, 22 June 1990, ACDP 08-001-624/3.

66 Note on the session of the EDU steering committee, 26 October 1990, ACDP 07-001-10310.

67 Compare with the CDUCE protagonist testimony of Stanisław Gebhardt, "The Christian Democratic Union of Central Europe," in *Christian Democracy across the Iron Curtain*, ed. Kosicki and Łukasiewicz, 423: "Even some representatives of the Christian Democratic parties of Western Europe, often acting in an official capacity, assumed that they could and should judge who was or was not a Christian Democrat. Western Europeans thereby killed the prospects for rebuilding Christian Democratic forces based on historical continuities with movements that had survived the many Cold War decades in exile."

68 Position paper on collaboration with Christian Democratic parties in Central, Eastern, and Southeastern Europe, 22 June 1990, ACDP 08-001-624/3.

69 Ibid.

Conclusions

Throughout his political career, Helmut Kohl expressed interest in the communist East and especially in the GDR. His contempt for the communist dictatorships, paired with his firm belief in the superiority of the Western, democratic, market-based system, was an inherent driving force behind his politics. It thus does not come as a surprise that he closely and sympathetically followed the peaceful revolutions in Central and Eastern Europe as well as the emergence of democratic parties. As a Christian Democrat, he of course showed a special interest in parties of similar ideological backgrounds. The CDU attempted early on to establish contacts to possible political partners but dispensed its support according to three conditions: considerations of *realpolitik*, programmatic proximity of the partners to its own positions, and the partners' prospects for success. Once a partner had been identified – as was the case in Hungary – the CDU rendered important support: assistance in setting up the faction and the party machine, political coordination talks at all levels, guidance for the principal figure (in Hungary's case, József Antall) on the integration of diverging party wings.

Kohl assigned a special role in all these countries to the KAS. As soon as possible, the Foundation established branches in Central and Eastern European countries, leading to a mushrooming of new offices all around the region. The Foundation could then more closely monitor the political developments on the ground, establish back-door communication channels with new parties, and report back to Bonn. Equally, it provided assistance for promising political partners.

All in all, in doing so Kohl and the CDU managed to weave a tight web with the numerous parties in all the countries of the former Eastern Bloc. The sustainability of this work was, however, limited in many cases because of the unstable landscape of political parties. In retrospect, however, it is conspicuous in the EPP that today a reliable party scene brought together in the course of the revolutions of 1989 does not exist. Contrary to what Kohl believed in 1989–1990, Christian Democratic parties were few and far between. Why the concept of Christian Democracy could not gain acceptance throughout Central and Eastern Europe after 1989 as it did in Western Europe is a separate matter.[70]

70 See, e.g., Szczerbiak and Bale, "Explaining the Absence of Christian Democracy in Contemporary Poland"; Anna Grzymała-Busse, "Why there is (almost) no Christian Democracy in post-communist Europe," *Party Politics* 19, no. 2 (2001): 319–342.

7

THE ITALIAN CHRISTIAN DEMOCRATIC PARTY CONFRONTS THE REVOLUTIONS OF 1989*

Giovanni Mario Ceci

On 19 October 1978, just a few hours after the elevation of Karol Wojtyła to the papacy, the Central Intelligence Agency (CIA), probably not surprisingly, issued a detailed memorandum on the impact of a Polish pope on the USSR, and more in general, on communism in the Eastern European and Western countries. In general, CIA analysts predicted a relevant and long-term impact on the Socialist societies in Eastern Europe. Much more complex was the judgment about the impact of the election of John Paul II on Western countries. According to the CIA, "having successfully coexisted with a communist regime in Poland, the new Pope will [actually] have more than symbolic impact on those communist parties in such heavily Catholic countries as Italy, France, and Spain." Of particular interest to the CIA, "the communists in these countries may now feel more free to stress their independence from Moscow." Maybe more surprisingly, the CIA also took into consideration the impact of the new pope on Italian Christian Democrats (CDs). It would be now "more difficult" for the Italian Christian Democratic Party (DC) – Langley's analysts wrote – "to use the influence of the Church" against the communists. Conversely, the CIA did not mention any possible (new) role, also in the light of Wojtyła's election, that Italian and non-Italian CDs could play in communist Eastern Europe.[1] Exactly twelve years later, facing the unexpected (for many including the CIA) fall

* This chapter presents the first conclusions of broader research carried out by the author on the reactions and the attitudes of the Italian Christian Democratic Party and the Italian Catholic world towards the collapse of communism in Central and Eastern Europe and the end of the Cold War (1989–1991). In this chapter, the author has merely indicated a few fundamental bibliographical references and only the essential sources.

1 CIA, National Foreign Assessment Center, *The Impact of a Polish Pope on the USSR*, 19 October 1978, National Archives and Record Administration (NARA), College Park (MD, USA), RG 263, Records of the Central Intelligence Agency, Directorate of Intelligence, Box 19, 22617, RP 78-10935.

of communism in Eastern Europe, important leaders of the DC proudly would claim, instead, to have significantly contributed (even if in an indirect way) to that rebirth of freedom that was taking place behind the (then-demolished) Iron Curtain.

This chapter examines the reactions, the analyses, and the attitudes of Italian Christian Democrats towards the revolutions of 1989 in Central and Eastern Europe and the fall of the Iron Curtain. Since the end of World War II, the DC had uninterruptedly been the cornerstone and the key actor of the Italian political system. In 1989, the DC still played this pivotal and dominating role. Since the 1970s, the party had actually come to face a relevant political and cultural crisis, but never resulting in a significant electoral decline. Not surprisingly, at the beginning of the 1980s, several prominent observers – like the CIA itself – had even come to define the future of the DC as "uncertain."[2] Nevertheless, in 1989, even if marked by an increasing degree of factionalism, the DC was still by far the largest Italian party. In July 1989, a prominent DC leader, Giulio Andreotti, again became Prime Minister. The new government – based on the exclusion of the Italian Communist Party (PCI) and on a five-party governing coalition (the so-called *Pentapartito*) – was the result of the opening of a new phase in the history of the DC. Some months earlier Arnaldo Forlani had replaced Ciriaco De Mita as secretary of the party. In contrast to De Mita's position, consisting in a strong and sometimes extremely bitter competition with the Socialists led by Bettino Craxi, the new DC headed by Forlani and the new government ruled by Andreotti aimed at reducing the tensions between the DC and the Italian Socialist Party (PSI). Also in order to make this cooperation closer, Andreotti symbolically appointed Gianni De Michelis, a prominent leader of the PSI very close to Craxi, as foreign minister.[3]

This chapter – based mainly on the documents of the DC preserved at the Archivio Storico Istituto Luigi Sturzo (ASILS) in Rome and on the party press – contains three levels of analysis. The first introduces the reactions, discussions, and interpretations about the revolutionary events of 1989 in

2 CIA, Directorate of Intelligence, A Research Paper, *The Italian Christian Democrats: An Uncertain Future*, 1 March 1982, NARA, Central Intelligence Agency (CIA) Records Search Tool (CREST).

3 On the history of the DC and, more generally, of the Italian political system (especially of the *Pentapartito*) in those years, see above all: Agostino Giovagnoli, *Il partito italiano: La Democrazia Cristiana dal 1942 al 1994* (Rome: Laterza, 1996); Piero Craveri, *La Repubblica dal 1958 al 1992* (Turin: UTET, 1995); Simona Colarizi, Agostino Giovagnoli and Paolo Pombeni, eds., *L'Italia contemporanea dagli anni Ottanta a oggi* (Rome: Carocci, 2014), vol. 3; Martin Bull, "The Pentapartito," in *Oxford Handbook of Italian Politics*, ed. Erik Jones and Gianfranco Pasquino (Oxford: Oxford University Press, 2015).

Eastern Europe that emerged within the DC.[4] The second level takes into consideration the hypotheses of the Italian CDs about the possible effects of these historic events on the international system. The third and last level of analysis deals with the analyses and judgments expressed by the DC about the consequences of the collapse of communism in Eastern Europe and of the end of the Cold War on Italian politics.

In brief, it is possible to affirm that the fall of communism in Eastern Europe and the end of the Cold War represented, for the Italian CDs, an unexpected event. Because the collapse was in many respects unforeseen, the reaction of the members of the DC to the "new course" in Eastern Europe (as well as their attitude towards the effects of the fall of communism on the international order and its consequences on Italian domestic politics) was characterized, in the immediate aftermath of the events, by a mixture of different, if not contrasting, feelings and stances: satisfaction and triumphalism, on one side; caution, realism, and concern, on the other. Not surprisingly, sharing this mixture of feelings, the Italian CDs adopted an overall position – with regard to both the domestic and the international new order – that can be described as a policy of *discontinuity within continuity*.

Before the revolutions: a sense of crisis and a profound uncertainty

On 18 February 1989, the DC opened its Eighteenth (XVIII) National Congress in Rome.[5] History would reveal that it would be the last Congress for the DC, which collapsed some years later at the beginning of the 1990s – a collapse certainly due to several factors, but which was decisively intertwined with the history reconstructed in the next pages. As usual, the

4 More generally, on the Italian reactions to the revolutions of 1989 (and to German unification), it is impossible not to cite at least the excellent analyses by Leopoldo Nuti, "Italy, German Unification, and the End of the Cold War," in *Europe and the End of the Cold War: A Reappraisal*, ed. Frédéric Bozo et al. (London: Routledge, 2008), 191–203; and by Antonio Varsori, "Italy, the East European Revolutions, and the Reunification of Germany (1989–92)," in *The Revolutions of 1989: A Handbook*, ed. Wolfgang Mueller, Michael Gehler and Arnold Suppan (Vienna: Verlag der Österreichischen Akademie der Wissenschaften, 2015), 403–418; Antonio Varsori, *L'Italia e la fine della guerra fredda* (Bologna: Mulino, 2013).

5 Archivio Storico Istituto Luigi Sturzo (ASILS), Rome, Fondo Democrazia cristiana (FDC), Serie Congressi Nazionali, *XVIII Congresso Nazionale*, boxes 27–34. The proceedings of the Congress were later published: *Atti del XVIII Congresso Nazionale della Democrazia cristiana: Relazioni e documenti*, ed. Carlo Dané, vol. 1: *Le relazioni, le conclusioni, i documenti*; vol. 2: *La discussione generale* (Rome: DC Spes/Cinque Lune, 1991).

debate among the several factions of the party was extremely lively, sometimes even heavily bitter and polemical. However, in contrast to all the previous Congresses of the party (at least those celebrated until the end of the 1970s), international issues were almost completely absent from the hundreds of pages presented by the many CDs participating in the Congress. Extremely scarce attention was paid also to the "Eastern issue," and more in general, to the "international communist question." Only some of the most prominent leaders dealt with international and Eastern Europe issues in their speeches. If we take into consideration the positions expressed during the Congress and, more in general, the analyses elaborated by the DC leaders and the party press in the weeks following, it is possible to identify two keywords which perfectly express the beliefs and the attitudes of the Italian CDs with regard to the Soviet Bloc in Eastern Europe in the first half of 1989: a sense or a feeling of *crisis*; and profound *uncertainty*.

In fact, between January and July, crisis definitely was the dominant word in CDs' reflections about communist regimes in Eastern Europe. Significantly, by June, some important leaders even came to write that the "phase of post-communism" had actually begun.[6] According to the CDs, a multifaceted crisis was affecting those countries behind the Iron Curtain: *economic, social, ideological*. However, for the CDs, it was undoubtedly the *political* crisis the most relevant one, being potentially fraught with revolutionary consequences. In particular, it was above all a crisis of political legitimacy (and it is relevant to highlight that according to some important leaders of the DC a very similar crisis, even if related to different causes and with different manifestations, was simultaneously affecting Western political regimes too, Italy included). The political crisis primarily consisted of a deep fracture between the institutions of the state (and/or the party system) and society, and in a consequent loss of support and confidence in the political system. Therefore, for the DC leaders, it was not surprising that a rising quest for freedom, a mounting, bottom-up push (also aided by an increasing re-discovery of religious sensibility) for "more democracy" and "more pluralism" were spreading in the Eastern European countries behind the Iron Curtain.

It was this new longing for freedom expressed by a growing number of people that represented for the Italian CDs the main *positive* change marking the Eastern European development during the first months of

6 See, e.g., the point of view clearly expressed by the vice-secretary of the party, Guido Bodrato: "La democrazia dopo il socialismo reale," *La Discussione*, 17 June 1989, 5.

1989. However, in those months, it was not only encouraging signals and good news that reached Rome from the Eastern Bloc. According to the Italian DC leaders and press, the overall picture of politics in the Soviet bloc between January and July presented new positive developments and traditional negative manifestations, ups and downs, events inducing optimism immediately followed by news of the opposite. In other words, the DC overall perception of the situation in Eastern Europe was made up of both light and shadows.

The most relevant and potentially revolutionary lights were especially identified by the Italian CDs in the "new courses" in Poland and Hungary, but also in Gorbachev's Soviet Union, where the new tendencies epitomized by *perestroika* seemed to have some successes. In particular, the elections to the Soviet Congress of People's Deputies (the "first more or less free vote in the USSR since 1918," even if they were not "multi-party elections" and their "outcome was largely pre-determined"), which took place in March (when about ninety percent of voters went to the polls and "many" anti-establishment, "independent and critical voices" demanding "further change" and reforms were elected[7]), were seen by the CDs as extremely revealing and promising. Every relevant step, every significant manifestation of these "new courses" attracted extraordinary attention and induced much optimism within DC headquarters. The main reasons and merits of what optimistically could be judged as the beginning of a real turning point for Eastern Europe and for international relations (significantly, many authoritative leaders of the party by February had begun to announce the end of the "Détente Age," replaced by a more peaceful, even if not clearly defined yet, "new condition") were evident for the Italian CDs. According to them these "new courses" were essentially a "revolution from below," the result of new pushes and quests by the citizens.[8] Nevertheless, they had certainly been inspired, encouraged and helped by other factors such as Western perseverance and firmness and especially by the "Helsinki Spirit."

And what about Gorbachev? Did he deserve some credit? The evaluation of his role during those months by the Italian CDs was rich in nuances.

7 Tony Judt, *Postwar: A History of Europe since 1945* (New York: Penguin, 2005), 600.

8 For an analysis of the most relevant interpretations of the causes, the factors, and the protagonists of the revolutions of 1989 (bottom-up perspective *vs.* top-down perspective; revolution from below approach *vs.* revolution from above approach; intentionalist explanation *vs.* structuralist explanation; etc.) see above all: Silvio Pons and Federico Romero, eds., *Reinterpreting the End of the Cold War: Issues, Interpretations, Periodizations* (London: Routledge, 2014); Wolfgang Mueller, "The Revolutions of 1989: An Introduction," in *The Revolutions*, ed. Mueller, Gehler and Suppan, 3–30.

On one hand, the Italian CDs agreed on the fact that Gorbachev was really playing a positive part in the Polish and Hungarian developments and that, above all, he was trying to improve political, economic, and social conditions in his own country. On the other side, they also aimed at not overestimating his role. In other words, the Italian CDs presented him not as the main actor, but only as an important protagonist who was "following" the new courses rather than promoting them. They highlighted also the contradictions and the limits of *perestroika* and of Gorbachev's action in general, citing: his policies towards nationalities in the USSR, discouraging actions/reactions in the domestic sphere after the aforementioned March elections, and the not yet explicit overcoming of the Brezhnev Doctrine. In the CDs' evaluations, the communist leaders in Hungary and Poland deserved even less credit. In fact, they merely *had* to accept the "new courses." Adopting new attitudes towards pluralism and allowing more freedom were actually evaluated by the CDs not as an action but only as a reaction. If, in the perspective of the DC, Poland and Hungary undoubtedly represented the most important lights, Czechoslovakia definitely symbolized the worst and most relevant shadow. "In Prague, it's still 'Brezhnev Time,'" *La Discussione* (the DC's weekly) headlined in March commenting on the new arrest of Václav Havel for his activities in protest demonstrations and the subsequent trial against him (during which, significantly, three representatives of the DC were sent to assist).

Therefore, between January and July, the Italian CDs held a "wait and see" attitude. This position was certainly characterized – on one hand – by a positive and hopeful stance about the new "liberal" tendencies, but also marked on the other hand by an abundance of caution, some skepticism, and several reservations. As a consequence, the DC expressed during the first months of 1989 – and this is the second keyword for this first phase – a profound uncertainty about future developments in Eastern Europe. This time, would tendencies towards pluralism and reformism finally prevail? Would those countries once and for all get rid of Stalinism and obtain full sovereignty and autonomy from Moscow? Did the recent events – especially in Poland and Hungary – really represent, finally, the initial steps towards a liberation from communism? Or, on the contrary, did they represent merely the umpteenth illusion, going to be betrayed (as happened so many times in the past and as the harsh repression in Beijing in those days further confirmed)? In short: would Eastern Europe experience a real and definitive "spring"? Or would a "wintry winter" (as the weekly of the DC wrote) still dominate in Prague and in the other Eastern capitals as well?

In those weeks, some Italian CDs were more optimistic; others more skeptical; others even pessimistic. Nevertheless, all the party leaders agreed on the fact that events occurring in Eastern Europe in those weeks represented a still *reversible* process. Above all, no one among them – and they were not the only ones in the Western hemisphere – was expecting or even imagining what would happen next.

Towards the earthquake: between confidence and confusion

On 24 August 1989, the Catholic intellectual Tadeusz Mazowiecki became Polish Prime Minister. He was the first non-communist premier of an Eastern European country after about forty years. The turning point in Poland probably constituted a turning point for the other countries in the Eastern Bloc, if not for history as well. Certainly, it was perceived and seen in this sense by the Italian CDs, who followed the succession of events in Poland with extraordinary attention and pathos. There is no doubt that the "revolutionary" and (hopefully) "proselytizing" turning point in Poland – as the newspaper of the DC, *Il Popolo*, used to describe it – weakened the sense of uncertainty which had characterized the attitude of the DC leaders to that point, and made them much more confident and optimistic. *Irreversible* and *unrestrainable* were significantly the two most recurring adjectives in CDs' speeches about the developments taking place not only in Poland but also in the Soviet Bloc in those days. Opening a National Council (*Consiglio Nazionale*, CN) of the party that took place only some hours after Mazowiecki's appointment, the secretary of the DC, Forlani, clearly stated: in Eastern Europe we face "the new age of the reversibility from communism" and the "irreversible crisis" of Marxism (and, more in general, of "closed ideologies"). The president of the CN and former secretary of the party, De Mita, echoed: "We are experiencing an extraordinary moment in the world history (...). The equilibrium of power, which had been established and which had guaranteed for better or worse the development of international relations, fell through and something new and deeply different is replacing it."[9]

9 ASILS, Fondo DC, Serie Consiglio Nazionale, *Consiglio Nazionale del 29-31 Agosto 1989*, Box 75, Folder 192.

During the following weeks (beginning in mid-September and increasing to the end of October), the never-ending succession of news from the Eastern Bloc further corroborated these beliefs. Extremely relevant and influential on the DC's attitude were the crisis in the GDR and, above all, the new course in Hungary. Decisive in the evolution of the DC's stance were the Hungarian policy toward Eastern Germans, and in particular, the decision to adopt a new constitution permitting a multiparty system and to change the country's name to the Republic of Hungary. All these revolutionary events increased even more optimism and confidence among the Italian CDs – and confidence is the first keyword related to this second phase. Revolution was evidently spreading behind the Iron Curtain. According to the most widespread analyses and points of view within DC headquarters, Eastern European countries were not merely experiencing a deep crisis and a significant evolution. Indeed, in those weeks, the Italian CDs became more and more confident that the Eastern Bloc was actually undergoing a radical transformation and a fundamental change, that a real earthquake was about to explode behind the Iron Curtain, that, in conclusion, communism in Eastern Europe was on the verge of collapse. Nothing better than the headlines in the party's newspaper, *Il Popolo*, expresses this widely shared perception and the escalation of confidence in the always more likely fall of communism in the Soviet Bloc already before the collapse of the Berlin Wall: "The East in Turmoil" (24 August); "The East Crumbles" (14 September); "The Decline of the Great Utopia" (23 September); "Chronicle of post Yalta" (23 September); "Communism Collapses" (24 October); "The Empire is on the Verge of the Fall" (25 October); "Communist Regimes Smashed to Pieces" (8 November).

Exactly this widely shared idea that the Soviet Bloc was undergoing a radical and irreversible (even if, maybe, not definitive yet) transformation and decline, and that Eastern Europe communism was most likely on the verge of the collapse provoked a relevant confusion in the Italian CDs – and this is the second keyword related to this phase. What does it mean that they were confused? It means that, between the summer and the fall of 1989 (at least until the collapse of the Berlin Wall), overlapping – and sometimes contrasting – feelings, positions, attitudes, beliefs, points of view coexisted, were fused together (in this sense: *con*fused) in the Italian CDs. A confusion that was in some cases perceived and admitted by the same CDs, and was essentially related to a specific condition: awareness of the fact they were facing an extraordinary turning point, an uncommon "acceleration of History" (as the head of the DC's Department of Foreign Affairs, Bruno Orsini, defined it).[10] An "acceleration" that was radically transforming well-established scenarios, shattering traditional paradigms, opening a new era for humankind and a new phase in history. This new era – and this was the real cause of the "confusion" among the CDs – was however still unclear, indefinite. Above all it was rich in hopes, but also full of unknowns. The confusion – exactly resulting from this perception – was particularly evident in the three issues most debated by the CDs with regard to the revolutionary events in Eastern Europe.

Italian CDs were first confused (in the sense just explained) about the future of Eastern Europe. The leaders of the party expressed great satisfaction for the extraordinary and extraordinarily positive events occurring behind the Iron Curtain, and for the astonishing struggle for freedom, pluralism, and democracy by Central and Eastern Europeans. A struggle which, significantly, some CDs did not hesitate to promote as a model for themselves and as a source of inspiration for a moral and cultural renewal. However, many Italian CDs also acknowledged that the collapse of communism could likely create a vacuum, certainly positive but also potentially dangerous. It would, in fact, provoke the decline of a source of hope for millions of people. Consequently, it would certainly represent a dramatically complex challenge. Dealing with this challenge by simply declaring the victory of the "market" as the unique regulating principle; or by replacing communism with a mere pragmatist approach; or by moving towards more conservative stances, as some German Christian Democrats seemed to suggest, were the wrong answers, for the majority of Italian CDs.

This challenge was particularly complex in Central and Eastern Europe. Even if the Italian CDs remained optimistic about the future, they considered the path to the end of communism and to pluralism in the former Soviet Bloc as not easy and rich in traps – also due to the increasing economic crisis affecting those countries. Between the summer and the fall, the leaders of the party were especially worried about the risks of (not so unlikely) dangerous backlashes, backward steps, and false moves. At the same time, they also feared evolution in the other countries of the Soviet Bloc not yet affected by revolutionary developments and, above all, they feared the situation in the USSR. They were in fact convinced that the fate of all Central and Eastern European countries – both those already "liberated" and those not yet – as well as the future of international relations was, at least partially, linked to the success of Gorbachev and his *perestroi-*

10 Bruno Orsini, "Aspettando Gorbaciov," *La Discussione*, 4 November 1989, 9.

ka in the USSR. For these reasons and especially due to the precariousness of the ongoing process, in those weeks the policy suggested by important DC leaders (such as Andreotti and Flaminio Piccoli) was to support Gorbachev. Above all there was a desire to launch an "aid program" (hopefully orchestrated with other European countries), a sort of new Marshall Plan for Eastern Europe. This idea had been already launched some months earlier in Moscow by the then Italian Prime Minister and DC Secretary, De Mita. Facing the revolutionary events and the emerging difficulties, it was relaunched in those weeks and resulted in some proposals presented by DC deputies to the Italian Parliament aimed at economically supporting those countries (Poland, first of all) struggling to free themselves from communism.[11]

The same confusion was expressed in the same weeks by the Italian CDs with regard to the international order. Also in this case the future appeared potentially rich in hopes: a new post-Yalta, more peaceful era could potentially begin. However, according to the DC, the unknowns were not less than the hopes. In particular, between the summer and the fall the most widespread doubts and questions about the new international order (which commonly remained unanswered) included: what to do with the traditional organizations essentially linked to the reality of the Cold War, like NATO for example? How to deal with the USSR? Do the Soviets accept being no longer considered a superpower, an empire? How to reach new steps towards disarmament without compromising and weakening the necessary conditions of full collective security? Is European integration a process to be abandoned or, on the contrary, to be improved (and quickly)? And should the new republics (hopefully) emerging from the collapse of communism be integrated and involved in this process of European integration?

Finally, a similar coexistence of different, if not contrasting, positions can be traced in the Italian CDs' attitude toward Italian communists during this phase. The crucial question, increasingly emerging in DC headquarters already before the fall of the wall in Berlin, was: is the crisis in Eastern Europe affecting the PCI too? If yes, how much, how deeply? Similarly, different points of view co-existed on this question as well. On one hand, many important DC leaders noticed some (even if only potential, for the moment) positive signals and developments emerging from the debate among the Italian communists (positive not only for them but for the whole political system), and consequently thought that the PCI deserved

11 "Solidarietà DC," *Il Popolo*, 20 October 1989, 2.

at least some confidence. Nonetheless, on the other hand, all the most important leaders of the DC were also strongly convinced that beyond the Italian communist leaders' statements and potentially positive signals, the crisis of the PCI was not necessarily going to bring about and actually had not brought about until then its transformation in a Social Democratic party. In short, according to them, the crisis of the PCI did not involve – at least not yet – the possibility that it would become a credible and realistic political alternative to the DC.

As this last point clearly shows, for the CDs, the (ever more likely) collapse of communism in Central and Eastern Europe could have some very relevant consequences on Italian domestic politics too. Indeed, one of the first and most relevant conclusions it is now possible to draw is that, especially since the end of the summer, the Italian CDs not only considered the revolutions in Central and Eastern Europe and their repercussions on the international sphere a crucial issue in their own political agenda, but they also began to devote progressively growing attention (and anxiety) to the domestic consequences of these events. "Internationality is the preeminent fact," Piccoli explicitly stated in August, during the aforementioned National Council of the party. "Underestimate the new facts" on the international arena – the head for foreign affairs of the party echoed during the same meeting – which are "radically modifying the features of one of the essential elements of our political system, the Communist Party" and which, therefore, inevitably will also "bring about changes in all the other elements," would be a "fundamental mistake." In particular, the main fears emerging among DC leaders in those days were: would the communist crisis (both global and domestic) involve an irreversible crisis also for the DC? Would the collapse of communism in Eastern Europe and the subsequent probable transformation of the PCI deprive the DC of one of the most relevant factors of support from its supporters and voters? In other words, after more than forty years, due to these extraordinary changes, could the DC be expelled from government and forced to become an opposition party?

The never-ending succession of events in the weeks immediately following made these fears even more widespread.

Facing the collapse and the birth of a new international and domestic order: between moderate triumphalism, strong realism, and abundant caution

Between November and December, what the large majority of the CDs still considered as unreal became real. The fall of the Berlin Wall, the deposing of Todor Zhivkov in Bulgaria, the Velvet Revolution in Czechoslovakia which brought Havel to power, and the definitely less velvet revolution which overthrew Ceaușescu's communist government in Romania made a deep impression on DC leaders and marked a fundamental turning point in their stance. Doubts almost completely disappeared in the headquarters of the party: "A Historical Turn in the Heart of Europe" (10 November), "A New World in Eastern Europe" (12–13 November), "The Collapse of Communism" (23 December), *Il Popolo* headlined without any hesitation. The historical experiences of communism in Central and Eastern Europe really seemed to come to an end *irreversibly* – Forlani stated on 22 December, during a press conference he decided to attend specifically in order to comment on the recent revolutions in Central and Eastern Europe. The real process of transition had begun, Forlani added.[12]

Different feelings dominated CDs' attitudes in those days. First of all, they certainly expressed great satisfaction and also an ill-concealed, even if moderate, triumphalism. At the same time, the way (i.e. *how* communism had collapsed) as well as the extraordinary speed of the process induced the Italian CDs to be strongly cautious and realistic, also because – as they recognized – the events had actually taken them by surprise. Satisfaction and hope as well as realism and caution were evident, first of all, in CDs' evaluations about the new course of Central and Eastern European countries. Transition (rich in expectations and opportunities but also marked by tensions and unknowns), and therefore uncertainty were undoubtedly the most recurrent categories adopted by the leaders of the party to describe the future of Eastern Europe. Not surprisingly, the party press and, significantly, also some DC leaders began to visit Eastern European countries frequently and prepare detailed reports aimed at informing the rank and file of the party on the developments in those areas. Nor was it surprising that DC leaders constantly and vigorously relaunched the proposal of an aid program aimed at economically but also politically and culturally supporting the countries of Central and Eastern Europe in order to guarantee a peaceful and smooth transition, help the sister parties, and in

12 *Il Popolo*, 23 December 1989.

this way hopefully avoid the possibility (perceived as not so unlikely) of a dangerous power vacuum.

The mix of triumphalism and satisfaction, on one hand, and caution, realism and concern, on the other, marked even more the attitude and the stance of the DC with regard to the two main issues on which the CDs focused in the immediate aftermath of the collapse of communism: the effects of the fall of communism on the international order ("characterized by high hopes but also by risks and relevant tensions," as the DC declared in the final document of the Directorate [*Direzione*] which took place on 16 January),[13] and its consequences on the domestic political sphere.

The Italian CDs were immediately and firmly convinced that the end of communism in Eastern Europe also meant the end of the Cold War; the end of the "Yalta Age" and of the order imposed by the "Yalta framework"; the beginning of a complex and unpredictable transition in the international sphere, and the likely birth of a new international order.[14] Accordingly, the DC also immediately and firmly recognized the need of devising a *new* foreign policy and forging a *new* Weltanschauung of the international order, which had to be independent from those expressed and conducted by Kohl, Bush, or Mitterrand. In particular, according to the large majority of the CDs, this new foreign policy agenda (which did not always coincide even with the foreign policy of the Italian government itself or of the socialist Italian Foreign Minister, Gianni De Michelis) necessarily had to include some essential, firm and unquestionable top priorities, strategies, and policies, in order to secure the process of transition and (re-) construct a new international order assuring peace, stability, and security.

The DC had no doubts about what the keystone of this new foreign policy had to be: Europe. Europeanism, aspiration to a real European integration had certainly been one of the cornerstones of the DC's foreign policy since 1945. Undoubtedly, the revolutions of 1989 vigorously relaunched it. In fact, all high-profile members of the party strongly believed that the collapse of communism in Central and Eastern Europe and the end of the Cold War meant, first of all, the expiration of the bipolar condominium, determined by "the mistake of Yalta." And, therefore, it meant (or better: could mean) the chance for Europe, after too long an era of decline, to rediscover – or to discover, probably, for the first time – its geographical

13 ASILS, Fondo DC, Serie Direzione Centrale, *Direzione del 16 gennaio 1990*, Box 53, Folder 752.

14 This position was for example clearly expressed in the immediate aftermath of the fall of the Berlin Wall by the prominent leader of the DC, Emilio Colombo, during a parliamentary debate which exactly dealt with international issues: *Atti Parlamentari, Camera dei Deputati, X Legislatura, Discussioni, Seduta del 14 novembre 1989*, 40490.

and political centrality, to become the independent architect of its own destiny and "common house," and to play a crucial and autonomous role in the international arena. However, in order to "regain the right to speak" and to become a prominent actor, Europe – CDs thought – had at long last to learn to "speak with one voice."[15] As a matter of fact, the leaders of the DC were firmly convinced that the revolutions in Eastern Europe clearly imposed the necessity of a more and more united Europe. In fact, according to them – and Secretary Forlani himself clarified the party line on several occasions between November and December –, the recent events in Central and Eastern Europe did "not clash at all with the construction of a united Europe" and did not devalue or, worse, involve the end of the process of European integration. Instead, for CDs – as Forlani unambiguously declared during a National Council of the party which took place on 17-18 November and, some days later, at the European Parliament –, the new scenario set in motion by the collapse of communist regimes in Eastern Europe necessarily had to involve not an "attenuation" or a "stall" but, on the contrary, an "acceleration" of the process of European unification.[16] What about the role in this process of Eastern European countries struggling to free themselves from communism? The line of the DC was extremely clear and was in many respects similar to Jacques Delors's plan for a "Europe of concentric circles" (which many of the DC leaders explicitly referred to). As Orsini, the head of the DC's Department of Foreign Affairs, explained during the National Council of the party which took place in November, in the first place it was fundamental to ensure and make more integrated the first of those circles, namely "the Europe of the Twelve." Only after the European Community had internally integrated and consolidated, further "integrations" of the countries of "the other Europe" would have been "possible and fruitful": "Heaven help – Orsini significantly warned – if what we may earn in terms of enlargement, we should lose in terms of depth; if what we may earn in terms of extent, we should lose in terms of cohesion."[17]

For the leaders of the DC, this renewed faith in Europeanism and effort to build a more integrated, stronger and autonomous Europe, had not to

15 This extraordinarily widespread point of view within the DC was perfectly summed up in those days by Gerardo Bianco, "Il compito dell'Europa"; Arturo Pellegrini, "Il dialogo tra i grandi e il ruolo dell'Europa," both in *Il Popolo*, 5 December 1989, 2.

16 ASILS, Fondo DC, Serie Consiglio Nazionale, *Consiglio Nazionale del 17-18 novembre 1989*, Box 75, Folder 192. For Forlani's speech at the European Parliament, see *Il Popolo*, 22 November 1989.

17 Beyond his speech at the National Council of November, see also "Aspettando Gorbaciov," *La Discussione*, 4 November 1989, 9.

undermine the second essential pillar of their foreign policy since 1945: Atlanticism and the strong relationship with the USA. As a matter of fact, in the aftermath of the collapse of communism in Central and Eastern Europe, all the major leaders of the party clearly expressed a strong opposition to any proposal damaging Italians' and Europeans' links with the USA or at expelling the USA from the European context (whose safety, according to them, could be guaranteed only by the active American presence and involvement). At the same time, the large majority of Italian CDs – Andreotti, first of all – expressed a strong opposition to any proposal immediately breaking up the two blocks or aimed at overcoming and breaking traditional alliances like NATO, still seen as a crucial "stabilizing factor."[18] "As things currently stand" – Andreotti affirmed during a long interview to the influential newspaper *Corriere della Sera*, expressing the predominant belief within his party:

> NATO and the Warsaw Pact are still necessary, and I think the Europeans' link with the USA constitutes a relevant balancing factor, which makes the dialogue possible, and which, therefore, meets the Soviets' interests too. I would go as far as saying that exactly the Soviets should be currently the most convinced supporters of NATO, while the West has no interest in the crumbling of the Warsaw Pact.[19]

As a consequence of that, CDs were also firmly in favor of any solution promoting only a controlled, gradual, and balanced disarmament. "Disarmament" – one of the most influential DC leaders on international issues, Emilio Colombo, clearly warned during the already mentioned National Council of the party in November – "[must] always be combined with security." Exactly for this reason, disarmament could be possible only if realized *within* the framework of the traditional military alliances and within safety. And – Colombo added – "this time" we have to consider "not only the safety of the Europeans or of the Americans" but also "the safety of the USSR."

For the Italian CDs, keeping into account the perspective and interest of the Soviets had to be an imperative priority not only when dealing with international security, but also when dealing with what they perceived as the number one problem: the issue of German unification. In the immediate aftermath of the fall of the Berlin Wall, extremely cautionary, worried,

18 Franco Maria Malfatti, "Alleanza Atlantica, per l'Europa una scelta da confermare," *Il Popolo*, 7 December 1989, 2.
19 "Andreotti: che dirò a Gorbaciov," *Corriere della Sera*, 26 November 1989, 1–2.

and rather cold stances and tones with regard to German unification were not absent within the headquarters of the DC in Rome. This attitude was in particular expressed by Andreotti, as Helmut Kohl would later recall in his memoirs.[20] Already in the past, Andreotti had frequently considered the possibility of a unified Germany without much enthusiasm and actually with some concern. In the immediate aftermath of the collapse of the Berlin Wall, he did not change his stance. He was rather worried, skeptical, and distrustful about the reunification of Germany. This attitude was certainly due to his longstanding personal point of view. At the same time it was also related to (or, at least, reinforced by) the fact that he was Prime Minister of a coalition government in those weeks – a coalition made up of very different positions, also on the German issue.

Still, at least on the basis of the sources taken into consideration, it is possible to conclude that this view – perfectly expressed by Andreotti – probably was a minority position in the debate within the DC. In the weeks immediately following the fall of the Berlin Wall, the large majority of CDs seemed to be undoubtedly in favor of the process of German unification. Indeed, quite a few of them came to express even a strong and deeply enthusiastic support to German reunification, also stressing the *inevitability* of the process and vigorously arguing against what they significantly defined "the culture of suspicion." A culture which, according to them, was improperly and exaggeratedly emphasizing the dangers of Pan-Germanism.

If, therefore, it is possible to say that the line largely shared by the members of the DC was in favor of German reunification (in some cases with moderate tones, in some others with much more enthusiasm), it is important as well to point out that all of those who supported this line did not conceal the dramatic difficulties related to the "German Question." They suggested that the hoped for goal of reunification had necessarily to be achieved by acting with extreme caution and by respecting some essential conditions. In particular, the DC identified five general conditions in order to secure the process of German unification: a) dealing with the "German Question" not as merely a German issue but as an European issue; b) guaranteeing the right of the Germans to self-determination, by allowing them to freely and democratically express their real will; c) not raising the question of the borders again and, in particular, respecting

20 Helmut Kohl, *Erinnerungen 1982–1990* (Munich: Droemer Knaur Verlag, 2005), 961–963, 1015. On Andreotti's position towards German unification, see the aforementioned publications by Nuti and by Varsori.

the borders established by the Helsinki Accords; d) making sure that the (eventual) new united Germany did not become a neutral country but, on the contrary, could be integrated in a united Europe; and e) reassuring and collaborating also with the Soviets during the process.

There is no doubt that the collapse of the Berlin Wall and the following events until the end of Ceaușescu's regime marked a fundamental turning point in the debate among the leaders of the DC with regard also to another crucial issue. In fact, those historic events dramatically increased their attention on the possible effects of the revolutions in Central and Eastern Europe on the Italian political system. The same mix of feelings characterizing the attitude of the CDs towards the fall of communism in Eastern Europe and its consequences on the international sphere also characterized their stance, attitude, and analyses with regard to the repercussions of the Central and Eastern European upheavals on Italian domestic politics. In fact, on the one hand, the leaders of the DC expressed triumphalism and satisfaction; on the other, they were at the same time extremely cautious and even concerned.

Actually, at least in the immediate aftermath of the collapse of communism, a widespread concern dominated the state of mind of the CDs. They were worried that the fall of the Berlin Wall could result in making the image of the PCI more "acceptable," strengthening its position (especially in terms of legitimacy to govern). This could make possible a new political formula and alliances largely considered unimaginable until then. In particular, one of the nightmares which began to circulate within DC headquarters was a possible *mitterrandizzazione* of the Italian political system, namely an alliance between socialists and communists to be promoted as an alternative to the DC. At the same time, CDs strongly feared – and many leaders of the party openly and often expressed this concern between November and January – that voters would no more consider the DC as indispensable. In other words, the members of the DC were extraordinarily worried that as the fall of communism could bring about the end of anti-communism, they would lose one of the fundamental motives of their own *raison d'être* and one of the main factors which had induced until then their constituency to back them. In conclusion, their concern was that the end of communism in Eastern Europe would bring about the decline of the DC rather than that of the PCI. And this would make almost inevitable the success of political formulas based merely on being an "alternative to the DC."

This extremely widespread concern induced Italian CDs to hold a defensive attitude. However, such a defensive attitude did not result in a passive position. On the contrary – as the leaders of the DC strongly believed it was absolutely necessary to make their own contribution, to play a key and autonomous role, to take an original political initiative and line – it gave rise to an extremely proactive approach and an offensive strategy. "We need a Christian Democracy on the attack," Luigi Granelli, member of the left-wing sectors of the party, came to affirm during the National Council of November. Schematically, it is possible to identify four essential building blocks in this approach and strategy.

Firstly, the DC launched an extremely polemical and harsh campaign against the PCI, with definitely heavier tones than those of the previous months. The Italian communists were blamed for their *past.* According to the CDs, the recent events in Eastern Europe unambiguously revealed the total senselessness and wrongness of all the major cultural and political positions of the PCI in the previous forty years and its historical responsibility for holding them. Moreover, the Italian communists were blamed by the members of the DC for the analyses and positions they took in the immediate aftermath of, and in reaction to, the revolutions in Central and Eastern Europe. Even if some more positive comments circulated within DC headquarters, the large majority of CDs categorically dismissed the PCI's debate and evolution taking place in those days. For the DC, the PCI had come to deal with the "communist question" and its eventual overcoming too late, and only because it had been forced by the events. In short, the PCI seemed not to be dealing with its own past and more in general with what communism had actually been. Not surprisingly, CDs concluded that the debate taking place among communists clearly showed a party without any identity and any precise cultural point of reference. The DC strongly criticized the PCI for its ideas about the *future* too. Their plans and their projects were judged by the CDs as worrying and untrustworthy. In fact, according to the CDs, the unique goal the PCI really wanted to reach consisted of "removing the DC," while it was not able to suggest a positive and reliable proposal.

Influencing public opinion, mobilizing the likely constituency of the party, and involving the members of the DC at all levels (from the top leaders to the local sections) – giving them extremely "clear instructions and guidelines," as Secretary Forlani affirmed during the National Congress of the party in November – was the second building block of the strategy pursued by the CDs in the weeks immediately following the fall of the

Berlin Wall. On 16 January 1990, according to the minutes of the meeting preserved at the ASILS, Andreotti significantly stated at the opening of an important Directorate of the party: "We need to broadly outline how we have to deal with the extraordinary events occurring in Eastern Europe." The "connection to public opinion" – other prominent leaders immediately echoed after Andreotti during the same Directorate – obliges us to consider the "great turn" taking place in Eastern Europe as a "top priority" and obliges us both to get our "periphery" (namely the local sections of the party) extraordinarily involved and to be much more present in the media, in contrast to the previous weeks, to promote our position.[21] The main goal – as Andreotti would add ten days later during the successive Directorate of the party – was unambiguous: make it clear that the DC was (and had to be perceived as) still undoubtedly "indispensable."[22]

In the following days and weeks, the DC implemented exactly this strategy. The leaders of the party realized it by promoting and advancing (and this was the third building block of the approach of the DC) especially a key message: the recent events had unquestionably validated the rightness and the forcefulness of the decisive choices and "historical position" of the DC. In other words, the dissolution of communism in Central and Eastern Europe had unambiguously revealed that the DC had always been and still was on the right side. "Today" – Pier Ferdinando Casini, one of the most important emerging leaders in the party, said during the 16 January Directorate – the DC can see "its forty-year political stance wholly realized."[23] "Marx's Manifesto is dead; the *Rerum Novarum* is not, it is alive and vital," Andreotti concluded some days later during a DC meeting specifically focused on the recent revolutions in Central and Eastern Europe.[24] Therefore, the large majority of CDs interpreted the collapse of communism also in terms of their own political (and cultural) victory.

Not surprisingly, one of the main immediate effects of the collapse of communism in Eastern Europe was a relaunch of the pride of being Christian Democrat and a deeply proud rereading of the history of the party. In brief, in the days following the fall of the Berlin Wall, there was in DC headquarters the triumph of triumphalism, which would even increase in the next weeks. A triumphalism further reinforced by the widespread belief that the collapse of communism was strongly linked not so much to

21 ASILS, Fondo DC, Serie Direzione Centrale, *Verbale della Direzione del 16 gennaio 1990*, Box 53, Folder 752.

22 Ibid., *Verbale della Direzione del 29 gennaio 1990*, Box 53, Folder 753.

23 Ibid., *Verbale della Direzione del 16 gennaio 1990*, Box 53, Folder 752.

24 *La Discussione*, 24 March 1990, 14–15.

the appeal of capitalism but much more to the rebirth, the power, and the influence of Christian feelings (and the initial successes of the Christian Democratic parties in the new republics seemed to validate this); and by the idea – expressed by the secretary of the party himself – that the DC had not only preserved freedom in Italy, but had also contributed to cause the recent revolutions in Central and Eastern Europe, thanks to its foreign policy and thanks to the overall success of its own experience.

The fourth and correlated building block consisted of the rediscovery of the Christian Democratic identity. According to the large majority of the members of the DC, there was no doubt that one of the lessons that it was good to learn from what was happening behind the Iron Curtain was the necessity of a cultural renewal of the party in order to refresh the identity of the DC. This was exactly the point. The leaders of the DC strongly believed that the collapse of communism imposed only a "refresh" of their political and cultural platform. They were absolutely convinced that the identity and the line of the party were not only right, but also definitely still effective and able to respond to the challenges emerging abroad and from the Italian context. Or better, as the final motion of the National Council of the party, which took place in November, they were absolutely convinced that the rediscovery and the relaunch of the identity and the line of the DC was actually the *only* way to deal with the new national and international condition. In contrast to the PCI, they did not have to rethink, reject, or replace their identity or their political line. Rather, they had only to rediscovery, restore, refresh and strengthen them: "Be careful," Granelli admonished during that same National Council, "not to say that, as everything is changing, we have to change too. Why? If anything, the DC has to strengthen its identity in order to prove that it won."

The end (of the Italian DC, not of history)

From this brief analysis of the DC reactions to the revolutions of 1989, it is possible to draw some general conclusions.

First of all, it is important to point out that the collapse of communism in Eastern Europe and the end of the Cold War represented all in all, an *unexpected* event for the Italian CDs. Certainly, most of them clearly understood that since the very beginning of 1989 both Marxism and "really existing socialism" were experiencing an extremely deep political, social, cultural, economic, and ideological crisis. This crisis was so seriously threatening the legitimacy of the communist regimes that their collapse in an indeterminate (but probably not so distant) future began to be perceived as not unlikely. However, no one among the DC leaders seemed to expect a so immediate and brief process of dissolution involving all the European communist regimes. Significantly, even after the fall of the Berlin Wall some uncertainties kept circulating. Only after the events in Czechoslovakia and especially in Romania, did hesitation start to disappear and the CDs begin to gain a fuller awareness of the end of communism in Central and Eastern Europe and of the Cold War.

Because the collapse was in many respects unforeseen, in the immediate aftermath of the events (in particular between November and January), the reaction of the members of the DC – rather disoriented and even shocked by the exceptional speed of the events, and uncertain about the transition and the features of the new (international and domestic) order – was made up of a mixture of different, if not opposite, feelings and stances. They certainly showed great satisfaction and triumphalism (which would increase in the following months, also because of dynamics related to Italian politics). However, they also expressed caution, realism, and concern. This mixture characterized the attitude and the stance of the DC not only with regard to the "new course" in Central and Eastern Europe (whose outcome still appeared as profoundly uncertain), but also – and above all – with regard to the two main issues on which the CDs mostly focused immediately after the dissolution of Eastern regimes: the consequences of the collapse of communism on the international order and its effects on Italian domestic politics.

Not surprisingly, with this mixture of feelings, the Italian CDs adopted an overall position that can be perfectly described as a policy of "discontinuity within continuity." This is extremely clear if we take into account the stances and points of view of the DC with regard to the new international system to be built on the ruins of the Berlin Wall. The members of the DC (or better: the large majority of them) accepted and sometimes enthusiastically welcomed some of the most relevant changes marking the new international order. For example, they strongly favored the overcoming of the order imposed by the "Yalta framework" or supported (in some cases, warmly supported) the process of German reunification. At the same time, the leaders of the DC were firmly convinced that these "discontinuities" had necessarily to be safely couched within an overall "continuity" framework in order to avoid a serious (and likely) earthquake. In particular, the DC thought it was absolutely necessary not to undermine, but on the contrary, to relaunch the two essential pillars which had been the cornerstones of its foreign policy since 1945: Atlanticism and the strong relationship with the USA, and Europeanism. With regard to the latter in particular, the DC actually identified in the collapse of communism not a factor of attenuation or stall in the process of European unification but, on the contrary, a chance to accelerate this process and to finally build a more integrated, stronger and autonomous Europe.

"Discontinuity within continuity" was also the policy, the line that the leaders of the DC adopted with regard to Italian domestic politics. They were fully aware of the revolutionary effects the fall of the Berlin Wall was likely to have on the Italian political system too. And, not rarely, many CDs also welcomed and positively judged changes, developments, discontinuities which could result from the post-Yalta Age. Nevertheless, also in this case, they were strongly convinced that these discontinuities had to be couched within the continuity. At the same time, the leaders of the DC firmly believed that, in contrast to the PCI, they did not need to reject or replace their identity or their political line, marking a complete fracture with the past. Rather, what seemed necessary was just restoring and refreshing the party identity and platform, achieving a perfect balance between continuity and discontinuity.

In conclusion, there is no doubt that the Italian CDs immediately perceived the revolutions of 1989 in Central and Eastern Europe as a fundamental turning point. Was the world facing the end of History, as some scholars (above all, the political scientist Francis Fukuyama) suggested in those days? Of course not, also for the Italian CDs, who explicitly and vigorously rejected this idea. Evidently, History – according to the DC too – was experiencing the beginning of a new era and had definitely not come to an end. Rather, it was the history of the Italian Christian Democratic Party to come to an end some months later. And undoubtedly the events here reconstructed – as well as their consequences on both the international order and the domestic sphere – played a fundamental role in determining its demise.

SECTION III

MADE BEHIND THE IRON CURTAIN: HOMEGROWN CATHOLIC POLITICS AND THE RISE AND FALL OF CHRISTIAN DEMOCRACY IN EASTERN EUROPE

8

THE CHRISTIAN DEMOCRAT WHO WASN'T

Tadeusz Mazowiecki and the End of Catholic Politics in Poland

Piotr H. Kosicki

> Our approach to socialism had as its starting point a moral motivation. We were attracted by the socialist tradition of social rebellion, or, to put it another way, by the social question, understood as the need for the transformation of society. We felt that the road to socialism would develop in such a way as to open up to personalist values. This was the basis of our involvement and the standard by which we judged the unfolding events.
>
> Tadeusz Mazowiecki, 1970[1]

The first Soviet Bloc country to choose a non-communist head of government was Poland. That leader was Tadeusz Mazowiecki, a life-long Catholic activist whose career in public life began when he joined a Christian Democratic party in 1946. And yet the revolutions of 1989 brought no Christian Democratic revival to Poland. As prime minister, Mazowiecki famously declared to West German Chancellor Helmut Kohl, "I am a Christian and a democrat, but I am not a Christian Democrat."[2]

This chapter has two goals: to reconstruct Mazowiecki's intellectual and political trajectory with a particular eye to Christian Democracy, and to tease out the implications of his 1990 statement to Kohl. Throughout his career in communist Poland, Mazowiecki understood himself to be a "Catholic socialist," committed to combining the best elements of both Catholicism and Marxism into a workable "third way" in political economy and governance – neither capitalist, nor communist.[3] Beginning already in

1 Tadeusz Mazowiecki, *Rozdroża i wartości* (Warsaw: Biblioteka WIĘZI, 1970), 195.

2 Tadeusz Mazowiecki, interview, 25 January 2006; Andrzej Brzeziecki, *Tadeusz Mazowiecki: Biografia naszego premiera* (Kraków: Znak Horyzont, 2015), 471.

3 On the origins and content of "Catholic socialism," see Piotr H. Kosicki, *Catholics on the Barricades: Poland, France, and "Revolution," 1891–1956* (New Haven, CT: Yale University Press, 2018).

the late 1950s, he had meaningful transnational encounters with Western European Christian Democrats, whose personalities, intellectual struggles, and political agendas influenced Mazowiecki's own choices. With the collapse of state socialism, however, this life-long advocate of a Catholic third way turned away from Catholic socialism and Christian Democracy alike.[4] In the end, convinced that the third way had failed as a viable option of governance, the man who represented Poland's greatest hope for Catholic politics instead became a reluctant liberal.

Beyond social Catholicism

Throughout his life, Mazowiecki referred to the "social question" as the driving force behind his philosophy of political and social action.[5] The social teaching of the Roman Catholic Church crystallized in the late nineteenth century as a program of ameliorating the condition of the poorest of the poor, the industrial proletariat brought into existence by Europe's Industrial Revolution. The premise was that solidarity across class lines might reverse the atomization and anomie afflicting industrial societies; the question was how.[6]

From the vantage point of the Holy See, the bedrock of Catholic responses to the social question was Leo XIII's 1891 encyclical *Rerum novarum*. This document inspired a revolution in Catholic thought about politics and society. *Rerum novarum* echoed far and wide across the Catholic world, including the lands of partitioned Poland, which in 1918 were rejoined into an independent Polish state.[7]

Since the nineteenth century, Catholic thinkers and activists have used the broad heading "social Catholicism" to describe a diverse assortment of responses to "the industrialization process and its consequences in the social classes."[8] In the mid-twentieth-century – the era in which Mazowiecki came of age amidst war, occupation, and genocide – a generation of

4 Piotr H. Kosicki, "After 1989: The Life and Death of the Catholic Third Way," *TLS - Times Literary Supplement*, 13 December 2013.

5 See, e.g., Mazowiecki, *Rozdroża i wartości*, 195.

6 Paul Misner, *Social Catholicism in Europe: From the Onset of Industrialization to the First World War* (New York: Crossroad, 1991); Lex Heerma van Voss, Patrick Pasture and Jan De Maeyer, eds., *Between Cross and Class: Comparative Histories of Christian Labor in Europe, 1840–2000* (Bern: Peter Lang, 2005).

7 See, e.g., Antoni Szymański, *Poglądy demokracyi chrześcijańskiej we Francyi, 1892–1907* (Poznań: Księgarnia św. Wojciecha, 1910); Kosicki, *Catholics on the Barricades*, 21–61.

8 See, e.g., Misner, *Social Catholicism in Europe*, 3.

radical thinkers reversed the grammar of "social Catholicism," reframing Catholic social teaching as a matter of "Catholic socialism." France's André Mandouze and Poland's Wojciech Kętrzyński were not the first Catholic writers to use this phrase, but in their hands it took on a revolutionary meaning: not merely a Catholic approach to social justice, but a literal fusing of Catholicism and socialism.[9] As the Red Army guaranteed the rise to power of Soviet-backed communist parties across Central and Eastern Europe in 1944–1945, Catholics, too, wrestled with the implications of the social "revolution" that Marxists claimed to enact. The hotbed of postwar "Catholic socialism" in the region was the Polish lay movement known first by the name of its weekly journal *Dziś i Jutro* (Today and tomorrow), then from 1952 onward as PAX.[10] As I have demonstrated at length in my book *Catholics on the Barricades*, it was this organization that launched Tadeusz Mazowiecki's career in public life.

With the ascent of John XXIII to the papacy in 1958, the conceptual world of social Catholicism absorbed also his language of *aggiornamento* ("updating"). In Poland, *aggiornamento* inspired several generations of Catholic intellectuals – including Mazowiecki – to take up German Jesuit theologian Karl Rahner's call for an *offene Kirche* (an "open Church"), predicated on "inclusivism."[11] The long-time "social Catholic" agenda of fostering cross-class solidarity remained, but beginning in the 1960s the path was presumed to be not confessional politics, but the embrace of a secular, pluralistic ethics undergirded by "dialogue" and "dignity of the human person."

A young "Catholic socialist"

At face value, this genealogy of "social Catholicism" seems relatively straightforward. And yet any serious reflection on Catholic social teaching should question "Catholic socialism" as an apparent oxymoron. After all,

9 See, e.g., André Mandouze, "Prendre la main tendue," in *Les Chrétiens et la politique* (Paris: Temps Présent, 1948), 39–78; Wojciech Kętrzyński, "Konsekwencje encyklik społecznych," *Dziś i Jutro*, 6 June 1948. The term had originally come from *fin-de-siècle* critics of "social Catholicism," see, e.g., Francesco Saverio Nitti, *Il Socialismo cattolico* (Rome: L. Roux, 1891).

10 Kosicki, *Catholics on the Barricades*, 218–302; Mikołaj Stanisław Kunicki, *Between the Brown and the Red: Nationalism, Catholicism, and Communism in Twentieth-Century Poland – The Politics of Bolesław Piasecki* (Athens, OH: Ohio University Press, 2012), 77–110.

11 Karl Rahner, *Strukturwandel der Kirche als Aufgabe und Chance* (Vienna: Herder, 1972), 100; Piotr H. Kosicki, "Vatican II and Poland," in *Vatican II Behind the Iron Curtain*, ed. Piotr H. Kosicki (Washington, DC: Catholic University of America Press, 2016), 170–174.

the Holy See has been steadfast in its dismissal of collaboration, certainly with communism, but even with socialism, already since the papacy of Pius IX. Leo XIII's *Rerum novarum*, too, was directed against socialism, as was Pius XI's 1931 *Quadragesimo Anno*. Six years later, the same pontiff railed against "bolshevistic and atheistic Communism" in *Divini Redemptoris*. Finally, in 1949, Pius XII's Holy Office threatened excommunication against "any Catholic faithful professing anti-Christian doctrine as communists, and above all those who defend or propagate such doctrine."[12]

To identify as a "Catholic socialist" after 1949, then, was to challenge over a century of papal teaching, risking outright identification with the communist camp. And yet at no point in his life did Tadeusz Mazowiecki, a Catholic socialist, identify either as a Marxist or a communist. Quite the opposite – he remained proud of the traditionalism of his Catholic upbringing.[13] His father Bronisław, a local leader of Catholic Action in Mazowiecki's Mazovian hometown of Płock, raised the future prime minister in a mix of nationalist and social-Catholic traditions. In 1946, fresh out of high school, the nineteen-year-old Mazowiecki joined a Christian Democratic party – his first-ever political affiliation.

As a novice in public life, Tadeusz Mazowiecki quickly proved himself rather radical. But it was geopolitics, rather than family tradition, that conditioned his approach: he sought not to abandon social Catholicism, but to smuggle it into the thoroughly circumscribed political arena of early communist Poland. A whole generation born in the 1920s looked to help rebuild Poland without hiding the fact that they were Catholics; they wanted neither to hide at home, nor to take up arms against the new communist government, but instead to roll up their sleeves and ensure a visible Catholic presence in postwar Polish public life. Mazowiecki later explained that Catholic socialism "reached out to the young, offering them a way of getting involved in the new reality – something that everyone was seeking because the division [between communism and capitalism] seemed permanent. It seemed that Poland might be able to preserve a certain measure of distinctiveness, and so we should be searching for some kind of *modus vivendi*."[14] Just as a whole generation of young Catholic intellectuals in 1920s Western Europe was caught "between Maurras and Mar-

12 Decree of the Holy Office of the Roman Catholic Church, 1 July 1949, in Yvon Tranvouez, *Catholiques et communistes: La crise du progressisme chrétien, 1950–1955* (Paris: Cerf, 2000), 42.

13 Tadeusz Mazowiecki, "Co wyniosłem z Płocka," *Więź* (2012) 4: 77; Brzeziecki, *Tadeusz Mazowiecki*, 11–22.

14 Mazowiecki, interview, 25 January 2006, quoted at Kosicki, *Catholics on the Barricades*, 112.

itain," young postwar Polish intellectuals were caught two decades later "between Thorez and Christ."[15]

For these Catholics in their early-to-mid-twenties, the idea was simple: to chart a "third way" between capitalism and communism, while assuring an autonomous space for Catholicism in a world defined by Marxist "revolution." Only the pursuit of revolution in a socialist order – they reasoned – gave Catholics the chance of building a more just society. Believing that the Gospels and *Das Kapital* could be brought into constructive partnership, Mazowiecki and his fellow postwar young intellectuals fashioned themselves as "Catholic socialists."[16]

In the summer of 1946, Tadeusz Mazowiecki had declared himself a Christian Democrat, enrolling in the Christian Labor Party (*Stronnictwo Pracy,* SP) and volunteering to lead its youth organization in Płock. Within two months, however, the party had imploded nationwide. SP's president was Karol Popiel, who had spent World War II in London as a leading figure in the Polish emigré government. In June 1945, Popiel had returned to Poland, inspired by the Yalta Agreements to believe that, under his leadership, Polish Christian Democracy could guarantee that communists would make good on the "free and fair elections" that Stalin had promised.[17] Instead, the communists prevented SP from holding party congresses and used a small faction within the party to coopt it and strip the party of its confessional Catholic identity. When Popiel suspended SP's activities in 1946, his pro-communist colleagues refused to yield. Ultimately, fearing for his freedom, Popiel returned into exile, where he transformed Polish Christian Democracy into a major front for American Cold War efforts to influence young intellectuals behind the Iron Curtain.[18] On Polish soil, however, the postwar attempt at reviving Christian Democracy had failed.

For the young Warsaw University law student Tadeusz Mazowiecki, only one option remained: *Dziś i Jutro*. Although its founder Bolesław Piasecki was infamous for having led a fascist organization in the 1930s, there was no other choice for young Polish Catholics seeking to join in Po-

15 Philippe Chenaux, *Entre Maurras et Maritain: Une génération intellectuelle catholique (1920–1930)* (Paris: Cerf, 1999); Lucien Pélissier, "Mounier et les communistes," in *Emmanuel Mounier ou le combat du juste* (Bordeaux: Guy Ducros, 1968), 105.

16 Kosicki, *Catholics on the Barricades*, 218–256.

17 Karol Popiel, *Od Brześcia do "Polonii"* (London: Odnowa, 1967), 8.

18 See, respectively, Jarosław Rabiński, "The Elimination of Christian Democracy in Poland after World War II," in *Christian Democracy across the Iron Curtain: Europe Redefined*, ed. Piotr H. Kosicki and Sławomir Łukasiewicz (London: Palgrave Macmillan, 2018), 153–176; Piotr H. Kosicki, "Christian Democracy's Global Cold War," in *Christian Democracy across the Iron Curtain*, ed. Kosicki and Łukasiewicz, 221–256.

land's postwar reconstruction without hiding their spiritual and intellectual commitments as Catholics. Mazowiecki joined Piasecki's movement in 1948, rapidly ascending through its ranks as a writer, editor, and recruiter. In the late 1940s, he read deeply in European Catholic thought and worked systematically to develop his own coherent philosophy of social and political action. By 1950, Mazowiecki had embraced Catholic socialism, and this is why he wrote in 1950, "It is *the complete development and integration of personalism into the content of the socialist revolution that ought to endow Catholic thought with the proper form.* For it is the struggle for personalism in a socialist order that falls to us as Catholics."[19]

Mazowiecki was only twenty-three when he wrote these words. But what he was reading in those years were canonical philosophical tracts; in response, he himself produced reasoned, well-informed philosophical reflections. In 1951, at the age of twenty-four, he went beyond producing articles for *Dziś i Jutro*'s eponymous weekly journal, undertaking a book-length project. His goal was to produce a blueprint for harmonizing Catholicism and Marxism under the umbrella of Poland's "socialist revolution." Mazowiecki succeeded in writing approximately sixty pages before he realized that his movement's publishing house was not, in fact, going to issue the book.[20]

From his late teenage years onward, Mazowiecki took part in both Polish and European debates. Paradoxically, he became more engaged in transnational conversations as Stalinism's hold over the Soviet Bloc tightened between 1948 and 1953. The young Pole was most interested in path-breaking French tracts written in the 1930s and 1940s: some with Catholic authors, like the Dominican theologian Yves Congar and the lay philosopher Emmanuel Mounier; others by communists, like Roger Garaudy. Mazowiecki did not know French, but his first wife Krystyna Kulesza systematically translated these tracts into Polish for him. It was through the devoted labors of his bed-ridden wife – who perished from consumption in the first year of their marriage – that Mazowiecki developed an intimacy with mid-century French thought.

Despite Mazowiecki's extensive intellectual engagement with the world outside Poland, he embraced the most paradoxical feature of *Dziś*

19 Tadeusz Mazowiecki, "Kierunek myśli społecznej," *Dziś i Jutro*, 2 July 1950. Emphasis in the original. See also Kosicki, *Catholics on the Barricades*, 252.

20 Tadeusz Mazowiecki, "Marksizm a personalizm wobec zagadnienia osoby ludzkiej", unpublished manuscript, May 1951, Archiwum Katolickiego Stowarzyszenia *Civitas Christiana* (Archives of the *Civitas Christiana* Catholic Association, Warsaw), VI/189; Janusz Zabłocki, "Mazowiecki mój przeciwnik (10): Dni-burze, o których wiesz tylko ty," *Ład*, 6 January 1991.

i Jutro's Catholic socialism: an aggressive ethnonationalism bred by the horrors of wartime occupation and mass violence. Anti-Germanism united the full range of postwar Polish Catholics – from the anti-communist underground through the Catholic socialists, from bishops to the lowliest of laymen. This animus even turned Polish Catholics against their coreligionists, including suspected "counter-revolutionaries" at home and Catholics identified with the American Cold War camp abroad. Christian Democrats became suspect on both counts.

On the pretext of curbing German influence in Polish public life, Mazowiecki, too, contributed to divisions within the Church. Prior to 1945, the Silesian city of Wrocław had been called Breslau, and – despite a sizable Polish-language minority – it had long been under German (Prussian) control.[21] Together with Pomerania and the city of Gdańsk, Lower Silesia was transferred from German to Polish jurisdiction by Allied agreement at Potsdam in August-September 1945. These were Poland's new western lands – propagandistically termed the "Recovered Territories" – taken from Germany as compensation for the loss of prewar Poland's easternmost third, which the Soviet Union had annexed.

In the summer of 1953, PAX relocated Mazowiecki to Wrocław with a simple but crucial mission: to assure a Catholic-socialist voice in the postwar Polish project of "polonizing" the formerly German lands. As founding co-editor of the new *Wrocław Catholic Weekly* (*Wrocławski Tygodnik Katolicki*, WTK), the twenty-six-year-old assembled an intrepid young staff that published articles insisting on the "eternal" Polishness of Silesia and Pomerania, as well as advice columns and comics tailored to the experience of Polish settlers recently transplanted from the east.[22] Thanks above all to Mazowiecki, WTK was a great success.

Polish communist propaganda made great hay of the argument that wartime German fascism was alive and well in the postwar – not only in the Federal Republic of Germany, but also the United States. In advance of WTK's fifth issue, the editor received a press pass to cover the most notable Polish show trial of the year, in which Kielce bishop Czesław Kaczmarek and four subordinates were convicted of espionage on behalf of the United States, the Holy See, and West Germany.[23] Mazowiecki wrote Kaczmarek

21 Gregor Thum, *Uprooted: How Breslau became Wrocław during the Century of Expulsions*, trans. Tom Lampert and Allison Brown (Princeton: Princeton University Press, 2011), 53–104.

22 See, e.g., Tadeusz Mazowiecki, "W sprawie Niemiec," *Wrocławski Tygodnik Katolicki*, 20 September 1953; Aleksander Rogalski, "Kościół na Śląsku w XI i XII w.," *Wrocławski Tygodnik Katolicki*, 4 October 1953.

23 Jan Śledzianowski, *Ksiądz Czesław Kaczmarek – biskup kielecki 1895–1963* (Kielce: Kuria Diecezjalna, 1991), 225–305.

into the communist narrative as both villain and exemplar, lamenting, "This is why we not only express our sorrow but indeed renounce the erroneous views of Bishop Kaczmarek, which have driven him to sabotage People's Poland." In Mazowiecki's rendering, the benighted bishop was an agent of Konrad Adenauer's "neo-Hitlerite Wehrmacht."[24]

Yet Mazowiecki's 1953 essay is no simple propaganda piece. Kaczmarek's presumed crimes, after all, did not exist in a discursive vacuum, but were instead painted by prosecutors as part of an international conspiracy of American and German crimes – against peace and against humanity. In the very year of Kaczmarek's trial, the European Coal and Steel Community came into being, the legacy of a plan announced by France's Christian Democratic foreign minister Robert Schuman. In the eyes of Catholic socialists on both sides of the Iron Curtain, Franco-German cooperation was but a fig leaf for German revanchism. The specter of (West) Germany's rehabilitation was at the forefront of young Catholic socialists' minds – along with the understanding that Christian Democrats were to blame.

Tadeusz Mazowiecki ultimately came to regret the role that he played in fomenting ethnonational hatred in the name of Catholic politics, but it took the better part of the Stalinist era for him to excise nationalism from his own Catholic socialism. Even after he abandoned PAX in 1955, the Polish activist continued to believe that the transnational Christian Democratic vision of an integrated European political economy would inevitably lead to war with the Soviet Bloc.

Aggiornamento

Mazowiecki's 1955 departure from PAX began his gradual evolution toward the status of a leading anti-communist dissident, co-founder of the *Solidarność* (Solidarity) trade-union movement, and de-communizing prime minister of Poland. His path paralleled the progression of the Soviet Bloc as a whole through the dashed hopes of de-Stalinization in the mid-1950s, the shattered illusions of the Prague Spring in 1968, the global turn to détente and human rights in the 1970s, and the growth of animosity between working classes and the communist establishments that claimed to govern in their name.[25] Over the quarter century separating Poland's

24 Tadeusz Mazowiecki, "Wnioski," *Wrocławski Tygodnik Katolicki*, 27 September 1953.

25 See, e.g., David Ost, *Solidarity and the Politics of Anti-Politics: Opposition and Reform in Poland since 1968* (Philadelphia: Temple University Press, 1990).

de-Stalinization from the birth of *Solidarność*, Mazowiecki enjoyed a career in public activism that was nothing short of miraculous for a Catholic intellectual in a communist-run country.

In broad terms, he pursued three entangled trajectories: publishing, national politics, and transnational networking. Together with a half-dozen other lay activists, Mazowiecki co-founded in October 1956 a network of discussion circles known as the Catholic Intelligentsia Clubs (*Kluby Inteligencji Katolickiej*, KIK), described by one of Mazowiecki's colleagues as "a set of educational circles, an open university, and finally a kind of research institute."[26] The clubs became one of several features of the new lay movement called Znak (Sign).

These were all fruits of de-Stalinization, with the approval coming personally from reinstated communist general secretary Władysław Gomułka. As a reward for Catholic intellectuals' support, Gomułka also invited Znak to put up candidates for election to the Polish parliament. It was under Znak's auspices that Mazowiecki co-founded the monthly journal *Więź* (Bond) in 1958, became an MP (1961–1972), and forged transnational partnerships through regular travels to Western Europe. Znak created an autonomous space for Catholic intellectuals in communist Poland to shape the world around them, independently of the communist agenda.[27] Nonetheless, Znak's autonomy never translated into party politics. Mazowiecki, in particular, viewed Catholic politics with suspicion. In this respect, the failure of the Christian Democratic party of his teenage years, as well as the fear ingrained in him under Stalinism that European integration would push the world into nuclear war, forever marred Mazowiecki's political imagination.

With his Znak colleagues, the Pole traveled extensively back and forth across the Iron Curtain throughout the 1950s and 1960s, exploring Austria, Belgium, France, Italy, Switzerland, and West Germany.[28] It was none other than Karol Popiel's Christian Democratic emigrés who made these travels possible. Chosen by the US-backed Free Europe Committee's Exile Rela-

26 Stefan Wilkanowicz, 3 October 1965, quoted in Andrzej Friszke, *Oaza na Kopernika: Klub Inteligencji Katolickiej, 1956–1989* (Warsaw: Biblioteka WIĘZI, 1997), 59.

27 Piotr H. Kosicki, "L'avènement des intellectuels catholiques: Le mensuel *Więź* et les conséquences polonaises du personnalisme mounierien," *Vingtième Siècle: Revue d'histoire*, 102 (2009): 31–46; Stefania Szlek-Miller, "Catholic Personalism and Pluralist Democracy in Poland," *Canadian Slavonic Papers* 25, no. 3 (1983): 425–439; Małgorzata Strzelecka, *Między minimalizmem a maksymalizmem: Dylematy ideowe Stanisława Stommy i Janusza Zabłockiego* (Toruń: UMK, 2015), 133–206.

28 See his passport applications at, e.g., Archiwum Instytutu Pamięci Narodowej (Archives of the Institute of National Remembrance, Warsaw), BU 1533/7667, 3–20.

tions Division to facilitate "counter-penetration" of the Soviet Bloc, the SP exiles provided funds and suggested candidates to NGOs like Pax Romana and political parties like the Democrazia Cristiana (DC), which then invited and hosted Znak activists in Western Europe.[29]

The Free Europe Committee leadership wanted to challenge communist regimes by exposing youth to the "free world." For the exiled Christian Democrats of SP, meanwhile, this was their last best hope to train new "cadres" of Polish Christian Democracy that might rebuild the party on Polish soil. A few Znak activists – like Mazowiecki's one-time friend and *Więź* co-founder Janusz Zabłocki – met SP's expectations, entering into extensive contacts with Western European Christian Democrats and vowing to transplant Christian Democracy back to Poland.[30] Most of Znak's activists, however, were like Mazowiecki: fascinated by their experiences in the "West," but wary of exiles and Western European politicians alike. In part, this reflected a desire not to be drawn into the international games of intelligence agencies – on either side in the Cold War – but also a genuine belief that Christian Democracy represented the way of the past.

Despite his commitment to Catholic social teaching, for Tadeusz Mazowiecki, the secular implications of Church doctrine pointed not to party politics, but instead to new forms of engagement by laity in the life of the "modern world." Although he was a child of World War II, the era that best expressed Mazowiecki's deepest intellectual and spiritual aspirations was the papacy of John XXIII. *Aggiornamento* and Karl Rahner's "open Catholicism" embodied the essence of Christian teachings on social justice.[31]

One of the defining moments of Mazowiecki's life was the June 1963 funeral of John XXIII, for which he was able to travel to Rome, having already traveled to Belgium for a conference organized by the French Catholic publication *Informations catholiques internationales*.[32] The pairing of these two events speaks volumes. The "spirit of Vatican II" tasked Catholic laity with exploring new forms of engagement in secular life, through the studied infusion of Catholic teachings into the realms of publishing, trade unionism, and international development. In Mazowiecki's mind, de-Stalinization and decolonization represented the defining issues of the

29 See, e.g., Paweł Ziętara, "Christian Democrats across the Iron Curtain," in *Christian Democracy across the Iron Curtain*, ed. Kosicki and Łukasiewicz, 177–220; Kosicki, "Christian Democracy's Global Cold War."

30 Janusz Zabłocki, *Dzienniki*, I: *1956–1965* (Warsaw: IPN-KŚZpNP, 2008), 492.

31 See, e.g., "Motywy, dążenia i braki postawy otwartej - dyskusja wokół książki Juliusza Eski *Kościół otwarty*," *Więź* 81 (1965): 19–46.

32 Tadeusz Mazowiecki, interview, 9 June 2006.

day for Catholics, posing questions for which Christian Democrats did not seem to have compelling answers.[33]

The one exception was Florentine mayor Giorgio La Pira. This leading figure of postwar Italian Christian Democracy was a man of the Left, identified with the radical *dossettiani* faction of the DC.[34] Time and again, La Pira bucked his party's agenda in the 1950s and 1960s in both national and international affairs: he pushed for ever greater rights for organized labor; he traveled to Moscow; he even wrote to Władysław Gomułka urging the communist to make Poland "the grand bridge that joins the West to the East."[35] In Mazowiecki's mind, La Pira had struck the perfect balance between principled commitments to Catholicism and a workable politics respectful of secular pluralism.

The two men first met in the summer of 1959 when Znak brought Mazowiecki to Florence. Four years later, however, they had the opportunity to speak at length at the Brussels conference, where both were among the headline speakers. These conversations deeply marked the future Polish prime minister – particularly the ease with which the Italian statesman reconciled "progress" with calls to evangelize the postcolonial world and to remember the obligation to protect the dignity of the human person ("the temple of the living God"). As La Pira put it, the bottom line for Catholic laity in the era of *aggiornamento* was to "launch dialogues between East and West; North and South; and the sons of Abraham, Israel, and Ishmael."[36]

Giorgio La Pira's version of dialogue inspired a new turn in Mazowiecki's political philosophy. Already in the early 1950s, he had argued that Catholics behind the Iron Curtain must work to broker successful dialogue between Catholics and Marxists. In 1963, he took this a step further. Invited to Brussels to speak on behalf of "the socialist countries," Mazowiecki defined dialogue between believers and non-believers, Catholics and Marxists, as the great ethical calling of Soviet Bloc Catholics. The challenge was to work out a "method of coexistence in which both sides constantly and reciprocally act upon one another, instead of turning their backs on

33 Piotr H. Kosicki, "The Catholic 1968: Poland, Social Justice, and the Global Cold War," *Slavic Review* 77, no. 3 (2018): 638–660.

34 Gerd-Rainer Horn, *Western European Liberation Theology: The First Wave (1924–1959)* (Oxford: Oxford University Press, 2008), 120–125; Massimo de Giuseppe, *Giorgio La Pira: Un sindaco e le vie della pace* (Milan: Centro Ambrosiano, 2001).

35 Giorgio La Pira to Władysław Gomułka, 10 April 1966, Archivio della Fondazione Giorgio La Pira (Florence), Box 10/6inse2/40.

36 Giorgio La Pira, "La vocation prophétique du laïc," in *Mission et liberté des laïcs dans le monde* (Paris: Cerf, 1964), 126, 130–131; Mazowiecki, interview, 25 January 2006.

each other and shutting themselves off."[37] "Dialogue" was the key to adapting Catholic socialism to the challenges of a global Church increasingly focused on international development and human rights. Mazowiecki was responding at once to Polish Marxists, to a Church of *aggiornamento*, and to radicals like La Pira.

Catholic and socialist, but anti-communist

As the 1960s gave way to the 1970s, Mazowiecki found it harder to pursue this kind of ecumenical agenda in communist Poland. In the Soviet Bloc, the year 1968 brought more than the brutal suppression of the Prague Spring. In Poland, March 1968 witnessed nationwide student demonstrations shut down by civic militia with truncheons and water cannons. Political repressions followed, and many of Mazowiecki's closest Marxist interlocutors – most notably, the revisionist philosopher Leszek Kołakowski – lost their public positions and went into exile.[38]

Two years later, following the bloody suppression of worker protests in the shipbuilding city of Gdańsk in December 1970, Mazowiecki himself fell into disfavor. After he called for an investigation into militia violence, the communist party barred him from standing for reelection to parliament.[39] Joining forces with the "secular left" that had protested in 1968, Mazowiecki and many Znak colleagues turned Poland's Catholic journals into ecumenical forums for anti-regime opposition. After communist Poland signed the Helsinki Final Act in 1975, Tadeusz Mazowiecki became one of its most vocal exponents, taking the regime to task again and again for infringing on the human rights of protesting workers and intellectuals.[40] At the same time, he became an ardent advocate of Polish-German reconciliation, developing extensive contacts not only within the Social Democratic Party of the Federal Republic of Germany, but also with Christian Democrats like future West German president Richard von Weizsäcker.[41]

37 Tadeusz Mazowiecki, "En pays socialiste," in *Mission et liberté des laïcs dans le monde*, 43.

38 See, e.g., Jerzy Eisler, "March 1968 in Poland," in *1968: The World Transformed*, ed. Carole Fink, Philipp Gassert and Detlef Junker (Cambridge: Cambridge University Press, 1998), 237–252.

39 Brzeziecki, *Tadeusz Mazowiecki*, 236–242.

40 This is the Catholic counterpart to the story told in Samuel Moyn, *The Last Utopia: Human Rights in History* (Cambridge, MA: Belknap Press of Harvard University Press, 2010), 120–175.

41 "'Für uns Protestanten waren die polnischen katholischen Beiträge sowohl im deutsch-polnischen als auch im europäischen Verhältnis von großem Gewicht': Gespräch mit Richard von Weizsäcker," in *"Wir vergeben und bitten um Vergebung": Der Briefwechsel der polnischen und deutschen Bischöfe von 1965 und seine Wirkung* , ed. Basil Kerski, Thomas Kycia and Robert Żurek (Osnabrück: Fibre, 2006).

By the late 1970s, Tadeusz Mazowiecki was one of the leading Catholic anti-communists behind the Iron Curtain. And yet, this did not mean that he had turned away from Catholic socialism. He first abandoned nationalism, then loyalty to the Polish communist state. Nonetheless, Mazowiecki continued to believe that Marxism had important lessons to offer Catholics seeking to make good on the social teaching of their Church.

In this conviction, he followed – perhaps paradoxically – on the writings among others of his friend Karol Cardinal Wojtyła, who in 1978 was elected Pope John Paul II. In his youth, Wojtyła had written approvingly of the French worker-priest experiment, and his philosophical work in phenomenology and ethics engaged seriously with a range of socialist thought.[42] To Mazowiecki, the young pope from Wadowice had revealed the ethical imperative for Christians in the modern world: to fight for the betterment of the secular world without presupposing its confessionalization. This is how Mazowiecki arrived at an aconfessional formula for Christian human rights, published in *Esprit* in 1978: "there are many ways of fighting for and serving the rights of man, but there is one thing that a Christian can never allow himself: wherever human liberty and dignity are oppressed and wherever one fights for the rights of man, a Christian cannot allow himself the gesture of Pilate."[43]

In August 1980, Mazowiecki's prominence as a defender of human rights behind the Iron Curtain made him a natural choice when Gdańsk electrician and strike leader Lech Wałęsa decided to invite intellectuals to advise him on how to negotiate with the regime. Mazowiecki co-founded the Solidarity trade-union movement, in which he saw the perfect expression of a Catholic third way between capitalism and communism: at once Catholic-inspired and deconfessionalized (following the example he had first seen in Belgium and France in the 1960s), driven by the promise of social justice without the ideological baggage of Marxism.[44]

As Solidarity spread across Poland in 1980–1981, growing its membership to more than one-quarter of the Polish population, Mazowiecki nonetheless began to lose faith in its potential as an exemplar for the Catholic

42 Kosicki, *Catholics on the Barricades*, 189–217; Rocco Buttiglione, *Karol Wojtyła: The Thought of the Man Who became Pope John Paul II*, trans. Paolo Guietti and Francesca Murphy (Grand Rapids, MI: Eerdmans, 1997), 293–302.

43 Tadeusz Mazowiecki, "Protester et éduquer," *Esprit* no. 7–8 (1978): 78–83.

44 Tadeusz Mazowiecki, *Rok 1989 i lata następne* (Warsaw: Prószyński i s-ka, 2012), 491–495; Jan Kułakowski and Leszek Jesień, *Spotkania na Bagateli: Polska, Europa, świat* (Warsaw: Rhetos, 2004), 57–84; Bronisław Geremek, interview, 2 July 2007.

third way.[45] On the one hand, John Paul II endorsed *Solidarność*: his September 1981 encyclical *Laborem Exercens* spelled out a model of political economy that corresponded to the founding precepts of the Polish movement. And yet, for Mazowiecki and other intellectuals standing on the movement's margins, watching its new leadership struggle to define the proper limits of Solidarity's role in politics and society, the union brought more dilemmas than solutions. In December 1981, communist leader Wojciech Jaruzelski imposed martial law, banned Solidarity, and imprisoned or interned its activists, including Mazowiecki. Martial law froze in time the concerns that had begun to gnaw at Mazowiecki.[46]

A Christian and a democrat, but...

And so, just as catastrophic economic decline in communist Poland met Mikhail Gorbachev's loosening grip on the Bloc in the late 1980s, Mazowiecki was at a crossroads in his political and philosophical commitments. The life-long Catholic socialist remained loyal to *Solidarność*. When Polish communists agreed to round-table discussions in February 1989 to relegalize the union, Mazowiecki was Wałęsa's immediate choice to negotiate with the communists.[47] After he succeeded, Mazowiecki resumed the post he had held eight years earlier, as editor of the *Solidarity Weekly* magazine (*Tygodnik Solidarność*).

And yet, when Mazowiecki received the greatest surprise of his life in August 1989 in the form of an invitation to become communist Poland's first non-communist prime minister, Catholic socialism failed him. Although the round-table negotiations had included an entire host of economists who shared Mazowiecki's third way sympathies, he chose a completely different direction for his government. Lacking any economic training, he relied on the advice of close collaborators from *Solidarność* who did not share his background in Catholic philosophy. Rather than look to Mounier or Maritain, his trusted economic advisor Waldemar Kuczyński – who spent most of the 1980s in Paris – heralded a more controlled liberal turn. Under Kuczyński's influence, Mazowiecki decided to eject

45 On Mazowiecki's evolving views of the dilemma faced by Solidarity in 1981, see Brzeziecki, *Tadeusz Mazowiecki*, 299–319.

46 Tadeusz Mazowiecki, *Internowanie* (London: Aneks, 1983).

47 Alojzy Orszulik, *Czas przełomu: Notatki ks. Alojzego Orszulika z rozmów z władzami PRL w latach 1981-1989* (Warsaw: Obserwator/Apostolicum, 2006), 462–466; Czesław Kiszczak, interview, 21 June 2007.

both the state and Solidarity's old guiding idea of *autogestion* from the heart of Poland's political economy. In his own words, Mazowiecki went looking for "his own Erhard."[48]

The invocation of Konrad Adenauer's long-time economy minister was both revealing and misleading. At face value, it sounded as though Mazowiecki had, after four decades, returned to the Christian Democracy of his teenage years. Certainly, the new prime minister became fascinated with the political choices made by Adenauer and Erhard at the launching of the Federal Republic of Germany in 1949. Mazowiecki had clearly disavowed the anti-Germanism of his years in PAX, and Polish-German reconciliation became one of his top priorities. Nurturing a warm relationship with West Germany's Christian Democratic chancellor Helmut Kohl, Mazowiecki succeeded in securing German recognition of Poland's long-disputed western border.[49] Likewise, the Poles developed cordial relations with Austrian Christian Democrats such as ÖVP leader and future vice-chancellor Erhard Busek.[50]

And yet, Mazowiecki's programmatic aversion to Christian Democracy never dissipated. The fascination with Adenauer and Erhard had been less about ideology and more about their willingness to pursue aggressive reforms in a time of transition. After all, the liberal Erhard had developed his own sort of third way in political economy – the social market economy – which became a staple of Christian Democracy's program for postwar Western Europe. Four decades after the birth of West Germany, Mazowiecki chose Leszek Balcerowicz as his finance minister and deputy prime minister. For his part, Balcerowicz made no pretense of building a social market economy, instead pursuing aggressive privatization at the expense of the welfare state.[51]

The prime minister parted ways definitively with Christian Democracy in March 1990, at a Budapest meeting of the European Democrat Union. In 1988–1989, a handful of surviving Christian Democrats from SP had reactivated the Christian Labor Party on Polish soil, but factionalism and confusion ensued, and the party made a historic miscalculation, declining

48 See, e.g., Waldemar Kuczyński, *Zwierzenia zausznika* (Warsaw: BGW, 1992), 56, 84; Leszek Balcerowicz with Jerzy Koźmiński, *800 dni: Szok kontrolowany* (Warsaw: BGW, 1992), 10.

49 See, e.g., Aleksander Hall, "Polska," in *Architekt wolnej Polski: Świat wartości i idei Tadeusza Mazowieckiego*, ed. Aleksander Hall (Kraków: Znak, 2017), 75–88.

50 Erhard Busek, *Mitteleuropa: Eine Spurensicherung* (Vienna: K & S, 1997), 48–53. See also Helmut Wohnout's chapter in this volume.

51 See, e.g., Tadeusz Kowalik, *From Solidarity to Sellout: The Restoration of Capitalism in Poland*, trans. Eliza Lewandowska (New York: Monthly Review Press, 2012), 107–110.

to side with *Solidarność* in the round-table negotiations.[52] Shut out of Solidarity's parliamentary revolution in the summer of 1989, SP was no more than an afterthought to the Christian Democrats of Western Europe. West Germany's CDU refused even to consider offering financial assistance to SP.[53] And so it was to Mazowiecki, instead of SP, that Helmut Kohl offered the full support and financial resources of Western Europe's Christian Democratic parties in order to rebuild Christian Democracy in Poland. The Polish prime minister rebuffed his German counterpart, however, with the dictum: "I am a Christian and a democrat, but not a Christian Democrat."[54]

This was not the final word on Christian Democracy in Poland. The Center Alliance (*Porozumienie Centrum*), the first political party founded by Law and Justice leader Jarosław Kaczyński, joined the EDU and actively participated in the union from 1991 to 1993.[55] Even Mazowiecki corresponded with the EDU following his departure from office in 1991, and his new political party (Democratic Union, later renamed Freedom Union) sent pamphlet literature to EDU headquarters and met with its representatives.[56] In the end, however, no electorally viable Christian Democratic party emerged in post-communist Poland.[57]

The greatest opportunity for political Catholicism in Poland in the second half of the twentieth century had rested with Tadeusz Mazowiecki. The prime minister who shepherded Poland from communism to liberal democracy had begun his career in public life as a Christian Democrat, yet after 1946 he never again considered Christian Democracy a viable option. He ultimately shed his fears of West Germany and European integration, prioritizing as prime minister his country's reconciliation to both. Loyal as he was to Catholic social teaching, however, Mazowiecki resisted throughout his public career the belief that Catholic social teaching should translate into programmatic politics and ideology. In his travels back and forth across the Iron Curtain in the 1950s and 1960s, Poland's future

52 See, e.g., Dominika Sozańska, *Chrześcijańska Demokracja w Polsce: Przyczyny słabości i szanse rozwoju* (Kraków: AFM, 2011), 119–120.

53 See Alexander Brakel's chapter in this volume.

54 Mazowiecki, interview, 25 January 2006; Brzeziecki, *Tadeusz Mazowiecki*, 471.

55 Jarosław Kaczyński to Andreas Khol, 7 October 1993, Archiv des Karl von Vogelsang-Instituts (AKVI, Vienna), European Democrat Union (EDU) Collection, Polen - L - PC (Sept. 1991 – 1995/96). See also Helmut Wohnout's chapter in this volume.

56 See, e.g., Tadeusz Mazowiecki to Andreas Khol, 24 April 1992, AKVI, EDU Collection, Polen - Ł - PC (Sept. 1991 – 1995/96); Piotr Nowina-Konopka to Andreas Khol, 14 September 1995, AKVI, EDU Collection, Polen - L - PC (Sept. 1991 – 1995/96).

57 Tim Bale and Aleks Szczerbiak, "Explaining the Absence of Christian Democracy in Contemporary Poland," in *Christian Democracy across the Iron Curtain*, ed. Kosicki and Łukasiewicz, 343–410.

prime minister rejected the mainstream of Western European Christian Democracy in favor of the radical *avant-garde* of Catholic lay activism. By 1980, Mazowiecki had established himself as an anti-communist dissident, but he remained committed to "Catholic socialism."

Paradoxically, it was *Solidarność* that dashed his hopes for a third way. When he became head of government in 1989, Mazowiecki broke with both statism and Catholic socialism, becoming a reluctant liberal. In so doing, he virtually guaranteed that, freed of its Soviet Bloc shackles, the most Catholic country in post-1989 Europe would not turn to Christian Democracy.

9

HUNGARY: A DECISIVE TRANSITION - BUT A REVOLUTION?

Anton Pelinka

The political transformation in Central and Eastern Europe – a transition from one-party dictatorship to pluralistic democracy – was a decisive victory for democracy, understood as majority rule, free competition between two or more parties, guarantees for the basic rights of minorities, and an independent judiciary. This development was as dramatic as the establishment of liberal democracies in Western Europe after the defeat of Nazi Germany.

Like 1945, the transition in 1989 had a national dimension. Starting with the Polish elections in June 1989, in all communist countries the communist rule imploded under circumstances that significantly differed, from Tirana to East Berlin, but the overall phenomenon was predicated on the transformation in the USSR itself. The attempted transformations in the GDR in 1953, in Hungary in 1956, and in Czechoslovakia in 1968 could not succeed because Moscow crushed those attempts by military means. And even in Poland, the end of power sharing between *Solidarność* and the communists in 1990 was the product of strong pressure that came from Moscow.

When a new generation had come to power within the framework of the Marxist-Leninist system in Moscow and within the leadership of the Communist Party of the Soviet Union, everything started to change. The "Gorbachev factor" opened the door for reforms in all communist countries in Europe – directly, or indirectly even in countries that were not under immediate Soviet control, like Albania and Yugoslavia.[1] The transformation of Central and Eastern Europe started at the center of an empire that had not permitted transformations at the periphery.

Within the member states of the Warsaw Pact, the communist leaders of the less totalitarian countries – Poland and Hungary – responded

1 Archie Brown, *The Gorbachev Factor* (Oxford: Oxford University Press, 1997).

rather favorably to the signals sent from Moscow beginning in 1985.[2] In Poland, the repressions of the freedoms that had been won in 1980–1981 had never been as severe as in Hungary after 1956. The Catholic Church had long been allowed a certain degree of autonomy in communist Poland, and the Catholic umbrella for civil society in Poland persisted for the most part even through martial law and the remainder of the 1980s. In Hungary, János Kádár's regime (his "Goulash communism") had instituted economic reforms that led to an improvement of the economic situation of the average Hungarians. The communist leaders in Poland and Hungary were Gorbachev's most important partners in his attempt to liberalize the communist regimes.[3] It was Poland first and Hungary second that took the first steps toward transition by introducing "round tables," giving the (until then not yet recognized) opposition forces some degree of official legal standing.

The specifics of Hungary's situation

However the transition from communist one-party system to multi-party system in 1989 is best described – it was not a revolution, at least not a revolution like the transition in France in 1799 or in Russia in 1919 had been. It was a non-violent regime change, within a geopolitical framework, defined by the end of the Cold War and the USSR's decision to accept defeat. Hungary's old political elite, still following the signals coming from Moscow and realizing that the old system could not be sustained any longer, negotiated with the (until 1989 not officially legal) opposition forces about how to engineer the transformation.

This transformation was not a specific Hungarian development. It followed a script, written by political, economic, and social necessities accepted by the Soviet core that had for such a long time defended the one-party dictatorship. Without the transformation that had started in Moscow in 1985 and without the end of the Brezhnev Doctrine, the transformation in Hungary would have not been possible – not in 1989, at least. In that respect, the transformation in Hungary was not different from the transformations in other Central and Eastern European countries – and very similar to the Polish case. For all of the cases in Central and Eastern Europe's political transitions after 1989, Ágnes Heller has highlighted one

2 Robert Service, *The End of the Cold War, 1985–1991* (London: Pan Books, 2015), esp. 314–318.
3 William Taubman, *Gorbachev: His Life and Times* (New York: W.W. Norton, 2017), 480–486.

decisive factor: "after 1989, the political class which took over from the former ruling party had zero practice in democratic politics."[4]

This did not mean that there were not specific Hungarian aspects visible in the process of transformation. Hungary was in a unique geographic situation. In contrast to Poland, it had a common border with a non-communist state – and the impact of the Hungarian-Austrian border played a significant role in 1989. Also, in contrast to the ČSSR and Romania, the Hungarian communist party – the Hungarian Socialist Workers' Party (MSZP) – had accepted Gorbachev's leadership from the very beginning of *glasnost* and *perestroika*. The combination of geography and the pro-Gorbachev attitude of Hungary's communist rulers had its particular impact in August 1989, when the Hungarian government decided – against the protests of the communist GDR government, but with the tacit agreement of the USSR – to open Hungary's border to Austria for GDR citizens. This resulted in the escape of East Germans, who had come to Hungary as tourists, to West Germany via Austria.[5] This was the beginning of the fall of the Iron Curtain – a month before the fall of the Wall in Berlin. In many ways, the example on the Hungarian-Austrian border made the end of the Soviet Empire unavoidable. In that respect, the transformation in Hungary had pan-European consequences.[6]

In contrast to the GDR, Hungary had to deal with the end of a political system – and not with the end of nationhood. And, as opposed to Yugoslavia, a post-communist Hungary was not in danger of being destroyed by ethnonational conflicts raging out of control. Meanwhile, in the GDR immediately, and in Yugoslavia not too much later, transitions destroyed the nation. That being said, Hungary did have an ethnonational problem, in a different sense than Yugoslavia: it was the only communist country in Central and Eastern Europe that had reason to feel victimized by the post-Versailles and post-Trianon order of 1919 and 1920, a geopolitical arrangement that had put a significant number of ethnic Hungarians under the rule of other nations and was responsible for giving rise to a victimization narrative.[7] The perception that Hungary was specifically pun-

4 Ágnes Heller, "Twenty Years After 1989," in *The End and the Beginning: The Revolutions of 1989 and the Resurgence of History*, ed. Vladimir Tismaneanu and Bogdan C. Iacob (Budapest - New York: CEU Press, 2012), 64.

5 Charles S. Maier, *Dissolution: The Crisis of Communism and the End of East Germany* (Princeton, NJ: Princeton University Press, 1997), esp. 125–129.

6 Service, *The End of the Cold War*, esp. 400–415. See Helmut Wohnout's chapter in this volume.

7 On the so-called "Trianon syndrome," see, e.g., Béla K. Király, Peter Pastor and Ivan Sanders, eds., *Essays on World War I: Total War and Peacemaking: A Case Study on Trianon* (New York: Social Science Monographs/Brooklyn College Press, 1982).

ished – by “the West” and by “the world” – played a role in the policy of revisionism that the Hungarian interwar regime followed and was one of the motivations for Horthy to side with Hitler in World War II.

The victors of World War II had decided to accept the borders designed in Trianon for the post-1945 European order. As especially the USSR had no interest whatsoever in allowing strong anti-Trianon sentiment to disturb Moscow’s control over Central and Eastern Europe, the ethnonationalist sentiment had to go underground – for as long as the parameters of Hungarian politics were decided in Moscow. The end of Soviet control was the thawing of nationalistic sentiments in general, all over Central and Eastern Europe; and for Hungary, this implied the thawing of the strong resentments directed against the Trianon Treaty.[8]

The Polish transition had been significantly defined by the specific role that Roman Catholicism had played in the history of Poland, including the period when *Solidarność* played the role of a semi-recognized opposition in 1980–1981. The situation in Hungary was different: Hungary was a “Catholic country,” populated by a Catholic majority. But in Hungary’s history, Protestantism (the “Reformed Church” in the Calvinist tradition) had played an important role – as a voice opposing the Habsburg-led Counter-Reformation and the rule of Habsburg Austria until the Compromise of 1867. Within the traditional aristocratic and bourgeois elite, Protestants had a visible role. Most prominent within this segment of Hungary’s society was Miklós Horthy, Hungary’s authoritarian ruler between 1920 and 1944.[9]

The history of Christian Democracy in Europe during the twentieth century demonstrates that there is a significant correlation between Catholicism – with respect to the strength of other Christian denominations – and Christian Democracy. The more dominant Catholicism was, the more important Christian Democratic parties became. This has been especially true in the European post-1945 party systems: the model cases for Christian Democratic parties were the French MRP, the Italian DC, and the Belgian Christian Socials – in countries without significant Protestant populations. Even in the West German Federal Republic, the CDU and the CSU parties, designed to overcome the historical gap between Catholicism and Protestantism, were more successful among Catholics than among Protestants.

8 For the concept of “thawing” see Urs Altermatt, *Das Fanal von Sarajevo: Ethnonationalismus in Europa* (Zurich: Neue Zürcher Zeitung, 1996), esp. 9–18.

9 See, e.g., Paul A. Hanebrink, *In Defense of Christian Hungary: Religion, Nationalism, and Anti-Semitism, 1890–1944* (Ithaca, NY: Cornell University Press, 2006).

In addition to this specific Hungarian cleavage between the Catholic and the Protestant (Reformed) tradition, the churches had to live with the burden of collaboration with the semi-fascist Horthy regime.[10] After 1945, the churches had to justify the *modus vivendi* with a non-democratic regime. This drive to atonement was used by the ruling communists to delegitimize the churches (e.g. in the trials against prominent members of the clergy). This was also specific to Hungary, although perhaps similar to Slovakia.[11] Despite some cases of anti-fascist resistance, the Catholic Church in Hungary could not credibly claim a role like that of the French MRP, the Italian DC or mainstream Polish Catholicism with a history of anti-fascist (anti-Nazi) traditions.

At last: free elections, liberal democracy

In Hungary, round-table talks started in June and ended in September 1989.[12] The result was an agreement that established a framework for a multi-party system and free elections, including constitutional amendments. Hungary became a republic with a parliamentary system based on competition between parties.[13] In that respect Hungary – like Poland and Czechoslovakia – did not try to invent a new form of democracy. Hungary explicitly followed the example of liberal democracies as they had already been established, especially in Western Europe.

The newly achieved freedom resulted in the creation of a multitude of – legally existing – parties. As of 1990, eighty political parties existed in Hungary. The central question was how to translate the huge number of parties and their competition for votes into a parliament that was supposed to become the main source of political authority. The electoral system that was chosen for the first elections, planned for 1990, was a complex mixture of nationwide proportional and single-district representa-

10 Csaba Fazekas, "Collaborating with Horthy: Political Catholicism and Christian Political Organizations in Hungary 1918–1944," in *Christdemokratie in Europa im 20. Jahrhundert / Christian Democracy in 20th Century Europe / La Démocratie Chrétienne en Europe au XXe siècle*, ed. Michael Gehler, Wolfram Kaiser and Helmut Wohnout (Vienna-Cologne-Weimar, 2001), 224–249.

11 James Mace Ward, *Priest, Politician, Collaborator: Jozef Tiso and the Making of Fascist Slovakia* (Ithaca, NY: Cornell University Press, 2016).

12 Tamás Fricz, "Democratization, the Party System and the Electorate in Hungary," in *Transition with Contradiction: The Case of Hungary, 1990–98*, ed. Mária Schmidt and László Gy. Tóth (Budapest: Kairosz, 1999), 93–124; Iván Bába, *The Hungarian Transition: Parties and Movements in the Political Regime Change in Hungary between 1987 and 1994* (Budapest: ICDT, 2011), esp. 96–132.

13 Fricz, "Democratization, the Party System and the Electorate in Hungary," 98 f.

tion – a kind of combination of the systems that the French Fifth Republic and the German Federal Republic had established.

This system was designed to, and did, prevent an extreme de-concentration of parliament. In 1990, six parties won seats. It was not too difficult to form a majority coalition – consisting of the national-conservative MDF (Hungarian Democratic Forum, 164 seats), the radical-conservative FKGB (44 seats), and the Christian Democratic KDNP (21 seats). The opposition consisted of the "radical liberal" SZDSZ (92 seats), the (post-Communist) Social Democratic MSZP (33 seats), and the "pragmatic liberal" Fidesz (21 seats).[14] The dominant force within the coalition was the MDF under Prime Minister József Antall. The only explicitly Christian Democratic Party – the KDNP – was in all respects the junior partner of another dominant party that also claimed to belong to the European Christian Democratic Party family.[15]

The results of the elections were in some respects surprising. Parties that had established systematic links to (Western) European party families did not do as well as expected. This was especially true for the KDNP, but the European party families had not fully made up their minds as to which Hungarian party should be backed. In 1990, the European Union of Christian Democrats (EUCD) had accepted as members the KDNP as well as the MDF and the (agrarian) Smallholders' Party (ISP), which did not win enough votes to get representatives in parliament. The party family of European Liberals followed this pattern when both SZDSZ and Fidesz were accepted as members of the Liberal International. Among the major party families, only the Social Democrats were able to focus on one Hungarian member exclusively, the MSZP – but not before 1996, years after the first free elections.[16]

In addition to the lack of traditional links between the Hungarian Christian Democrats and the European party family (represented first and foremost by the DC, MRP, and CDU/CSU), the EUCD, the European Democrat Union (EDU), and Germany's CDU all had difficulties deciding which party in Hungary should be backed – through consultations or financial

14 Fricz, "Democratization, the Party System and the Electorate in Hungary," 101.

15 See also, generally, Attila Ágh and Sandor Kurtán, eds., *Democratization and Europeanization in Hungary: The First Parliament (1990–1994)* (Budapest: Hungarian Center for Democracy Studies, 1995).

16 Gabor Török, "External Influences on the Hungarian Party System," in *Democratic Consolidation: The International Dimension – Hungary, Poland and Spain*, ed. Gerhard Mangott, Harald Waldrauch and Stephen Day (Baden-Baden: Nomos, 2000), 194.

support.[17] This was one of the reasons that – after the implosion of the MDF following Antall's untimely death from cancer in 1993 – the EUCD accepted Fidesz after the party had switched its European outlook from the Liberal to the Christian Democratic/Conservative party family. The only Hungarian party that could claim to represent the Christian Democratic tradition in full during the two first decades, the KDNP, was bound to play the role of a junior partner – first to the MDF and later to Fidesz.

From the very beginning, the (Western) European Christian Democratic party family – still represented by the European Democrat Union (EDU) in 1990 – could not make up its mind which Hungarian political party it should favor, accept as a member, or back (especially financially) in the first period of Hungary's regained political pluralism. In August 1990, at the EDU meeting in Helsinki, three Hungarian parties participated – the MDF, the KDNP, and the FKgP (the Smallholders' party), which was attempting to exploit its place in Hungarian historical memory as the dominant party in the brief period between the German occupation (followed by the "Arrow Cross" rule in 1944) and the beginning of the Soviet-style Marxist-Leninist one-party system in Hungary.[18]

In post-1945 Italy, the internal pluralism of the *Democrazia Cristiana* was expressed by the power-sharing arrangement of the "*correnti*," the factions within the party. In (West) Germany, a different kind of internal pluralism was expressed by the duality of the CSU (which only exists in Bavaria) and the CDU (organized in all of the German federal states outside of Bavaria). In Hungary, starting in 1990, it was not possible to establish a common umbrella under which all different interests, all different understandings, of what Christian Democracy was about could be united. One reason for the weakness of Hungarian Christian Democracy in the first period after the democratic transition was the inability to form a common platform representing all Christian Democratic forces.

Compared with Western European democracies in the decades after 1945, the post-1989 Hungarian party system was characterized by the weaknesses of an explicit Christian Democratic party.[19] This was one of

17 See Alexander Brakel's chapter (on the CDU) and Michael Gehler and Johannes Schönner's chapter (on the EDU) in this volume.

18 Jenö Gergely, "Towards the One-Party State: Nascent Christian Democracy in Hungary," in *Christian Democracy in Europe since 1945*, vol. 2, ed. Michael Gehler and Wolfram Kaiser (London - New York: Routledge, 2004), 135–150.

19 For a similar explanation of Christian Democracy's weakness, and ultimate failure, in post-1989 Poland, see Aleks Szczerbiak and Tim Bale, "Explaining the Absence of Christian Democracy in Contemporary Poland," in *Christian Democracy across the Iron Curtain: Europe Redefined*, ed. Piotr H. Kosicki and Sławomir Łukasiewicz (London: Palgrave Macmillan, 2018), 343–410.

the reasons that there was an "empty spot" in the center-right of Hungary's party system. According to the classification by public opinion polls in 1990, 1999, and 2003, among the relevant political parties – as classified on the left-to-right scale – only two parties were seen as more "left" than "right," the MSZP and the SZDSZ. The others were seen as more "right" than "left," including the KDNP. The MDF's demise after 1999 as the dominant party right of center left a vacancy in this area of the political spectrum, and this spot was obviously filled not by the Christian Democratic KDNP, but by Fidesz – which moved from a centrist, liberal position to a rightist conservative, nationalistic position. This move was not only the result of an "ideological" transformation, but also of an evolution in perceptions by the Hungarian electorate.[20] The KDNP lost: first, against the MDF – and later against Fidesz.

The perception of the Hungarian parties by the electorate was an important signal for Christian Democracy in Hungary. In Western Europe after 1945, Christian Democratic parties perceived themselves as centrist parties. This was not always identical with the perception of the electorate, but – as the example of the French MRP demonstrates – as long as Christian Democratic parties were considered to be between left and right, they helped to balance the party system and to stabilize democracy. Not so in Hungary: the KDNP was seen as being to the right of the political center and was never allowed to play a distinct or a unique role in Hungary's democracy.

The democratic quality of Hungary was illustrated by the acceptance of the change of governing coalitions in 1994, 1998, 2002, and 2010. After the center-right coalition, which represented the majority in parliament, a center-left majority came to power in 1994, a coalition formed by MSZP and SZDSZ, followed by a Fidesz-led center-right coalition in 1998. In 2002, again, the center-left returned to power. Since 2010, Fidesz has become the dominant party within a center-right majority, sustained by the elections of 2014 and 2018. The rise of Fidesz was of particular significance, due to the party's move from defining itself as "liberal" to becoming conservative, with significant nationalistic aspects, taking over this role from the MDF, which in the meantime had disappeared. The KDNP – and therefore Christian Democracy on the whole – was unable to become a decisive player in Hungary's post-1989 democratic pluralism.

20 András Körösényi, Csaba Tóth and Gábor Török, *The Hungarian Political System* (Budapest: Hungarian Center for Democracy Studies Foundation, 2009), 170.

The lingering shadow of revisionist nationalism

Hungarian political self-perception is based on a high degree of identification with Hungarian nationhood spanning more than one thousand years. This identification includes the kingdom which existed within the Austro-Hungarian Dual Monarchy between 1867 and 1918 and also with the Hungary of the interwar period, which was defined by the authoritarian regime under Miklós Horthy.[21] The identification does not include, at least not necessarily or universally, any identification with the Horthy regime's authoritarian character, but there is a rather general tendency to excuse Horthy's revisionist foreign policy. Still, that revisionism was (and would be, again) directed against Central and Eastern European neighbors.

The contemporary Hungarian debate – at least, in its openly accepted form – does not show signs of identification with the period of German occupation in 1944 and 1945 or with the Arrow Cross dictatorship, which existed as a puppet government on behalf of Nazi Germany. The post-1989 debate is about Horthy – and about Horthy's co-responsibility for the implementation of the Holocaust in 1944. The political right tends to place all responsibility on "the Germans," and the political left stresses Horthy's collaboration with Nazi Germany, including participation in the Holocaust. This is not so different from other post-communist countries (and European countries in general). The years before and during World War II dominate a sometimes heated national discourse.[22]

There is a broad consensus in Hungary that has recast the communist decades as a dictatorship, forced upon Hungary by foreign (Soviet) interests, but there is no consensus concerning the pre-communist past and how it should be integrated into any general and widely accepted national narrative. What Ágnes Heller has written about all former communist countries is especially true for Hungary: "Whereas Frenchmen and Germans succeeded in forgetting their past enmities, post-communist nations cling to the ghosts of their pasts."[23]

Hungary, beginning 1990, has been part of the Visegrád Group – together with Poland and (following the so-called Velvet Divorce) the sep-

21 Ibid., 1–11.

22 For the contemporary debate concerning Hungarian active participation in the Holocaust, see: Randolph L. Braham and András Kovács, eds., *The Holocaust in Hungary: Seventy Years Later* (Budapest: CEU Press, 2016); Árpád von Klimó, *Remembering Cold Days: The 1942 Massacre of Novi Sad, Hungarian Politics and Society, 1942–1989* (Pittsburgh, PA: University of Pittsburgh Press, 2018).

23 Heller, "Twenty Years after 1989," 63.

arate states of the Czech Republic and Slovakia. These four states have in common not only the history of communist dictatorship forced upon them by the USSR at the end of World War II. Post-1945 history needs to be seen as their common fate – as victims of the USSR's repressions. The events of 1956 in Hungary and of 1968 in Czechoslovakia, the military intervention to secure the geopolitical interests of Moscow, and the Polish martial law declaration of 1981, also under massive pressure from Moscow, created a kind of transnational narrative. The Visegrád countries are also bound by their "Western orientation" – the backbone of the European Union's policy that favors their fastest possible entry into the EU.

But there is a difference between Hungary and the other Visegrád countries concerning pre-1945 history: Hungary and Hungary alone voluntarily, as a sovereign country, sided with the Axis Powers, while the three other nations (even taking into consideration the compromising history of the fascist Slovak Republic under Jozef Tiso) have grounds to perceive themselves as victims of Nazi Germany. Hungary and Hungary alone profited from its alliance with Germany since its territory grew as a result of Hitler's strategic orientation, at the cost of Slovakia (and Romania). In Hungary, these territorial gains (significant parts of southern Slovakia and Romanian Transylvania) were perceived as compensation for the unjustified loss that the Treaty of Trianon had dictated.

When the Allies decided that the Hungarian borders after 1945 should be exactly the same as those that the Treaty of Trianon had forced upon Hungary, this had to be accepted – especially under communist rule, when any kind of border revision would have been directed against communist neighbors. But when the end of communism allowed the opening of a free discourse, it became evident that Hungary (and Hungarian society at large) still saw Trianon as a major injustice, an indicator for Hungarians that the dominant global forces were defined by an anti-Magyar bias. Hungary – so went the narrative – was once again left alone to defend its rights against the overwhelming forces of enemies. Who are these enemies? They can be seen as "Western," or as communists, or just a vague global conspiracy.

In Hungary today, Trianon is still a kind of battle cry, which can be used as an instrument for transforming national sentiments into political activism.[24] But being permanently reminded of the deep injustice of Trianon is also a reminder of Hungarian revisionism, which played a dominant role in Central and Eastern Europe between 1920 and 1945, leaving a lasting mark on some of Hungary's neighbors (Romania, Slovakia, Serbia). Dem-

24 Körösényi, Tóth and Török, *The Hungarian Political System*, 20 and 30.

ocratic Hungary does not seem to have any interest in acting "revisionist" along the lines of Horthy's Hungary. Democratic Hungary (even under the leadership of Viktor Orbán) respects the role of the Council of Europe, which does not allow any changes of international borders within Europe against the will of any states. Contemporary Hungary's tentative sympathy with Russia's annexation of the Crimea must be seen as the survival of some revisionist sentiment – even if it does not explicitly define Hungary's foreign and European policies.

The trauma of 1956 plays an important role in Hungary's perception of its place within Europe. In 1956, there was a real revolution. A mass movement in Hungary used the first steps of de-Stalinization to confront both the USSR's control over the spheres of influence, as negotiated in the Yalta and Potsdam Agreements and shaped by the American policy of "containment"; and the one-party dictatorship in Hungary. But one was linked to the other: the post-Stalinist USSR would have accepted a decrease in totalitarian control in Hungary, but was unwilling to accept the dissolution of the Warsaw Pact. The revolution of 1956, based on an alliance between reform communists like Imre Nagy and various anti-communist factions, was crushed. Yet, until its tragic end, Hungarians thought that they had reason to hope for help from the West. In the mainstream of Hungarian public opinion, the behavior of "the West" in 1956 bordered on treason: "The West," to appease the USSR, had sacrificed Hungary – and in doing so, the credibility of "the West" had suffered.[25]

The Hungarian hopes of 1956 were an illusion, a complete misunderstanding of US, NATO, and Western European interests. The American (and, generally, the Western) policy of containment was oriented towards preventing an increase in Soviet influence – not challenging the existing East-West division of Europe. The feeling of have been "abandoned" by the West, despite the promises of the "Free World," had an impact on post-1989 Hungary and strengthened the feeling that Hungary was still alone – despite NATO and EU membership.

The persistence of this conviction also helps to explain a growing distance from "liberal democracy" within contemporary Hungarian political culture. Liberal democracy has become identified with a wave of decadence that Hungary should no longer accept – a distance that became important

25 Paul Lendvai, *Der Ungarn-Aufstand 1956: Eine Revolution und ihre Folgen* (Munich: Bertelsmann, 2006); Charles Gati, *Failed Illusions: Moscow, Washington, Budapest, and the 1956 Hungarian Revolt* (Washington, DC - Stanford, CA: Woodrow Wilson Center Press/Stanford University Press, 2006).

in the years when Fidesz began to define Hungary's position in Europe. The insistence that Hungary is not bound to follow a specific "Western" way of democracy, that Hungary is entitled to develop a – to some extent – different understanding of democracy, has its roots in Hungary's victimization narrative – from 1848 to 1920 and from 1945 to 1956.[26]

The weaknesses of Christian Democracy – as understood in Western Europe beginning with 1945 – played a role in the changing Hungarian perception of European integration. The European Community, designed by Jean Monnet as a process of creating an ever "closer" Europe and built especially on the transnational political consensus formulated by Christian Democrats like Robert Schuman, Alcide De Gasperi, and Konrad Adenauer, was not so easy to reconcile with the Hungarian understanding that the transition of 1989 was the rebirth of full national sovereignty.[27] To opt for membership in the European Union, a union designed among others by Monnet and his Christian Democratic founding colleagues of post-1945 Europe, was not the return to a past Europe; it was the foundation of a very new Europe.

In contrast, the European Union that democratic Hungary wanted to join after the transition was not just a confederation of still-fully sovereign states. The EU that Hungary joined was (and is) a federation in the making. Yet there is not much space for a specific Hungarian role – just as there is not much space for a specific German or French or Spanish position.

Conclusions: 1989, reason and pragmatism – but not much of heroism and revolution

The events leading to the Hungarian transition were very different from the events of 1956. The transition of 1989 was negotiated between representatives of the old system and representatives of a system that had yet to be born. It is important to underscore that the transition was not violent.

The reason for the successes of 1989–1990 was not the heroism of the Hungarian anti-communist opposition. If heroism had been a decisive factor, no liberation movement could have ever been more heroic than the revolutionaries of 1956. The democratic dissidents realized that a win-

26 See, e.g., Paul Lendvai, *Orbán: Hungary's Strongman* (Oxford: Oxford University Press, 2017); Jan-Werner Müller, "The Problem with 'Illiberal Democracy,'" *Project Syndicate*, 21 January 2016.

27 Michael Gehler, "Begegnungsort des Kalten Krieges: Der 'Genfer Kreis' und die geheimen Absprachen westeuropäischer Christdemokraten 1947–1955," in *Christdemokratie in Europa im 20. Jahrhundert*, ed. Gehler, Kaiser and Wohnout, 642–694.

dow of opportunities had presented itself, a window opened not by the dissidents themselves but by the reform communists in Moscow. The communists in Hungary did not have much choice but to follow the path defined by Mikhail Gorbachev and already implemented in Poland.

The dissidents – politically split among right, left, and center – acted reasonably. There was no need to replay the heroism of 1956. For 1989, the 1956 revolution was a point of reference, a reminder of the brutality any revolutionary heroism was unable to overcome within the political framework in place at that time.[28] Still, there was no need to repeat 1956. There was every need to negotiate the best possible solution presented by a completely new geopolitical situation.

Gorbachev had tried not to destroy but to renew Marxism-Leninism and had realized – too late – that no "third way" existed between a communist one-party system and a liberal, pluralistic democracy. The outcome of Hungary's negotiated transition was not a compromise: the representatives of the old system just had to accept defeat. There was not much that the dissidents could have done to prevent this defeat. The dissidents had only to take what was offered by the process that had started in Moscow in 1985.

There is an understandable tendency to look for more heroism behind the transition of 1989. There is some criticism that the end of communism has not been radical enough, that the victory over the Stalinist and post-Stalinist dictatorships had no deeper consequences. Obviously, a revolution without blood is not easily accepted as a real revolution. The failed revolution of 1956 had many martyrs, while the revolution of 1989 had none.

There are two different (but not necessarily conflicting) interpretations of the dramatic changes during 1989: was the result of this year a national liberation from foreign dictates, or was it the replacement of dictatorship by democracy? Considering the EU's basic philosophy to tame nationalism by building a democratic federation out of sovereign states, the second interpretation must be seen as dominant – at least for countries that had decided to join the European Union.[29] If Hungary gives priority to the first interpretation, Hungary will play a significant role in a policy of undoing the already existing, but unfinished, European Union.[30]

28 See, e.g., István Rév, *Retroactive Justice: Prehistory of Post-communism* (Stanford, CA: Stanford University Press, 2005).

29 Daniel Cohn-Bendit and Guy Verhofstadt, *For Europe! Manifesto for a Postnational Revolution in Europe* (Munich: Hanser, 2012).

30 Ivan Krastev, *After Europe* (Philadelphia: University of Pennsylvania Press, 2017).

10

AMONG THE HUSSITES, COMMUNISTS, AND NEO-LIBERALS

Christian Democratic Political Actors in Communist Czechoslovakia and the Democratic Transition*

Ladislav Cabada

After World War II, Czechoslovakia was among the most enthusiastic followers of Stalin's Soviet Union. As early as April 1945, when the restoration of Czechoslovak independence was announced in the Slovak city of Košice, the newly created National Front (NF) system banned all political parties with a conservative ideological profile. Christian Democratic and perhaps Christian socialist programs survived in one NF party, the Czechoslovak People's Party. This party was, however, the target of communist sabotage and, after February 1948, it became a satellite of the communist "state party," with its leaders fully subordinated to the totalitarian political leadership. During the first months and subsequent years of the communist regime, churches – with the partial exception of the Pan-Slavonic Hussite Church – were targeted and suppressed and the monastic orders were dispersed. Many representatives of the clergy were arrested, tortured, and even killed.

This situation threatened the very survival of Christian Democratic and conservative political and social actors in Czechoslovakia. This chapter focuses on the development of Christian Democratic and conservative political groups in the country, in spite of communism's arrival in power. To this end, it poses a series of research questions:

* The author would like to thank his colleagues Jan Bureš and Markéta Kolarčíková for their help, including useful feedback on interpretation. This chapter was prepared with the support of an internal grant from Metropolitan University Prague's Central European Politics department, internal code 57-01.

1. To what extent did the communist regime use pre-existing anti-Catholic and radical atheist sentiments in Czech society to aggressively displace the Christian Democratic – and, more to the point, clerical – political movement from official politics?
2. Was there any continuity in terms of ideology and/or personnel within Christian Democratic political groups in the country between 1948 and 1989?
3. Were there any important differences between the separate parts and regions of Czechoslovakia, i.e. between the Czech and Slovak parts of the country and society? Were there any aspects of Moravia that might make it a significant player in Christian Democratic politics?
4. Finally, given that this study extends to developments in the transition period and beyond, I ask:
   How did Christian Democratic groups formed before 1989 influence the transition and subsequent development of the new democratic regime in Czechoslovakia? What impact have these surviving groups had on the two independent states – the Czech Republic and Slovakia – that were established in 1992?

My analysis begins with a short historical overview of the position of Christian Democratic political actors in the Czech and Slovak political systems before the creation of a common state in 1918. I then examine the influence of Christian Democratic political parties on Czechoslovak politics over two decades of democratic development. These parties, I show, were able to strengthen their positions under the authoritarian regime of the second Czechoslovak Republic and again under the totalitarian clerico-fascist regime of the quasi-independent Slovak Republic from 1939 to 1945.

The study next turns to the period of the communist totalitarian regime between 1948 and 1960, when the Christian Democratic political movement was almost destroyed. These years were followed by a rebirth of Christian Democratic and to some extent also conservative politics during the liberalization era (1964–1969), and I trace these developments alongside activities and ideological debates within these groups in the two decades preceding the transition out of communism. At the heart of this study is an analysis of the important activism of the Christian Democratic groups that were transformed into anti-communist political parties and movements in and around November 1989, as well as their impact on the transition. Last but not least, I consider key themes and policies that have been stressed and promoted by Christian Democratic actors since November 1989.

Historical preconditions for the rise of conservative and Christian Democratic parties

Analyzing the development of Christian Democratic political movements in Czechoslovakia prior to the democratic transition is a complicated and challenging task. One key reason for this difficulty is the range of very different paths followed by these political actors in various parts of the country, specifically Bohemia, Moravia, and Slovakia. As I will show, these differences were so important and so striking that separate analyses are required for the Czech lands and Slovakia. At the same time, we need to recognize the clear differences between Bohemia and Moravia, especially concerning Christian Democratic politics, and more generally, political clericalism and the role of the Catholic Church in politics and society.

In the case of the Czech lands, the rise of clericalism was greatly limited historically by conflicts among Christian party leaders. Immediately before World War I, there were seven clerical parties in the Czech lands. For this reason, the Catholic political camp in Bohemia failed to win any seats in the 1911 parliamentary elections.[1] During the war, the parties integrated and after 1918, the Czechoslovak People's Party (*Československá strana lidová,* ČSL) was established with the support of a potential ten percent of the electorate.

This party was, however, also affected by factionalism. In 1922, ČSL broke ties with a Slovak group that then resumed its independence as Hlinka's Slovak People's Party (*Hlinkova slovenská ľudová strana*, HSLS), dedicating itself to the promotion of Slovak autonomy and later independence. After this step, ČSL had a different profile in Bohemia (where it had substantial anti-democratic tendencies but weak electoral support) and Moravia (where it took on a Christian socialist position and had relatively good electoral results).[2] The position of the party – and of clericalism more generally – was greatly restricted by the new independent state authorities headed by President Tomáš G. Masaryk. The Catholic Church and ČSL were branded former collaborators with the Habsburg dynasty and "Vienna," and the new state actively supported reformist churches and

1 Ladislav Cabada and David Šanc, *Český stranický systém ve 20. století* (Pilsen: Aleš Čeněk, 2005), 17.

2 Some Moravian Christian Democrats stressed the social dimension and criticized the cooperation with the right-wing parties. In 1929, this Christian Socialist stream left the ČSL as newly established the Czechoslovak Christian Socialist Party. Indeed, the party did not achieve any important electoral success; see Jiří Malíř, Pavel Marek et al, *Politické strany 1861–1938* (Brno: Doplněk, 2005), 675–677.

the related myth of Jan Hus as one of the most important Czech martyrs and fighters against Catholicism and "Germanness" (*Deutschtum*). Even so, with his shrewd centrist politics, ČSL leader Jan Šrámek succeeded in ensuring the party's participation in the majority of more than twenty coalition governments in the interwar period.[3]

The situation was very different for HSLS, which grew out of the former Slovak National Party. While, in the Czech lands and especially Bohemia, national revival processes were historically connected with anti-Catholicism and even atheism, in Slovakia, the Catholic Church was the main driver of national consciousness. HSLS had the support of most Slovak voters throughout the entire interwar period, and it declared Slovak autonomy after the so-called Munich Crisis in the autumn of 1938. In December 1938, HSLS was the only Slovak party in the non-competitive Slovak parliamentary elections. The party had many wings, including clerical-fascist and National Socialist arms that succeeded in internal conflicts after Hlinka's death in August 1938 and ruled the quasi-independent totalitarian Slovak Republic after 14 March 1939. Although these policies made it impossible for HSLS to continue its rule after World War II, they generated vital grassroots support in the postwar decades, both among the Slovak population and those in exile.

As regards ČSL, after the Munich crisis, the party split into two camps. While the majority endorsed the new concept of authoritarian democracy,[4] Šrámek and his followers rejected this idea after the Nazi occupation of the Czech lands. They joined the government in exile in London, then returned after the war as part of the new government and regime. Becoming part of the National Front in April 1945, ČSL agreed on a grand coalition with three left-wing parties – Communist, Socialist, and Social Democratic. Within such coalitions, as well as during the electoral campaign, ČSL tried to behave more independently, but the pro-communist wing also operated within the party. In the 1946 parliamentary elections, ČSL received 16.27 percent of the votes and again joined the grand coalition. The result was understood as a failure insofar as the party had hoped to attract the for-

3 Cabada and Šanc, *Český stranický systém ve 20. století*, 81–84; see James Ramon Felak, *At the Price of the Republic: Hlinka's Slovak People's Party, 1929–1938* (Pittsburgh: University of Pittsburgh Press, 1995).

4 Authoritarian democracy was the term used by the leader of the Second Czechoslovak Republic (30 September 1938 – 15 March 1939) Rudolf Beran. The doctrine was based on the idea of limited pluralism – only one party has to exist and the pluralism should be implemented within this party, Party of National Unity (*Strana národní jednoty*). The doctrine also included a devoted position towards Nazi-Germany, anti-liberalism, and antisemitism. See Jan Rataj, *O národní autoritativní stát* (Prague: Karolinum, 1998).

mer voters from the Agrarian party. Within the party, a group was formed around the party's Vice Chairman Adolf Procházka, who asked for a more critical approach towards the dominant Communist Party of Czechoslovakia. Nevertheless, the most visible members of the group (Bohdan Chudoba, Pavel Tigrid[5]) were persecuted or even expelled (Helena Koželuhová) from the party.[6] After the communists came to power, ČSL became one of two "satellite" parties, and its new leadership – Alois Petr and Josef Plojhar (party chairman in 1951–1968) – declared their support for the new totalitarian regime.

In addition to Christian Democratic parties and Catholic political actors more generally, we should also mention the role of the National Conservative Party in the Czech lands. From the former National Party (divided since the 1870s into two entities, the Conservative and Liberal Conservative Parties), the Czech(oslovak) National Democratic Party emerged between 1918 and 1919, with Karel Kramář serving as a strong leader and the first Czechoslovak Prime Minister. Nevertheless, this party experienced a gradual loss of support, and by 1919, it was already the weakest of the five members of the all-state coalition of Czech(oslovak) parties. In the 1920s, the Czech(oslovak) National Democratic Party began to flirt with authoritarianism and fascism, and in the 1930s, it cooperated with authoritarian and fascist entities to form the so-called Aryan Front. In the autumn of 1938, it also endorsed authoritarian democracy and aligned itself with the anti-liberal and anti-democratic National Unity Party. Like HSLS, the Czech(oslovak) National Democratic Party was banned after World War II.[7]

As we have seen, even before communists came to power, conservative and/or Christian Democratic political actors were relatively weak in the Czech lands, and after the war, HSLS was banned in Slovakia as a totalitarian state party. In 1947, the Democracy Party, also the only non-communist party in Slovakia, was dismantled following accusations that it included many former HSLS members and was promoting HSLS's agenda. All this transpired even before February 1948, when the communists became the

5 After 1948, both left Czechoslovakia and became active Christian Democrats in exile. In Paris, Tigrid established the review *Svědectví*, the most important periodical from a Czechoslovak exile. In Brussels, Chudoba established the Christian Democratic Movement in 1949; Ladislav Mrklas, "Exilová demokratická pravice," *CEVRO-Revue* 3 (2004), 6 April 2004, www.cevro.cz/cs/30164-exilova-demokraticka-pravice (20 December 2018).

6 Bradley F. Abrams, *The Struggle for the Soul of the Nation: Czech Culture and the Rise of Communism* (Lanham, MD: Rowman & Littlefield, 2004).

7 See Rataj, *O národní autoritativní stát.*

only relevant actors under Czechoslovakia's newly established totalitarian regime.

The new regime understood churches and the Catholic Church above all as dangerous ideological rivals that should be intimidated and destroyed in the near future. As Cuhra puts it, "in communist Czechoslovakia, the Catholic Church was the target of strict persecution by the regime."[8] In addition to the imprisonment, internment, and political assassination of members of the clergy and the destruction of monastic orders, the regime undertook a brutal persecution campaign mainly targeting religious intellectuals, such as teachers who could influence the public. One of the most visible of these collectives was the "Family" (*Rodina*), a group inspired by Tomislav Kolaković, which later became very important.

Kolaković (who had given up his surname Poglajen during World War II and adopted his mother's maiden name) had left fascist Croatia in 1943 and, on the recommendation of the archbishop of Zagreb, Alojzije Stepinac, started a mission in Slovakia. At first in Slovakia and also in Prague after 1945, he cooperated with his students and co-workers to create the Family, a group that aspired to influence politics and play an active role in political life. This group's most important activity was the protection of Slovakia's Jewish population during the war, i.e. after the Nazi occupation of the country provoked by the Slovak national uprising. The Family included many personalities who worked on an illegal (or as Vaško put it, "clandestine"[9]) basis, and these individuals were persecuted in a draconian manner during the communist period after 1948. (Silvester Krčméry and Vladimír Jukl, for instance, were each imprisoned for twelve years, while people like Růžena Vacková, Oto Mádr, and Josef Zvěřina faced similar or even tougher penalties.) Kolaković left Czechoslovakia illegally at the beginning of August 1946 as part of a group of Belgian repatriates.[10] The Family and its legacy were responsible for some of the most important Catholic structures in communist Czechoslovakia. Many of its mem-

8 Jaroslav Cuhra, "Katolická církev a odpor vůči 'normalizačnímu' režimu," in *Opozice a odpor proti komunistickému režimu v Československu 1968–1989*, ed. Petr Blažek (Prague: Ústav světových dějin and Dokořán, 2005), 67.

9 Václav Vaško, "Legendární profesor Kolakovič," *Teologické texty: Časopis pro teoretické a praktické otázky teologie* 30, no. 4 (2007), www.teologicketexty.cz/casopis/2007-4/Legendarni-profesor-Kolakovic.html (accessed 28 October 2016).

10 Ján Čarnogurský, "Disent na Slovensku," in *Za svobodu a demokracii I: Odpor proti komunistické moci*, ed. Jaroslav Cuhra and Václav Veber (Prague: Evropské hnutí v České republice, 1999), 211–212; Id., "Christian Democracy in Slovakia," in *Christian Democracy across the Iron Curtain: Europe Redefined*, ed. Piotr H. Kosicki and Sławomir Łukasiewicz (London: Palgrave Macmillan, 2018), 426.

bers hovered on the edge of official and unofficial roles from the 1960s onwards.

After more than a decade of Stalinism, the 1960s brought no significant shift in the communists' aggressive anti-confessional rhetoric and active suppression of religious activities. Indeed, as Cuhra observes, "the regime created and maintained pro-regime priest associations, beginning with the Velehrad Committee (*Velehradský výbor*) and Catholic clergy's Peace Movement (*Mírové hnutí katolického duchovenstva*) and extending to the 'normalizing' Association of Catholic Clergy (*Pacem in Terris*), which 'corrupted' and divided."[11] As such, the organization of underground priests and secret studies of theology was the most visible act of resistance before the Prague Spring. These activities were, however, understood within the Catholic Church to be non-political.[12]

Normalization, Charter 77, and conservative and Christian Democratic groups

The Prague Spring and, more generally, the continued relaxation of the communist regime during the 1960s revealed the limits of conservative politics in the Czech lands. During 1968, there were no discernable efforts to set up a public group based on conservative ideology. As regards Christian activities, ČSL (and also the second satellite party – the Czechoslovak Socialist Party) membership grew impressively in 1968, highlighting the popularity of Christian Democratic politics, especially in Moravia. The new members were attracted by both their family traditions and the general wave of political activism in the short Prague Spring period, but the ideological background was proclaimed only in a very vague manner in both non-communist parties. Before the planned extraordinary ČSL Congress could propose a new – "purely Christian" – party manifesto, the Warsaw Pact invasion and occupation suspended intra-party changes. The Slovak population remained politically passive during the reform period; as a result, there was a clear extension of non-political activities in Slovakia despite the occupation of the country and changes within the Communist Party leadership.

11 Cuhra, "Katolická církev a odpor vůči ′normalizačnímu′ režimu," 67–68.

12 James Ramon Felak, "Vatican II and Czechoslovakia," in *Vatican II Behind the Iron Curtain*, ed. Piotr H. Kosicki (Washington, DC: The Catholic University of America Press, 2016), 99–126.

In the first half of the 1970s, "small communities" (*malé spoločenstva*) were organized in Slovakia, laying the foundations for the underground church. Kmeť identifies this period with the continued development of two groups – "one around J. Beňo, and the second represented by Jukl, Krčméry, and Bishop Ján Chryzostom Korec."[13] Čarnogurský also stresses the role of both of these groups in the Catholic dissent movement and the underground church in Slovakia. Beňo's supporters did not take part in pilgrimages or other public activities, and Čarnogurský sees this group as a curiosity. The second group was far more important; it was made up of activists surrounding Krčméry and Jukl, and Čarnogurský stresses that their origins lay in the Family network that drew inspiration from Kolaković. Beginning in the early 1980s, there was an observable "boom in the underground church and associated structures (…) The real head of the secret church was Bishop Korec (…) He was the authority who succeeded in unifying different activities of the secret church at least in terms of labor."[14]

Aside from Bishop Korec, Ján Čarnogurský was the most important figure in the Christian Democratic dissent movement in Slovakia and he showed an important ability to overcome the tensions between the Catholic and civic dissent movements. According to Marušiak, these were the two groups of dissidents in Slovakia: on the one hand, the civic dissent movement focused mainly on human rights issues and was represented by well-known personalities with close ties to their Czech counterparts in Charter 77; on the other, there was the Catholic dissent group. This Christian resistance was far stronger in Slovakia than in the Czech lands, even though the so-called underground Church was created and promoted as primarily a non-political institution.[15]

Within the Slovak dissent movement, Ján Čarnogurský was the most prominent individual who came from Catholic circles. His father, Pavol (Paľo) Čarnogurský had been a member of parliament in the autonomous (1938–1939) and later quasi-independent (1939–1945) Slovak Republic. In February 1945, he crossed the battlefront and joined the Czechoslovak army. Pavol Čarnogurský was also close to Kolaković, and he remained one of the most important Slovak dissidents within postwar and later commu-

13 Norbert Kmeť, "Opozícia a hnutie odporu na Slovensku 1968–1989," in *Opozice a odpor proti komunistickému režimu v Československu 1968–1989*, ed. Blažek, 42.

14 Čarnogurský, "Disent na Slovensku," 211.

15 Juraj Marušiak, "Nezávislé inciativy na Slovensku v rokoch normalizácie," in *November 1989 na Slovensku: Súvislosti, predpoklady a dôsledky*, ed. Jan Pešek and Soňa Szomolányi (Bratislava: Nadácia Milana Šimečku, Historický ústav SAV and Katedra politológie FF UK, 1999), 70–71.

nist Czechoslovakia. As early as 1947, he was arrested on the grounds he was a "Slovak nationalist," and he spent 18 months in prison. He suffered the same fate in the 1951–1953 period, and by the time of the communist regime, had been labelled a bourgeois nationalist. In 1976, at the age of 68, he was arrested again, and almost his entire archive was confiscated by the communist secret police.[16]

Pavol Čarnogurský's five children all also became politically active. His son, Pavol, left Czechoslovakia and went into exile in Canada, where he was an important member of the Slovak World Congress (*Svetový kongres Slovákov)*. The other sons, Ján and Ivan, were both active politicians, while his two daughters – Marina and Oľga – served in the Slovak diplomatic service. With all due respect to his siblings, Ján was the most inspiring personality. While studying in Prague between 1967 and 1969, he formed ties with Václav Benda and Václav Malý.[17] After completing his studies in law, he became an attorney in 1970 and established a reputation as a defender of religious activists. In 1981, the regime organized his expulsion from the Bar Association. As such, Ján belonged to a very small group of Slovak dissidents, becoming the single most prominent individual within the Christian Democratic stream in Slovakia.[18] In contrast, the vast majority of the Slovak population remained politically inactive, preferring to participate in underground church activities.

As regards the Czech lands, the situation was even worse before the development of Charter 77. In the first half of the 1970s, there was almost no opposition and only the Helsinki process, with its promise of respect for human rights, created the potential for the appearance of critics of the regime. During the 1970s, we can detect three basic sources of resistance activities in this period – communist reformers, democratic and liberal actors, and members of the religious underground. Otáhal mentions that the third group also included Christians, but he gives no further details. According to Malý, who was one of the most important members of the resistance to originate from the Catholic clergy, Charter 77 had no effect on the Christian community and changes took place only after Cardinal Tomášek revised his position at the beginning of the 1980s and strengthened the criticism against the communist leaders.[19]

16 Paľo (Pavol) Čarnogurský, *Boj s komunismom* (Bratislava: Kalligram, 2013).

17 Čarnogurský, "Disent na Slovensku," 214.

18 See Id., "Christian Democracy in Slovakia."

19 Milan Otáhal, "K některým otázkám dějin tak zvané normalizace v českých zemích," in *Za svobodu a demokracii I: Odpor proti komunistické moci*, ed. Cuhra and Veber, 122–124.

Tomášek had been very reserved about Charter 77, not least because of the involvement of former Communist Party members, including Jiří Hájek – known for "recently mocking the Church" and as formerly having been "a militant communist atheist" – at the top. The Catholic and Czech Brethren Churches declared their neutral position on the issue; however, they did not reject the document. In fact, a general mistrust of underground movements and in some cases also longstanding anti-Semitism were evident within the Catholic clergy, especially after 1977. Nevertheless, Christians represented an important part of Charter 77 – as Cuhra notes, "it is symbolic that [if we look at] the signatories in alphabetical order, we find the priest Milan Balabán, and in last place, another priest, J. Zvěřina."[20] Zvěřina, Mádr and the evangelical activists Ladislav Hejdánek, Božena Komárková, and Miloš Rejchrt all criticized the loss of solidarity among religious leaders. Zvěřina also stressed his alarm that while the pope had been positive about the Charter, Czech Catholic leaders took the opposite view. Together with Malý, Zvěřina might be seen as the driving force (*spiritus agens*) behind Tomášek's change of heart.[21]

It is worth reiterating that Cardinal Tomášek had reservations about Charter 77. Even so, a relatively large group of important Catholic figures decided to sign the document, including the priests Josef Zvěřina, Václav Malý, František Lízna, and Josef Kordík and laypeople such as Charles University Professor Růžena Vacková as well as Radim Palouš, Ivan Medek, Jan Sokol, Dana Němcová, Augustin Navrátil, and Václav Benda. Cardinal Tomášek began to change his position mainly under the influence of the new Polish pope John Paul II, abandoning the Eastern policy of his predecessors John XXIII and Paul VI,[22] and also under the influence of the Catholic dissidents.[23]

This assessment suggests that Catholic dissent was expressed partly through Charter 77. Still, an independent Catholic dissident movement also existed in Czechoslovakia, and Catholics were mostly active via that route. Protestant movements were generally less persecuted, but they were also largely missing from the Charter 77 activities.[24] An exception was the New Orientation (*Nová orientace*) group with its unofficial ties to

20 Josef Cuhra, "Křesťané a počátky života Charty 77," *Katolická revue* 74, no. 3 (2007): 25–26.

21 Ibid., 27–28.

22 See Hansjakob Stehle, *The Eastern Politics of the Vatican, 1917–1979*, trans. Sandra Smith (Athens, OH: Ohio University Press, 1981).

23 Milan Otáhal, *Opoziční proudy v české společnosti 1969–1989* (Prague: Ústav pro soudobé dějiny AV ČR, 2011), 148–149.

24 Id., "K některým otázkám dějin tak zvané normalizace v českých zemích," 124.

the Czech Brethren Church. Ladislav Hejdánek should be singled out as the most important representative of this group.[25] Cuhra refers to the end of the 1970s as a "period of turnover." Religious *samizdat*, petitions and protest letters appeared; the regime was confronted with Catholics' involvement in Charter 77 activities. It was not just the election of John Paul II and his appeal for greater bravery that provoked this change. The 1983 protest letter of Cardinal Tomášek that accused the communist regime of violating the freedom of religion can be seen as some kind of culmination of these measures, with official and unofficial Church representatives clamoring increasingly loudly against the pro-regime *Pacem in Terris* [association].[26] Slovak theology students went on a hunger strike in October 1980 to protest the *Pacem in Terris* seminar at the faculty. As a result, eleven of these students were expelled from the university; however, they received personal encouragement from Pope John Paul II, and in March 1983, the Holy See officially "banned" the association.[27]

Even so, the role of the "official," i.e. supported by (part of) the Catholic clergy, resistance in Czechoslovakia was not as significant as was the case in Poland or the German Democratic Republic. We can identify just two events whose importance went beyond the internal life of the Catholic Church and which had major civic repercussions – the Velehrad Pilgrimage in 1985 and the document known as Navrátil's Petition.[28]

The Velehrad Pilgrimage took place on 6 and 7 July 1985 to commemorate the 1100th anniversary of Saint Methodius's death. The event was expected to align generally with communist – and even more pan-Slavic – ideology and assumptions since the age of Greater Moravia was understood as a milestone for Czechoslovak identity and its interconnection with eastern civilizations and Slavic nations. Nevertheless, the clergy and believers saw the pilgrimage in quite a different way. With the support of 22,000 citizens, Cardinal Tomášek invited the pope to attend the event; Benda highlights the fact that this petition attracted more support than any other in fifteen years. The communist regime succeeded in promoting the event as domestic, and foreign participants were not invited. Still, as Otáhal observes, "the authorities did not manage to change the pilgrimage

25 Id., *Opoziční proudy v české společnosti 1969–1989*, 149–150.

26 Important impulse for such critics was the apprehension of 15 Franciscans in March 1983; see Jan Hartmann, Bohumil Svoboda and Václav Vaško, *Kardinál Tomášek. Generál bez vojska ...?* (Prague: Vyšehrad, 2003).

27 Cuhra, "Katolická církev a odpor vůči ´normalizačnímu´ režimu," 77.

28 Otáhal, *Opoziční proudy v české společnosti 1969–1989*, 7.

into a peaceful vehicle for the official policy framework."[29] He continues, "On the first day of the event, believers refused to leave the area in front of the basilica and stayed there praying overnight. On the second day, about 150,000 citizens took part, coming primarily from Moravia and Slovakia (…) At the same time, 100,000 joined the pilgrimage to the eastern Slovak city of Levoča."[30]

The most visible protest against the regime came in the form of a petition for religious freedom, which was organized by the Catholic layperson Augustin Navrátil with support from Cardinal Tomášek and the Catholic clergy. More than 600,000 people signed this document.[31] The petition was prepared by a group of Moravian Catholics led by Navrátil, and it was presented in November 1987. The document put forward 31 policy points, including a demand for the separation of church and state, the restoration of the theology faculty in Olomouc, the reinstatement of members of the clergy, and the revival of monastic orders, along with a more general call for respect for human rights across the country.

The majority of the petition's signatories were of Slovak origin, a fact that underscores the strength of the Church in this part of the federation. The success of the petition was also made clear by the large number of agnostic signatories. The regime could not punish such a massive group. Instead, it sanctioned Navrátil with an extraordinary, although for a totalitarian regime very typical, penalty: he was placed in a psychiatric hospital against his will.[32]

With all due respect for the anti-communist position of the Catholic clergy in the 1980s, a standpoint also expressed through the activities of the "decade of spiritual renewal" (*Desetiletí duchovní obnovy*) that began in 1985, the most important conservative and Christian Democratic activists were to be found in dissident groups. In Slovakia, the activities of Ján Čarnogurský should once again be highlighted. In 1988, he began to publish the *samizdat* review *Bratislava Letters* (*Bratislavské listy*) together with Ján Langoš and František Mikloško. Among Čarnogurský's collaborators were also Milan Šimečka, Hana Ponická, and Miroslav Kusý. Yet neither Čarnogurský nor Šimečka signed Charter 77. In this regard, Char-

29 Otáhal, *Opoziční proudy v české společnosti 1969–1989*, 249.

30 Ibid., 250. Čarnogurský mentions 200,000 participants. See Čarnogurský, "Christian Democracy in Slovakia," 427.

31 Otáhal, "K některým otázkám dějin tak zvané normalizace v českých zemích," 128. Again, Čarnogurský offers different information – 500,000 signatories, most of them from Slovakia. Čarnogurský, "Christian Democracy in Slovakia," 427.

32 Otáhal, *Opoziční proudy v české společnosti 1969–1989*, 556–558.

ter 77 was seen as basically a "Czech" activity, a view that was particularly strong in the Slovak Catholic community, which – unlike the equivalent community in the Czech lands – was actually functional during the communist period.[33]

As regards the Czech lands, we can discern several important communities with a conservative and/or Christian Democratic orientation in the post-1977 era. Turning first to the Christian Democratic group in Charter 77, we should mention Václav Benda, a Catholic intellectual closely allied with critics of Cardinal Tomášek's indecision about the regime and Charter 77. Benda signed Charter 77 and was imprisoned from 1979 to 1984. After returning home, he became the most important voice of the Catholic position within Charter 77. From the outset, Benda was involved in debates with other streams within Charter 77, especially communist reformists and leftists more generally. A typical example was his ongoing exchange with Petr Uhl, one of the most important proponents of Marxist and Trotskyist ideology within Charter 77. As early as 1985, Uhl criticized Benda as an ideologue.[34] Uhl was himself an ideologue of equal conviction, although one with a very different ideology.

A second group that warrants mention consisted of the conservatives surrounding Daniel Kroupa and Pavel Bratinka. In 1978, Kroupa created his own seminary for young philosophers. The group included Bratinka and Jiří Skalický among others, and it was greatly influenced by the work of Eric Voegelin.[35]

Last but not least, we should highlight a group of dissidents who demanded a de-ideologized debate about Czech history. In 1984, Rudolf Kučera and the conservative dissidents around him began to publish the journal *Střední Evropa* (Central Europe). Kučera was himself one of the two authors (the other being his namesake Jan P. Kučera) of Charter 77 Document No. 77, which was published in November 1984 under the title "The Right on History" (*Právo na historii*). That document was written from a conservative and "Catholic" perspective, and it opened a major debate not only between the Charter and the official historiography, but also among different groups of historians.[36] It is worth adding that in 1987, the Moravian chapter established the quarterly *Střední Evropa – brněnská verze* (Central Europe – Brno version) based on limited cooperation with

33 Cuhra, "Křesťané a počátky života Charty 77," 29.

34 Otáhal, *Opoziční proudy v české společnosti 1969–1989*, 312.

35 Petr Dimun and Milan J. Hamerský, *10 let na straně svobody: kronika ODA z let 1989–1999* (Brno: Bachant, 1999), 9.

36 Otáhal, *Opoziční proudy v české společnosti 1969–1989*, 291.

the Prague group. Key members of the Brno group included Petr Fiala, František Mikš, and Pavel Švanda.

To sum up, in Bohemia, Christian Democracy was restricted to relatively small groups of dissidents with mostly intellectual backgrounds, while in Moravia and above all in Slovakia also the grassroots level was important and quite active before 1989.

The final years of the communist regime

Czechoslovakia was one of the communist states that remained subject to a very rigid regime and ideology even after Mikhail Gorbachev came to power. The replacement of Czechoslovak Communist Party General Secretary Gustáv Husák with Milouš Jakeš, the leader of the party's screening commission after the Warsaw Pact occupation in 1968, showed how unprepared the regime was for any kind of liberalization. At the same time, the rhetoric of the new party leadership included Gorbachev's terminology – *perestroika*, "new thinking," and *glasnost* – which would also become an important part of the public debate in Czechoslovakia.

In this period, the Charter 77 group also prepared for its third forum. According to Benda, who reflected on the position of Christian participants, no reforms of communism were possible. Nevertheless, after Tomášek's change of heart, Benda understood that the Catholic Church had a key role as a result of its mass membership.[37] Similarly, Václav Malý pointed to the changing position of Catholicism in Czechoslovakia despite persistent dissent, mainly from the Czech side. Initially, Charter 77 did not mention religious rights. Nevertheless, Catholics understood that the movement for human dignity did not distinguish between civil and religious rights. As an example of the potential for cooperation between believers and other citizens, Benda highlighted Navrátil's petition.[38]

Reflecting on the position of Charter 77, Benda came up with the idea of a new organization – the Movement for Civic Freedom (HOS). According to Otáhal:

> [t]he catalyst for the creation of the Movement for Civic Freedom was the attempt to overcome the social isolation of Charter 77 and create an organization that would apply competitive political methods. The immediate

37 Otáhal, *Opoziční proudy v české společnosti 1969–1989*, 291.
38 Ibid., 308.

reason for its constitution was the dispersal of participants in Charter 77's Third Forum in January 1988. The birth of the movement was beset with difficulties, and it was not until 15 October 1988 that the manifesto *Democracy for All* (*Demokracii pro všechny*) was published, making the organization known to the public.[39]

In fact, this movement inherently had the same ideological basis as Charter 77 and, as such, contained several ideological streams. "HOS was not an ideologically coherent organization, but rather a free association of political groups and clubs that were not subordinated to any center. Soon, the individual streams took form: around V. Benda, there was a Christian Democratic one; around D. Kroupa and P. Bratinka, a civic democratic one; and around Rudolf Battěk, a curbed Socialist one."[40]

In the Slovak part of the Czechoslovak Federation, Ján Čarnogurský, Miroslav Kusý, Hana Ponická, and Milan Šimečka were among those who joined in this new undertaking, whose creation was announced shortly before the 70th anniversary of the declaration of an independent Czechoslovakia.[41] As we will see, HOS became an important tool for integrating Czech and Slovak Christian Democratic groups. The *Democracy for All* manifesto also created new divisions, with Benda on one side and Petr Uhl, who refused to support the Movement for Civic Freedom, on the other. Uhl claimed that his position was mainly due to absence of the word "Socialism" from the declaration. Šimečka formulated a response to Uhl's criticisms using Christian Democratic arguments.[42]

Along with these observable changes in the dissident movement, we should also mention some developments within ČSL. I have already stressed the negative role of the party, which supported the regime from a "satellite" position. In this vein, Pehr notes:

> On the one hand, the People's Party was seen as a collaboration between the National Front satellite party and the Communist Party of Czechoslovakia (...) On the other, the communists understood membership of the People's Party as some kind of "stigma" that marked a person for life.

39 Milan Otáhal, "Programová orientace disentu 1969–1989," in *Opozice a odpor proti komunistickému režimu v* Československu *1968–1989*, ed. Blažek, 38.

40 Ibid., 39.

41 Kmeť, "Opozícia a hnutie odporu na Slovensku 1968–1989," 52; Růžena Hlušičková and Blanka Císařovská, eds., *Hnutí za občanskou svobodu 1988–1989: Sborník dokumentů* (Prague: Maxdorf, 1994), 12.

42 Hlušičková and Císařovská, eds., *Hnutí za občanskou svobodu 1988–1989: Sborník dokumentů*, 118–119.

> Being a member of the People's Party usually meant being treated like an official reactionary, who was tolerated out of compassion (…) The People's Party was viewed as some kind of edifying (Catholic) association that put hundreds and thousands of hours of volunteer work hours into maintaining churches, cultural heritage, village squares, and other places. In many cases, activities that would usually have been organized by the Catholic Church (pilgrimages, excursions, balls etc.) were done with the patronage of the People's Party.[43]

Changes in the USSR, Poland, Hungary, and East Germany also prompted a new internal debate within ČSL. Pehr observes:

> In the communist *perestroika* period, dissatisfied members created a group within the People's Party (…) This group is usually referred to as the revivalist movement (*Obrodný proud*) (or "Christians for *perestroika*") (…) Among the main voices of this group, we can identify Richard Sacher, the Minister of Internal Affairs after November; Josef Bartončík, the future party chair; and Bohumil Svoboda, the chair of the Prague 6 party district committee.[44]

Nevertheless, this group could hardly be seen as conservative or Christian Democratic at this stage.

In the final year of Czechoslovak communist rule, the regime became increasingly violent and repressive as it lost its self-confidence. Cuhra emphasizes the importance of "Palach Week," held in January 1989, which mobilized young Christians against the communist regime.[45] In his opinion, Palach Week reinforced the interconnectedness of religious and civic circles of opposition. In the summer of 1989, the celebrations of Cardinal Tomášek's 90th birthday also drew attention to Tomášek as a protector of human rights. Tomášek responded to the brutality of the secret police in January 1989 in a letter to the federation's Prime Minister Ladislav Adamec, which stressed the existence of a right to liberty that could not be overridden by violence. This position was much closer to the stance of Charter 77 than the one taken by ČSL at the time.

In the autumn of 1989, a group of Slovak dissidents associated with HOS was accused of sedition and subversion of the communist regime in Czechoslovakia. The group comprised Čarnogurský, Kusý, and Ponická,

43 Michal Pehr, "ČSL na konci komunismu," in *Josef Lux a česká politika 90. let*, ed. Milan Znoj and Michal Pehr (Prague: Ústav politologie FF UK, 2005), 28.

44 Ibid., 28–29.

45 This was a week of activities commemorating the 20th anniversary of the self-immolation of the student Jan Palach.

along with Anton Selecký and Vladimír Maňák; Čarnogurský and Kusý were arrested. The leaders of HOS called on Czechoslovakia's official leaders to release both these activists, with similar appeals to the new Polish and Hungarian leadership established during the transition and Soviet leader Mikhail Gorbachev.[46] This, however, occurred only after 17 November 1989.

Christian Democratic groups and parties in November 1989

HOS's Christian Democratic Club was established on 15 November 1989, not long before the start of the Czechoslovak democratic transition. The club was created in Prague, with organizers expressing the hope that similar clubs would soon be founded in other Czechoslovak cities and regions. The new club's spokespersons were Václav Benda, Josef Cuhra, and Michaela Freiová; other founding members were Petr Burian, Ivan Dejmal, Jan Dus, Markéta Fialková, Přemysl Fialka, Jiří Gruntorád, Libor Holman, Michal Holeček, Josef Kříž, Petr Kůrka, Jan Litomiský, Stanislav Novotný, Martin Palouš, Radim Palouš, Michal Semín, Petruška Šustrová, Miroslav Tyl, and Tomáš Vlasák.[47] The club did not declare any comprehensive manifesto. However, in the works of the signatories and the ideological profile of the Christian Democratic Party as the successor of the club, Christian Democracy might be distinguished as the most important impulse.

Only two days after the establishment of the club, the democratic revolution began in Czechoslovakia, and on 19 November 1989, the Civic Forum (*Občanské forum*, OF) was created. Benda – like Rudolf Battěk, the most prominent leader of the movement's Social Democratic stream – chose to end his involvement with HOS.[48] As a result, the new Christian Democratic Party first found a place within the Civic Forum and went on

46 Hlušičková and Císařovská, eds., *Hnutí za občanskou svobodu 1988–1989: Sborník dokumentů*, 181–182; 208–211.
47 Ibid., 243–244.
48 Ibid., 249–250.

to become an independent political party in the Christian and Democratic Union.[49] As Benda's son Marek, also an active politician, points out:

> The Christian Democratic Party (KDS) had already been formed on 3 December 1989, and from the very start, we stressed the need to dissolve the catch-all Civic Forum movement and set up standard political parties. Even so, at this time, we defended the idea of KDS remaining in the OF until the first free elections. Only KDS's defeat at the March party congress, where we failed to convince delegates that this was the correct approach, brought us into an electoral coalition with the People's Party.[50]

In the case of ČSL, this group from the revivalist stream assumed power after November 1989. As Pehr notes, "During the night of 27 November 1989, the old party leadership resigned in response to recent developments. The new Central Committee was elected with the following members: J. Bartončík (Chairperson), B. Svoboda (First Deputy Chairperson), and František Reichel (Second Deputy Chairperson). A. Baudyš and Richard Sacher also joined the new party leadership. On 9 December, the party rejected the National Front system."[51] Nevertheless, such changes in the leadership did not ensure the democratization of the party, its break with the pro-communist legacy, or any reorientation towards a clear ideological profile.

I would add that it is highly questionable whether any of this new group of leaders from the Czechoslovak People's Party can be considered conservative. To begin with, there is insufficient information about their independent political preferences since the party joined the coalition of Czechoslovak Christian Democratic parties that was established before the first contested elections in May 1990. Known as the Christian Democratic Union (KDU), this coalition was dominated by the Slovak Christian Democratic Movement, headed by Čarnogurský, and the Czech Christian Democratic Party led by Benda. This state of affairs was reinforced only

49 The Christian and Democratic Union (KDU) was the electoral coalition of the ČSL and a group of newly established parties for the first competitive elections in post-November 1989 Czechoslovakia. Next to the ČSL it included the Christian Democratic Party, Free Peasant Party, Union of Czechoslovak Entrepreneurs, Moravian Civic Movement; and Senior Club. The ideological profile was rather unclear, although Christian values were repeatedly mentioned in public speeches by the leaders. The Slovak Christian Democratic Movement (KDH) rejected joining the coalition and decided for individual ballots. Čarnogurský, "Christian Democracy in Slovakia," 431.

50 Marek Benda, "Konzervatismus v 90. letech. Odkaz Václava Bendy," in *Česká konzervativní a liberální politika. Sborník k desátému výročí založení revue Proglas*, ed. Petr Fiala and František Mikš (Brno: Centrum pro studium demokracie a kultury, 2000), 131.

51 Pehr, "ČSL na konci komunismu," 29.

a few days before elections, when news broke of the Bartončík Affair in which the ČSL leader was accused of collaborating with the communist secret police.

Along with KDS, another political party was formed at the core of HOS. This was the liberal conservative Civic Democratic Alliance (*Občanská demokratická aliance*, ODA). According to Dimun and Hamerský:

> Within the HOS Christian Democratic Club, the nucleus of ODA was also created – these were people who held Christian values so sacred that they objected to their use in political games. They understood Christianity as a personal challenge for every individual (...) In fact, no one stood more closely by ODA than KDS. Along these lines, Kroupa also stressed that Christians should be involved in every political party,[52] arguing that Christianity did not mandate any particular political direction.[53]

In a piece in the year 2000 commemorating his father's activities, Marek Benda writes that the touchstone of Václav Benda's politics was the recognition that "communism has corrupted everything, and we have to try to (re-)establish normal, natural conditions." In this context, he recalls one of his father's "key sentences during one of our debates in 1989": "conservatives face difficulties in the Czech lands because there is nothing that should be conserved."[54] The elder Benda had joked that a radical conservative party was needed in the Czech context in order to enforce changes across almost all spheres:

> Already the name "Conservative Party" was ruled out by the historical context since that phrase was reserved for the hard-line Czech Communist Party. The issue of the party's name was one of the main reasons why long-time colleagues in the dissent movement (Benda, Tyl, and Litomiský; Bratinka, Kroupa, and Mašek) dispersed into two parties, forming KDS and ODA. KDS represented the logical continuation of the Christian Democratic Club in the Movement for Civic Freedom, and the group around my father insisted on the need to state clearly that the party's ideological anchor lay in the general confusion about the political terms already contained in its name. In contrast, the founders of the future ODA made the argument that the Czech public was not ready for a "Christian" party.[55]

52 Daniel Kroupa, member of HOS and later ODA.
53 Dimun and Hamerský, *10 let na straně svobody*, 10.
54 Benda, "Konzervatismus v 90. letech. Odkaz Václava Bendy," 126.
55 Ibid.

Politicians from conservative, and especially Christian Democratic, parties, made up an important part of the newly established post-November 1989 political elite. The new ČSL leaders played a key role in both the federal and Czech governments, and KDS and ODA members were significant players in the post-November political scene. In fact, the most prominent actor from within this group was Ján Čarnogurský. He was released from prison on 25 November 1989 and just two weeks later became the first Deputy Prime Minister of the federal government and head of the Legislative Council. In February 1990, he was made the first chair of the Christian Democratic Movement, the party he continued to lead until 2000. Nevertheless, even before the first contested elections, there were signs that Čarnogurský's first priority was Slovak nationalism rather than Christian Democratic politics. After the elections, he refused to endorse the new federal government even as the other members of the KDU electoral coalition gave it their support. Later, he reflected that the defeat of communism had cleared the way for him to take up new political challenges: "During the communist period, the basic division in the world was the one between communism and democracy. Every political movement was important only insofar as it took part in the struggle against communism (…) The anti-communist movement which emerged out of Christian and civic dissent in Slovakia performed its duty in the service of the Slovak national interest."[56] After 1989, Čarnogurský had new priorities, specifically the struggle to create an independent Slovakia. His position and later the dissolution of the Czechoslovak Federation significantly weakened Christian Democratic politics in the Czech lands.

In addition to political parties, we should also briefly consider the development of important conservative and Christian Democratic think tanks and communities. The Moravia/Brno group behind *Střední Evropa* were responsible for creating the journal *Proglas* in early 1990:

> In the first issue, the journal announced its support not just for conservatism and Christian values but also the idea of European integration, in parallel with maintaining particular national communities and cultures. From the very outset, this ideological position was complemented by a stress on the Anglo-Saxon form of modern liberal (neo)-conservatism that was the second basic ideological pillar of the journal.[57]

56 Čarnogurský, "Disent na Slovensku," 217.

57 Petr Fiala and František Mikš. "Intelektuálové, novináři a česká politika," in *Česká konzervativní a liberální politika*, ed. Fiala and Mikš, 11.

Similar positions were also put forward by the newly established think tank and publishing house the Centre for Studies of Democracy and Culture (*Centrum pro stadium demokracie a kultury*, CDK). Both outlets greatly influenced political discourse in the Czech lands (Petr Fiala, the current leader of the Civic Democratic Party, came up from within these forums.)

Turning to the subsequent development of *Střední Evropa* and the Prague group, it is clear that in later years, the focus on neo-conservatism and especially its economic component (Thatcherism, Reaganomics), was distinctly weaker and limited to "only" a small number of the original group. Most of the group, including the journal's editor Rudolf Kučera, who was also president of the Czechoslovak section of the Pan-European Union and founder of the Institute for Central European Culture and Politics (*Institut pro středoevropskou kulturu a politiku*, ISE) think tank and publishing house, drew on the "social market economy" model. More generally, they followed examples from Germany (especially Bavaria, given their close ties with Sudeten German groups) and Austria. Alena Hromádková, the founder of the liberal conservative party, Democratic Union (*Demokratická unie*, DEU), should be singled out as a most important "exception" to this trend since she strongly favored the Anglo-Saxon school of political thought. We should also note that the "Proglas Group" greatly influenced the establishment of new social science departments and faculties at Masaryk University. Similarly, Rudolf Kučera and others from *Střední Evropa* established the Political Science Department at the newly established Faculty of Social Sciences at Charles University.

In May 1990, the Civic Institute (*Občanský institut*, OI), a think tank for the ODA, was created.[58] The founders of OI included important figures such as Michaela Freiová, Michal Semín, and Roman Joch, the future chief advisor to Prime Minister Petr Nečas.

Christian Democratic politics after 1990

Seen from a distance of three decades, the history of Christian (Democratic) politics in the Czech lands does not appear to be the greatest success story of the Velvet Revolution. In terms of electoral success, the prospects of Bohemian and Moravian Christian politics are not very noteworthy, as Hanuš suggested in 2000: "The attempt to establish a new political party (KDS) after 1989 failed; amending its policies in the supraconfessional

58 Dimun and Hamerský, *10 let na straně svobody*, 12.

(non-religious) direction, the longstanding People's Party was, in fact, a little more successful."[59] According to Hanuš, the fate of the KDS party was not so bad since it was at least partially transformed into a "certain civic party," i.e. the Civic Democratic Party (ODS).[60]

The reasons for the limited success – or even failure – of Christian politics may be found in the years before November 1989. As this analysis has shown, we need not confine ourselves to the time of communist dominance but should also consider the years before 1948. In fact, as we have seen, the Czech (Bohemian) experience is very distinct when compared to both the Moravian and Slovak contexts. In particular, the Catholic Church in Bohemia did not succeed in carrying out any discernible grassroots activism for larger groups in society. Both the clergy and the Catholics within Charter 77 failed to develop strategies that would address these broader social groups. To paraphrase Hanuš once again, the Catholic Church did not find its way into Bohemian and Moravian society. Among the reasons for this, he cites the Church's resistance to the presence of democracy in its own internal activities. Furthermore, "its programs such as the decade of spiritual renewal (*Desetiletí duchovní obnovy*) that were rooted in the communist period were no longer impressive in the new democratic atmosphere, and went unacknowledged."[61]

Slightly more successful were the former dissident movements that developed relationships with at least a small segment of non-Christian society. In this context, the specific connection between the Christians within Charter 77 and "ordinary" citizens is often stressed – in other words, the tendency to move between the church and the pub. Václav Benda is presented as the prototype of a Catholic intellectual, who "should think (if he is truly doing so) in a way that is by definition universal, 'with the community and within the community' and should stop himself from taking on a ghetto mentality."[62]

In fact, after the transition, Benda led his party into a state of deep isolation, and the same might also be said about his personal situation. Nevertheless, the isolation was not exclusively negative, at least insofar as it was based on an effort to develop (highly) principled policies, with a special focus on the past. Christian Democratic groups became the most promi-

59 Jiří Hanuš, "Má církev v České republice budoucnost?," *Proglas* 11, no. 5–6 (2000): 38.
60 Ibid., 39.
61 Ibid., 40.
62 Ibid., 36–37.

nent anti-communist movement in Czech politics.[63] This was true of ODA, DEU, and the above-mentioned think tanks as well as of ODS and KDS, for whom this status became important in 1995. Regarding anti-communism, Pečínka points out: "right-leaning politicians were among the main advocates for radical restitution, opening up the lustration question and helping to set up Benda's Institute for the Documentation and Investigation of Communist Crimes (*Úřad pro dokumentaci a vyšetřování zločinů komunismu*, ÚDV); they prepared the Act on the Publication of State Security Materials."[64]

For Benda, restitution and de-communization became the most important political goals. Commenting on his activities for the Institute for the Documentation and Investigation of Communist Crimes, Benda – who called himself a "hunter of communists" – advanced this view in 1993: "We cannot yet forgive the communists who continue to sin and behave arrogantly and aggressively; savoring defeatism is not a Christian sentiment."[65]

In a country where millions of citizens were (former) members of the Communist Party and had cooperated with the normalization regime in many different ways, this stance naturally did not have much political weight or support. Moreover, Benda appears to have been someone who never moved beyond the basic black-and-white framework of anti-communism even after the transition. As an example, it is worth noting that, in 1994, Benda supported the visit of Augusto Pinochet to the Czech Republic, inviting the leader to lunch and stating that he would proceed in the same way as Pinochet were he in the latter's position. Among the negative fallout, this view prompted another dispute between Benda and Uhl. Uhl criticized Benda for supporting the desecration of human rights. In response, Benda stressed that he "would behave decently towards [another person], but in a conflict where the other person stood for evil and violence, [he] could respond with violence too."[66] Otáhal claims that both Benda and Uhl were radicals.[67] Pithart, on the other hand, offers this sketch of Benda: "He was one of the hardcore dissenters. He was a fighter who would not go

63 Ladislav Cabada, "Anti-Communism in Czech Society and Politics after 1989: Analysis of the Background and Development of the Phaenomenon," *Journal of East European and Asian Studies* 3, no 1 (2012): 55–75.

64 Bohumil Pečinka, "Formování české občanské pravice," in *Česká konzervativní a liberální politika*, ed. Fiala and Mikš, 70.

65 Jan Lipold, "Václav Benda se nikdy nevezl s proudem," *Mladá fronta DNES*, 3 June 1999, 2.

66 Ibid., 2.

67 Otáhal, *Opoziční proudy v české společnosti 1969–1989*, 517–518.

with the flow even after joining a political party."[68] Benda was a strong personality, a fact confirmed when he succeeded in the first Senate elections in 1996 based on the two-round voting majority system. In the second round for the Prague 1 district, Benda defeated another giant of the Czech conservative and Christian Democratic political scene, Pavel Tigrid. In June 1999, Benda died at not quite 53 years of age.

Only five months later, a second key Christian Democratic politician, Josef Lux, the leader of KDU, also died. He was just ten years younger than Benda. As Hanuš notes, Lux saved the party after the Bartončík Affair and slowly steered it back onto the Christian Democratic path. The most visible sign of this change was the slogan "social market economy," which was used to oppose Václav Klaus's phrase "market without adjectives." After Lux's death, the party descended into conflicts between two factions of which one was left-leaning ("socialists visiting church," as Miroslav Kalousek put it in 2009 when he left the party to start the TOP09 Party with Karel Schwarzenberg), while the other was led by Kalousek and neo-liberals. Neither group followed Lux's approach.

ODA eventually collapsed in 1998 as a result of internal financial difficulties, factionalism, and a loss of support. KDS, the second arm of the conservative group established under communism, was also subsequently dissolved. This group (KDS, ODA) had emerged from the "politicization of dissenting intellectuals."[69] Another group presented young opponents of communism from the Czech dissent movement – most visible members of this group were Stanislav Devátý, Jan Ruml, and Hana Marvanová. The latter two were the first chairpersons of the Freedom Union, which was established in 1998 and recruited a large number of former ODA voters. In fact, this party was predominantly liberal, and conservatism was not an important part of its ideology.

As the most successful of the conservative groups, we can identify the 40–50-year-old liberal economists who worked for the Economic Institute and Forecasting Center. Among its best-known members were Václav Klaus, Josef Zieleniec, Dušan Tříska, Tomáš Ježek, Vladimír Dlouhý, and Karel Dyba. In my view, this group should not be seen as either Christian Democratic or conservative since these individuals and their associates stressed the economic aspects of transformation and (ultra-)liberal economic positions. Furthermore, many of them – and especially Klaus – un-

68 Lipold, "Václav Benda se nikdy nevezl s proudem," 2.
69 Pečinka, "Formování české občanské pravice," 71.

derestimated and even mocked the role of values, religion, and churches in the transformation process.

The majority of these individuals went on to create ODS, one of two catch-all parties in the Czech Republic until 2013. Nevertheless, conservatives made up only a small group within the party, and many of them embraced protectionist, Euroskeptic, and anti-globalization rhetoric. Former Prime Minister Petr Nečas, probably the party's most prominent Christian Democrat, also promoted ultra-liberal economic policies during his 2010–2013 government, although he did make an effort to bring anti-communism back into the political debate.

Since the collapse of Nečas's government and the subsequent decline of both liberal conservative parties – ODS and TOP09 – which each received less than ten percent of votes in the 2013 parliamentary elections,[70] the only winner among conservative and Christian Democratic actors has appeared to be KDU-ČSL. This party had its power restored in both parliament and government, but it remains to be seen whether its leadership will adopt Christian Democratic policies. Certainly, the most recent October 2017 parliamentary elections have revealed the presence of a purely conservative (and economically neo-liberal) movement around ODS. To date, KDU-ČSL and ODS have shown only minimal overlap in their policy priorities and strategies. While KDU-ČSL appears to be a pro-European and even Euro-federalist party that emphasizes social market economics, ODS sees itself as a voice of Euroskepticism and an unconditional defender of the small state and the market economy. For many years, KDU-ČSL has also seemed to prioritize shrewd office-seeking measures over policy. In contrast, ODS has billed itself as the sole protector of democratic politics and the national interest from more conservative/right-wing positions. TOP09, which also has only a small number of deputies, lies in the middle of these parties. This splintering of the Christian Democratic and conservative camp does not bode well for the future.

70 Ladislav Cabada, "The Czech Party System in the Year 2016: Strenghtening Populism, Personalization Tendencies and Anti-Political Attitudes," in *The Czech Center-Right Solutions to the Political Challenges of 2017*, ed. Lucie Tunkrová et al. (Prague: Wilfried Martens Centre for European Studies, Konrad-Adenauer-Stiftung & TOPAZ, 2016), 81–90.

Conclusions

As this analysis has shown, clerical and conservative political forces had already faced mistrust and opposition from within Czech society before the establishment of an independent Czechoslovakia in 1918. In Slovakia, the situation was different, and political clericalism also played an important role in the development of national identity within Hungary and later the First Czechoslovak Republic. For Czech progressives – and liberals and socialists in particular – this was a key reason for ideological distrust in the Slovak elite, and indeed it has remained a permanent source of tension between Czech and Slovak politics. Certainly, this is partially due to the anti-democratic tendencies of an important faction of the dominant Slovak party – Hlinka's Slovak People's Party – as well as similar tendencies among some Czech clerical actors and a critical part of the Czech conservative movement before World War II. We can thus see that there were significant reasons for the exclusion of clerical and conservative political voices from the political contest even before the communist putsch of 1948. In this regard, the communists extended earlier political practices and exploited the anti-clerical/conservative mood within Czech society, albeit with a new totalitarian brutality.

One of the chief ways that Christian Democratic and conservative political consciousness survived the 1950s and managed to evolve was through the continuity of key personnel. Despite the oppression, arrest, and even murder of many thinkers and actors in this political camp during the totalitarian period, some Christian Democrats and conservatives were able to regroup and train a new generation of the movement during the 1960s. It was precisely these members of the new Christian Democratic/conservative intellectual wave who became very active during the transition and subsequent years.

The differences between the Czech lands and Slovakia that had emerged before 1948 remained in place during the communist period. As we have seen, in the Czech lands – and especially Bohemia – the clerical and conservative movement was weak and its support was mostly confined to small epistemic communities. In Slovakia and Moravia by contrast, the Christian Democratic movement had much stronger backing, and an important part of this activism happened at grassroots level.

Finally, we have observed the role of Christian Democratic and conservative political actors in post-communist Czechoslovakia and in the two new independent states that were established in 1992. While in the Czech

Republic conservative but predominantly neo-liberal actors steered the economic transition in the first half of the 1990s, in Slovakia these actors re-established a pro-democratic political path after Mečiar's "*democratura*." Significantly, the Czech conservative parties ODS and ODA were unable to include important conservative norms and values in their policies and their "conservative" character seems debatable, particularly given the activities of important leaders of these parties during the communist period. The main heir of clerically based politics, KDS, was also weak, although it managed to influence government policies in some key areas (lustration, overhauls, restitution). In my view, it is has only been since 2009 that we have seen signs of the (re-)creation of a genuine conservative and Christian Democratic movement in the Czech context, although this too remains weak. In Slovakia, by contrast, conservative and Christian Democratic parties have found much stronger grassroots support in the post-transition years. Nevertheless, their political performance since 2006 has been poor, and this includes the unstable government led by Prime Minister Iveta Radičová. This is, I would suggest, largely due to the fragmentation of the Christian Democratic and conservative camp, and some of these splits have followed the embrace by several actors of more authoritarian political ideologies and styles.

11

THE RESTORATION OF CHRISTIAN DEMOCRACY IN LITHUANIA, 1989-1990

Continuities and Ruptures

Artūras Svarauskas

The Christian Democrats are a political party with a long historical tradition in Lithuania. In the interwar republic, they were the strongest political force, dominating the Lithuanian Parliament from 1920 to 1926. Later, in the 1930s, they became the most influential opposition group to the authoritarian regime. Throughout the Soviet occupation, that spanned the entire second half of the twentieth century (from 1944 to 1989), they controlled most important positions in the Senior Committee of Liberation of Lithuania (SCLL), part of the unofficial Lithuanian government-in-exile in the USA. Still, in 1989, when the party was restored in Soviet Lithuania, it never regained the influence that it had had during the interwar years.

This chapter begins by exploring the origins and ideology of the Christian Democratic Party (LCDP) in the early twentieth century. However, my focus here is on the circumstances of its re-establishment in Lithuania during 1989–1990. I will also survey the aims of the party's political program. Finally, I will discuss the views of Christian Democrats on the road to re-establishing Lithuania's independence in the context of Gorbachev's reforms.

There is a lack of studies on Christian Democracy in Lithuania.[1] Only the ideas of Christian Democracy in the early twentieth century and the party's activities before World War II have received more thorough academic attention.[2] However, its history in the late twentieth century has

1 Algirdas Kasulaitis, *Lithuanian Christian Democracy* (Cleveland: Leo XIII Fund, 1976), 7–244.

2 Artūras Svarauskas, *Krikščioniškoji demokratija nepriklausomoje Lietuvoje (1918–1940): politinė galia ir jos ribos* (Vilnius: Lietuvos istorijos institutas, 2014), 45–374.

still not been researched. There are only some encyclopedia entries that have appeared since 1990.[3] In 2013, a publication appeared that includes extracts from various party documents.[4] The newest and most thorough study on the restoration of independent Lithuania largely fails to discuss the activities of the Christian Democrats.[5]

The origins of Christian Democracy and the challenges to the restoration of the party in 1989-1990

The impulse for the creation of Christian Democracy in Lithuania was given by Pope Leo XIII's corpus of late-nineteenth-century encyclicals, first and foremost *Rerum novarum* (1891). However, specific historical circumstances in the Western provinces of the Russian Empire – which exercised political sovereignty over Lithuania – such as the "national revival" that began at the end of the nineteenth century among ethnic Lithuanians, influenced the perception of Christian Democracy in their own way. In this region, the theses of *Rerum novarum* were interpreted differently than elsewhere in Europe. The first promoters of Christian Democracy were the nationally oriented Lithuanian Catholic clergy, who emphasized nationality and Catholicism, rather than the issue of workers. Due to the agrarian nature of Lithuanian society, the ideas of *Rerum novarum* were adapted to the social condition of the peasantry. In addition, Lithuanians were a confessional minority in the largely Orthodox Russian Empire.[6] Therefore, the joint emphasis on nationality and Catholicism became the basis for politicizing Catholicism, i.e. for the emergence of the Christian Democratic party.[7] At that time, the question of workers – in other words, the very question that *Rerum novarum* had been written to address – was not a priority for Lithuanians.

3 Albinas Gražiūnas, *Krikščioniškoji demokratija Lietuvoje: Lietuvos krikščionių demokratų partijos istorijos bruožai* (Vilnius: Tėvynės sargas, 1994), 15–165; Viktoras Petkus, *Krikščioniškoji demokratija pasaulyje ir Lietuvoje* (Vilnius: Lietverslas, 1991), 3–79.

4 Pranas Povilaitis and Viktorija Škiudaitė, *Lietuviai krikščionys demokratai išeivijoje* (Vilnius: Leono XIII fondas, 2013), 7–1200.

5 Česlovas Laurinavičius and Vladas Sirutavičius, *Sąjūdis: nuo "Persitvarkymo" iki Kovo 11-osios* (Vilnius: Baltos lankos, 2008), 3–579.

6 See, e.g., Mikhail D. Dolbilov, *Russkii krai, chuzhaia vera: Etnokonfessianal'naia politika imperii v Litve i Belorussii pri Aleksandre II* (Moscow: Novoe literaturnoe obozrenie, 2010).

7 Svarauskas, *Krikščioniškoji demokratija*, 53.

Thus, in 1905–1907, a distinctive feature of the Christian Democratic Party in Lithuania was its combination of nationalism and Catholicism.[8] This aspect also characterized the party's priorities following World War I in the newly independent Republic of Lithuania (1918–1940). Until the Second World War, LCDP leaders believed that Catholicism should be the main tool for mobilizing ethnic Lithuanians, but not the only incentive for mobilization. In other words, the leaders of the Lithuanian Christian Democratic Party were not oriented to multicultural Catholics living in Lithuania or Christians of other denominations, but to an integralist understanding of "Lithuanian Catholics." In 1921, the long-time leader of the interwar Central Committee of the LCDP and one of the most prominent Lithuanian politicians, Rev. Mykolas Krupavičius, described the purpose of Christian Democrats as follows: "Whether it is a university, a school or temperance activity, sports or gymnastics, everything must be Catholic (...). The method of 'taking care of your own' must be maintained not only in purely economic and national terms, but also in Catholic affairs."[9] The phenomenon of "insularity" was characteristic of some Catholic parties in the first half of the twentieth century.[10] The Lithuanians preserved this party direction until the middle of the twentieth century.

Christian Democrats were the most powerful and one of the most influential political forces in the Republic of Lithuania (1918–1940). From 1920 to 1926, Christian Democrats maintained about fifty percent of mandates in the parliament, and they prepared and passed the most important laws of the young state. For example, Christian Democrats were behind pushing through the first and the only democratic constitution; land reform, which was a very significant achievement at the time; and the laws that helped to launch a new currency.

In 1940, the first Soviet occupation, followed by German occupation, and, finally, the second Soviet occupation that lasted from 1944 to 1990 forced part of the population into emigration. The Christian Democrats, who had retreated to West Germany, restored their party in exile in 1946. During this period, it became involved in the international activities of European Christian Democrats, becoming a member of the Christian Dem-

8 For a comparison of the origins of political Catholicism in *fin-de-siècle* Russian Poland, see, e.g., Piotr H. Kosicki, *Catholics on the Barricades: Poland, France, and "Revolution," 1891–1956* (New Haven, CT: Yale University Press, 2018), 21–61; Robert Blobaum, "The Revolution of 1905–1907 and the Crisis of Polish Catholicism," *Slavic Review* 47, no. 4 (1988): 667–686.

9 *Ateitis*, 7 (1919), 203.

10 Kees van Kersbergen, *Social Capitalism: A Study of Christian Democracy and the Social Welfare State* (London - New York: Routledge, 1995), 31.

ocrat International (initially the *Nouvelles Équipes Internationales,* NEI) and the Christian Democratic Union of Central Europe (CDUCE). After 1950, the party core moved to the US and renamed itself as the Lithuanian Christian Democratic Union (LAC). During the Soviet occupation, Lithuanian emigrants distanced themselves from the population living in the Lithuanian homeland. Contacts with the reviving party in Soviet Lithuania were established just prior to Lithuania restoring its independence in 1989–1990.

Throughout the entire 45-year occupation period, Christian Democrats isolated themselves and took the radical position of avoiding contacts with residents of occupied Lithuania. Their reasoning was that if contacts were established with occupied Lithuania, this would be tantamount to recognition of the occupation of Lithuania and the Lithuanian Soviet Socialist Republic (SSR).[11] In exile, Christian Democrats used a strategy of separation from the residents of the Lithuanian SSR. They supported only sparse dissident activities.

For these reasons, Lithuanians living behind the Iron Curtain had no possibility of being introduced to Christian Democracy. Its ideas faded from the minds of the people over five decades of Soviet, German, and again Soviet occupation. One of the people who re-founded the LCDP in 1989, the dissident Vytautas Bogušis, wrote that he had secretly searched antique bookshops for any materials about the party, its program, and ideas. He acknowledged that he accidentally used interwar documents and LCDP brochures he had found to familiarize himself with Christian Democracy.[12]

The second factor that hindered mass expansion of Christian Democracy and limited the party's influence in the restoration of an independent state is related to the position of party leaders. The process of political liberation in Lithuania started in the summer of 1988 when the *Sąjūdis* Popular Front was established. In early 1989, it officially announced the implementation of Mikhail Gorbachev's *perestroika* in Soviet Lithuania. However, the years 1989–1990 witnessed an interesting political constellation in the country: the duality of government. The Communist Party represented an official government, while *Sąjūdis* initiated new political developments that could not be ignored by communists. *Sąjūdis* quickly became a political umbrella that attracted people of different ideologies and various organizations that were seeking their own restoration.

11 Povilaitis and Škiudaitė, *Lietuviai krikščionys demokratai*, 24.
12 *Tėvynės sargas* 3/4 (1999), 85.

Christian Democrats were one of those organizations. The LCDP became the second political party to be re-established on Lithuanian soil. It chose a symbolic date for its restoration – 16 February 1989, in this way stressing the symbolic continuity with the interwar Lithuanian Republic, which had been established on 16 February 1918. For a long time, the re-created Christian Democrats kept solidarity with *Sąjūdis* and acted more on behalf of *Sąjūdis* than their own party. Even during the first democratic elections for Lithuania's Supreme Council (Parliament) in 1990, they participated under the banner of *Sąjūdis*. Having won three mandates, they did not form a separate parliamentary faction. During the *perestroika* period, the party did not announce its program of action. In numerous cases, it positioned itself as a party interested only in specific questions: teaching religion in schools, protection of the rights of the Catholic Church, implementation of Christian values in public life, and the promotion of the anti-Soviet stance.[13] Therefore, the re-created party did not have a visible identity in the general struggle for freedom in Lithuania.

The third factor that limited the party's influence was a series of internal conflicts and leadership problems. It seems to be symptomatic, but these tendencies were also visible in the party during the interwar period. The party that was founded in 1918 was greatly divided. The interwar LCDP had several political wings. The first was oriented towards the proletariat, while the second one to more conservative and wealthy farmers. The third group represented the interests of intellectuals and the clergy. Each wing had its own autonomy and its own leaders. It was frequently difficult, if not impossible, to accommodate the interests of all of these factions. As a result, one of the features of the prewar LCDP was its institutional and ideological fragmentation.[14]

A similar situation could be observed in the late 1980s. In February 1989, the LCDP established a core group that was responsible for its restoration. Its membership included thirteen persons living in Soviet Lithuania, while their leader was an ex-political prisoner named Viktoras Petkus. At the time, they still did not have any contacts with Christian Democrats living in exile. No one officially elected the leader of this core group. Petkus as the leader was chosen by a collective consensus. However, the group survived only for a month: it split apart just before the elections to the Supreme Council of the USSR in March 1989. The majority (nine of thirteen) members of the group distanced themselves from Petkus, pointing out as

13 *Tėvynės sargas* 1 (1997), 3–20.
14 Svarauskas, *Krikščioniškoji demokratija*, 60–86.

the main reason his authoritarian methods and arbitrariness. Petkus had radical views and supported the Christian Democrats in exile and their desire to isolate themselves from Soviet Lithuania. Before the elections, he penned an open letter to the leaders of the Lithuanian Church on behalf of the LCDP. In his opinion, "participation in the elections of Soviet Lithuania will only enforce slavery and legitimize the Soviet occupation."[15] However, other members of the core group opposed this idea. During the elections, they supported candidates of *Sąjūdis* (they had no delegates of their own) and stood by the position that all available legal efforts and peaceful measures must be used to achieve independence. They argued that the refusal to participate in the elections amounted to "capitulation."[16]

These principal disagreements over the tactics split the newly restored party. Petkus was deprived of his authority to speak on behalf of the LCDP. After this conflict, he founded a separate party – the Lithuanian Christian Democratic Union (LCDU). Therefore, since 1989 there have been two parties of Christian Democrats. Both of them considered themselves to be successors of the interwar LCDP. There had been a similar situation in Lithuania during World War I, when there were also two independent Christian Democratic parties. One of them was founded by Lithuanian war refugees in the spring of 1917 in Moscow and Petrograd. Another one, in the autumn of 1917, was founded by Catholic intellectuals who remained in Vilnius. After the war, the returning refugees initiated a joint party conference in Vilnius in November 1918. It was difficult to align the programs of both parties: Lithuanian returnees from Russia were influenced by the revolutionary mood of Russia, and, as a result, had a quite radical social program (nationalization of land, etc.). Meanwhile, local Lithuanians were moderate and argued for a conservative social program. However, because of the rigid German occupation, the latter did not have an organizational network; only the party leadership was active. Therefore, in the long run, Christian Democrats who returned from Russia and were better organized, started to dominate the party. Two parties were merged into one only after a long negotiation.

In 1989, Lithuanian exile activists accepted and treated as "legitimate" the group of Christian Democrats led by Viktoras Petkus. Nevertheless, this party performed a destructive role in the process of state's restoration. It chose the tactic of open confrontation and negation: it boycotted all elections and institutions of the Lithuanian SSR. Later on it started opposing

15 Petkus, *Krikščioniškoji demokratija*, 31.

16 Povilaitis and Škiudaitė, *Lietuviai krikščionys demokratai*, 24–25.

even *Sąjūdis*. However, in the course of time, this party became marginal. The Christian Democrats who distanced themselves from Petkus avoided a single-person party leadership and pursued a different direction of actions. They intentionally refused to elect a chairman of the party. The leadership of the party was in the hands of a three-member secretariat where each member had a right of "veto."

The internal conflict hindered Lithuanian Christian Democracy's expansion and reduced its significance in the process of state's re-establishment. The evolution of the party stopped, and the inaugural conference was convened only after a year, in January 1990. Only then was an abstract party program approved. However, the official program of the party was adopted only as late as 1993. While the wider independence movement was preparing for the new democratic elections to the Supreme Council of the Lithuanian SSR, the LCDP was still trying to solve its internal problems of tactics and organization.

Aims, tactics, and approaches of the LCDP to re-establish independence

The restored LCDP had several well-defined directions of its activity. First of all, the party tried to revive its relationship with those Christian Democrats who had emigrated after World War II. This was supposed to assure long-term continuity in the party's activities.

Yet this ambition produced some unforeseen complications. Christian Democrats in exile supported the strategy of the radical Viktoras Petkus which manifested itself in the "non-recognition" and "total separation" from Soviet Lithuania. At the same time, Lithuanians in exile were skeptical about attempts by *Sąjūdis* to achieve independence by means of peaceful negotiation with the Soviets. The LCDP acted as part of *Sąjūdis*. Therefore, at least formally, Christian Democrats in exile demonstrated distrust towards those Christian Democrats who re-established the organization in Soviet Lithuania.

There were several reasons for this suspicion. First, it was difficult for Lithuanians in exile to accept that the process of Lithuania's liberation from the USSR has been started by local activists in Lithuania, i.e., Soviet citizens living behind the Iron Curtain. There were many members of the Communist Party of the Soviet Union among them, who in the late 1980s turned to the path of euro-communism and started distancing themselves from Moscow. In December 1989, the Lithuanian Communist Party left the Communist Party of the Soviet Union. Lithuanians in exile were dissatisfied with the involvement of communists in the national movement. There were some rumors floating around among the Lithuanians in exile that allegedly the KGB could have been involved in the liberation of Lithuania. Such rumors disappeared after the announcement of independence in 1990. These suspicions existed despite the fact that the LCDP had strict requirements for party membership. For example, former KGB employees, Soviet security agents, and informants were not allowed to join the LCDP.[17]

Another aspect of great importance to the LCDP in 1989 was the question of its organizational structure and the relationship with the Catholic Church. The party program ensured that the Church would be the key moral authority for Christian Democrats and that the party would collaborate with the Church in solving all political, social, economic, and moral problems.[18] There were three clergymen among the thirteen members of the LCDP core group responsible for the party's restoration.[19] During *perestroika*, the first branches of the party were created within church parishes. In addition, throughout the Soviet occupation, the Church had strongly promoted the national and Catholic identity of Lithuanians. The Church also was an initiator of reforms and was openly anti-Soviet. Therefore, the re-established LCDP tried to use the authority of the Catholic Church to recruit new members into the party more effectively. However, such a strategy proved ineffective compared to the original party-building efforts from seven decades earlier, during the interwar period. Within a matter of years, part of the society started challenging the party's strategy of using the Church for its political aims.

The third conflict within the re-established party concerned the revision of its programmatic aims. One of them was to highlight the old historical tradition of the party. However, it was difficult to accommodate the original program of a party that had been written at the beginning of the twentieth century to the political realities of the end of that same century. Formally, in 1989 the LCDP acted according to the first party program. It had been written in 1905, but failed to come into force. In 1905, the party's program remained only aspirational – a project that was never used in practice, because at the time it lacked the approval of Church leaders.

17 Viktorija Škiudaitė, *Krikščionys demokratai Lietuvoje, 1989–2015* (Vilnius: Baltijos kopija, 2015), 72.

18 Algimantas Jankauskas, Egidijus Kūris and Jūratė Novagrockienė, eds., *Lietuvos politinės partijos ir partinė sistema* (Vilnius: Naujasis Lankas, 1997), I, 326–389.

19 *Sąjūdžio žinios*, 73 (1989), 294.

And due to the changing political situation in the Russian Empire after the Revolution of 1905, it became impossible to establish the party formally until 1917–1918. Thus, the original LCDP program's aims were entirely incompatible with the requirements of 1990s.

One of the problematic issues was the fact that, when Lithuania was part of tsarist Russia before World War I, at the time the Christian Democrats wanted only autonomy (self-government) for Lithuania. They did not speak about its independence. This political argument flew in the face of the mood of 1989: Lithuania's determination to leave the USSR. The LCDP program of 1917–1918 was ignored during the interwar democratic period of 1920–1926. Therefore, there was a lack of ideological continuity within the party as re-established in 1989–1990. Similar problems hindered the preparation of the LCDP program. It was, finally, prepared and approved in 1993, i.e. three years after the restoration of independence.

In 1989, discussions about the party program revealed another conceptual problem. Christian Democrats tried to find a middle ground among several competing strategies in the process of Lithuania's re-establishment. Despite the fact that Lithuanians in exile had been engaged in anti-Soviet propaganda for almost five decades, they did not have a specific strategy for re-founding an independent Lithuania. Some believed that after leaving the USSR, Lithuania would have to "return" to the situation that had existed before the occupation of 1940, i.e., that Lithuania would reconstitute the old political order. Others stated that such a scenario was not realistic; alternatives had to be found. There was a fundamental disagreement on how they should respond to the existence of Soviet Lithuania. They could "reject" it as absolute evil and try to re-create the state that had existed before World War II. The other perspective was that the Lithuanian Soviet Socialist Republic could not be ignored, and an effort should be made to "transform" it into an independent state. Nevertheless, the Christian Democrats in exile chose the first option with a clear orientation towards re-creation of the interwar state and a rejection of Soviet Lithuania.[20]

After the re-establishment of independence in 1990, Christian Democrats had a distinctive feature: they escalated various requirements to consider Russia as the successor to the USSR. One of the LCDP's leaders, Algirdas Saudargas, was the first Minister of Foreign Affairs of the restored Republic of Lithuania. His activities also reflected the party's priorities. During the years 1990–1992, his, as Minister's, most important foreign

20 Laurinavičius and Sirutavičius, *Sąjūdis*, 527.

policy priorities were negotiations with the USSR, renewal and implementation of pre-World War II international treaties, and an improvement in relations with Lithuanian emigrés. He also aimed at developing relations with the Scandinavian countries and the establishment of relations with Lithuania's northern neighbors, as well as achieving international recognition for Lithuania and building a diplomatic network with the countries of Western Europe.

In addition, the LCDP initiated a referendum on the withdrawal of Soviet troops from Lithuania. The party constantly demanded that the Russian government compensate Lithuania for the damage done by the Soviet occupation. The party also took an interesting position regarding the international status of a future independent Lithuanian state. In the context of the collapse of the USSR, Christian Democrats considered international neutrality to be a priority for Lithuania's foreign policy. At that time, there were no thoughts about integrating Lithuania into the Euro-Atlantic organizations. This idea was born after the re-establishment of independence.

Despite the diversity of their tactics, Christian Democrats were very actively involved in the re-establishment of Lithuania's independence. Their key strategy, however, was to seek the realization of their political aims peacefully, using legal measures. Still, it is quite difficult to track the activities of the LCDP in this process for two reasons. First, there are no academic studies concerning the party in Lithuania. Second, the analysis of its activities is complicated by its subtly chosen strategy during the last years of *perestroika*. This can be summarized as "the aim of the party is not to gain power, but to participate in government." This meant that the party did not try to assume a leading role in Lithuania's politics. After all, it did not have a single popular leader who would have allowed Christian Democrats to dominate the political stage.

Conclusions

During the years 1989–1990, Christian Democrats used quite unconventional political strategies. They did not participate in public politics as a separate political force. Instead, they supported the national umbrella movement of Lithuanian independence, *Sąjūdis*. Also, not having a strong political leader, the party re-established itself as a small political organization that had only limited political ambitions. It became a "catch-all" party only after the proclamation of independence. Such a strategy differed from the one followed by interwar Christian Democrats, who from 1920 to 1926 had sought to form several governments dominated by a single party. In the post-1918 republic, the Christian Democrats were a dominant political force, but they could not establish their identity in Lithuania in the early 1990s. As a result, in 2008 they ceased to exist as an independent party and merged with the Conservative Party of Lithuania. The reconstructed LCDP did not have a single well-articulated position on the question of re-establishing independence. From 1989 onward, they promoted the strategy of gaining Lithuania's independence by legal means. Thus they supported national candidates in the political institutions of the USSR and tried to achieve independence through peaceful negotiations and compromise. The result was not only Christian Democratic collapse on Lithuanian soil, but also a failure to integrate into any transnational Christian Democratic structures, canceling for example the legacy of the Lithuanian exile members of the Christian Democratic Union of Central Europe.

12

ABANDONED PATTERNS

1989 and the Discontinuation of Cold War Cooperation among Emigré Central and Eastern European Christian Democrats

Sławomir Łukasiewicz

The year 1989 was a breaking point not only for the history of Central and Eastern European states, but also for Central and Eastern European Cold War exiles. Over four decades, emigrés in the West had organized themselves in the fight against communism, and after the collapse of communism it seemed that their return to the home countries was something natural, if not indeed pre-ordained. The fate of the Christian Democratic Union of Central Europe (CDUCE), created in 1950 in New York on the basis of cooperation among Central and Eastern European Christian Democrats in exile, is a symbolic one. The history of the CDUCE has already inspired substantial research,[1] but its dissolution after 1989 deserves more attention. After the relocation of its headquarters to Paris and eventually to Rome, this specific organization survived until the beginning of the 1990s. Its last congresses were organized in 1990 in Budapest and Bratislava. Both places symbolized an attempt to transfer the framework of emigré politics from exile into political activity within a new, post-communist reality back in the homelands. Apart from a few individual success stories, the attempt turned out to be a fiasco.

The case of the CDUCE gives us an additional benefit by creating the framework for a comparative analysis of at least a few key Central and Eastern European cases. My approach draws on four crucial works. The first is the monograph by Peter Van Kemseke comparing the Socialist In-

1 Peter Van Kemseke, *Towards an Era of Development: The Globalization of Socialism and Christian Democracy: 1945–1965* (Leuven: Leuven University Press, 2006). See Sławomir Łukasiewicz, *Third Europe. Polish Federalist Thought in the United States 1940–1970s* (Budapest: Helena History Press, 2016).

ternational with the Christian Democratic Union of Central Europe; unfortunately, he stopped in the 1960s.[2] Second, Tim Bale and Aleks Szczerbiak began with the observation that there is no Christian Democracy in contemporary Poland and then asked: why not?[3] Their work is one of the key contributions among the comparative and connective analysis featured in a volume edited by Piotr H. Kosicki and Sławomir Łukasiewicz concerning the functioning of European Christian Democracy during the Cold War, up until the breakthrough of 1989 (with multiple chapters exploring the activities and fate of the CDUCE).[4] And the fourth key point of reference here is the book on the European People's Party by Thomas Jansen and Steven Van Hecke, containing parts on the CDUCE.[5]

The conviction that Poland, although a mostly Catholic country, has a problem with the creation of a strong Christian Democratic party similar to the case of Western European countries, was expressed by the emigrés themselves. I experienced this in conversation with Zofia Fedorowicz-Grzelak (one of the oldest members of the emigré Polish Christian Labor Party, personally involved in the activities of the party in exile) in 1999 in New York. The natural question was – why was Christian Democracy not the dominant strain in Polish political life after 1989? Why is the legacy of the CDUCE almost unknown in Poland, and why are only a few witnesses and experts still interested in it? These questions can be applied to each of the countries with active representations in the CDUCE throughout the Cold War.

2 Van Kemseke, *Towards an Era of Development.*

3 Tim Bale and Alex Szczerbiak, "Why is there no Christian Democracy in Poland (and why does it matter)?" Sussex University Institute Working Paper No 91, www.sussex.ac.uk/webteam/gateway/file.php?name=sei-working-paper-no-91.pdf&site=266, accessed on 22 June 2017. Recently, a similar thesis has been posed by Dominika Sozańska in her very interesting book on Polish Christian Democratic initiatives after 1989, *Chrześcijańska Demokracja w Polsce. Przyczyny słabości i szanse rozwoju* (Kraków: Krakowskie Towarzystwo Edukacyjne - Oficyna Wydawnicza AFM, 2011).

4 Piotr H. Kosicki and Sławomir Łukasiewicz, eds., *Christian Democracy across the Iron Curtain: Europe Redefined* (London: Palgrave Macmillan, 2018). The volume is principally a product of a conference held in Lublin in May 2015. For present purposes, the eyewitness testimony of Stanisław Gebhardt included in the volume is of the greatest importance.

5 Thomas Jansen and Steven Van Hecke, *At Europe's Service: The Origins and Evolution of the European People's Party* (Berlin: Springer; Brussels: Centre for European Studies, 2011).

CDUCE - a model of cooperation

The Christian Democratic Union of Central Europe was a unique initiative, created in exile, thanks to funds organized under the Cold War umbrella of the National Committee for a Free Europe (NCFE), better known from its later name: the Free Europe Committee (FEC). It was the consequence of the American Cold War policy toward Central and Eastern European emigrés. The CDUCE became one of the instruments of this policy, which strengthened the US-driven anti-communist campaign, helped to mobilize Catholic emigré youth in the West, and gave the signal that the American government supports Catholics in captive Central and Eastern European countries.[6]

This initiative, though financed by the NCFE/FEC until 1964, needed a European framework for effective activity. Such a framework came in the form of the *Nouvelles Équipes Internationales* (NEI), a type of Christian Democratic international which emerged in 1947 on the basis of Christian Democratic cooperation. Such facts generated the atmosphere for the meeting of the leaders of emigré Central and Eastern European Christian Democratic parties that took place in New York in May 1950. They decided to create a common organizational home, and two months later, on 26 July 1950, the Christian Democratic Union of Central Europe was founded. Its headquarters were originally supposed to be in Washington DC, but eventually they were opened the next year in New York.[7] From the beginning, the CDUCE had its representation also in Europe, e.g. in France, Italy, Belgium, and West Germany.

Because Europe was the real Cold War theater after 1956, the headquarters were moved to Paris and in 1962 to Rome. The CDUCE consisted of Christian Democratic representatives from Czechoslovakia, Hungary, Latvia, Lithuania, Poland, and Slovenia (the last of these represented the whole of Yugoslavia). Such party representation was therefore limited only to a few countries from Central and Eastern Europe. Comparing this with other, similar initiatives falling under the NCFE umbrella, which embraced more countries (including Bulgaria and Romania), the CDUCE's initial structural limitations conditioned also its potential expansion after 1989.

6 Anna Mazurkiewicz, *Uchodźcy polityczni z Europy Środkowo-Wschodniej w amerykańskiej polityce zimnowojennej (1948–1954)* (Warsaw-Gdańsk: Instytut Pamięci Narodowej/Uniwersytet Gdański, 2016), 346–351; Piotr H. Kosicki, "Christian Democracy's Global Cold War," in *Christian Democracy across the Iron Curtain*, ed. Kosicki and Łukasiewicz, 221–256.

7 Łukasiewicz, *Third Europe*, 89.

Moreover, the representation was based on individuals, even though the Polish Christian Labor Party (*Stronnictwo Pracy*, SP) in exile was rather small (though with a big Youth Section). The president of the organization was a Catholic priest, József Közi-Horváth from Hungary, and there were several vice-presidents: Miha Krek representing Yugoslavia, Kazys Pakštas representing Lithuania, Karol Popiel representing Poland, and Ivo Ducháček (later also Adolf Procházka) representing Czechoslovakia.

Congresses organized by the CDUCE in 1953 and 1955 were relatively great successes. To the participants of the first one (ca. 900 people, organized after the death of Joseph Stalin), Konrad Adenauer, Georges Bidault, Robert Schuman, and Paul van Zeeland sent their greetings. This meeting generated a document entitled "The Union's Political and Ideological Platform." For the latter meeting, themed "Freedom, a Prerequisite to Lasting Peace," Bidault and Van Zeeland together with Luigi Sturzo belonged to the honorary committee.

A relatively great achievement of the CDUCE was the creation of its Youth Section, with Dimitri Pavlista as president and Edward Bobrowski as secretary-general and leader of this section in France. Another affiliated organization was the Central European Federation of Christian Trade Unions, created in 1952 with Jan Straszak and Karol Balon as the leaders. The union had also its own journal: *Christian Democratic Review*.

The program of the CDUCE reflected the wishes of the individual emigrés it assembled as exiled representatives of their homelands. They referred to many universal values such as freedom, democracy, or human rights. They also formulated the methods and the goals of CDUCE transnational activities, among them informing the world about the persecution of the Catholic Church in the home countries, liberation of the latter in accordance with the slogans of American policy of the time, and the broadly understood struggle against communism.[8] However, Christianity remained the core of the program. During the first congress, the organization adopted "a platform (...) incorporating the basic principles on which the Christian Democratic parties of six Central European countries agree to work together toward the liberation of their respective fatherlands as well as toward the inauguration of the political, social, and cultural order based on Christian principles."[9] These principles were formulated in a

8 Van Kemseke, *Towards an Era of Development*, 173.

9 "Union of European Countries," *Christian Democratic Review* no. 1 (March 1954): 11.

very spiritual and symbolic way: "Union of God and man. Union of people. Union of peoples (nations)."[10]

The consequence of such an approach was a vision of a future Central European federation, based upon cooperation between Central and Eastern European countries, especially among the region's Christian Democratic parties. The process of Western European integration was a great inspiration for them.[11] Prominent emigré politicians got involved in such extraordinary projects, among them Jan Kułakowski, participant in youth Christian Democratic movements and later one of the most influential global leaders of Christian Democratic trade unions (especially the World Confederation of Labor) or Stanisław Gebhardt, who began his political career as head of the London branch of the CDUCE Youth Section and became a globally recognized Christian Democratic activist. Both symbolized the interest in global politics in which the CDUCE engaged especially after 1956, when the First World Conference of Christian Democratic Movements took place, gathering representatives of the NEI, Latin America's Christian Democratic Organization, and the CDUCE. On this basis, a few years later the World Christian Democratic Union was founded. Although these actions were consistent with the policies outlined in the founding document of the CDUCE, they had little to do with searching for a concept of international order in Europe, especially in its Central part.

This experiment of cooperation among the Central and Eastern European emigré Christian Democrats, though it took place under pressure from the Cold War philosophy of anti-communism, is the legacy under examination in this chapter. Since the middle of the 1960s, without American support yet, the CDUCE was still active, though on a smaller scale. In the opinion of Thomas Jansen and Steven Van Hecke, the CDUCE was recognized as a regional organization of the Christian Democrat International (CDI).[12] But since the 1970s, the importance of the Union had diminished. Jansen and Van Hecke attribute this to the politics of détente, in which there was no place for sharp anti-communist organizations.

The Central and Eastern European Christian Democrats played certain crucial roles and held positions of importance in European Christian Democratic initiatives during the Cold War. They were even trying to strengthen this position, at least in the 1950s and 1960s. Idesbald Goddeeris has

10 "Platforma Ideowo-Polityczna Unii" [The Union's ideological and political platform], *Odnowa* no. 3/15 (March 1953): 2.

11 "Resolution on Federalism," *Christian Democratic Review* no. 3 (May-June 1954); Kazys Pakštas, "Middle European Federation," *Christian Democratic Review* no. 2 (April 1954): 6–8.

12 Jansen and Van Hecke, *At Europe's Service*, 93.

argued that they failed to find effective lobbying strategies.[13] The lack of a common Central and Eastern European Christian Democratic representation after 1989 is a kind of confirmation of Goddeeris's thesis.

Jansen and Van Hecke noted in their book two factors that caused the decline of the CDUCE. First, after 1989 the organization of the CDUCE was dispersed, and their ideas were not treated seriously by their in-country counterparts. Second, the representatives from particular countries demonstrated an unwillingness to have a common Central and Eastern European representation. Probably we can add to this picture the trauma of long-term compulsory cooperation between communist states under Moscow's umbrella. Moreover the new Central and Eastern European Christian Democrats preferred to be a part of pan-European organizations such as the European Union of Christian Democrats (EUCD), not of the regional one. EUCD membership guaranteed "cooperation with the Western European parties and the EPP."[14] Certain personal ambitions of politicians also might have played a certain role – "they did not want to take orders from the 'old men' (however highly respected) who had returned from exile."[15]

With these tensions as a backdrop, two CDUCE congresses took place in 1990: in Budapest on 2–4 March, and with a General Assembly in Bratislava on 7–9 December. Stanisław Gebhardt's impression was that Western Europe's Christian Democratic parties were trying to impose their own vision on their new counterparts in post-communist Europe, creating confusion greater than that caused by the collapse of communism.[16] Eventually, after many talks and considerations, the representatives of the CDUCE decided to dissolve the organization during the EUCD congress in Warsaw, 21-23 June 1992.

13 Idesbald Goddeeris, "Exiles' Strategies for Lobbying in International Organizations. Eastern European Participation in Nouvelles Equipes Internationales," *European Review of History* 11, no. 3 (2004): 383–400.

14 Jansen and Van Hecke, *At Europe's Service*, 94.

15 Ibid., 94.

16 Stanisław Gebhardt, "The Christian Democratic Union of Central Europe," in *Christian Democracy across the Iron Curtain*, ed. Kosicki and Łukasiewicz, 411–424.

Attitude of the Central and Eastern European Christian Democrats in exile toward the revolutions of 1989

There is not sufficient research on the impact of the revolutions of 1989 and beyond on the encounters between Christian Democrats in exile and similar groups in Central and Eastern Europe under communist regimes. The Christian Democratic parties in exile had their contacts in the home countries and moreover tried to revive those contacts in moments of political crisis. The Polish case is a significant one. There was an attempt to establish a Christian Democratic Party in the Polish People's Republic just after World War II. It failed because of the communist policy, which supported so-called progressive Catholics at the same time. Catholics gathered around the Catholic Church hierarchy in Poland were in a bad situation, but they maintained their channels of expression (like *Tygodnik Powszechny*).[17] Following 1956, such groups had their symbolic representation in the Parliament, and eventually, this caused the fragmentation of the movement – a topic deserving of separate attention. For our purposes, it is enough to note that some of these Catholics were looking for cooperation with the communist authorities even into the late 1970s and early 1980s, hoping that it could enable the creation of a Christian Democratic party within that system. Simultaneously, many other people identifying with the Catholic Church worked for the opposition, and especially for the Solidarity trade union network. Some of them carved out a middle ground, somewhere between the dissidents and the communist authorities.

Polish Christian Democrats in exile worked hard at building networks of contacts with groups and individuals in Poland who shared their Christian values. Analysis of the beneficiaries who received help thanks to the fellowships organized, for example, by Stanisław August Morawski and Stanisław Gebhardt in Rome, confirms this thesis. Before 1989, such help was both necessary and practical, but after the collapse of communism it muddied the waters. Relatively good contacts in Poland did not help Polish emigré Christian Democrats to properly predict political trends back in the home country or to prepare them effectively for the transition from communist rule to pluralistic democracy.

The Christian Democratic milieu in Poland was deeply fragmented. Dominika Sozańska mentions several groups with Christian Democratic

17 See Piotr H. Kosicki, *Catholics on the Barricades: Poland, France, and "Revolution," 1891–1956* (New Haven, CT: Yale University Press, 2018).

profiles that were active in Poland after 1989, among them *Chrześcijańsko-Demokratyczne Stronnictwo Pracy* (Christian Democratic Labor Party) – a continuation of the old *Stronnictwo Pracy* (Polish Christian Labor Party) with Władysław Siła-Nowicki as its chairman; *Chrześcijańska Partia Pracy* (Christian Labor Party); and *Partia Chrześcijańskich Demokratów* (Party of Christian Democrats). But their relative successes could be noted only at the beginning of the 1990s, when several Christian Democrats won parliamentary or municipal elections. In subsequent years, all similar groupings went through multiple crises and splits.[18] Some of them joined other parties like *Porozumienie Centrum* (Center Agreement)[19] or *Zjednoczenie Chrześcijańsko-Narodowe* (Christian-National Union), whose programs comprised certain Christian Democratic elements. Neither *Porozumienie Centrum* nor *Zjednoczenie Chrześcijańsko-Narodowe* built their political strategies on the basis of these elements.

The Polish case is just a fragment of the broader Central and Eastern European landscape. A similar scenario took place in Hungary, where the Christian Democratic People's Party (*Kereszténydemokrata Néppárt*), referring to the interwar party, nearly ceased to exist in the decade that followed 1989. At the same time, Christian Democracy came into being in Slovakia under the name Christian Democratic Movement (*Kresťanskodemokratické hnutie*, KDH). The potential of this party survived despite even more destructive oppression that almost expunged the Catholic Church from Slovakia during communist times.[20] Similarly, in Romania, at the beginning of the 1990s a weak Christian Democratic party named *Partidul Național Țărănesc Creștin Democrat* (a token continuation of the old Romanian Peasant Party), became a leading political force.

But these cases compel us to supplement the picture painted by Jansen and Van Hecke. Maintaining the unity of the Central and Eastern European representation was a utopian goal, when some countries were not even able to create their own strong Christian Democratic representations, or created only very weak and short-lived ones. Unfortunately, we have at our disposal only rather scattered pieces of documentation that incom-

18 A detailed and convincing description of those processes was given by Dominika Sozańska, *Chrześcijańska Demokracja*, 117–157. Supplementary information can be found in *Chrześcijańska demokracja we współczesnym świecie* [Christian Democracy in the contemporary world], ed. Katarzyna Krzywicka and Edward Olszewski (Lublin: Wydawnictwo Uniwersytetu Marii Curie-Skłodowskiej, 1999) – especially in texts by Stefan Stępień, Michał Gołoś, and Maria Marczenko-Rytko.

19 *Porozumienie Centrum* evolved into *Prawo i Sprawiedliwość* (Law and Justice).

20 Ján Čarnogurský, "Christian Democracy in Slovakia," in *Christian Democracy across the Iron Curtain*, ed. Kosicki and Łukasiewicz, 425–437.

pletely illustrate the situation in particular countries. The comprehensive picture of cross-border contacts between emigrés and country politicians before 1989 still needs to be drawn. In such circumstances, assessment of the Christian Democratic initiatives in Central and Eastern Europe after 1989 becomes even more difficult.

Perhaps the work of Andrzej Antoszewski comes closest to this aim, although he unfortunately combined Christian Democrats with Conservatives, and he concentrated instead on the transition from the 20th to the 21st centuries, narrowing the scope of analysis of the transformation processes.[21] Antoszewski repeats the conclusion that there was no strong Christian Democratic party in this part of Europe after 1989. He states that good results were achieved in such countries as Bulgaria, Slovenia, Poland, and Romania, but there were some fundamental problems: with unambiguous identification of the parties as Christian Democratic, and with the failure of the coalition building process, which could have strengthened the position of the united Christian Democrats. Individually, the respective Christian Democratic parties lacked the clout to exercise real influence in national politics. In his opinion, there is a lack of large or even medium Christian Democratic parties in Central and Eastern Europe comparable with the Western European giants. He claimed additionally that there was no connection (as in Western Europe) between the religious structure of the society and the existence of a strong Christian Democracy.[22] In Central and Eastern Europe, such parties operate in mostly Orthodox Bulgaria or Romania, mostly Protestant Latvia, or even the mostly atheist Czech Republic.

Party politics and political transformation in Central and Eastern Europe: lessons for Christian Democracy

Maybe an answer for the question as to why Christian Democrats were not able to strengthen their position in Central and Eastern Europe after 1989 lies in more objective factors. Analyzing the beginnings of the party systems in Central and Eastern Europe after 1989, the experts dis-

21 Andrzej Antoszewski, *Partie i systemy partyjne państw Unii Europejskiej na przełomie wieków* (Toruń: Wydawnictwo Adam Marszałek, 2009), 128ff.

22 Ibid., 154.

tinguish three main models of party origins.[23] First of all, former dominant parties, i.e. the communist ones, were transformed into completely new formations (so-called successor parties), retaining the former structures, possessions as well as the general political profile. They have been mostly morphed into different sorts of Social Democracy, making them resemble Western European Social Democracy. This was the case with the Polish United Workers' Party (*Polska Zjednoczona Partia Robotnicza*, PZPR) which became the Social Democracy of the Polish Republic (*Socjaldemokracja Rzeczypospolitej Polskiej*, SdRP).

The former satellite (bloc) parties mostly followed this pattern. After 1989, they absolutely dissociated themselves from their communist past, searching for counterparts in Western Europe, and emphasizing the continuities with historical parties that had existed before 1939. This was the case also for the United People's Party (*Zjednoczone Stronnictwo Ludowe*, ZSL) which became the Polish Peasants' Party (*Polskie Stronnictwo Ludowe*, PSL), evoking the historical party of this same name; PSL today is a member of the EPP.

The second model included parties of a forum type that had originated within democratic movements and initiatives, very often anti-system (anti-communist) movements prior to 1989. In Poland, the parties originated from the Solidarity movement. Nonetheless similar (but not the same) processes were observed in other countries in the region, taking into account the acceleration of political life in Central and Eastern European countries. Many parties were created within the first years, and over 100 took part in the 1991 elections in Poland! Many of the initiatives had only a temporary character, responding to the need for articulation of previously stifled social and political interests.

Finally, there is the third model discussed in political science by Polish author Katarzyna Sobolewska-Myślik as well as Czech authors (Ladislav Cabada, Vit Hloušek, Petr Jurek) – the rebuilding of so-called historical parties,[24] i.e. parties that "were active before World War II and shortly after the war, and whose activities were suspended for various reasons – by dissolution, a ban on activity imposed by the state or inclusion in com-

23 Katarzyna Sobolewska-Myślik, *Partie i systemty partyjne na świecie* (Warsaw: Wydawnictwo Naukowe PWN, 2010), 20–22; Ladislav Cabada, Vit Hloušek and Petr Jurek, *Party Systems in East Central Europe* (Lanham, MD: Lexington Books, 2014), 53.

24 Sobolewska-Myślik distinguishes parties of opposition type origins, "historical" groupings, communist parties, and satellite parties: *Partie i systemy partyjne Europy Środkowej po 1989 roku* [Parties and party systems in Central Europe after 1989] (Kraków: Księgarnia Akademicka, 1999), 54–69.

munist formations."[25] This type of party origin is not accepted by all authors.[26] Danish political scientist Søren Riishøj suggests that "contrary to South[ern] European countries like Greece, Spain, and Portugal, before 1989 the parties in the CEECs had not been in a position to establish institutionalized structures internally or externally, i.e. in exile."[27] Such an approach neglected those traditions of socialist, Christian Democrat, or peasant movements and parties, which had supporters both in the home countries and in exile. Moreover, such political parties still existed in exile in 1989, and they should be added to the list of historical parties. Their political aim in exile was first of all an attempt at preservation and continuation of such historical projects. This was the case, for example, with Central and Eastern European Christian Democrats. Their "historical" model is omitted by numerous political scientists, probably because Central and Eastern European Christian Democratic parties were not able to build a common foundation across national lines, and the individual cases amount rather to stories of failure. Particular attempts to transfer the emigré structures into the new party systems that had emerged in Central and Eastern Europe mostly failed.

The imposition of communist systems in Central and Eastern European countries divided political life into two parts – into a homeland and exile. The process started at different moments (e.g. for Czechoslovakia it was 1948,[28] for Poland 1944–1945), but everywhere, it resulted in a discontinuation of the former political projects and structures. Their preservation in good condition during the decades of communism was almost a miracle for many reasons – biological ones, an internal emigré rivalry, and the divisions as well as the destructive measures used against the emigrés by the communist states. The restoration of such projects and structures in 1989 posed an extremely difficult task. After decades of separation from the homeland, the exile community had lost most of its political potential, not to mention any claim to serve as legitimate representation.

Due to the heritage of communism, the new party systems were based on the opposition circles and a rivalry between the post-communist parties and the new ones, also those restored on the assumption of a conti-

25 Ibid., 59–61.

26 See Jean-Michel De Waele, *L'Emergence des partis politiques en Europe centrale* (Brussels: Editions de l'Université de Bruxelles, 1999); James Toole, "The Historical Foundations of Party Politics in Post-Communist East Central Europe," *Europe-Asia Studies* 59, no. 4 (June 2007): 541–566.

27 Søren Riishøj, "Development of Parties and Party Systems in Central Europe 1989–2007," *Politologiske Skrifter* no. 19 (2007): 12.

28 Cabada, Hloušek and Jurek, *Party Systems in East Central Europe*, 5.

nuity with parties of the 1930s and 1940s.[29] The rivalry tended, however, to work in the favor of former opposition groups, rather than the historical parties. In the case of the national Christian Democratic initiatives, a troublesome question was their lack of an unequivocal profile relative to the past communist regime: some such politicians had their own phase of political opposition in the past, while others were treated as collaborators of the former systems, or at least as opportunists.[30] The opposition and post-communist components were mixed in such cases. In other words, the Christian Democrats were deemed neither sufficiently oppositionist nor sufficiently post-communist to fit within the post-1989 political spectrum of Central and Eastern European states. This basic fact fundamentally differentiated the origins of Central and Eastern European parties from the model observed in the Western European democracies following the end of the Second World War.

For the Czech authors, such a diagnosis render useless Rokkan's classic model of cleavages (based on "social stratification and political representation") for use in analysis of the Central and Eastern European political transition from communism. They state that this new

> cleavage consists of two concurrent processes. From above, the motivating factor is the strategy and the efforts of political parties to clarify their ideological and program profiles and to structure the party competition on the basis of those long-term preferences and topics. From below, even in post-communist societies, the gradual process of the structuring of voters, who formed certain blocs or clusters based on their political and social preferences, took place. Social structuring, however, proceeded in a slower manner and the appearing phenomena, such as the significant volatility of the voters' preferences, the weak institutionalization and frequent trans-

29 Cabada, Hloušek and Jurek, *Party Systems in East Central Europe*, 6, 53.

30 A separate question, not analyzed in this chapter, but important for understanding political change in the region, is so-called "vetting," "lustration," or purification of public life within the Central and Eastern European countries, based on the examining of the files of former security apparatus in search for clandestine collaborators of secret police. The revelation of such a past in the case of a public person very often effects his/her "public death." See, e.g., Kieran Williams, Aleks Szczerbiak and Brigid Fowler, "Explaining Lustration in Eastern Europe: A Post-communist politics approach," *Sussex European Institute Working Paper* No. 62, March 2003 (www.sussex.ac.uk/webteam/gateway/file.php?name=sei-working-paper-no-62.pdf&site=266, accessed on 7 April 2017). It harmed e.g. Josef Bartončík, the leader of Czechoslovak Christian and Democratic Union (*Křesťanská a demokratická unie* – KDU); Vít Hloušek and Lubomír Kopeček, *Origin, Ideology, and Transformation of Political Parties: East-Central and Western Europe Compared* (Farnham-Burlington: Ashgate, 2010), 142–143. Recently in Poland there has also been a discussion about the past of Wiesław Chrzanowski, a symbolic figure for Christian Democrats as well as National Democrats. Sławomir Cenckiewicz and Roman Graczyk, "Wiesław Chrzanowski w sidłach bezpieki," *Rzeczpospolita – Plus Minus*, 12 December 2016.

formations of the parties themselves, as well as the individualization of the political behavior, prevented the application of Rokkan's concept.

In the opinion of those authors, the nature of this split is strictly a political one based on the opposition between communism and anti-communism.[31] This division is dominant especially for a transformation period. The Czech authors are aware that some other classical cleavages played an additional role, although not as important as in the postwar founding era of Western Europe's political party systems. Church-state relations, value-oriented rivalries, or social and economic divisions – in Central and Eastern Europe, these seemed to be only secondary factors during the transition period.[32]

We can test the Czech authors' hypothesis against recent research by French political scientist Daniel-Louis Seiler. Just before the European Union's "Eastern Enlargement" (2004), he asked: Is it possible to apply Rokkan's model to Central and Eastern Europe?[33] In the same volume, Jean-Michel De Waele attempted to propose different schemata for understanding political cleavages in this part of Europe. He examined the basic categories of divisions like urban/rural, center/periphery, and church/state. But, perceiving a difficulty in their consistent application, De Waele proposed also new categories, like maximalist/minimalist (related to the dynamics of economic transformation), authoritarian/democratic, and communist/anti-communist, with particular emphasis on the importance of this last element.[34] A few years later, Daniel-Louis Seiler further confirmed the thesis of Cabada, Hloušek, and Jurek,[35] namely that the Rok-

31 Cabada, Hloušek and Jurek, *Party Systems in East Central Europe*, 53–54. Similar diagnosis was given by Antoszewski, *Partie i systemy partyjne*, 295ff.

32 Cabada, Hloušek, and Jurek, *Party Systems in East Central Europe*, 58.

33 Daniel-Louis Seiler, "Peut-on appliquer les clivages de Rokkan à l'Europe centrale?," in *Partis politiques et démocratie en Europe centrale et orientale*, ed. Jean-Michel De Waele (Brussels: Éd. de l'Université de Bruxelles, 2002), 115–144.

34 Jean-Michel De Waele, "Consolidation démocratique, partis et clivages en Europe centrale et orientale," in *Partis politiques et démocratie en Europe centrale et orientale*, ed. De Waele, 150–158.

35 Vít Hloušek with Lubomír Kopeček (*Origin, Ideology, and Transformation*) propose an overview of the consequences of such new splits for particular party families in Central and Eastern Europe, taking into account also Christian Democratic parties from Czechoslovakia, later the Czech Republic (mainly Christian and Democratic Union, i.e. *Křesťanská a demokratická unie* – KDU) and Slovakia (at the beginning of the 1990s, the very strong Christian Democratic Movement, i.e. *Kresťanskodemokratické hnutie* – KDH), Poland as well as Hungary (especially the Christian Democratic Party i.e. *Kereszténydemokrata Néppár* – KDNP) and Slovenia.

kan's model has only limited applicability in the case of the Central and Eastern European transitions.[36]

The implications of this discussion of the literature go beyond mere heuristic challenges with the implementation of Rokkan's model in this part of Europe. It means, first of all, that after the collapse of communist regimes political splits formed completely differently than in Western Europe. Without a doubt, the dynamics of the collapse hindered, or even disrupted, the creation of parties analogous to their Western European counterparts, as well as a return to historical antecedent parties. In turn, both halves of Christian Democratic Europe differed with regard to language, key political concepts, and even underlying axiology. It would be hard to imagine the construction of a common, mutually intelligible political project under such circumstances.

Weakness of the emigré patterns

Knowing that such a transnational organization as the Christian Democratic Union of Central Europe operated throughout the Cold War, we can pose the question: why, under such circumstances, did the emigré patterns not work? The patterns built on the basis of inter-party cooperation were part of a Western political culture of the Cold War. First, Central and Eastern European states respected Western European patterns, but only at a specific universal level. In the early 1990s, the process of Europeanization was strengthened by the fact that the candidate countries for admission to the European Union agreed to the so-called pre-accession Copenhagen criteria, including democracy, rule of law, and the free market economy.

Still, in the case of the profiles of political parties, a more important role was played by the domestic cleavages. This is one of the explanations for why the Western European Christian Democratic patterns represented by emigré movements did not arouse sufficient interest. There are some cases where the emigrés were treated as an instrument of legitimization, but nothing more. The emigré parties were deprived of a chance to become a part of the new, pluralistic party systems emerging in Central and Eastern Europe. In a sense, they constituted a family of the historical parties that failed to adapt to the new conditions. For their part, the emigré parties

36 Daniel-Louis Seiler, "Qu'est-ce qu'un clivage politique? Le cas de l'Europe centrale: limites et extension du modèle de Rokkan," in *Clivages et familles politiques en Europe*, ed. Jean-Michel De Waele (Brussels: Éd. de l'Université de Bruxelles, 2011), 79–103.

felt the need for great caution in selecting partners back in the homeland, especially with regard to the role that individuals and groups alike had played during the communist period.

The state politics, as well as the contacts before 1989 between Christian Democrats remaining in the homeland and their emigré counterparts, were the crucial factors. After the so-called *annus mirabilis*, the Central and Eastern European Christian Democratic initiatives comprised (in different proportions, depending on the country) all four types of parties that had emerged during the transition: the historical party, the emigré party, the opposition movement, and former partners of the communist parties. This heterogeneity hindered creation of a cohesive Christian Democratic representation. Together with individual politicians' ambitions, these were the factors fragmenting the Christian Democratic political scene in Central and Eastern Europe after 1989. Countries that witnessed lower levels of fragmentation saw the creation of stronger Christian Democratic representation, as was the case in Slovakia. The Polish Christian Democratic scene, meanwhile, was entirely fragmented.

Was the Catholic Church able to help in the transfer of emigrés back to Christian Democracy in the homeland? Especially the Polish case compels us to ask this question. Partial answers were proposed by Dominika Sozańska, who stated that the strong position of the Catholic Church in Poland in fact amounted to an obstacle. During communist times, the Catholic Church had played the roles characteristic for political parties and civil society. In contrast to Western Europe, in Poland after 1989 there was no strong split between the Church and the state. Nor had Poland experienced a strong process of secularization which could also have stimulated a stronger, more coherent response on the part of Catholics.[37] The point is illustrated by the paradoxical case of Ryszard Bender, treated by the Polish emigrés as the pillar and even a certain symbol of Polish Christian Democracy, who instead quickly abandoned Christian Democracy and became one of the principal lay faces of the emerging Redemptorist-run media empire known as *Radio Maryja* (Radio Mary). Bender remained active until his death in 2016 in Polish right-wing politics, but showed no interest in European Christian Democracy.

37 Sozańska, *Chrześcijańska Demokracja*, 39–40; Bale and Szczerbiak, "Why is there no Christian Democracy in Poland"; Alar Kilp, "L'influence de l'Église sur le développement du clivage politique religieux dans sept pays d'Europe centrale et orientale," in *Les clivages politiques en Europe centrale et orientale*, ed. Jean-Michel De Waele (Brussels: Editions de l'Université de Bruxelles, 2004), 119–135.

At the same time, the split between liberal or conservative Catholic politicians and the hierarchy of the Catholic Church played its role. Within the framework of European party politics, it was the liberal *Unia Wolności* (Freedom Union), which gained the status of an observer and member of the EPP (beginning in 1996), with Tadeusz Mazowiecki as its leader. Yet Mazowiecki, as Piotr H. Kosicki has pointed out, despite a long career as a Catholic activist decisively rejected identification with the Christian Democratic family.[38] How did the Christian Democrats of Western Europe understand this seeming contradiction? Did Western Christian Democrats show sufficient interest in party declarations and identifications? Did they have sufficient knowledge of what these declarations meant? Were they in a position to recognize mistakes and to reverse course eventually? Were they even interested in this?

In the final analysis, internal Central and Eastern European processes, with emerging new splits and factions, prevailed over the influence (and money) of the Western European partners, although their role cannot be ignored. They helped both materially and with expertise. Some emigrés, like Stanisław August Morawski and Stanisław Gebhardt in Rome, worked to continue in their long-standing Cold War roles as bridges between Central and Eastern Europe on the one hand and the Western world on the other. But the impassioned engagement of such individuals was insufficient to overcome the trends described above. Polish emigré Jan Kułakowski, long-time leader in Western European Christian trade unions, returned to Poland after 1989 at Mazowiecki's request and became a diplomat with close ties to *Unia Wolności*. Stanisław Gebhardt returned to Poland, but his hopes that such people as Ryszard Bender could create a strong and stable, internationally recognized Polish Christian Democratic Party were dashed. Maybe this failure additionally caused a certain radicalization of those who persisted in their attachments to Catholic politics: in Poland, the consequences included the creation of *Radio Maryja*, which has long exercised outsized political influence as the largest Catholic broadcasting corporation in Poland.

38 See Piotr H. Kosicki's chapter in this volume.

Conclusions

This lack of a united representation of Central and Eastern European Christian Democrats proved to be a problem not just for Central and Eastern Europe, but also for the European People's Party, in which the revolutions of 1989 triggered substantial long-term changes. The EPP, which by 2004 in reality represented not only the Christian Democratic parties of Western Europe, but also many conservatives, was forced to look for reliable partners in Central and Eastern Europe, where most potential partners were in truth neither Christian Democratic nor conservative. The case of the Civic Platform in Poland is striking: only a handful of individual members of this later governing party of Poland would have called themselves Christian Democrats, but the party's public stature sufficed for it to become a part of the EPP. As Alexander Brakel has shown in this volume, this flexibility in the quest for partners was in fact nothing new: the Civic Platform's predecessor, the Liberal Democratic Congress (KLD) had been aggressively courted by the German CDU as a potential partner even as Polish Prime Minister Jan Krzysztof Bielecki of the KLD consistently demonstrated that his loyalties lay with neoliberalism, rather than the political economy of Christian Democracy.[39]

The EU's eastern enlargement and the processes of Europeanization at work in Central and Eastern European parties also influenced their western counterparts, although the eastern parties in many cases ignored the legacy of pre-World War II and pre-Soviet Bloc Christian Democracy. Likewise, the changes did not lead to the creation of a strong and unified bloc of Western and Eastern European Christian Democrats within the European Union. This chance was lost in the 1990s. It was a lost opportunity for creating a regional Christian Democratic framework, and a lost opportunity for a true Europeanization, for example, of Polish Christian Democracy.

There are still experts in Eastern Europe who contemplate the prospects for a revival of Christian Democracy (like Dominika Sozańska in Poland), but can the emergence of a new Christian Democracy in Poland (or in other Central and Eastern European countries) create an opportunity for reviving the long Cold War history of cooperation between Western European parties and Central and Eastern European emigrés? For now, the heritage of specifically Central and Eastern European divisions effectively precludes such a scenario.

39 See Alexander Brakel's chapter in this volume.

CONCLUSION

Beyond 1989: The Disappointed Hopes of Christian Democracy in Post-Communist Central and Eastern Europe

Piotr H. Kosicki

> If one had to choose one movement in ideas and party politics that has created the political world in which Europeans still live today, the answer has to be Christian Democracy.
>
> Jan-Werner Müller[1]

In 1989, one of Poland's leading philosophers (Marcin Król) held impromptu seminars on the work of Friedrich Hayek and commended a generation of aspiring young statesmen to neo-liberalism; one of those statesmen was Donald Tusk, now President of the European Council. This same philosopher – Tusk's mentor – recently looked back on the direction in which he once pointed his young charges with the bitter self-criticism: "We were stupid."[2]

As the thirtieth anniversary of Central and Eastern Europe's anti-communist turn draws near, the face of that region seems to resemble less and less the hopes that many Western intellectuals and politicians held for it as the Cold War drew to a close. A range of prominent commentators have used the term "illiberal international" to describe the region's turn (and now, with an eye to Donald Trump, Rodrigo Duterte, and others – the world's turn) toward "illiberal" democracy as inspired by Russian President Vladimir V. Putin. In Central and Eastern Europe proper, the clarion voice of "illiberal" democracy has consistently been that of Hungarian

1 Jan-Werner Müller, *Contesting Democracy: Political Thought in Twentieth-Century Europe* (New Haven, CT: Yale University Press, 2011), 5–6.

2 Marcin Król, "Byliśmy głupi," interview with Grzegorz Sroczyński, *Gazeta Wyborcza*, 2 February 2014.

prime minister Viktor Orbán – himself a one-time hero of 1989.[3] Yale historian Timothy Snyder has put the matter most dramatically, looking back (with a nod to Hayek) on the past three decades as a "road to unfreedom" – with the post-communist region heralding liberal democracy's presumptive death knell.[4]

One of the defining tropes of modern and contemporary European history has been the multi-faceted, if not indeed deeply problematic, relationship between liberalism and nationalism. Beginning with the French Revolution, proceeding through the revolutions of 1848, until (and beyond) the "self-determination" revolutions that followed the World War I armistice, nationalists and liberals were occasionally one and the same force.[5] But the key term is *occasionally*. In the *fin-de-siècle*, nationalism and socialism, too, began to find one another, sometimes on an ad hoc basis, sometimes – and especially in the lands of partitioned Poland – on the assumption that national liberation was a precondition for achieving social justice.[6]

In the wake of the Bolshevik Revolution of 1917, a simple (and deeply misleading) equation was made by global observers of the international order: nationalism equals anti-communism.[7] As several decades' worth of historical scholarship across multiple fields has now documented, however, the *fin-de-siècle* phenomenon of context-dependent collaboration between nationalism and socialism never really disappeared. In the interwar period, fascism, too, could not have functioned without absorbing key elements of the broadly understood socialist program. As in the interwar, so after World War II did revolutionary socialism – now installed with brutal heavy-handedness by the Soviet Union, with Red Army boots enforcing the

3 See, e.g., Jan-Werner Müller, "The Problem with 'Illiberal Democracy,'" *Project Syndicate*, 21 January 2016; Sławomir Sierakowski, "The Illiberal International," *Project Syndicate*, 9 September 2016.

4 Snyder looks especially to post-Soviet Russia, but also to Poland: Timothy Snyder, *The Road to Unfreedom: Russia, Europe, and America* (New York: Tim Duggan Books, 2018).

5 See, e.g., Pieter Judson, *Exclusive Revolutionaries: Liberal Politics, Social Experience, and National Identity in the Austrian Empire, 1848–1914* (Ann Arbor: University of Michigan Press, 1996); F.L. Carsten, *Revolution in Central Europe, 1918–1919* (Aldershot, UK: Wildwood House, 1988); Ray Taras, *Liberal and Illiberal Nationalisms* (Basingstoke, UK: Palgrave Macmillan, 2002).

6 See, e.g., Timothy Snyder, *Nationalism, Marxism, and Modern Central Europe: A Biography of Kazimierz Kelles-Krauz, 1872–1905* (Oxford: Oxford University Press, 2017 edition).

7 Francine Hirsch, *Empire of Nations: Ethnographic Knowledge and the Making of the Soviet Union* (Ithaca, NY: Cornell University Press, 2005); Paul A. Hanebrink, *A Specter Haunting Europe: The Myth of Judeo-Bolshevism* (Cambridge, MA: The Belknap Press of Harvard University Press, 2018).

"revolution" – often proceed hand in hand with nationalist mobilization.[8] Ethnic hatred and nationalist violence proved in the 1940s and 1950s, especially, to be a remarkably effective means for Soviet-backed communists to create a modus vivendi – if not elicit outright collaboration – with local populations.[9]

By contrast with studies of Stalinism, de-Stalinization, and the upheavals of 1968, few historians have tackled the relationship – by turns collegial and antagonistic – between nationalism and liberalism in the 1980s. Francis Fukuyama famously argued – as part of his much-maligned thesis that 1989 marked a definitively liberal "end of history" – that liberalism's victory did not preclude the survival (even the empowerment) of nationalist pride, hatred, and violence.[10] This would imply that nationalism's fate need not, in fact, correlate with the fate of communism.

The trend of world politics in the 2010s suggests that, however wrong Fukuyama might have been about liberalism's victory, he was certainly correct that nationalism would survive the caesura of 1989. *New York Times* columnist Ross Douthat has even gone so far as to suggest that the revolutions of 1989 in Central and Eastern Europe were not principally – or perhaps even at all – about liberalism, but instead about nationalism. In its 1980s incarnation, nationalism in Central and Eastern Europe implied a set of sovereignty claims against the Soviet Union, but since the USSR's collapse, nationalism's semantic content has been reinvented again and again against a Western "other" (most often: "Brussels," the metonym for all imagined consumerist and technocratic ills of European integration – if not indeed more nefarious imagined foes).[11] Douthat surely takes the point too far, but from the vantage point of 2019 it is difficult not to see a

8 Jan Gross, "War as Revolution," in *The Establishment of Communist Regimes in Eastern Europe, 1944–1949*, ed. Norman Naimark and Leonid Gibianskii (Boulder, CO: Westview Press, 1997), 17–40; Piotr H. Kosicki, *Catholics on the Barricades: Poland, France, and "Revolution," 1891–1956* (New Haven, CT: Yale University Press, 2018).

9 See, e.g., Michael Fleming, *Communism, Nationalism, and Ethnicity in Poland, 1944–50* (London: Routledge, 2010); Norman M. Naimark, *Fires of Hatred: Ethnic Cleansing in Twentieth-Century Europe* (Cambridge, MA: Harvard University Press, 2001); Hugo Service, *Germans to Poles: Communism, Nationalism, and Ethnic Cleansing after the Second World War* (Cambridge: Cambridge University Press, 2013).

10 For the original argument, see Francis Fukuyama, "End of History?," *National Interest*, Summer 1989. For the expanded, book-length version, see Francis Fukuyama, *The End of History and the Last Man* (New York: Free Press, 1992).

11 Ross Douthat, "The Fall of the German Empire," *New York Times*, 16 May 2018; see also, e.g., Ivan Krastev, "Central Europe is a lesson to liberals: Don't be anti-nationalist," *The Guardian*, 11 July 2018.

telos of nationalist illiberalism embedded already within the revolutionary events of the late 1980s.[12]

The missing piece of this puzzle is (neo-)liberalism – and, even more importantly, the social and cultural mythology surrounding it. Stephen Metcalf writes, "'neo-liberalism' is not simply a name for pro-market policies, or for the compromises with finance capitalism made by failing social democratic parties. It is a name for a premise that, quietly, has come to regulate all we practice and believe: that competition is the only legitimate organizing principle for human activity."[13] In the region's collective memory, the turn to the free market in post-1989 Central and Eastern Europe has become as much a matter of biography as of economics, singling out, most notably, Leszek Balcerowicz, János Kis, and Václav Klaus.[14] These free-market thinkers and statesmen became the right men, in the right place, at the right time, so to speak – stepping into the role of intermediaries between economic theories incubated in the West and real social and economic pressures faced by former Soviet Bloc populations.

In twenty-first-century Poland, former Deputy Prime Minister Leszek Balcerowicz's name is virtually synonymous with the decline of Polish heavy industry and its selling-off to foreign investors – in other words, with the impoverishment of entire swathes of the post-1989 Polish population. And yet, Balcerowicz rose to power thanks to Tadeusz Mazowiecki, a long-time Catholic advocate of social justice who had been vigorously engaged since the 1950s in shaping public opinion and policy in communist Poland.[15] Conversely, from a North American vantage point, it is all too

12 Douthat is hardly the only author to explore the causes of liberalism's twenty-first-century crisis in Central and Eastern Europe: see, e.g., Timothy Garton Ash, "Liberal Europe isn't dead yet: But its defenders face a long, hard struggle," *The Guardian*, 9 July 2018; Jacques Rupnik, "Explaining Eastern Europe: The Crisis of Liberalism," *Journal of Democracy* 29, no. 3 (2018): 24–37; Ellen Hinsey, *Mastering the Past: Contemporary Central and Eastern Europe and the Rise of Illiberalism* (Candor, NY: Telos Publishing, 2017).

13 Stephen Metcalf, "Neoliberalism: The idea that swallowed the world," *The Guardian*, 18 August 2017; more generally, see Quinn Slobodian, *Globalists: The End of Empire and the Birth of Neoliberalism* (Cambridge, MA: Harvard University Press, 2018).

14 See, e.g., Leszek Balcerowicz, *Socialism, Capitalism, Transformation* (Budapest: Central European University Press, 1995); János Kis, *Mi a liberalizmus? Esszék, Tanulmányok, 1985–2014* (Pozsony: Kalligram, 2015); Václav Klaus, *Renaissance: The Rebirth of Liberty in the Heart of Europe* (Washington, DC: Cato Institute, 1997). For an important corrective, see Grzegorz W. Kołodko, *From Shock to Therapy: The Political Economy of Postsocialist Transformation* (Oxford: Oxford University Press, 2000).

15 On Mazowiecki's embrace of Balcerowicz, see Piotr H. Kosicki, "After 1989: The Life and Death of the Catholic Third Way," *TLS – Times Literary Supplement*, 13 December 2013. For the case "against" Balcerowicz, see, e.g., Henryk Pająk, *Piąty rozbiór Polski: 1990–2000* (Lublin: Retro, 2005). On Balcerowicz's appointment by Mazowiecki, see Waldemar Kuczyński, *Zwierzenia zausznika* (Warsaw: BGW, 1992), 54–59.

easy to see the political and economic fate of post-communist Central and Eastern Europe as having been conceived and carried out – like Zeus giving birth to Athena – in the minds of American economist Jeffrey Sachs and Hungarian-American philanthropist (and now favorite bogeyman of the Euro-American alt-right) George Soros.[16] "Fake news" and disinformation aside, there is of course more to the story.

The neo-liberalism particular to Central and Eastern Europe since 1989 was the product of multiple crossroads and conversations: between imported and homegrown ideas, between communists and non-communists, and between politics and anti-politics.[17] As Quinn Slobodian has shown, the word "neo-liberalism" is no mere placeholder for the technocratic rubber-stamping of a dramatic post-imperial redrawing of the international order. Rather, "neo-liberals" are, and have been, real historical actors with local and national roots, whose ideas achieved transnational reach and consequence.[18] European Council president Donald Tusk himself exemplifies perfectly this balancing act.

If post-1989 Central and Eastern Europe has been dominated first by neo-liberalism, then by nationalism, then what happened to the middle road? As the death knell tolled for the communist system of Central and Eastern Europe in the late 1980s, the victory of capitalism – *pace* Fukuyama – was hardly inevitable. Certainly, to observers from outside the region, and even to many from within, various "third ways" amounted to little more than – in Tony Judt's words – a "short-lived optimistic alternative."[19] Principal among these were the Left's non-revolutionary answer to communism – read: Social Democracy – and another political force, difficult to equate with any other: Christian Democracy.

16 See, e.g., Kenneth P. Vogel, Scott Shane, and Patrick Kingsley, "How Vilification of George Soros Moved from the Fringes to the Mainstream," *New York Times*, 31 October 2018. For the protagonists' perspective, see, e.g., Jeffrey Sachs, *Poland's Jump to the Market Economy* (Cambridge, MA: MIT Press, 1993); George Soros, *Underwriting Democracy: Encouraging Free Enterprise and Democratic Reform among the Soviets in Eastern Europe* (New York: PublicAffairs, 2004).

17 On anti-politics, see George [György] Konrad, *Antipolitics: An Essay*, trans. Richard E. Allen (New York: H. Holt, 1987); David Ost, *Solidarity and the Politics of Anti-politics: Opposition and Reform in Poland since 1968* (Philadelphia: Temple University Press, 1990).

18 Slobodian puts it thus: "the neoliberal project focused on designing institutions – not to liberate markets but to encase them, to inoculate capitalism against the threat of democracy, to create a framework to contain often-irrational human behavior, and to reorder the world after empire as a space of competing states in which borders fulfill a necessary function." Slobodian, *Globalists*, 2.

19 Tony Judt, "The 'Third Way' is No Route to Paradise," *New York Times*, 27 September 1998.

Christian Democracy and the fall of communism

This book has reconstructed the story of Christian Democracy's role in the "long" fall of communism – looking before and after the revolutions of 1989, inside and outside the region, and situating "third way" options in the broader political imaginary of late-Cold War Europe.[20] Despite its oft-noted similarities of policy priority to Social Democracy, Christian Democracy is undoubtedly an ideological sui generis in virtue of its declared inspiration by Christianity. Christian Democracy, of course, implies neither evangelization nor theocracy; its long history in modern Europe has been one of progressive – if reluctant – reconciliation with liberal democracy.

Yet the broader narrative of European Christian Democracy says little about the continent's eastern half.[21] Despite the vigorous activism of political emigrés who fled the communization of Central and Eastern Europe in the 1940s and 1950s, four decades of Soviet domination effectively eliminated Central and Eastern European Christian Democracy's capacity to shape the fate of the region. As Sławomir Łukasiewicz and I have written elsewhere with regards to Poland, "since the communist collapse in 1989, Christian Democracy (...) has arguably fared worse than while the Soviet Bloc still existed."[22] Emigré Christian Democrats in the 1950s and 1960s helped to promote Catholic-identified political forces worldwide, but it was not until the Helsinki human rights turn of the mid-1970s that new generations of homegrown Christian Democrats began to emerge behind

20 Piotr H. Kosicki and Kyrill Kunakhovich, eds., *The Long 1989: Decades of Global Revolution* (Budapest: Central European University Press, 2019).

21 The crucial exceptions are: Michael Gehler, Wolfram Kaiser and Helmut Wohnout, eds., *Christdemokratie in Europe im 20. Jahrhundert – Christian Democracy in 20th-Century Europe* (Vienna: Böhlau, 2001); Piotr H. Kosicki and Sławomir Łukasiewicz, eds., *Christian Democracy across the Iron Curtain: Europe Redefined* (London: Palgrave Macmillan, 2018). Monographs on political Catholicism published since 2000 have, however, helped to create a scholarly canvas for thinking in genuinely pan-European terms continent as a whole about the intellectual, cultural, and political entanglements of Christian Democracy. See, e.g., Giuliana Chamedes, *A Twentieth-Century Crusade: The Vatican's Battle to Remake Christian Europe* (Cambridge, MA: Harvard University Press, 2019); James Chappel, *Catholic Modern: The Challenge of Totalitarianism and the Remaking of the Church* (Cambridge, MA: Harvard University Press, 2018); Marco Duranti, *The Conservative Human Rights Revolution: European Identity, Transnational Politics, and the Origins of the European Convention* (Oxford: Oxford University Press, 2017); Wolfram Kaiser, *Christian Democracy and the Origins of European Union* (Cambridge: Cambridge University Press, 2007); Kosicki, *Catholics on the Barricades*; Jan-Werner Müller, *Christian Democracy: A New Intellectual History* (Cambridge, MA: Harvard University Press, forthcoming); Carolyn M. Warner, *Confessions of an Interest Group: The Catholic Church and Political Parties in Europe* (Princeton, NJ: Princeton University Press, 2000).

22 "Editors' Introduction," in Kosicki and Łukasiewicz, *Christian Democracy across the Iron Curtain*, v-xvii, at vii.

the Iron Curtain.[23] These, in turn, found themselves caught in generational and political scissors between the international renown of their emigré elders and the leading (often post-Marxist) dissidents who paved the way to the revolutions of 1989. Even József Antall and Ján Čarnogurský – despite their rapid ascent to prominence as statesmen in the early 1990s – enjoyed only brief moments in the sun before their agendas were coopted or supplanted by neo-liberal technocrats and post-communist populists.

For the non-specialist in the affairs of this region, this is a difficult story to process: too many minor movements or parties, too many names that are difficult to spell or pronounce (the eternal curse of Europe's eastern half!). Therefore, Michael Gehler, Helmut Wohnout, and I undertook this project with a calculated two-fold strategy:

1. to examine Central and Eastern Europe from the outside in, reconstructing the efforts of Western European actors to foster or support Christian Democratic efforts in the region; and
2. to examine the (re-)emergence of homegrown Christian Democratic formations in the 1980s and 1990s.

The resulting volume has presented the reader with twelve scholarly chapters. These are neither exhaustive nor definitive of the subject, but rather were intended to launch a conversation. Three questions have guided this conversation, as outlined in the volume's introduction by Michael Gehler:

1. What was the perception of Central and Eastern Europe before and after 1989 by Christian Democrats?
2. What ideas, plans, and visions did Christian Democrats develop on the future of Europe before and after 1989?
3. What was the result and the outcome of Christian Democratic efforts and initiatives?

In particular, the material contained in this volume removes debates about Christian Democracy's role in Central and Eastern Europe from the "ghetto" of national historiographies, presenting the state of the art and the latest research in the academic lingua franca of English in hopes of – finally! – connecting scholarship on the Iron Curtain's collapse with scholarship on political Catholicism. The three sections of this volume have assessed the balance of who did what in complex transitional years, focusing especially

23 In this volume, see the contributions by Ladislav Cabada and Anton Pelinka. For the broader context, see – on the emigrés – Kosicki and Łukasiewicz, *Christian Democracy across the Iron Curtain*. On the human rights turn of the 1970s – Samuel Moyn, *The Last Utopia: Human Rights in History* (Cambridge, MA: Belknap Press of Harvard University Press, 2010); Michael Cotey Morgan, *The Final Act: The Helsinki Accords and the Transformation of the Cold War* (Princeton, NJ: Princeton University Press, 2018).

on the years of collapse of the Soviet Bloc and the Soviet Union in 1989–1991, reassessing the thinking and actions of global Catholic politicians invested in the outcome of political events in Central and Eastern Europe.

Even in the mid-nineteenth-century heyday of ultramontanism, Catholic politics could never be divorced from its secular counterparts, with whom Catholic politicians frequently competed for their constituency.[24] This was still true 150 years later, as Christian Democratic activists in political and social movements confronted the tectonic shifts in the international system that marked the final stages of the Cold War. In Section One of this book, we find three chapters that have guided the reader through a maze of heretofore-unexplored (or underexplored) international players that created the conditions of possibility for Christian Democratic actors to facilitate the revolutions of 1989. The book opens with Kim Christiaens's study of the World Confederation of Labor (WCL) as a post-Christian Democratic institution: "post" in the sense not only of having experienced secularization in the 1960s, but also in its choice not to affiliate automatically with independent trade unions in predominantly Catholic countries like Poland (a choice made in reference to the Global South as much as Europe).

The complexity of the WCL's relationship with *Solidarność* in the 1980s helps to set up also the stories told by Andrea Brait, Michael Gehler, and Johannes Schönner. The Vienna follow-up to the celebrated Helsinki Conference of the 1970s and the resultant Conference on Security and Cooperation in Europe (CSCE) – as reconstructed by Brait and Gehler – helps to explain both the role of the concept of "human rights" in the run-up to the revolutions of 1989 and, specifically, the agency of Christian Democrats (and of the Austrian statesman Alois Mock, in particular). Theirs is a story that takes the "global Cold War" scholarship on the CSCE beyond détente into ideological and institutional entanglements rarely explored outside the study of political Catholicism.[25]

Finally, Gehler and Schönner examine the case of the European Democrat Union (EDU), a distinctive Christian Democratic network whose peculiar history vis-à-vis the political constellation of the European Communities (EC) – in particular, the Christian Democracy-derived European

24 See, e.g., Austin Gough, *Paris and Rome: The Gallican Church and the Ultramontane Campaign, 1848–1853* (Oxford: Clarendon Press, 1986); Emiel Lamberts, *The Struggle with Leviathan: Social Responses to the Omnipotence of the State, 1815–1965*, trans. Maria Kelly (Leuven: Leuven University Press, 2017).

25 The canonical work that defined the paradigm of the "global Cold War" is Odd Arne Westad, *The Global Cold War* (Cambridge: Cambridge University Press, 2005).

People's Party (EPP) – led it to embrace also conservative, non-Christian Democratic parties. As a transnational network unbound either by nation-state logic or by the party politics of the EC (by contrast with the EPP), the EDU had by the late 1980s achieved remarkable maneuvering room in Central and Eastern Europe. This – in spite of the shifting sands of national communist politics in the region following the imposition of martial law in Poland (1981) and the rise of Mikhail Gorbachev to the leadership of the Communist Party of the Soviet Union (1985). As a result, the EDU made possible one of Western European Christian Democracy's greatest achievements across the collapsing Iron Curtain: sponsoring the creation of the Hungarian Democratic Forum, the political alliance that brought to power the one distinctly Christian Democratic prime minister of the post-1989 transition, József Antall. This is a connection not to be underestimated in terms of its continent-wide implications for Europe.

Having established the ideological and institutional parameters within which European Christian Democracy sought to carve out a place for itself in the transformation of the communist world, this book then examined in two separate sections the story from both sides of the collapsing Iron Curtain. Sections Two and Three, therefore, cannot stand alone, but rather tell entangled stories that should be considered in conversation with one another.

In Section Two, four chapters reconstructed the efforts of Christian Democrats in Europe's "West" to reshape its "East." Section Two began, perhaps a bit unusually for a book about Christian Democracy, with Thomas Gronier's ground-breaking case study of a transnational Catholic network that helped to shape the revolutions of the 1989 – *without* identifying with Christian Democracy. The Taizé community, founded in France in 1940, created an avowedly Christian, but still distinctly ecumenical, umbrella for cross-Iron Curtain network formation that began to achieve its best results already in the 1960s and 1970s. Through openings in the Iron Curtain that Taizé helped to expand, young Catholics from behind the Iron Curtain encountered, among others, the Christian Democratic movements of the West. But Christian Democracy played only a minor role in this story, and therein lies one of the paradoxical lessons of Section Two: that, at the institutional level, perhaps the most impactful contribution of Western European Catholics to the collapse of the communist system came not through the political parties of Helmut Kohl or Giulio Andreotti, but rather through communities of prayer and reflection.

Gronier's Taizé story helps to frame a necessary backdrop for assessing both the tremendous achievements and the important limitations of the efforts of Austrian, (West) German, and Italian Christian Democrats to engage in movement building across Central and Eastern Europe: first, as the Iron Curtain was collapsing; and then, as post-communist political systems were crystallizing in the region. To be clear: Alois Mock, Erhard Busek, Helmut Kohl, and Ciriaco De Mita built a wide range of contacts in the region well before the Iron Curtain's collapse. The support of the EDU, the CDU, and other national and transnational movements affiliated with Christian Democracy played a decisive role in convincing many Iron Curtain dissidents that they could – and indeed would – ultimately succeed in shaping a successor political system to the collapsing communist world. Four decades of success in reshaping the face of Western Europe – indeed, of creating a new model for transnationalism in the pursuit of peace and economic cooperation – seemed a powerful countervailing model to that of the discredited Soviet empire.[26]

At a practical level, too, the Western European project of recasting communist Europe as a Christian Democratic haven was no fool's errand. The considerable resources – financial as well as personal – invested especially by the Germans and the Austrians in Czechoslovakia, Hungary, and elsewhere led to tangible and substantial results. From the perspective of mid-1990 – with the possible exception of Poland – Christian Democracy seemed poised to become one of the defining forces of post-communist Central and Eastern Europe. Even in Lithuania – which declared independence in 1990, only to await the USSR's collapse in 1991 – Christian Democracy entered into government and drew heavily on the legacy of its pre-World War II prominence.

But the Christian Democratic moment of 1990 was just that: a moment. In Hungary, József Antall died soon thereafter, and Christian Democrats split across several different formations (surviving even today as part of Viktor Orbán's grand "Christian nationalist" coalition).[27] In Czechoslovakia, Christian Democracy never recovered from the Velvet Divorce, after which Čarnogurský's party fought a losing battle against the aspiring authoritarian Vladimír Mečiar.[28]

26 On the collapse of the "Soviet empire," see, e.g., Vladislav Zubok, *A Failed Empire: The Soviet Union in the Cold War from Stalin to Gorbachev* (Chapel Hill: University of North Carolina Press, 2007).

27 See, e.g., Paul Lendvai, *Orbán: Hungary's Strongman* (Oxford: Oxford University Press, 2017), 213.

28 Minton F. Goldman, *Slovakia since Independence: A Struggle for Democracy* (Westport, CT: Praeger, 1999).

In the region's largest and also most Catholic country, Poland, there was barely a Christian Democratic moment at all. Upon offering resources to build a Polish counterpart to the CDU, Helmut Kohl famously heard from his Polish counterpart Tadeusz Mazowiecki – the region's first non-communist head of government since the 1940s – that he was "a Christian and a democrat, but not a Christian Democrat."[29] In Poland, Mazowiecki's rebuff of Christian Democratic money meant that aspiring Catholic statesmen repositioned themselves instead more in line with the long legacy of Polish integral nationalism – dating back to the *fin-de-siècle* and to the anti-Semitism and xenophobia of Roman Dmowski.[30] Seeking Western European support, these nascent post-1989 formations competed for scraps, alternately adopting and dropping the "Christian Democratic" label as they saw fit, in largely instrumental fashion.

The Polish case – while unique and unrepresentative of the region as a whole – is nonetheless particularly telling. If Christian Democracy could not flourish in one of the world's most Catholic countries, then where could it? Political scientists Aleks Szczerbiak and Tim Bale have explained the absence of a successful Christian Democratic option in post-communist Poland by comparison with Western Europe after World War II, where, famously, the Christian Democratic moment of the late 1940s spawned not only European integration, but virtual Christian Democratic hegemony over national politics in West Germany and Italy, and a strong presence in Austria, Belgium, France, and the Netherlands.[31] Szczerbiak and Bale identify six factors that obtained in Western Europe in 1945, but not in Poland in 1990:

1. "a real and pervasive fear" of a "potentially totalitarian left";
2. "bedrock support" from female, rural, and middle-class voters;
3. a delegitimized, post-totalitarian Right (in post-communist Poland, even the extreme Right held a trump card over the post-totalitarian Left);
4. unequivocal support of the Church hierarchy for Christian Democracy;
5. widespread civil society campaigns on Christian Democracy's behalf; and

29 See Piotr H. Kosicki's chapter in this volume.

30 See, e.g., Brian Porter, *When Nationalism Began to Hate: Imagining Modern Politics in Nineteenth-century Poland* (Oxford: Oxford University Press, 2001); Kosicki, *Catholics on the Barricades*, 21–61.

31 Kaiser, *Christian Democracy and the Origins of European Union*, 191–252.

6. autonomy for Christian Democratic parties from the Church hierarchy.[32]

Szczerbiak and Bale's is a profoundly important matrix for comparative study of European Christian Democracy's role in post-authoritarian transitions, but perhaps the most important facet of European Christian Democracy is missing from their list: its transnationalism. Section Two of this book has tested the hypothesis that Christian Democratic transnationalism – with Austrians, and Germans, and Italians at the helm – could suffice either to create or to re-create electorally viable Christian Democratic parties across Central and Eastern Europe. In the long term, the hypothesis fails. Yet both the short-term successes and long-term failures are of profound importance, as national as well as transnational narratives.

Unlike Thomas Gronier's story of Taizé as a successful transnational umbrella movement – an apolitical "catch-all" – Helmut Wohnout, Alexander Brakel, and Giovanni Mario Ceci have all told stories that say more about the Western European "donor" countries than about the intended recipients of their aid in Central and Eastern Europe. Wohnout's chapter paints portraits of Alois Mock and Erhard Busek in a time when their Austrian People's Party (ÖVP) was relegated to junior coalition partner status in government, rebuilding Austrian Christian Democratic prestige by spearheading movement-building efforts in Hungary and in Czechoslovakia. Wohnout's is undoubtedly the most successful of the stories told in these chapters – especially in reference to the three years that József Antall held power in Hungary, when the Austrian-led EDU played a profound role in Hungarian movement building.

The revelation that Western European Christian Democratic support split (re-)nascent Central and Eastern European Christian Democracy is a cruel irony, but also a crucial explanation for Christian Democracy's failure to take on the kind of dominant "catch-all" status in post-communist Europe that it enjoyed in post-World War II Western Europe.[33] Brakel's chapter, in conversation with the various chapters of Section Three, has established how the West German CDU dismissed older generations of Christian Democrats who had been holding down the fort in exile since the

32 Aleks Szczerbiak and Tim Bale, "Explaining the Absence of Christian Democracy in Contemporary Poland," in *Christian Democracy across the Iron Curtain*, ed. Kosicki and Łukasiewicz, 388–389.

33 Otto Kirchheimer, "The Transformation of Western European Party Systems," in *Political Parties and Political Development*, ed. Joseph LaPalombara and Myron Weiner (Princeton, NJ: Princeton University Press, 1966), 177–200.

1940s, seeking instead to empower new self-styled Christian Democratic movements, like József Antall's Hungarian Democratic Forum, with no electoral experience and no competing ties in the West. Seeking to imprint themselves upon the future of Central and Eastern European Christian Democracy, the Christian Democrats of the Federal Republic of Germany instead helped to insure its transience.

It is unsurprising, therefore, that Giovanni Mario Ceci's chapter on Italian Christian Democracy (DC) focuses entirely on how the revolutions of 1989 in Central and Eastern Europe complicated internal debates within the DC. On the one hand, the DC had long provided resources and a home for Christian Democrats fleeing the Iron Curtain throughout the Cold War. On the other, Italian governments had actively supported the politics of détente since the 1960s, and had great difficulty establishing a consistent line on Central and Eastern Europe's post-communist future.[34] Ceci has shown that, rather than provide a source of inspiration for counterparts to the east, Italy's Christian Democrats found in the revolutions of 1989 yet another source of disagreement in what was rapidly proving to be the party's unraveling. Instead of a story of support for Christian Democratic expansion, Ceci has told the story of the collapse of one of the pillars of the post-1945 Christian Democratic order.

The five chapters that comprise Section Three have shown what was on the other side of the looking glass into which the Austrians, Germans, and Italians gazed (and into which they sent their resources). Piotr H. Kosicki's chapter has shown why Tadeusz Mazowiecki – a former Catholic socialist who reluctantly embraced neoliberalism, but not party politics – was the wrong person to invite to build a Christian Democratic movement. In the subsequent chapters in this section, Anton Pelinka and Ladislav Cabada respectively explore the long-range conditions and explanations for the limited success – if not outright failure – of Christian Democracy to shape the post-communist face of Hungary and Czechoslovakia. Pelinka provides a corrective to the EDU, Austrian, and German perspectives on Hungary by showing that, instead of a Christian Democratic success story, Hungarian political culture after 1989 did not coalesce around Europe or Christianity, but instead wrestled with the nationalist demons of Hungarian historical memory. Ladislav Cabada, in turn, has charted the emergence of a range of homegrown Catholic political initiatives in the Czech and Slovak lands: in

34 See the contributions in Antonio Varsori and Benedetto Zaccaria, eds., *Italy in the International System from Détente to the End of the Cold War: The Underrated Ally* (London: Palgrave Macmillan, 2018).

Czech lands, pre-war Christian Democracy made a brief comeback, while in Slovakia, the generation of Ján Čarnogurský set the tone. Yet in Czechoslovakia, too, the story was one of discontinuity and difficulty establishing a stable place in the political spectrum for the ideology and agenda of Christian Democracy.

The term "velvet divorce" accurately describes not only the political fate of Czechoslovakia in the early 1990s, and not only a separation between nationalities, but also a broader point regarding the emergence of generational fissures and ideological cleavages. Beginning in the early 1990s, growing numbers of Central and Eastern Europeans who had come up through dissident ranks proved their reluctance to commit to investing in transnationalism as much as their Western European benefactors had given them.

As Artūras Svarauskas has shown, Lithuania – though a world apart in virtue of its long history of subjugation within the USSR – was subject to the same pressures. The reactivation of the pre-Soviet party of Christian Democrats foundered on the question of how to treat the generations that had survived in exile, as both sides considered the other to be too tainted by accommodation – either with the West, or with the Gorbachev-era Soviet Union. This irreconcilable generational divide – a nail in the coffin of post-communist Europe's Christian Democratic potential – has been reconstructed synoptically at a regional level in this book by Sławomir Łukasiewicz, whose account of the quiet death of the long-standing pillar of Christian Democracy in exile, the Christian Democratic Union of Central Europe, documents the definitive displacement of the old by the new – and the consequent failure of the new to reclaim the position achieved by their elders.

Christian Democracy for export

How should we assess the balance of Christian Democracy's movement-building efforts in post-communist Central and Eastern Europe? Certainly, there is a crucial distinction to be drawn between homegrown projects and those hatched in the minds of statesmen and ideologues in Bonn, Rome, and Vienna. Seen through the heuristic lens of a scholarship positioned principally within the study of (Western) European Christian Democracy – even though the European People's Party benefited directly from the overall continental expansion of the political formation after

1989 – both projects failed. Indeed, these failures have likely contributed to the fact of Christian Democracy having reached its horizon line, if not indeed having been entirely eclipsed, across twenty-first-century Europe – West as well as East. The case of Italy's Democrazia Cristiana – which fell apart just as Central and Eastern Europe was regaining its sovereignty – is telling on this point.

Many homegrown Christian Democrats of post-communist Central and Eastern Europe sympathize today, in the 2010s, with the populist, illiberal agendas of Jarosław Kaczyński, Viktor Orbán, and Miloš Zeman.[35] Indeed, the political parties helmed by these men have absorbed most of the region's post-communist "first generation" of Christian Democrats, from the early 1990s. Kaczyński himself briefly flirted with the Christian Democratic label, and the place of his first political party – *Porozumienie Centrum* (Center Agreement, PC) – in the archives of the CDU and the EDU confirms the relative elasticity with which the label was applied in both directions.[36]

It is perhaps too tempting to compare the state of European Christian Democracy in 1989–1990 with that of 1945. After all, both moments offered the prospect of an unprecedented continental influence for political Catholicism in the wake of the delegitimation of a totalitarian system. In 1945, Christian Democracy gained a decisive position in mainstream politics following the discrediting of Europe's totalitarian Right.[37] By contrast, in 1989, it was the totalitarian Left that fell away.

In 1945, Western European Christian Democracy received outside support, from the United States – but the US was, of course, no Christian Democratic force. James Chappel has put it best: "While it would be absurd to deny the role of the Americans in the creation of democratic societies in non-communist Europe, they did not do the lion's share of the labor. Ideologically and economically, the main sources of Europe's reconstruction were native."[38] In 1989, meanwhile, ready-made models emerged in Western Europe for export to the "East." Unlike the synergy seen in the West after World War II the confluence of outside support and homegrown forces resulted in fragmentation.

35 See, e.g., Patrick Kingsley, "How a Liberal Dissident Became a Far-Right Hero, in Hungary and Beyond," *New York Times*, 6 April 2018.

36 See Michael Gehler's and Johannes Schönner's chapter and Alexander Brakel's chapter in this volume. In the EDU archives, the record of correspondence with Jarosław Kaczyński can be found in the folder "Polen – L – PC (Sept. 1991 – 1995/96)," in Archiv des Karl von Vogelsang-Instituts (Vienna): European Democrat Union (EDU) Collection.

37 See, e.g., Kaiser, *Christian Democracy and the Origins of European Union*, 163–190.

38 Chappel, *Catholic Modern*, 149.

Aleks Szczerbiak and Tim Bale have observed ruefully, "In the field of party politics, there is an implicit expectation that the party systems of East-Central Europe will over time come to resemble those of the western half of the continent."[39] If one scratches beneath the surface of scholarly inquiry – whose home, after all (especially for English-language publishing), has long been in the West – one encounters a foundational epistemic problem that blocks objective analysis of the relationship between European Christian Democracy East and West. Szczerbiak and Bale are right to question the prevailing teleology of "Eastern" convergence with the "West," not only on empirical grounds, but above all as smacking of Orientalism.

One need not be a devotee of Edward Saïd to recognize the dangers of a "West" looking to remake an imagined "East" in its own image. In reference to the late eighteenth century, historian Larry Wolff famously contended that, instead of encountering Europe's "East" on its own terms, as a vast array of peoples and territories with their own customs and traditions, Voltaire, Hume, and other *lumières* saw it through a glass darkly, as a backward, broken reflection of themselves. It is difficult to resist the temptation to see in similar terms the late-twentieth-century projects of Western European Christian Democrats seeking to "help" and "train" their cross-Iron Curtain brethren.[40]

To make this claim does not imply a value judgment, but rather a simple recognition of the shifting power dynamics of the global Cold War. Just as the "First" and "Second" Worlds competed beginning in the mid-twentieth century to impose their own models of international development on the post-colonial South, so did Germans and Italians seek to define the terms on which Catholic politics in the long-Soviet-dominated East would be reintegrated into a transnational European mainstream.[41] What they sought was a Catholic, self-styled Christian Democratic politics after their own image.[42] What they found instead was a pressure cooker combining

39 Szczerbiak and Bale, "Explaining the Absence of Christian Democracy in Contemporary Poland," 343.

40 Edward W. Saïd, *Orientalism* (New York: Vintage, 1979); Larry Wolff, *Inventing Eastern Europe: The Map of Civilization on the Mind of the Enlightenment* (Stanford, CA: Stanford University Press, 1994).

41 On European Catholics' approach to the Global South, see, e.g., Piotr H. Kosicki, "The Catholic 1968: Poland, Social Justice, and the Global Cold War," *Slavic Review* 77, no. 3 (2018): 638–660; Giuliana Chamedes, "The Catholic Origins of Economic Development after World War II," *French Politics, Culture, and Society* 33, no. 2 (2015): 55–75.

42 Patrick Pasture, "Catholic and Christian Democratic Views on Europe before and after World War II: Continuities and Discontinuities," in *Christian Democracy across the Iron Curtain*, ed. Kosicki and Łukasiewicz, 25–56.

forces long-suppressed by a repressive communist state apparatus and the illusion of a unified opposition. In that pressure cooker, nationalism dominated over transnationalism, and in fact integralism re-entered the political mainstream. In many ways, Central and Eastern European politics of the 1990s more closely resembled French or Austrian politics of the 1890s – with Karl Lueger or Charles Maurras seeming to lurk in the background – than of their own time.[43]

The attempt at a global assessment of the legacy of Central and Eastern Europe's transformation is therefore haunted by what George Orwell once described as problems of ideological translation.[44] Catholic politics, in particular, fell victim to ideological *mis*-translation across the former Iron Curtain. As a result, the single most successful import into the political ideology and political economy of Europe's "East" came not from Christian Democracy, nor any other third way, but rather from (neo-)liberalism. Reading Hayek, Ludwig von Mises, and Milton Friedman bred homegrown neo-liberals as well.[45] Perhaps among the most famous – as we have already seen – are Leszek Balcerowicz, Václav Klaus, and Donald Tusk.

However we assess the balance of nationalism and liberalism before, during, and since the revolutions of 1989, it is clear that post-communist Central and Eastern Europe has proven deeply inimical to the full range of "third way" solutions. This is perhaps understandable in the case of Social Democracy – tainted by the accession of former communist party members following the Soviet collapse – but why not Christian Democracy, especially in overwhelmingly Catholic Poland, or in traditionally Catholic Hungary or Slovakia? As this book has documented, all three of these countries witnessed in 1989 the meteoric rise of Catholic political leaders: in Poland, Tadeusz Mazowiecki; in Hungary, József Antall; and in Slovakia, Ján Čarnogurský. Of these three, only Čarnogurský would work to build a Christian Democratic political organization going by that name; while Antall died too soon, Mazowiecki overtly rejected the Christian Democratic label.

43 See, e.g., Pierre Birnbaum, *The Anti-Semitic Moment: A Tour of France in 1898*, trans. Jane Marie Todd (Chicago: University of Chicago Press, 2011); John W. Boyer, *Political Radicalism in Late-Imperial Vienna: Origins of the Christian Social Movement, 1848–1897* (Chicago: University of Chicago Press, 1981).

44 See, e.g., Ralf Dahrendorf, *Reflections on the Revolution in Europe* (New Brunswick, NJ: Transaction Publishers, 2005 edition), 15.

45 See esp. Slobodian, *Globalists*; Paul Dragos Aligica and Anthony J. Evans, eds., *The Neoliberal Revolution in Eastern Europe: Economic Ideas in Transition from Communism* (Cheltenham, UK: Edward Elgar, 2009).

Yet even Čarnogurský was a homegrown Catholic politician, rather than a Christian Democrat after the mold of the CDU, the DC, or the Christian Democrats of Austria or the Benelux countries. As Sławomir Łukasiewicz has shown in this volume, the active role of Christian Democrats from the region whose organizations had survived decades in exile ended – paradoxically – just as their home countries regained sovereignty. In other words, one of the defining facets of party politics in post-communist Central and Eastern Europe has been the non-starter status of Christian Democracy, either self-styled or as defined by existing scholarship. As Szczerbiak and Bale have noted with respect to Poland, "those parties that claimed to be Christian Democratic failed, while those that succeeded could not be described (nor did they describe themselves) as Christian Democratic."[46] While the epigraph of this essay, drawn from Jan-Werner Müller, is undoubtedly accurate, it is nonetheless also difficult to see Christian Democracy's active influence across all of "Europe" – understood in its geographical fullness – rather than traditional (Western Europe-centered) historiography.

Poland may be the most puzzling among these cases of post-1989 Christian Democratic stillbirth. Over a dozen post-1989 Polish parties have flirted with the Christian Democratic label to varying degrees, yet, as Aleks Szczerbiak and Tim Bale have contended, Christian Democracy as such had extremely weak roots on Polish soil. The Polish case indeed underscores how essential it is to distinguish between *soi-disant* Christian Democracy and the broader umbrella of political Catholicism – an umbrella so broad, frankly, as to elide a range of meaningful distinctions: between regional and national parties, between confessional and catch-all parties, and between confessionally partisan statesmen and those who (like, for example, Mazowiecki) merely sought guidance in religious belief and axiology, without defining their political programs through the political family of Christian Democracy. According to Szczerbiak and Bale, the "weakness" of Christian Democracy in post-communist Central and Eastern Europe was not merely a result of the revolutions of 1989, but rather of a long-standing structural failure of Christian Democracy to claim a durable position in the political imaginaries of the region.

46 Szczerbiak and Bale, "Explaining the Absence of Christian Democracy in Contemporary Poland," 388.

Christian Democracy eclipsed

When, in February 1989, Francis Fukuyama first used the term "end of history" to describe the arrival of communism's world-historical horizon line, the victor in his story was liberalism, not Christian Democracy. Indeed, there was no place for political Catholicism in Fukuyama's narrative. Even as Pope John Paul II was criss-crossing the Iron Curtain, making pilgrimages to his native (then still communist) Poland, Fukuyama saw religion as little more than an indulgence of false consciousness.[47] For Fukuyama – his thinking firmly imprinted by the Hegelian language he had imbibed through the writings of Alexandre Kojève – there was no third way for History to follow: with communism's collapse, liberalism was all that remained. Despite its resonance, Fukuyama's voice was but the first – and hardly the most accurate – to give meaning to the fall of communism in progress at the turn of the 1980s and 1990s. And yet, aside from the Vatican, no prominent actors in the international political arena asserted a dominant place for political Catholicism in the post-communist political episteme.[48]

To be clear – political Catholicism, expressed as a "third way" in the form of Christian Democracy, must be held as entirely distinct from the sort of integral nationalism inherited by Central and Eastern Europe from its nineteenth-century progenitors. The ideological rooting of Christian Democracy in a hybrid, yet distinctly modern approach to enacting social justice in secular politics – neither wholly corporatist, nor statist, nor market-driven, yet incorporating elements of all of these – left little room for restricting the definition of those deserving of justice to some imagined, exclusionary select few constituting a "nation" in the sense understood by Roman Dmowski or Gyula Szekfű.[49] By the end of the 1940s, in the wake of World War II and the Holocaust, Christian Democracy presupposed universalism – the idea that anyone, Christian or no, had the potential to belong, and therefore deserved the fruits of that belonging.

Ideologically, this universalism was grounded in Christian Democracy's declared prioritization of the dignity of human personhood, with the

47 James Ramon Felak, "Pope John Paul II, the Saints, and Communist Poland: The Papal Pilgrimages of 1979 and 1983," *Catholic Historical Review* 100, no. 3 (2014): 555–574.

48 On the Vatican's role, see, e.g., George Weigel, *The Final Revolution: The Resistance Church and the Collapse of Communism* (Oxford: Oxford University Press, 2003).

49 See, e.g., Porter, *When Nationalism Began to Hate*; Paul A. Hanebrink, *In Defense of Christian Hungary: Religion, Nationalism, and Antisemitism, 1890–1944* (Ithaca, NY: Cornell University Press, 2006), 118–121.

"consuming family" as the vehicle for its promotion in a modern industrial age. Ironically, the promotion of family values led Christian Democracy to embrace liberalism – first economic, then political. As James Chappel has noted, "Above all, the family required economic growth. (...) While they may have sought to smooth out the rough edges of organized capitalism, Christian Democrats had little interest in a fundamental transformation of the system. Economic development, they hoped, would solve problems of inequality – an ideology that occluded many forms of economic justice, a biting critique of consumerism, or a deep concern for the environment."[50]

As the twentieth century advanced through its second half, Christian Democracy became progressively more "liberal." The movement shed its confessional trappings, accepting technocrats like Ludwig Erhard at the helm of its parties, and dissolving the boundaries between Christian Democratic and Conservative parties through transnational partnerships like the European Democrat Union and the European People's Party.[51] "Ordoliberalism," for all its distinctiveness in the realm of political economy, was nonetheless still derivative of "liberalism."[52] At the point at which Christian Democracy became a "catch-all," it sided with the liberals.

From the perspective of the 2010s, when Hungarian prime minister Viktor Orbán derided "blah blah" as the heart of political liberalism, that characterization as "blah blah" pertained also to Christian Democracy – even as, however ironically, Orbán's Fidesz has remained at the EU level a member of the (post-)Christian Democratic EPP.[53] If the 2010s represent a post-liberal moment, then Christian Democracy, too, seems to have been eclipsed right alongside the liberals and neo-liberals. Social justice as an agenda has been torn asunder from the Cold War-era "third ways" – Christian Democracy and Social Democracy – and coopted by nationalist populists.

These contemporary reflections cast into stark relief the conditions that obtained as Western European Christian Democrats, Central and Eastern European Christian Democratic emigrés, and homegrown post-1989 Christian Democrats all sought to define the place of Christian Democra-

50 Chappel, *Catholic Modern*, 19, 226.

51 Beata Kosowska-Gąstoł, "A Truly 'European' Christian Democracy? The European People's Party," in *Christian Democracy across the Iron Curtain*, ed. Kosicki and Łukasiewicz, 127–152; Thomas Jansen and Steven Van Hecke, *At Europe's Service: The Origins and Evolution of the European People's Party* (Berlin: Springer Verlag, 2011).

52 See, e.g., Georg Milbradt, "The Prospects of Christian Democracy in Contemporary Europe: Experiences from Germany," in *Christian Democracy across the Iron Curtain*, ed. Kosicki and Łukasiewicz, 439–448.

53 Jan-Werner Müller, *What is Populism?* (Philadelphia: University of Pennsylvania Press, 2016), 53.

cy in the emerging political constellation of post-communist Europe. For life-long political activists committed to Catholic social teaching as a core value, like Tadeusz Mazowiecki, Christian Democracy was too liberal. For liberals, Christian Democracy was not liberal enough. The promise of a "third way" turned into a pitfall. As misunderstandings multiplied and generations divided in the course of ideological mis-translation between West and East, Christian Democracy found itself pushed into a *cul de sac* – on both sides of the former Iron Curtain. And so it became that, just as Austrian and German Christian Democrats were attempting to shape new Christian Democratic movements in Hungary and Poland, Italian Christian Democracy was retreating from the scene.

The lesson here is that structured transnationalism – Christian Democracy's hallmark – is enough to shape fundamental structures, but not to assure long-term agency. For European Christian Democrats of the 1980s and 1990s, this was a humbling conclusion, and yet also a mark of the movement's historical import and strength. Fukuyama may have been wrong about liberalism's decisive victory, but he was right that the Cold War-era "third ways" – Christian Democracy and Social Democracy – were on the wane. In some ways, therefore, the most telling chapters in this book are those authored by Kim Christiaens and Thomas Gronier, both of whom have documented the limitations of Christian Democracy.

At the same time, however, one of this volume's seminal contributions lies in its documentation of the decisive role that Christian Democracy played in supporting the political (and anti-political) forces that engineered the communist collapse from within between 1989 and 1991. However the epitaph of Christian Democracy will read, the movement's contribution to the fall of communism must be acknowledged.

LIST OF ABBREVIATIONS

ACV/CSC	Algemeen Christelijk Vakverbond/Confédération des syndicats chrétiens (Belgium)
AFL-CIO	American Federation of Labor and Congress of Industrial Organizations
CDs	Christian Democrats
CDI	Christian Democrat International
CDK	Centrum pro stadium demokracie a kultury (Center for Studies of Democracy and Culture)
CDU	Christlich Demokratische Union (Christian Democratic Union, Germany)
CDUCE	Christian Democratic Union of Central Europe
CEE	Central and Eastern Europe
CEEC	Central and Eastern European Countries
CFTC	Confédération Française des Travailleurs Chrétiens
CIA	Central Intelligence Agency
CIDSE	Coopération Internationale pour le Développement et la Solidarité
CISL	Confederazione Italiana Sindacati Lavoratori
CLAT	Central Latinoamericana de Trabajadores
CN	Consiglio Nazionale (National Council of the Italian Christian Democratic Party)
CNV	Christelijk Nationaal Vakverbond (the Netherlands)
Comecon	Council for Mutual Economic Assistance
CPSU	Communist Party of the Soviet Union
CSCE	Conference on Security and Cooperation in Europe (i.e. KSZE)
ČSL	Československá strana lidová (Czechoslovak People's Party)
CSU	Christlich Soziale Union (Christian Social Union, Germany)
DC	Democrazia Cristiana (Italy)
DEU	Demokratická unie (Democratic Union)
EBRD	European Bank of Reconstruction and Development
EC	European Community
EDU	European Democrat Union
EFTA	European Free Trade Agreement
EPP	European People's Party
EU	European Union
EUCD	European Union of Christian Democrats
EVP	Europäische Volkspartei (i.e. EPP)
FCG	Fraktion Christlicher Gewerkschafter im ÖGB (Association of Christian Trade Unions, Austria)
FDP	Freie Demokratische Partei (Free Democratic Party, Germany)
FEC	Free Europe Committee
FOPADESC	Fondation Panafricaine pour le Développement Économique, Social et Culturel
FPÖ	Freiheitliche Partei Österreichs (Freedom Party of Austria)
FRG	Federal Republic of Germany
GDR	German Democratic Republic
HOS	Movement for Civic Freedom
HSLS	Hlinka's Slovak People's Party
ICFTU	International Confederation of Free Trade Unions
IDU	International Democrat Union
IFCTU	International Federation of Christian Trade Unions
ILO	International Labor Organization
INF	Intermediate-Range Nuclear Forces
ISE	Institute for Central European Culture and Politics

ISP	Independent Smallholders' Party (Hungary)
KDH	Kresťanskodemokratické hnutie (Christian Democratic Movement, Slovakia)
KDNP	Kereszténydemokrata Néppárt (Christian Democratic People's Party, Hungary)
KDS	Křesťanskodemokratická strana (Christian Democratic Party, Czechoslovakia)
KDU	Křesťanská a demokratická unie (Christian and Democratic Union)
KGZE	Konferenz gewerkschaftlicher Zusammenarbeit in Europa (Conference of Trade Union Cooperation in Europe)
KIK	Kluby Inteligencji Katolickiej (Catholic Intelligentsia Clubs, Poland)
KLD	Kongres Liberalno-Demokratyczny (Liberal Democratic Congress, Poland)
KvVI	Karl von Vogelsang Institute (Vienna)
LCDP	Lithuanian Christian Democratic Party
MDF	Magyar Demokrata Fórum (Hungarian Democratic Forum)
MfS	Ministerium für Staatssicherheit (i.e. Stasi/GDR)
MP	Member of Parliament
MRP	Mouvement Républicain Populaire (Popular Republican Movement, France)
MSzMP	Magyar Szocialista Munkáspárt (Hungarian Socialist Workers' Party)
MSzP	Magyar Szocialista Párt (Hungarian Socialist Party)
NATO	North Atlantic Treaty Organization
NCFE	National Committee for a Free Europe
NEI	Nouvelles Équipes Internationales
ÖAW	Österreichische Akademie der Wissenschaften (Austrian Academy of Sciences)
ODA	Občanská demokratická aliance (Civic Democratic Alliance)
ODS	Občanská demokratická strana (Civic Democratic Party)
OF	Občanské forum (Civic Forum)
ÖGB	Österreichischer Gewerkschaftsbund (Austrian Trade Union Federation)
OI	Občanský institut (Civic Institute)
ORIT	Organización Regional Interamericana de Trabajadores (Inter-American Regional Organization of Workers)
ÖVP	Österreichische Volkspartei (Austrian People's Party)
PC	Porozumienie Centrum (Center Agreement, Poland)
PCI	Partito Comunista Italiano (Italian Communist Party)
PSC	Parti Social Chrétien (Christian Social Party, Belgium)
PSL	Polskie Stronnictwo Ludowe (Polish Peasants' Party)
PZPR	Polska Zjednoczona Partia Robotnicza (Polish United Workers' Party)
RPR	Rassemblement pour la République (France)
SdRP	Socjaldemokracja Rzeczypospolitej Polskiej (Social Democracy of the Polish Republic)
SED	Sozialistische Einheitspartei Deutschlands (Socialist Unity Party of Germany)
SI	Socialist International
SP	Stronnictwo Pracy (Polish Christian Labor Party)
SPD	Sozialistische Partei Deutschlands (Socialist Party of Germany)
SPÖ	Sozialistische Partei Österreichs (Socialist Party of Austria)
SZDSZ	Szabad Demokraták Szövetsége (Alliance of Free Democrats, Hungary)
TOP09	Tradition, Responsibility, Prosperity 09
ÚDV	Institute for the Documentation and Investigation of Communist Crimes
USO	Unión Sindical Obrera (Spain)
USSR	Union of Soviet Socialist Republics
WCL	World Confederation of Labor
WFTU	World Federation of Trade Unions
WTK	*Wrocławski Tygodnik Katolicki* (Wrocław Catholic Weekly, Poland)
ZSL	Zjednoczone Stronnictwo Ludowe (United Peasants' Party, Poland)

BIBLIOGRAPHY

Archival sources

Amsterdam, International Institute of Social History (IISH)
- Archives CLAT-Netherlands.
- Archives International Confederation of Free Trade Unions (ICFTU).
- Archives Solidarność Netherlands.

College Park, Maryland, United States National Archives and Records Administration (NARA), Records of the Central Intelligence Agency (CIA).

Florence, Archivio della Fondazione Giorgio La Pira (Archives of the Giorgio La Pira Foundation).

Leuven, KADOC, Archives of the World Confederation of Labor (WCL).

Louvain-la-Neuve, Université catholique de Louvain (UCL), Archives Jan Kułakowski (AK).

Munich, Archive of the Hanns-Seidel-Foundation (HSS).

Nijmegen, Katholieke Documentatie Centrum (KDC)
- Archives Pax Christi International.
- Archives Vincentius Vereniging Nederland (VVN).

Rome, Archivio Storico Istituto Luigi Sturzo (Historical Archives of the Luigi Sturzo Institute, ASILS), Fondo Democrazia cristiana (DC).

St. Augustin, Konrad-Adenauer-Stiftung (Konrad Adenauer Foundation, KAS)
- Archive of the Konrad-Adenauer-Foundation (KAS).
- Archiv für Christlich-Demokratische Politik (ACDP).

Vienna, Archives of the Association of Christian Trade Unions (*Fraktion Christlicher Gewerkschafter*, FCG) (FCG Archives).

Vienna, Austrian State Archives (ÖStA), Archiv der Republik (AdR), Archiv Bundesministerium für auswärtige Angelegenheiten (Federal Ministry for External Affairs, BMaA).

Vienna, Archiv des Karl von Vogelsang-Institutes (Archive of the Karl von Vogelsang Institute, AKVI)
- Archive of the European Democrat Union (EDU).

Warsaw, Archiwum Instytutu Pamięci Narodowej (Archives of the Institute of National Remembrance, AIPN).

Warsaw, Archiwum Katolickiego Stowarzyszenia *Civitas Christiana* (Archives of the *Civitas Christiana* Catholic Association).

Newspapers, magazines, and print media

Arbeiter Zeitung.
Ateitis.
Außenpolitischer Bericht (Jahrbuch der österreichischen Außenpolitik).
Austria Presse Agentur (Austria Press Agency, APA).
Christian Democratic Review.
Corriere della Sera.
La Croix.
La Discussione.
Dziś i Jutro.
EDU Yearbook.
Esprit.
Europäische Rundschau.
Flash.
Frankfurter Allgemeine Zeitung.
Gazeta Wyborcza.
The Guardian.
Kurier.
Ład.
Le Monde.
The National Interest.
Neue Zürcher Zeitung.
The New York Review of Books.
The New York Times.
Odnowa.
Österreichische Monatshefte.
ÖVP-Press Service.
Il Popolo.
Die Presse.
Project Syndicate.
Rzeczpospolita.
Sąjūdžio žinios.
Tėvynės sargas.
Wochenpresse.

Videos (available online)

The History Between Taizé and Prague. https://vimeo.com/109302099, 32 min., A&PT Production, 2014.
Wege des Vertrauens … Zur DDR-Zeiten. https://vimeo.com/317448924, 19 min., Ateliers et Presses de Taizé (A&PT) Production, 2011.

Books, book chapters, and articles

Abrams, Bradley F. *The Struggle for the Soul of the Nation: Czech Culture and the Rise of Communism.* Lanham, MD: Rowman & Littlefield, 2004.
Acanfora, Paolo. "Christian Democratic Internationalism: The *Nouvelles Équipes Internationales* and the Geneva Circles between European Unification and Religious Identity, 1947–1951." *Contemporary European History* 24, no. 3 (2015): 375–391.
Adamishin, Anatoly, and Richard Schifter. *Human Rights, Perestroika, and the End of the Cold War.* Washington, DC: United States Institute of Peace, 2009.
Ágh, Attila, and Sandor Kurtán, eds. *Democratization and Europeanization in Hungary: The First Parliament (1990–1994).* Budapest: Hungarian Center for Democracy Studies, 1995.
Aligica, Paul Dragos, and Anthony J. Evans, eds. *The Neoliberal Revolution in Eastern Europe: Economic Ideas in Transition from Communism.* Cheltenham, UK: Edward Elgar, 2009.
Altermatt, Urs. *Das Fanal von Sarajevo: Ethnonationalismus in Europa.* Zurich: Neue Zürcher Zeitung, 1996.
Altrichter, Helmut. *Russland 1989: Der Untergang des sowjetischen Imperiums.* Munich: Beck, 2009.
Altrichter, Helmut, and Hermann Wentker, eds. *Der KSZE-Prozess: Vom Kalten Krieg zu einem neuen Europa 1975 bis 1990.* Munich: Oldenbourg, 2011.
Antoszewski, Andrzej. *Partie i systemy partyjne państw Unii Europejskiej na przełomie wieków.* Toruń: Wydawnictwo Adam Marszałek, 2009.
Atti del XVIII Congresso Nazionale della Democrazia cristiana: Relazioni e documenti, edited by Carlo Dané. Volume 1: *Le relazioni, le conclusioni, i documenti*; Volume 2: *La discussione generale.* Rome: DC Spes/Cinque Lune, 1991.
Bába, Iván. *The Hungarian Transition: Parties and Movements in the Political Regime Change in Hungary between 1987 and 1994.* Budapest: ICDT, 2011.
Bachmann, Klaus. "Poland and Austria." In *"Peaceful Coexistence" or "Iron Curtain": Austria, Neutrality, and Eastern Europe in the Cold War and Détente, 1955–1989*, edited by Arnold Suppan and Wolfgang Mueller, 363–392. Vienna-Berlin: LIT Verlag, 2009.
Bachmann, Klaus. "Poland 1989: The Constrained Revolution." In *The Revolutions of 1989: A Handbook*, edited by Wolfgang Mueller, Michael Gehler and Arnold Suppan, 47–75. Vienna: Verlag der Österreichischen Akademie der Wissenschaften, 2015.
Balcerowicz, Leszek. *Socialism, Capitalism, Transformation.* Budapest: Central European University Press, 1995.
Balcerowicz, Leszek, with Jerzy Koźmiński. *800 dni: Szok kontrolowany.* Warsaw: BGW, 1992.
Bale, Tim, and Alex Szczerbiak. "Why is there no Christian Democracy in Poland (and why does it matter)?" Sussex University Institute Working Paper No. 91, online at www.sussex.ac.uk/webteam/gateway/file.php?name=-sei-working-paper-no-91.pdf&site=266. Accessed on 22 June 2017.
Bale, Tim, and Aleks Szczerbiak. "Why is there no Christian Democracy in Poland – and Why should We Care. *Party Politics* 14, no. 4 (2008): 479–500.
Ball, S. J. *The Cold War: An International History, 1947–1991.* London - New York - Sydney - Auckland: Arnold, 1998.
Bange, Oliver. "Der KSZE-Prozess und die sicherheitspolitische Dynamik des Ost-West-Konflikts 1970–1990." In *Wege zur Wiedervereinigung*, edited by Oliver Bange and Bernd Lemke, 87–104. Munich: Oldenbourg Verlag, 2013.
Bar, Joanna. "From Communism to Democracy: the Concept of Europe in Cracow's Press in the Years 1975–1995." In *Europa im Ostblock: Vorstellungen und Diskurse (1945–1991)*, edited by Christian Domnitz, José M. Faraldo and Paulina Gulińska-Jurgiel, 215–244. Cologne et al.: Böhlau, 2008.
Bartoszewski, Władysław. "Der Ostreisende." In *Erhard Busek: Ein Porträt*, edited by Elisabeth Welzig, 263–267. Vienna-Cologne-Weimar: Böhlau, 1992.

Baudet, Floribert. "'It was Cold War and We wanted to Win': Human Rights, 'Détente,' and the CSCE." In *Origins of the European Security System*, edited by Andreas Wenger, Vojtech Mastny and Christian Nuenlist, 183–198. London - New York: Routledge, 2008.

Bauquet, Nicolas. "Pouvoir, Église et société en Hongrie communiste, 1944–1964. Histoire intérieure d'une domination." PhD dissertation, Institut d'études politiques de Paris, 2013.

Bégin, Natalie. "Kontakte zwischen Gewerkschaften in Ost und West: Die Auswirkungen von Solidarność in Deutschland und Frankreich. Ein Vergleich." *Archiv für Sozialgeschichte* 45 (2005): 293–324.

Benda, Marek. "Konzervatismus v 90. letech. Odkaz Václava Bendy." In *Česká konzervativní a liberální politika. Sborník k desátému výročí založení revue Proglas*, edited by Petr Fiala and František Mikš, 125–137. Brno: Centrum pro studium demokracie a kultury, 2000.

Benziger, Karl P. "The Funeral of Imre Nagy: Contested History and the Power of Memory Culture." *History and Memory* 12, no. 2 (2000): 142–164.

Berger, Stefan. "*Solidarność*, Western Solidarity, and Détente: A Transnational Approach." *European Review* 16, no. 1 (2008): 75–84.

Bilandžić, Vladimir, Dittmar Dahlmann and Milan Kosanović, eds. *From Helsinki to Belgrade: The First CSCE Follow-up Meeting and the Crisis of Détente*. Göttingen-Bonn: V & R Unipress, 2012.

Birnbaum, Pierre. *The Anti-Semitic Moment: A Tour of France in 1898*. Translated by Jane Marie Todd. Chicago: University of Chicago Press, 2011.

Blobaum, Robert. "The Revolution of 1905–1907 and the Crisis of Polish Catholicism." *Slavic Review* 47, no. 4 (1988): 667–686.

Bloed, Arie, and Peter van Dijk, eds. *The Human Dimension of the Helsinki Process: The Vienna Follow-up Meeting and its Aftermath*. Dordrecht-Boston-Norwell: Nijhoff, 1991.

Borhi, László. *Dealing with Dictators: The United States, Hungary, and East Central Europe, 1942–1989*. Bloomington: Indiana University Press, 2016.

Bott, Sandra, Jussi M. Hanhimäki, Janick Marina Schaufelbueh and Marco Wyss, eds. *Neutrality and Neutralism in the Global Cold War: Between or within the Blocs?* Abingdon, Oxon-New York: Routledge, 2016.

Boyer, Christoph. "1989 und die Wege dorthin." *Vierteljahrshefte für Zeitgeschichte* 59, no. 1 (2011): 101–118.

Boyer, John W. *Political Radicalism in Late-Imperial Vienna: Origins of the Christian Social Movement, 1848–1897*. Chicago: University of Chicago Press, 1981.

Bozo, Frédéric. *Mitterrand, la diplomatie française et la fin de la guerre froide: De Yalta à Maastricht*. Paris: Odile, 2005.

Bracke, Maud. *Which Socialism, Whose Détente? West European Communism and the Czechoslovak Crisis of 1968*. Budapest - New York: Central European University Press, 2007.

Braham, Randolph L., and András Kovács, eds. *The Holocaust in Hungary: Seventy Years Later*. Budapest: CEU Press, 2016.

Brait, Andrea, and Michael Gehler, eds. *Grenzöffnung 1989: Innen- und Außenperspektiven und die Folgen für Österreich*. Vienna-Cologne-Weimar: Böhlau, 2014.

Bredow, Wilfried von. *Der KSZE-Prozess: Von der Zähmung zur Auflösung des Ost-West-Konflikts*. Darmstadt: Wissenschaftliche Buchgesellschaft, 1992.

Brenner, Christiane. "A Missed Opportunity to Oppose State Socialism? The People's Party in Czechoslovakia." In *Christian Democracy in Europe since 1945*, vol. 2, edited by Michael Gehler and Wolfram Kaiser, 173–192. London - New York: Routledge, 2004.

Brier, Robert. "Poland's Solidarity as a Contested Symbol of the Cold War: Transatlantic Debates after the Polish Crisis." In *European Integration and the Atlantic Community in the 1980s*, edited by Kiran Klaus Patel and Kenneth Weisbrode, 83–104. New York: Cambridge University Press, 2013.

Brix, Emil. "Die Mitteleuropapolitik von Österreich und Italien im Revolutionsjahr 1989." In *Italien, Österreich und die Bundesrepublik Deutschland in Europa / Italy, Austria, and the Federal Republic of Germany: Ein Dreiecksverhältnis in seinen wechselseitigen Beziehungen und Wahrnehmungen von 1945/49 bis zur Gegenwart / A Triangle Relationship: Mutual Relations and Perceptions from 1945/49 to the Present*, edited by Michael Gehler and Maddalena Guiotto, 455–467. Vienna-Cologne-Weimar: Böhlau, 2012.

Brown, Archie. *The Gorbachev Factor*. Oxford: Oxford University Press, 1997.

Brown, Archie. *Seven Years that Changed the World: Perestroika in Perspective.* Oxford: Oxford University Press, 2009.
Bruck, Elke. *François Mitterrands Deutschlandbild – Perzeption und Politik im Spannungsfeld Deutschland-, Europa- und sicherheitspolitischer Entscheidungen 1989–1992.* Frankfurt/Main: Lang, 2003.
Brüggemann, Karsten. "'One Day We Will Anyway': The 'Singing Revolution' in the Soviet Baltic Republics." In *The Revolutions of 1989: A Handbook*, edited by Wolfgang Mueller, Michael Gehler and Arnold Suppan, 221–246. Vienna: Verlag der Österreichischen Akademie der Wissenschaften, 2015.
Brunnbauer, Ulrich. "The End of Communist Rule in Bulgaria: The Crisis of Legitimacy and Political Change." In *The Revolutions of 1989: A Handbook*, edited by Wolfgang Mueller, Michael Gehler and Arnold Suppan, 177–197. Vienna: Verlag der Österreichischen Akademie der Wissenschaften, 2015.
Bruns, Wilhelm. "Mehr Substanz in Ost-West-Beziehungen. Zur dritten KSZE-Folgekonferenz in Wien." *Aus Politik und Zeitgeschichte*, B12 (1989): 3–9.
Brzeziecki, Andrzej. *Tadeusz Mazowiecki: Biografia naszego premiera.* Kraków: Znak Horyzont, 2015.
Bull, Martin. "The Pentapartito." In *Oxford Handbook of Italian Politics*, edited by Erik Jones and Gianfranco Pasquino. Oxford: Oxford University Press, 2015.
Bundesministerium für auswärtige Angelegenheiten. *Außenpolitischer Bericht 1989 (Jahrbuch der österreichischen Außenpolitik).* Vienna: Manz, 1990.
Busek, Erhard. *Lebensbilder.* Vienna: Kremayr & Scheriau, 2014.
Busek, Erhard. *Mitteleuropa: Eine Spurensicherung.* Vienna: Kremayr & Scheriau, 1997.
Busek, Erhard. *Ein Porträt aus der Nähe: Im Gespräch mit Jelka Kušar.* Klagenfurt-Vienna-Ljublijana et al.: Wieser, 2006.
Busek, Erhard, and Emil Brix. *Mitteleuropa Revisited: Warum Europas Zukunft in Mitteleuropa entschieden wird.* Vienna: Kremayr & Scheriau, 2018.
Busek, Erhard, and Emil Brix. *Projekt Mitteleuropa.* Vienna: Ueberreuter, 1986.
Busek, Erhard, and Gerald Stourzh, eds. *Nationale Vielfalt und gemeinsames Erbe in Mitteleuropa.* Vienna-Munich: Verlag für Geschichte und Politik, 1990.
Buttiglione, Rocco. *Karol Wojtyła: The Thought of the Man who became Pope John Paul II.* Translated by Paolo Guietti and Francesca Murphy. Grand Rapids, MI: Eerdmans, 1997.

Cabada, Ladislav. "Anti-Communism in Czech Society and Politics after 1989: Analysis of the Background and Development of the Phaenomenon." *Journal of East European and Asian Studies* 3, no. 1 (2012): 55–75.
Cabada, Ladislav. "The Czech Party System in the Year 2016: Strengthening Populism, Personalization Tendencies and Anti-Political Attitudes." In *The Czech Center-Right Solutions to the Political Challenges of 2017*, edited by Lucie Tunkrová et al., 81–90. Prague: Wilfried Martens Centre for European Studies, Konrad-Adenauer-Stiftung & TOPAZ, 2016.
Cabada, Ladislav, Vit Hloušek and Petr Jurek. *Party Systems in East Central Europe.* Lanham, MD: Lexington Books, 2014.
Cabada, Ladislav, and David Šanc. *Český stranický systém ve 20. století.* Pilsen: Aleš Čeněk, 2005.
Čarnogurský, Ján. "Christian Democracy in Slovakia." In *Christian Democracy across the Iron Curtain: Europe Redefined*, edited by Piotr H. Kosicki and Sławomir Łukasiewicz, 425–438. London: Palgrave Macmillan, 2018.
Čarnogurský, Ján. "Disent na Slovensku." In *Za svobodu a demokracii I: Odpor proti komunistické moci*, edited by Jaroslav Cuhra and Václav Veber, 209–217. Prague: Evropské hnutí v České republice, 1999.
Čarnogurský, Paľo (Pavol). *Boj s komunismom.* Bratislava: Kalligram, 2013.
Carsten, F.L. *Revolution in Central Europe, 1918–1919.* Aldershot, UK: Wildwood House, 1988.
Chamedes, Giuliana. "The Catholic Origins of Economic Development after World War II." *French Politics, Culture, and Society* 33, no. 2 (2015): 55–75.
Chamedes, Giuliana. *A Twentieth-Century Crusade: The Vatican's Battle to Remake Christian Europe.* Cambridge, MA: Harvard University Press, 2019.
Chappel, James. *Catholic Modern: The Challenge of Totalitarianism and the Remaking of the Church.* Cambridge, MA: Harvard University Press, 2018.
Chenaux, Philippe. *Entre Maurras et Maritain: Une génération intellectuelle catholique (1920–1930).* Paris: Cerf, 1999.

Chenaux, Philippe. *Une Europe vaticane? Entre le plan Marshall et les Traités de Rome*. Brussels: Editions CIACO, 1990.

Chimiak, Galia. "From Solidarność to Global Solidarity? The Engagement of Polish Civil Society in Development Cooperation." *Studia Socjologiczne* 222, no. 3 (2016): 165–198.

Chiron, Yves. *Frère Roger, le fondateur de Taizé*. Paris: Perrin, 2008.

Christiaens, Kim. "The Difficult Quest for Chilean Allies: International Labor Solidarity Campaigns for Chile in the 1970s and 1980s." In *European Solidarity with Chile, 1970s–1980s*, edited by Kim Christiaens, Idesbald Goddeeris and Magaly Rodríguez García, 97–129. Bern: Peter Lang, 2014.

Christiaens, Kim. "Globalizing Nicaragua? An Entangled History of Sandinista Solidarity Campaigns in Western Europe." In *Making Sense of the Americas: How Protest Related to America in the 1980s and Beyond*, edited by Jan Hansen, Christian Helm and Frank Reichherzer, 155–177. Frankfurt - New York: Campus, 2015.

Christiaens, Kim. "The ICFTU and the WCL: The International Coordination of Solidarity." In *Solidarity with Solidarity: Western European Trade Unions and the Polish Crisis, 1980–1982*, edited by Idesbald Goddeeris, 101–127. Lanham, MD: Lexington, 2010.

Christiaens, Kim. "Podstawy do współpracy? Międzynarodowa Konfederacja Wolnych Związków Zawodowych i Światowa Konfederacja Pracy wobec powstania, zawieszenia i delegalizacji NSZZ 'Solidarność.'" In *Świat wobec "Solidarności" 1980–1989*, edited by Paweł Jaworski and Łukasz Kamiński, 210–224. Warsaw: IPN, 2013.

Christiaens, Kim, and Idesbald Goddeeris. "Solidarność and Latin America: Encounters, Conflicts and Failures." *Archiv für Sozialgeschichte* 56 (2016): 445–461.

Christiaens, Kim, and Idesbald Goddeeris. "Solidarność a Trzeci Świat, Część I: Chrześcijańsko-demokratyczna droga do Ameryki Łacińskiej." *Dzieje Najnowsze* 50, no. 1 (2018): 281–308.

Christiaens, Kim, and Idesbald Goddeeris. "Solidarność i Trzeci Świat, Część II: Taktyczne sojusze z kluczowymi ruchami lat osiemdziesiątych XX wieku." *Dzieje Najnowsze* 50, no. 2 (2018): 247–272.

Cohn-Bendit, Daniel, and Guy Verhofstadt. *For Europe! Manifesto for a Postnational Revolution in Europe*. Munich: Hanser, 2012.

Colarizi, Simona, Agostino Giovagnoli and Paolo Pombeni, eds. *L'Italia contemporanea dagli anni Ottanta a oggi*. Vol. 3. Rome: Carocci, 2014.

Craveri, Piero. *La Repubblica dal 1958 al 1992*. Turin: UTET, 1995.

Cuhra, Jaroslav. "Katolická církev a odpor vůči 'normalizačnímu' režimu." In *Opozice a odpor proti komunistickému režimu v Československu 1968–1989*, edited by Petr Blažek, 67–78. Prague: Ústav světových dějin and Dokořán, 2005.

Cuhra, Josef. "Křesťané a počátky života Charty 77." *Katolická revue* 74, no. 3 (2007): 25–29.

Dahrendorf, Ralf. *Reflections on the Revolution in Europe*. New Brunswick, NJ: Transaction Publishers, 2005 edition.

Dakowska, Dorota. "Les fondations politiques allemandes en Europe centrale." *Critique internationale* 3, no. 24 (2004): 139–154.

de Giuseppe, Massimo. *Giorgio La Pira: Un sindaco e le vie della pace*. Milan: Centro Ambrosiano, 2001.

De Waele, Jean-Michel. "Consolidation démocratique, partis et clivages en Europe centrale et orientale." In *Partis politiques et démocratie en Europe centrale et orientale*, edited by Jean-Michel De Waele, 145–160. Brussels: Éditions de l'Université de Bruxelles, 2002.

De Waele, Jean-Michel. *L'Émergence des partis politiques en Europe centrale*. Brussels: Éditions de l'Université de Bruxelles, 1999.

Dimitrov, Martin K. "European Lessons for China: Tiananmen 1989 and Beyond." In *The Long 1989: Decades of Global Revolution*, edited by Piotr H. Kosicki and Kyrill Kunakhovich, 61–88. Budapest: CEU Press, 2019.

Dimun, Petr, and Milan J. Hamerský. *10 let na straně svobody: kronika ODA z let 1989–1999*. Brno: Bachant, 1999.

Dinkel, Jürgen. *Die Bewegung Bündnisfreier Staaten: Genese, Organisation und Politik (1927–1992)*. Berlin: De Gruyter Oldenbourg, 2015.

Dolbilov, Mikhail M. *Russkii krai, chuzhaia vera: Etnokonfessianal'naia politika imperii v Litve i Belorussii pri Aleksandre II*. Moscow: Novoe literaturnoe obozrenie, 2010.

Domber, Gregory F. *Empowering Revolution: America, Poland, and the End of the Cold War.* Chapel Hill: University of North Carolina Press, 2014.
Dülffer, Jost. *Jalta, 4. Februar 1945: Der Zweite Weltkrieg und die Entstehung der bipolaren Welt.* Munich: DTV, 1998.
Duranti, Marco. *The Conservative Human Rights Revolution: European Identity, Transnational Politics, and the Origins of the European Convention.* Oxford: Oxford University Press, 2017.

Eichtinger, Martin. "Österreichs Außenpolitik in Zentral- und Osteuropa nach dem Annus mirabilis 1989: Das Engagement des österreichischen Vizekanzlers und Außenministers Alois Mock nach dem Zusammenbruch des Kommunismus." In *Viribus unitis*, edited by Ilona Slawinski and Joseph P. Strelka, 103–122. Bern-Berlin-Frankfurt am Main et al.: Peter Lang, 1996.
Eichtinger, Martin, and Helmut Wohnout. *Alois Mock: Ein Politiker schreibt Geschichte.* Vienna-Graz-Klagenfurt: Styria Verlag, 2008.
Eisler, Jerzy. "March 1968 in Poland." In *1968: The World Transformed*, edited by Carole Fink, Philipp Gassert, and Detlef Junker, 237–252. Cambridge: Cambridge University Press, 1998.
Elster, Jon, ed. *The Roundtable Talks and the Breakdown of Communism: Constitutionalism in Eastern Europe.* Chicago: University of Chicago Press, 1996.
Elvert, Jürgen. "A fool's game or a comedy of errors?" In *European Union Enlargement: A Comparative History*, edited by Wolfram Kaiser and Jürgen Elvert, 189–208. London–New York: Routledge, 2004.
Engel, Ulf, Frank Hadler and Matthias Middell, eds. *1989 in a Global Perspective.* Leipzig: Leipzig University Press, 2015.
Englisch, Andreas. *Johannes Paul II: Das Geheimnis des Karol Wojtyła.* Munich-Berlin: Ullstein, 2003.
"Es war für Polen schwer verständlich, dass es für uns immer einen Zusammenhang zwischen der Grenzfrage und der Wiedervereinigung gab. Gespräch mit Bernhard Vogel." In *"Wir vergeben und bitten um Vergebung": Der Briefwechsel der polnischen und deutschen Bischöfe von 1965 und seine Wirkung*, edited by Basil Kerski, Thomas Kycia and Robert Żurek. Osnabrück: Fibre, 2006.
Escaffit, Jean-Claude, and Rasiwala Moïz. *Histoire de Taizé.* Paris: Le Seuil, 2008.

Fazekas, Csaba. "Collaborating with Horthy: Political Catholicism and Christian Political Organizations in Hungary 1918–1944." In *Christdemokratie in Europa im 20. Jahrhundert / Christian Democracy in 20th Century Europe / La Démocratie chrétienne en Europe au XXe siècle*, edited by Michael Gehler, Wolfram Kaiser and Helmut Wohnout, 224–249. Vienna-Cologne-Weimar: Böhlau, 2001.
Felak, James Ramon. *At the Price of the Republic: Hlinka's Slovak People's Party, 1929–1938.* Pittsburgh: University of Pittsburgh Press, 1995.
Felak, James Ramon. "Pope John Paul II, the Saints, and Communist Poland: The Papal Pilgrimages of 1979 and 1983." *Catholic Historical Review* 100, no. 3 (2014): 555–574.
Felak, James Ramon. "Vatican II and Czechoslovakia." In *Vatican II behind the Iron Curtain*, edited by Piotr H. Kosicki, 99–126. Washington, DC: The Catholic University of America Press, 2016.
Fiala, Petr, and František Mikš. "Intelektuálové, novináři a česká politika." In *Česká konzervativní a liberální politika. Sborník k desátému výročí založení revue Proglas*, edited by Petr Fiala and František Mikš, 9–32. Brno: Centrum pro studium demokracie a kultury, 2000.
Fischer, Thomas. "Austria and the Helsinki Process." In *"Peaceful Coexistence" or "Iron Curtain": Austria, Neutrality, and Eastern Europe in the Cold War and Détente, 1955–1989*, edited by Arnold Suppan and Wolfgang Mueller, 168–202. Vienna-Berlin: LIT Verlag, 2009.
Fischer, Thomas. *Keeping the Process Alive: The N+N and the CSCE Follow-Up from Helsinki to Vienna (1975–1986).* Zurich: Center for Security Studies, ETH Zürich, 2012.
Fischer, Thomas. *Neutral Power in the CSCE: The N+N states and the Making of the Helsinki Accords 1975.* Baden-Baden: Nomos, 2009.
Fischer, Thomas. "Die Sowjetunion, Österreich und die finnische KSZE-Initiative vom 5. Mai 1969." In *Osteuropa vom Weltkrieg zur Wende*, edited by Wolfgang Mueller and Michael Portmann, 313–339. Vienna: Verlag der Österr. Akad. der Wissenschaften, 2007.
Fleming, Michael. *Communism, Nationalism, and Ethnicity in Poland, 1944–50.* London: Routledge, 2010.

Fontaine, Pascal. *Herzenssache Europa: Eine Zeitreise 1953–2009: Geschichte der Fraktion der Christdemokraten und der Europäischen Volkspartei im Europäischen Parlament*. Brussels: Racine, 2009.

Foot, Rosemarie. "The Cold War and Human Rights." In *Cambridge History of the Cold War*, edited by Melvyn P. Leffler and Odd Arne Westad, 445–465. Cambridge: Cambridge University Press, 2010.

Fricz, Tamás. "Democratization, the Party System and the Electorate in Hungary." In *Transition with Contradiction: The Case of Hungary, 1990–98*, edited by Mária Schmidt and László Gy. Tóth, 93–124. Budapest: Kairosz, 1999.

Friszke, Andrzej. *Oaza na Kopernika: Klub Inteligencji Katolickiej, 1956–1989*. Warsaw: Biblioteka WIĘZI, 1997.

Friszke, Andrzej. "The Znak Movement as the Moderate Wing of 'Solidarity.'" In *The Polish Solidarity Movement in Retrospect: A Story of Failure or a Success?*, edited by Dariusz Aleksandrowicz, Stefani Sonntag and Jan Wielgohs, 128–144. Berlin: GSFP, 2009.

Fukuyama, Francis. *The End of History and the Last Man*. New York: Free Press, 1992.

"'Für uns Protestanten waren die polnischen katholischen Beiträge sowohl im deutsch-polnischen als auch im europäischen Verhältnis von großem Gewicht': Gespräch mit Richard von Weizsäcker." In *"Wir vergeben und bitten um Vergebung": Der Briefwechsel der polnischen und deutschen Bischöfe von 1965 und seine Wirkung*. Edited by Basil Kerski, Thomas Kycia and Robert Żurek. Osnabrück: Fibre, 2006.

Gabanyi, Anneli Ute. "The Romanian Revolution." In *The Revolutions of 1989: A Handbook*, edited by Wolfgang Mueller, Michael Gehler and Arnold Suppan, 199–220. Vienna: Verlag der Österreichischen Akademie der Wissenschaften, 2015.

Gabanyi, Anneli Ute. *Systemwechsel in Rumänien: Von der Revolution zur Transformation*. Munich: Piper, 1998.

Gabanyi, Anneli Ute. *Die unvollendete Revolution: Rumänien zwischen Diktatur und Demokratie*. Munich: Piper, 1990.

Gaddis, John Lewis. *The Cold War*. London - New York: Penguin, 2005.

Gala, Marilena. "From INF to SDI: How Helsinki Reshaped the Transatlantic Dimension of European Security." In *The Crisis of Détente in Europe*, edited by Leopoldo Nuti, 111–123. London: Routledge, 2009.

Galkin, Aleksandr, and Anatolij Tschernjajew [Anatoly Chernyaev], eds. *Michail Gorbatschow und die deutsche Frage: Sowjetische Dokumente 1986–1991: Deutsche Ausgabe herausgegeben von Helmut Altrichter, Horst Möller und Jürgen Zarusky, kommentiert von Andreas Hilger*. Munich: Oldenbourg, 2001.

Garton Ash, Timothy. *The File: A Personal History*. New York: Vintage Books, 1998.

Garton Ash, Timothy. *In Europe's Name: Germany and the Divided Continent*. London: Jonathan Cape, 1993.

Garton Ash, Timothy. *Ein Jahrhundert wird abgewählt: Aus den Zentren Mitteleuropas 1980–1990*. Munich-Vienna: Hanser, 1990.

Garton Ash, Timothy. *The Polish Revolution: Solidarity, 1980–82*. London: Cape, 1983.

Garton Ash, Timothy. *We the People: The Revolution of '89 witnessed in Warsaw, Budapest, Berlin and Prague*. Cambridge: Granta, 1990.

Gasteyger, Curt. "Europa nach dem INF-Abkommen." *Aus Politik und Zeitgeschichte* 10 (1988): 3–10.

Gati, Charles. *Failed Illusions: Moscow, Washington, Budapest, and the 1956 Hungarian Revolt*. Washington, DC – Stanford, CA: Woodrow Wilson Center Press/Stanford University Press, 2006.

Gebhardt, Stanisław. "The Christian Democratic Union of Central Europe." In *Christian Democracy across the Iron Curtain: Europe Redefined*, edited by Piotr H. Kosicki and Sławomir Łukasiewicz, 411–424. London: Palgrave Macmillan, 2018.

Gehler, Michael. "Die Affäre Waldheim: Eine Fallstudie zur Instrumentalisierung der NS-Vergangenheit zur politischen Vorteilsverschaffung 1986–1988." *Geschichte in Wissenschaft und Unterricht* 69, no. 1/2 (2018): 67–85.

Gehler, Michael. "Austria, the Revolutions, and the Unification of Germany." In *The Revolutions of 1989: A Handbook*, edited by Wolfgang Mueller, Michael Gehler and Arnold Suppan, 437–466. Vienna: Verlag der Österreichischen Akademie der Wissenschaften, 2015.

Gehler, Michael. "Austria: The Revolutions in Central and South Eastern Europe: Austrian Perceptions and International Reactions 1989–90." In *Disintegration and Integration in East-Central Europe 1919 – post-1989*, edited by Wilfried Loth and Nicolae Păun, 186–204. Baden-Baden: Nomos, 2014.

Gehler, Michael. "Begegnungsort des Kalten Krieges: Der 'Genfer Kreis' und die geheimen Absprachen westeuropäischer Christdemokraten 1947–1955." In *Christdemokratie in Europa im 20. Jahrhundert / Christian Democracy in 20th Century Europe / La Démocratie chrétienne en Europe au XXe siècle*, edited by Michael Gehler, Wolfram Kaiser and Helmut Wohnout, 642–694. Vienna-Cologne-Weimar: Böhlau, 2001.

Gehler, Michael. *Deutschland von der Teilung zur Einigung. 1945 bis heute.* Vienna-Cologne-Weimar: Böhlau Verlag, 2010.

Gehler, Michael. "'...eine grotesk überzogene Dämonisierung eines Mannes....' Die Waldheim-Affäre 1986–1992." In *Politische Affären und Skandale in Österreich*, edited by Michael Gehler, 614–665. Innsbruck: Studien Verlag, 2007.

Gehler, Michael. *Europa: Ideen – Institutionen – Vereinigung – Zusammenhalt.* Reinbek-Hamburg: Lau Verlag, 2018.

Gehler, Michael. "The Fall of the Iron Curtain: Causes, Structures, Timelines and Effects." In *The Republic of Austria, 1918–2018: Milestones and Turning Points*, edited by Heinz Fischer, Andreas Huber and Stephan Neuhäuser, 185–200. Vienna: Czernin, 2018.

Gehler, Michael. "The Geneva Circle of West European Christian Democrats." In *Christian Democracy in Europe since 1945*, vol. 2, edited by Michael Gehler and Wolfram Kaiser, 207–220. London - New York: Routledge, 2004.

Gehler, Michael. "Der 'Genfer Kreis:' Christdemokratische Parteienkooperation und Vertrauensbildung im Zeichen der deutsch-französischen Annäherung 1947–1955." *Zeitschrift für Geschichtswissenschaft* 49, no 7 (2001): 599–625.

Gehler, Michael. "Konferenzen über Sicherheit und Zusammenarbeit in Europa (KSZE)." In *Lexikon der deutschen Geschichte 1945–1990,* edited by Michael Behnen, 365–366. Stuttgart: Kröner, 2002.

Gehler, Michael. *Österreichs Außenpolitik der Zweiten Republik: Von der alliierten Besatzung bis zum Europa des 21. Jahrhunderts.* Innsbruck-Vienna-Bozen: StudienVerlag, 2005.

Gehler, Michael. "Paving Austria's Way to Brussels: Chancellor Franz Vranitzky (1986–1997): A Banker, Social Democrat, and Pragmatic European Leader." *Journal of European Integration History* 18, no. 2 (2012): 159–182.

Gehler, Michael. "Revolutionäre Ereignisse und geoökonomisch-strategische Ergebnisse: Die EU- und NATO 'Osterweiterungen' 1989–2015 im Vergleich." Zentrum für Europäische Integrationsforschung Discussion Paper C 239. Bonn, 2017.

Gehler, Michael, and Andrea Brait, eds. *Am Ort des Geschehens in Zeiten des Umbruchs: Lebensgeschichtliche Erinnerungen aus Politik und Ballhausplatzdiplomatie vor und nach 1989.* Hildesheim: Georg Olms Verlag, 2018.

Gehler, Michael, Marcus Gonschor, Hinnerk Meyer and Johannes Schönner, eds. *Mitgestalter Europas: Transnationalismus und Parteiennetzwerke europäischer Christdemokraten und Konservativer in historischer Erfahrung.* St. Augustin - Berlin: Konrad-Adenauer-Stiftung, 2013.

Gehler, Michael, Marcus Gonschor, Hinnerk Meyer and Hannes Schönner, eds. *Transnationale Parteienkooperation der europäischen Christdemokraten und Konservativen 1965–1979. Coopération transnationale des partis démocrates-chrétiens et conservateurs en Europe. Dokumente 1965–1979.* Berlin: De Gruyter Oldenbourg, 2018, 2 vols.

Gehler, Michael, and Maximilian Graf. "Austria, German Unification, and European Integration: A Brief Historical Background." *Cold War International History Project/CWIHP Working Paper* 86 (March 2018), Wilson Center, Washington, DC, www.wilsoncenter.org/publication/austria-german-unification-and-european-integration-brief-historical-background (quoted December 2018).

Gehler, Michael, and Maximilian Graf, eds. *Europa und die deutsche Einheit: Beobachtungen, Entscheidungen und Folgen.* Göttingen: Vandenhoeck & Ruprecht, 2017.

Gehler, Michael, and Maximilian Graf, eds. *Österreich und die deutsche Frage: Vom Honecker-Besuch in Bonn bis zur Einheit 1987–1990.* Göttingen: Vandenhoeck & Ruprecht, 2018.

Gehler, Michael, and Wolfram Kaiser, eds. *Christian Democracy in Europe since 1945*, vol. 2. London - New York: Routledge, 2004.

Gehler, Michael, and Wolfram Kaiser, eds. *Transnationale Parteienkooperation der europäischen Christdemokraten: Dokumente 1945–1965 / Coopération transnationale des partis démocrates-chrétiens en Europe: Documents 1945–1965 / Transnational Party Cooperation of European Christian Democrats: Documents 1945–1965.* Munich: Saur, 2004.

Gehler, Michael, Wolfram Kaiser and Helmut Wohnout, eds. *Christdemokratie in Europe im 20. Jahrhundert – Christian Democracy in 20th-Century Europe.* Vienna: Böhlau, 2001.

Gehler, Michael, and Hannes Schönner. "The European Democrat Union and the Revolutionary Events in Central Europe in 1989." In *Europa und die deutsche Einheit: Beobachtungen, Entscheidungen und Folgen*, edited by Michael Gehler and Maximilian Graf, 739–766. Göttingen: Vandenhoeck & Ruprecht, 2017.

Gehler, Michael, and Johannes Schönner. "Transnationale christdemokratische Parteienkooperationen in Europa 1965–1989: Der Beitrag österreichischer Ideen und Initiativen." In *Demokratie und Geschichte: Jahrbuch des Karl von Vogelsang-Instituts zur Erforschung der Geschichte der christlichen Demokratie in Österreich*, 11/12 (2007/2008), edited by Helmut Wohnout, 271–318. Vienna-Cologne-Weimar: Böhlau, 2009.

Geppert, Dominik. "Isolation oder Einvernehmen? Großbritannien und die deutsche Einheit, 1989/90." *Geschichte in Wissenschaft und Unterricht* 67, no. 1/2 (2016): 5–22.

Genscher, Hans-Dietrich. *Erinnerungen.* Berlin: Siedler, 1995.

Gergely, Jenö. "Towards the One-Party State: Nascent Christian Democracy in Hungary." In *Christian Democracy in Europe since 1945*, vol. 2, edited by Michael Gehler and Wolfram Kaiser, 155–172. London - New York: Routledge, 2004.

Ghebali, Victor-Yves. *La diplomatie de la Détente: La CSCE, d'Helsinki à Vienne (1973–1989).* Brussels: Bruylant, 1989.

Gilde, Benjamin. "Hüter des Dritten Korbes: Die humanitäre KSZE-Politik Österreichs in Belgrad und Madrid zwischen Bundeskanzler, Diplomaten und internationalen Spannungen." In *Die KSZE im Ost-West-Konflikt*, edited by Matthias Peter and Hermann Wentker, 155–172. Berlin-Boston: De Gruyter, 2013.

Gilde, Benjamin. *Österreich im KSZE-Prozess 1969–1983: Neutraler Vermittler in humanitärer Mission.* Munich: Oldenbourg Verlag, 2013.

Gimbel, John. *The Origins of the Marshall Plan.* Stanford, CA: Stanford University Press, 1976.

Giovagnoli, Agostino. *Il partito italiano: La Democrazia Cristiana dal 1942 al 1994.* Rome: Laterza, 1996.

Goddeeris, Idesbald. "Exiles' Strategies for Lobbying in International Organizations: Eastern European Participation in Nouvelles Équipes Internationales." *European Review of History* 11, no. 3 (2004), 383–400.

Goddeeris, Idesbald. "The limits of lobbying: ILO and Solidarność." In *ILO histories: Essays on the International Labour Organization and its Impact on the World during the Twentieth Century*, edited by Jasmien Van Daele, Magaly Rodríguez García, Geert Van Goethem and Marcel van der Linden, 423–441. Bern: Peter Lang, 2011.

Goddeeris, Idesbald. "Lobbying allies? The NSZZ Solidarność Coordinating Office Abroad, 1982–1989." *Journal of Cold War Studies* 13, no. 3 (2011): 83–125.

Goddeeris, Idesbald. "Ministerstwo Spraw Zagranicznych 'Solidarności': Biuro Koordynacyjne NSZZ 'Solidarność', 1982–1989, część 1." *Pamięć i Sprawiedliwość* 10, no. 2 (2006): 315–347.

Goddeeris, Idesbald, ed. *Solidarity with Solidarity: Western European Trade Unions and the Polish Crisis, 1980–1982.* Lanham, MD: Lexington, 2010.

Goeckel, Robert F. *The Lutheran Church and the East German State: Political Conflict and Change under Ulbricht and Honecker.* Ithaca, NY: Cornell University Press, 1990.

Goedertier, Wouter. "The Ambiguity of Solidarity: Belgium and the Global Struggle against Apartheid." DPhil thesis, KU Leuven, 2015.

Goldman, Minton F. *Slovakia since Independence: A Struggle for Democracy.* Westport, CT: Praeger, 1999.

Göls, Cornelia. *Die politischen Parteien in der Ukraine*. Frankfurt am Main: Peter Lang, 2008.
Gough, Austin. *Paris and Rome: The Gallican Church and the Ultramontane Campaign, 1848–1853*. Oxford: Clarendon Press, 1986.
Grachev, Andrei. "Gorbachev and the 'New Political Thinking.'" In *The Revolutions of 1989: A Handbook*, edited by Wolfgang Mueller, Michael Gehler and Arnold Suppan, 33–46. Vienna: Verlag der Österreichischen Akademie der Wissenschaften, 2015.
Graf, Maximilian. "European Détente and the CSCE: Austria and the East-Central European Theatre in the 1970s and 1980s." In *The CSCE and the End of the Cold War*, edited by Nicolas Badalassi and Sarah B. Snyder, 249–274. New York: Berghahn, 2019.
Graf, Maximilian. "Kreisky und Polen: Schlaglichter auf einen vernachlässigten Aspekt der österreichischen 'Ostpolitik.'" In *Bananen, Cola, Zeitgeschichte: Oliver Rathkolb und das lange 20. Jahrhundert*, vol. 2, edited by Lucile Dreidemy, Richard Hufschmied, Agnes Meisinger et al., 692–706. Vienna-Cologne-Weimar: Böhlau Verlag, 2015.
Graf, Maximilian. "Ein Musterbeispiel der europäischen Entspannung? Die österreichisch-ungarischen Beziehungen von 1964 bis 1989." In *Österreich und Ungarn im 20. Jahrhundert*, edited by Csaba Szabó, 261–280. Vienna: Institut für Ungarische Geschichtsforschung, 2014.
Graf, Maximilian. *Österreich und die DDR 1949–1990: Politik und Wirtschaft im Schatten der deutschen Teilung*. Vienna: VAW, 2016.
Graf, Maximilian. "Österreich und das 'Verschwinden' der DDR: Ostdeutsche Perzeptionen im Kontext der Langzeitentwicklungen." In *Grenzöffnung 1989: Innen- und Außenperspektiven und die Folgen für Österreich*, edited by Andrea Brait and Michael Gehler, 221–242. Vienna-Cologne-Weimar: Böhlau, 2014.
Graf, Maximilian. "Die Welt blickt auf das Burgenland. 1989 – Die Grenze wird zum Abbild der Veränderung." In *Das Burgenland als internationale Grenzregion im 20. und 21. Jahrhundert*, edited by Maximilian Graf, Alexander Lass and Karlo Ruzicic-Kessler, 135–179. Vienna: Neue Welt, 2012.
Gražiūnas, Albinas. *Krikščioniškoji demokratija Lietuvoje: Lietuvos krikščionių demokratų partijos istorijos bruožai*. Vilnius: Tėvynės sargas, 1994.
Gresch, Norbert. *Transnationale Parteienzusammenarbeit in der EG*. Baden-Baden, 1987.
Gross, Jan. "War as Revolution." In *The Establishment of Communist Regimes in Eastern Europe, 1944–1949*, edited by Norman Naimark and Leonid Gibianskii, 17–40. Boulder, CO: Westview Press, 1997.
Grosser, Pierre. *1989: L'année où le monde a basculé*. Paris: Perrin, 2009.
Groth, Michael. "Fortschritte im KSZE-Prozeß: Das dritte Folgetreffen in Wien." *Europa Archiv* (1989): 95–102.
Grzymała-Busse, Anna. "Why there is (almost) no Christian Democracy in Post-Communist Europe." *Party Politics* 19, no. 2 (2001): 319–342.
Guérin-Sendelbach, Valérie. *Frankreich und das vereinigte Deutschland: Interessen und Perzeptionen im Spannungsfeld*. Opladen: Leske + Budrich, 1999.

Haberl, Othmar Nikola, and Lutz Niethammer, eds. *Der Marshall-Plan und die europäische Linke*. Frankfurt am Main: Lang, 1986.
Hahn, Karl Josef, and Hans August Lücker. *Christliche Demokraten bauen Europa*. Bonn: Europa Union Verlag, 1987.
Hall, Aleksander. "Polska." In *Architekt wolnej Polski: Świat wartości i idei Tadeusza Mazowieckiego*, edited by Aleksander Hall, 75–88. Kraków: Znak, 2017.
Hanebrink, Paul A. *In Defense of Christian Hungary: Religion, Nationalism, and Antisemitism, 1890–1944*. Ithaca, NY: Cornell University Press, 2006.
Hanebrink, Paul A. *A Specter Haunting Europe: The Myth of Judeo-Bolshevism*. Cambridge, MA: The Belknap Press of Harvard University Press, 2018.
Hanhimäki, Jussi M. "Non-Aligned to What? European Neutrals and the Cold War." In *Neutrality and Neutralism in the Global Cold War*, edited by Sandra Bott, Jussi M. Hanhimäki, Janick Marina Schaufelbuehl and Marco Wyss, 17–32. Abingdon-New York: Routledge, 2016.
Hanisch, Anja. *Die DDR im KSZE-Prozess 1972–1985: Zwischen Ostabhängigkeit, Westabgrenzung und Ausreisebewegung*. Munich: De Gruyter, 2012.
Hanuš, Jiří. "Má církev v České republice budoucnost?" *Proglas* 11, no. 5/6 (2000): 36–40.
Hartmann, Jan, Bohumil Svoboda and Václav Vaško, eds. *Kardinál Tomášek: Generál bez vojska ...?* Prague: Vyšehrad, 2003.

Havel, Václav. *Letters to Olga*. New York: Knopf, 1988.

Heller, Ágnes. "Twenty Years After 1989." In *The End and the Beginning: The Revolutions of 1989 and the Resurgence of History*, edited by Vladimir Tismaneanu and Bogdan C. Iacob, 55–68. Budapest - New York: CEU Press, 2012.

Herf, Jeffrey. *War by Other Means: Soviet Power, West German Resistance, and the Battle of the Euromissiles*. New York: Free Press, 1991.

Hertle, Hans-Hermann. *Chronik des Mauerfalls: Die dramatischen Ereignisse um den 9. November 1989*. Berlin: Links Verlag, 2009.

Hertle, Hans-Hermann. *Der Fall der Mauer: Die unbeabsichtigte Selbstauflösung des SED-Staates*. Opladen-Wiesbaden: VS Verlag, 2nd edition, 1999.

Hertle, Hans-Hermann. "The October Revolution in East Germany." In *The Revolutions of 1989: A Handbook*, edited by Wolfgang Mueller, Michael Gehler and Arnold Suppan, 113–135. Vienna: Verlag der Österreichischen Akademie der Wissenschaften, 2015.

Hertle, Hans-Hermann. *Der Tag, an dem die Mauer fiel: Die wichtigsten Zeitzeugen berichten vom 9. November, 1989*. Berlin: Nicolai, 2009.

Hinsey, Ellen. *Mastering the Past: Contemporary Central and Eastern Europe and the Rise of Illiberalism*. Candor, NY: Telos Publishing, 2017.

Hirsch, Francine. *Empire of Nations: Ethnographic Knowledge and the Making of the Soviet Union*. Ithaca, NY: Cornell University Press, 2005.

Hloušek, Vít, and Lubomír Kopeček. *Origin, Ideology and Transformation of Political Parties: East-Central and Western Europe Compared*. Farnham-Burlington: Ashgate, 2010.

Hlušičková, Růžena, and Blanka Císařovská, eds. *Hnutí za občanskou svobodu 1988–1989: Sborník dokumentů*. Prague: Maxdorf, 1994.

Hogan, Michael J. *The Marshall Plan: America, Britain, and the Reconstruction of Western Europe 1947–1952*. Cambridge: Cambridge University Press, 1987.

Horn, Gerd-Rainer. *Western European Liberation Theology: The first Wave (1924–1959)*. Oxford: Oxford University Press, 2008.

Hutter, Roman. *Revolution und Legitimation: Die politische Instrumentalisierung des Umbruchs 1989 durch die Postkommunisten in Rumänien*. Berlin: Frank & Timme, 2015.

Isaacs, Jeremy, and Taylor Downing. *Der Kalte Krieg. Eine illustrierte Geschichte*. Munich-Zurich: Wilhelm Heyne, 2001.

Jackisch, Klaus-Reiner. *Eisern gegen die Einheit: Margaret Thatcher und die deutsche Wiedervereinigung*. Frankfurt am Main: Lang, 2004.

Jankauskas, Algimantas, Egidijus Kūris and Jūratė Novagrockienė, eds. *Lietuvos politinės partijos ir partinė sistema*. Vol. 1. Vilnius: Naujasis Lankas, 1997.

Jansen, Thomas. *Die Entstehung einer Europäischen Partei: Vorgeschichte, Gründung und Entwicklung der EVP*. Bonn: Europa-Union-Verlag, 1996.

Jansen, Thomas. *Die Europäische Volkspartei: Entstehung und Entwicklung*. Brussels: EDP, 2006.

Jansen, Thomas, and Steven Van Hecke. *At Europe's Service: The Origins and Evolution of the European People's Party*. Berlin: Springer, 2011.

Jaworski, Paweł, and Łukasz Kamiński, eds. *Świat wobec "Solidarności" 1980–1989*. Warsaw: IPN, 2013.

Judson, Pieter. *Exclusive Revolutionaries: Liberal Politics, Social Experience, and National Identity in the Austrian Empire, 1848–1914*. Ann Arbor: University of Michigan Press, 1996.

Judt, Tony. *Postwar: A History of Europe since 1945*. New York: Penguin, 2005.

Kaiser, Wolfram. *Christian Democracy and the Origins of European Union*. Cambridge: Cambridge University Press, 2007.

Karner, Stefan. "Von der Stagnation zum Verfall. Kennzeichen der sowjetischen Wirtschaft der 1980er Jahre." In *Der Zerfall des Sowjetimperiums und Deutschlands Wiedervereinigung*, edited by Hanns Jürgen Küsters, 15–45. Cologne-Weimar-Vienna: Böhlau, 2016.

Karner, Stefan, Mark Kramer, Peter Ruggenthaler and Manfred Wilke, eds. *Der Kreml und die deutsche Wiedervereinigung 1990: Interne sowjetische Analysen*. Berlin: Metropol Verlag, 2015.

Kasulaitis, Algirdas. *Lithuanian Christian Democracy*. Cleveland: Leo XIII Fund, 1976.

Kersbergen, Kees van. *Social Capitalism: A Study of Christian Democracy and the Social Welfare State*. London - New York: Routledge, 1995.

Kerski, Basil; Thomas Kycia and Robert Żurek, eds. *"Wir vergeben und bitten um Vergebung": Der Briefwechsel der polnischen und deutschen Bischöfe von 1965 und seine Wirkung.* Osnabrück: Fibre, 2006.
Khol, Andreas. "Österreich und Europa im *Annus mirabilis Europae* 1989." In *Österreichisches Jahrbuch für Politik 1989*, edited by Andreas Khol, Alfred Stirnemann and Günther Ofner, 813–841. Vienna: Oldenbourg, 1989.
Khol, Andreas; Lars Tobisson and Alexis Wintoniak, eds. *Twenty Years European Democrat Union 1978–1998.* Vienna: EDU, 1998.
Kilp, Alar. "L'influence de l'Église sur le développement du clivage politique religieux dans sept pays d'Europe centrale et orientale." In *Les clivages politiques en Europe centrale et orientale*, edited by Jean-Michel De Waele, 119–135. Brussels: Éditions de l'Université de Bruxelles, 2004.
Király, Béla K., Peter Pastor and Ivan Sanders, eds. *Essays on World War I: Total War and Peacemaking: A Case Study on Trianon.* New York: Social Science Monographs / Brooklyn College Press, 1982.
Kirchheimer, Otto. "The Transformation of Western European Party Systems." In *Political Parties and Political Development*, edited by Joseph LaPalombara and Myron Weiner, 177–200. Princeton, NJ: Princeton University Press, 1966.
Kis, János. *Mi a liberalizmus? Esszék, Tanulmányok, 1985–2014.* Pozsony: Kalligram, 2015.
Kiss, László J. "Politik und Wahrnehmung. Ungarns (Außen-) Politik im Übergang – Österreichs Außenpolitik im Zuge der Umbruchsjahre (1988–1991)." In *Grenzöffnung 1989: Innen- und Außenperspektiven und die Folgen für Österreich*, edited by Andrea Brait and Michael Gehler, 405–426. Vienna-Cologne-Weimar: Böhlau, 2014.
Klaus, Václav. *Renaissance: The Rebirth of Liberty in the Heart of Europe.* Washington, DC: Cato Institute, 1997.
Klimó, Árpád von. *Remembering Cold Days: The 1942 Massacre of Novi Sad and Hungarian Politics and Society, 1942–1989.* Pittsburgh, PA: University of Pittsburgh Press, 2018.
Kmeť, Norbert. "Opozícia a hnutie odporu na Slovensku 1968–1989." In *Opozice a odpor proti komunistickému režimu v Československu 1968–1989*, edited by Petr Blažek, 41–53. Prague: Ústav světových dějin and Dokořán, 2005.
Kohl, Helmut. *Berichte zur Lage, 1989–1998.* Edited by Günter Buchstab and Hans Otto Kleinmann. Düsseldorf: Droste, 2012.
Kohl, Helmut. *Erinnerungen 1982–1990.* Munich: Droemer Knaur Verlag, 2005.
Kołodko, Grzegorz W. *From Shock to Therapy: The Political Economy of Postsocialist Transformation.* Oxford: Oxford University Press, 2000.
Konrad, George. *Antipolitics: An Essay.* Translated by Richard E. Allen. New York: H. Holt, 1987.
Kopstein, Jeffrey. *The Politics of Economic Decline in East Germany 1945–1989.* Chapel Hill, NC: University of North Carolina Press, 1997.
Körösényi, András; Csaba Tóth and Gábor Török. *The Hungarian Political System.* Budapest: Hungarian Center for Democracy Studies Foundation, 2009.
Kosicki, Piotr H. "After 1989: The Life and Death of the Catholic Third Way." *TLS – Times Literary Supplement*, 13 December 2013, 13–15.
Kosicki, Piotr H. "L'avènement des intellectuels catholiques: Le mensuel *Więź* et les conséquences polonaises du personnalisme mounierien." *Vingtième Siècle: Revue d'histoire* 102 (2009): 31–46.
Kosicki, Piotr H. "The Catholic 1968: Poland, Social Justice, and the Global Cold War." *Slavic Review* 77, no. 3 (2018): 638–660.
Kosicki, Piotr H. *Catholics on the Barricades: Poland, France, and "Revolution," 1891–1956.* New Haven, CT: Yale University Press, 2018.
Kosicki, Piotr H. "Christian Democracy's Global Cold War." In *Christian Democracy across the Iron Curtain: Europe Redefined*, edited by Piotr H. Kosicki and Sławomir Łukasiewicz, 221–256. London: Palgrave Macmillan, 2018.
Kosicki, Piotr H. "Masters in their own Home or Defenders of the Human Person? Wojciech Korfanty, Anti-Semitism, and Polish Christian Democracy's Illiberal Rights-Talk." *Modern Intellectual History* 14, no. 1 (2017): 99–130.
Kosicki, Piotr H. "Vatican II and Poland." In *Vatican II behind the Iron Curtain*, edited by Piotr H. Kosicki, 127–198. Washington, DC: Catholic University of America Press, 2016.
Kosicki, Piotr H., and Kyrill Kunakhovich, eds. *The Long 1989: Decades of Global Revolution.* Budapest: CEU Press, 2019.
Kosicki, Piotr H., and Sławomir Łukasiewicz, eds. *Christian Democracy across the Iron Curtain: Europe Redefined.* London: Palgrave Macmillan, 2018.

Kosowska-Gąstoł, Beata. "A Truly 'European' Christian Democracy? The European People's Party." In *Christian Democracy across the Iron Curtain: Europe Redefined*, edited by Piotr H. Kosicki and Sławomir Łukasiewicz, 127–152. London: Palgrave Macmillan, 2018.

Kotkin, Stephen. *Armageddon Averted: The Soviet Collapse*. Oxford: Oxford University Press, 2001.

Kotkin, Stephen, with Jan T. Gross. *Uncivil Society: 1989 and the Implosion of the Communist Establishment*. New York: Vintage Books, 2010.

Kowalik, Tadeusz. *From Solidarity to Sellout: The Restoration of Capitalism in Poland*. Translated by Eliza Lewandowska. New York: Monthly Review Press, 2012.

Kramer, Mark, and Vít Smetana, eds. *Imposing, Maintaining, and Tearing Open the Iron Curtain: The Cold War and East-Central Europe, 1945–1989*. Lanham - Boulder - New York et al.: Lexington Books, 2014.

Krapfl, James. *Revolution with a Human Face: Politics, Culture, and Community in Czechoslovakia, 1989–1992*. Ithaca, NY: Cornell University Press, 2013.

Krastev, Ivan. *After Europe*. Philadelphia: University of Pennsylvania Press, 2017.

Krzywicka, Katarzyna, and Edward Olszewski, eds. *Chrześcijańska demokracja we współczesnym świecie*. Lublin: Wydawnictwo Uniwersytetu Marii Curie-Skłodowskiej, 1999.

Kuczyński, Waldemar. *Zwierzenia zausznika*. Warsaw: BGW, 1992.

Kułakowski, Jan, and Leszek Jesień. *Spotkania na Bagateli: Polska, Europa, świat: Z Janem Kułakowskim rozmawia Leszek Jesień*. Warsaw: Rhetos, 2004.

Kunicki, Mikołaj. "Between Accommodation, Resistance, and Dialogue: Church-State Relations in Communist Poland, 1945–1989." In *"Peaceful Coexistence" or "Iron Curtain": Austria, Neutrality, and Eastern Europe in the Cold War and Détente, 1955–1989*, edited by Arnold Suppan and Wolfgang Mueller, 393–411. Vienna-Berlin: LIT Verlag, 2009.

Kunicki, Mikołaj Stanisław. *Between the Brown and the Red: Nationalism, Catholicism, and Communism in Twentieth-Century Poland – The Politics of Bolesław Piasecki*. Athens, OH: Ohio University Press, 2012.

Kuper, Ernst. *Transnationale Parteienbündnisse zwischen Partei- und Weltpolitik*. Berlin - New York - Vienna: Peter Lang, 1995.

Küsters, Hanns Jürgen, ed. *Der Zerfall des Sowjetimperiums und Deutschlands Wiedervereinigung. The Decline of the Soviet Empire and Germany's Reunification*. Cologne-Weimar-Vienna: Böhlau, 2016.

Kwaschik, Anne, and Ulrich Pfeil, eds. *Die DDR in den deutsch-französischen Beziehungen / La RDA dans les relations franco-allemande*. Frankfurt am Main: Lang, 2013.

Lamberts, Emiel. *The Struggle with Leviathan: Social Responses to the Omnipotence of the State, 1815–1965*. Translated by Maria Kelly. Leuven: Leuven University Press, 2017.

La Pira, Giorgio. "La vocation prophétique du laïc." In *Mission et liberté des laïcs dans le monde*, 125–132. Paris: Cerf, 1964.

Laplane, Sabine. *Frère Roger de Taizé – Avec presque rien ...* Paris: Cerf, 2015.

Lappenküper, Ulrich. *Mitterrand und Deutschland: Die enträtselte Sphinx*. Munich: Oldenbourg, 2011.

Lappenküper, Ulrich. "Prekäres Vertrauen: François Mitterrand und Deutschland seit 1971." In *Diplomatie mit Gefühl: Vertrauen, Misstrauen und die Außenpolitik der Bundesrepublik Deutschland*, edited by Reinhild Kreis, 83–96. Berlin: Oldenbourg, 2015.

Larres, Klaus. "Margaret Thatcher and German Unification Revisited." In *The Revolutions of 1989: A Handbook*, edited by Wolfgang Mueller, Michael Gehler and Arnold Suppan, 355–384. Vienna: Verlag der Österreichischen Akademie der Wissenschaften, 2015.

Laurinavičius, Česlovas, and Vladas Sirutavičius. *Sąjūdis: nuo "Persitvarkymo" iki Kovo 11-osios*. Vilnius: Baltos lankos, 2008.

Lehne, Stefan. *The Vienna Meeting of the Conference on Security and Cooperation in Europe, 1986–1989: A Turning Point in East-West Relations*. Boulder - San Francisco - Oxford: Westview Press, 1991.

Lehne, Stefan. "Vom Prozeß zur Institution: Zur aktuellen Debatte über die Weiterentwicklung des KSZE-Prozesses." *Europa Archiv* 45, no. 16 (1990): 499–506.

Lehnguth, Cornelius. *Waldheim und die Folgen: Der parteipolitische Umgang mit dem Nationalsozialismus in Österreich*. Frankfurt am Main - New York: Campus, 2013.

Lendvai, Paul. *Der Ungarn-Aufstand 1956: Eine Revolution und ihre Folgen*. Munich: Bertelsmann, 2006.

Lendvai, Paul. *Orbán: Hungary's Strongman.* Oxford: Oxford University Press, 2017.

Liedermann, Helmut. "Österreichs Rolle beim Zustandekommen der KSZE." In *Mit anderen Augen gesehen*, edited by Oliver Rathkolb, Otto M. Maschke and Stefan August Lütgenau, 491–521. Vienna-Cologne-Weimar: Böhlau, 2002.

Lipold, Jan. "Václav Benda se nikdy nevezl s proudem." *Mladá fronta DNES*, 3 June 1999, 1–2.

Litván, György, and János M. Bak, eds. *Die Ungarische Revolution 1956: Reform – Aufstand – Vergeltung.* Vienna: Passagen Verlag, 1994.

Loth, Wilfried. "Der KSZE-Prozess 1975–1990: eine Bilanz." In *Die KSZE im Ost-West-Konflikt*, edited by Matthias Peter and Hermann Wentker, 323–331. Berlin-Boston: De Gruyter, 2013.

Loth, Wilfried. *Die Teilung der Welt: Geschichte des Kalten Krieges 1941–1955.* Munich: Taschenbuch Verlag, 4th ed., 1983; rev. ed., 2000.

Łukasiewicz, Sławomir. *Third Europe: Polish Federalist Thought in the United States 1940–1970s.* Budapest: Helena History Press, 2016.

Lukošaitis, Alvidas. "Moderniosios partinės sistemos formavimosi etapai Lietuvoje." In *Lietuvos politinės partijos ir partinė sistema.* vol. 1, edited by Algimantas Jankauskas, Egidijus Kūris and Jūratė Novagrockienė, 92–128. Vilnius: Naujasis Lankas, 1997.

Magenheimer, Heinz. "Konventionelle Stabilität und Sicherheit in Europa: Truppenreduktionen, Umrüstungen und Wiener VKSE-Konferenz." *Aus Politik und Zeitgeschichte*, B 36 (1990): 3–12.

Maier, Charles S. *Dissolution: The Crisis of Communism and the End of East Germany.* Princeton, NJ: Princeton University Press, 1997.

Maier, Charles S., and Günter Bischof, eds. *Deutschland und der Marshall-Plan.* Baden-Baden: Nomos, 1992.

Majchrowski, Jan. "Chadecja w III Rzeczypospolitej." *Znaki Nowych Czasów* nos. 5–6 (2003): 103–120.

Malíř, Jiří, and Pavel Marek et al. *Politické strany 1861–1938.* Brno: Doplněk, 2005.

Mandouze, André. "Prendre la main tendue." In *Les Chrétiens et la politique*, 39–78. Paris: Temps Présent, 1948.

Martini, Stephan. *Die sicherheitspolitische Funktion der KSZE im entspannungspolitischen Konzept der Bundesrepublik Deutschland 1975–1990.* Berlin: Mensch & Buch, 2006.

Marušiak, Juraj. "Nezávislé inciativy na Slovensku v rokoch normalizácie." In *November 1989 na Slovensku: Súvislosti, predpoklady a dôsledky*, edited by Jan Pešek and Soňa Szomolányi, 54–75. Bratislava: Nadácia Milana Šimečku, Historický ústav SAV and Katedra politológie FF UK, 1999.

Mastny, Vojtech. "Did Gorbachev Liberate Eastern Europe?" In *The last Decade of the Cold War*, edited by Olav Njølstad, 402–423. London - New York: Cass, 2004.

Mauthe, Jörg. *Demnächst oder Der Stein des Sisyphos.* Vienna: Edition Atelier, 1986.

Mazowiecki, Tadeusz. "Co wyniosłem z Płocka." *Więź* no. 4 (2012): 75–79.

Mazowiecki, Tadeusz. "En pays socialiste." In *Mission et liberté des laïcs dans le monde*, 33–50. Paris: Cerf, 1964.

Mazowiecki, Tadeusz. *Internowanie.* London: Aneks, 1983.

Mazowiecki, Tadeusz. "Protester et éduquer." *Esprit* no. 7–8 (1978): 78–83.

Mazowiecki, Tadeusz. *Rok 1989 i lata następne.* Warsaw: Prószyński i s-ka, 2012.

Mazowiecki, Tadeusz. *Rozdroża i wartości.* Warsaw: Biblioteka WIĘZI, 1970.

Mazurkiewicz, Anna. *Uchodźcy polityczni z Europy Środkowo-Wschodniej w amerykańskiej polityce zimnowojennej (1948–1954).* Warsaw-Gdańsk: Instytut Pamięci Narodowej/Uniwersytet Gdański, 2016.

McDermott, Kevin, and Matthew Stibbe, eds. *The 1989 Revolutions in Central and Eastern Europe: From Communism to Pluralism.* Manchester - New York: Manchester University Press, distributed in the United States exclusively by Palgrave Macmillan, 2013.

Meneguzzi Rostagni, Carla, ed. *The Helsinki Process: A Historical Reappraisal.* Padova: CEDAM, 2005.

Mertens, Christian. *Österreichische Christdemokraten im Dienste Europas.* Vienna: Medien und Recht, 1997.

Meyer, Hinnerk. "Participation on limited cooperation – Großbritanniens schwierige Rolle im deutschen Einigungsprozess 1989–90." *Europa und die deutsche Einheit: Beobachtungen, Entscheidungen und Folgen*, edited by Michael Gehler and Maximilian Graf, 141–160. Göttingen: Vandenhoeck & Ruprecht, 2017.

Miedema, Christie. "Struggling against the Bomb or Against the Bloc Divide? The Dutch Peace Movement and Eastern Europe." *Dutch Crossing: Journal of Low Countries Studies* 39, no. 3 (2015): 261–274.

Milbradt, Georg. "The Prospects of Christian Democracy in Contemporary Europe: Experiences from Germany." In *Christian Democracy across the Iron Curtain: Europe Redefined*, edited by Piotr H. Kosicki and Sławomir Łukasiewicz, 439–448. London: Palgrave Macmillan, 2018.

Misner, Paul. *Social Catholicism in Europe: From the Onset of Industrialization to the First World War*. New York: Crossroad, 1991.

Mitchell, Kristine. "The European Trade Union Confederation at 40: integration and diversity in the European labor movement." *Labor History* 55, no. 4 (2014): 403–426.

Morgan, Michael Cotey. *The Final Act: The Helsinki Accords and the Transformation of the Cold War*. Princeton, NJ: Princeton University Press, 2018.

Moyn, Samuel. *The Last Utopia: Human Rights in History*. Cambridge, MA: Belknap Press of Harvard University Press, 2010.

Mrklas, Ladislav. "Exilová demokratická pravice." *CEVRO-Revue* 3 (2004), 6 April 2004. Online at www.cevro.cz/cs/30164-exilova-demokraticka-pravice. Accessed 20 December 2018.

Müller, Jan-Werner. *Christian Democracy: A New Intellectual History*. Cambridge, MA: Harvard University Press, forthcoming.

Müller, Jan-Werner. *Contesting Democracy: Political Thought in Twentieth-Century Europe*. New Haven, CT: Yale University Press, 2011.

Müller, Jan-Werner. *What is Populism?* Philadelphia: University of Pennsylvania Press, 2016.

Mueller, Wolfgang. "'Die Lage gleitet uns aus den Händen': Motive und Faktoren in Gorbatschows Entscheidungsprozess zur Wiedervereinigung Deutschlands." *Zeitschrift des Forschungsverbundes SED-Staat* 39 (2016): 3–28.

Mueller, Wolfgang. "The Revolutions of 1989: An Introduction." In *The Revolutions of 1989: A Handbook*, edited by Wolfgang Mueller, Michael Gehler and Arnold Suppan, 3–30. Vienna: Verlag der Österreichischen Akademie der Wissenschaften, 2015.

Mueller, Wolfgang. "The USSR and the Reunification of Germany, 1989–90." In *The Revolutions of 1989: A Handbook*, edited by Wolfgang Mueller, Michael Gehler and Arnold Suppan, 321–353. Vienna: Verlag der Österreichischen Akademie der Wissenschaften, 2015.

Mueller, Wolfgang; Michael Gehler and Arnold Suppan, eds. *The Revolutions of 1989: A Handbook*. Vienna: Verlag der Österreichischen Akademie der Wissenschaften, 2015.

Naimark, Norman M. *Fires of Hatred: Ethnic Cleansing in Twentieth-Century Europe*. Cambridge, MA: Harvard University Press, 2001.

Naimark, Norman M. "The Superpowers and 1989 in Eastern Europe." In *The Revolutions of 1989: A Handbook*, edited by Wolfgang Mueller, Michael Gehler and Arnold Suppan, 249–270. Vienna: Verlag der Österreichischen Akademie der Wissenschaften, 2015.

Neuhold, Hanspeter, ed. *CSCE: N+N Perspectives: The Process of the Conference on Security and Cooperation in Europe from the Viewpoint of the Neutral and Non-aligned Participating States*. Vienna: Braumüller, 1987.

Neuhold, Hanspeter, and Stefan Lehne. "The Role of the Neutral and Non-Aligned Countries at the Vienna Meeting." In *The Human Dimension of the Helsinki Process*, edited by Arie Bloed and Pieter van Dijk, 30–53. Dordrecht-Boston-Norwell: Kluwer, 1991.

Nitti, Francesco Saverio. *Il socialismo cattolico*. Rome: L. Roux, 1891.

Njølstad, Olav, ed. *The Last Decade of the Cold War: From Conflict Escalation to Conflict Transformation*. London - New York: Cass, 2004.

Nuti, Leopoldo, ed. *The Crisis of Détente in Europe: From Helsinki to Gorbachev, 1975–1985*. London: Routledge, 2009.

Nuti, Leopoldo. "Italy, German Unification, and the End of the Cold War." In *Europe and the End of the Cold War: A Reappraisal*, edited by Frédéric Bozo, Marie-Pierre Rey, N. Piers Ludlow and Leopoldo Nuti, 191–203. London: Routledge, 2008.

O'Brennan, John. *The Eastern Enlargement of the European Union*. New York: Routledge, 2006.

O'Brennan, John. "EU Enlargement, 1989–2009." In *The Revolutions of 1989: A Handbook*, edited by Wolfgang Mueller, Michael Gehler and Arnold Suppan, 553–571. Vienna: Verlag der Österreichischen Akademie der Wissenschaften, 2015.

Oplatka, Andreas. *Der Eiserne Vorhang reißt: Ungarn als Wegbereiter*. Zurich: Neue Zürcher Zeitung, 1990.

Oplatka, Andreas. *Der erste Riss in der Mauer: September 1989 – Ungarn öffnet die Grenze*. Vienna: Zsolnay Verlag, 2009.

Oplatka, Andreas. "Hungary 1989: Renunciation of Power and Power-Sharing." In *The Revolutions of 1989: A Handbook*, edited by Wolfgang Mueller, Michael Gehler and Arnold Suppan, 77–91. Vienna: Verlag der Österreichischen Akademie der Wissenschaften, 2015.

Orszulik, Alojzy. *Czas przełomu: Notatki ks. Alojzego Orszulika z rozmów z władzami PRL w latach 1981–1989*. Warsaw: Obserwator/Apostolicum, 2006.

Ost, David. *Solidarity and the Politics of Anti-Politics: Opposition and Reform in Poland since 1968*. Philadelphia: Temple University Press, 1990.

Ostermann, Christian F. "The United States and German Unification." In *Europa und die deutsche Einheit: Beobachtungen, Entscheidungen und Folgen*, edited by Michael Gehler and Maximilian Graf, 93–116. Göttingen: Vandenhoeck & Ruprecht, 2017.

Otáhal, Milan. "K některým otázkám dějin tak zvané normalizace v českých zemích." In *Za svobodu a demokracii I: Odpor proti komunistické moci*, edited by Jaroslav Cuhra and Václav Veber, 117–129. Prague: Evropské hnutí v České republice, 1999.

Otáhal, Milan. *Opoziční proudy v české společnosti 1969–1989*. Prague: Ústav pro soudobé dějiny AV ČR, 2011.

Otáhal, Milan. "Programová orientace disentu 1969–1989." In *Opozice a odpor proti komunistickému režimu v Československu 1968–1989*, edited by Petr Blažek, 25–40. Prague: Ústav světových dějin and Dokořán, 2005.

Otáhal, Milan. "Die 'samtene' Revolution – ohne Alternative." In *Wandel durch Repräsentation – Repräsentation durch Wandel: Entstehung und Ausformung der parlamentarischen Demokratie in Ungarn, Polen, der Tschechoslowakei und der ehemaligen DDR*, edited by Uwe Thaysen and Hans Michael Kloth, 125–130. Baden-Baden: Nomos, 1992.

Paczkowski, Andrzej, and Malcolm Byrne. "The Polish Crisis: Internal and International Dimensions." In *From Solidarity to Martial Law: The Polish Crisis of 1980–1981*, edited by Andrzej Paczkowski and Malcolm Byrne, 1–43. Budapest: CEU Press, 2007.

Pająk, Henryk. *Piąty rozbiór Polski: 1990–2000*. Lublin: Retro, 2005.

Pasture, Patrick. "Catholic and Christian Democratic Views on Europe before and after World War II: Continuities and Discontinuities." In *Christian Democracy across the Iron Curtain: Europe Redefined*, edited by Piotr H. Kosicki and Sławomir Łukasiewicz, 25–56. London: Palgrave Macmillan, 2018.

Pasture, Patrick. *Christian Trade Unionism in Europe since 1968: Tensions between Identity and Practice*. Aldershot: Avebury, 1994.

Pasture, Patrick. *Histoire du syndicalisme chrétien international: La difficile recherche d'une troisième voie*. Paris: L'Harmattan, 1999.

Pasture, Patrick. "Jan Kułakowski, from Exile to International Trade Union Leader and Diplomat." In *Intégration ou représentation? Les exilés polonais en Belgique et la construction européenne*, edited by Michel Dumoulin and Idesbald Goddeeris, 99–120. Louvain-la-Neuve: Academia-Bruylant, 2005.

Paupert, Jean-Marie. *Taizé i Kościół jutra*. Warsaw: Instytut Wydawniczy PAX, 1969.

Pečinka, Bohumil. "Formování české občanské pravice." In Česká konzervativní a liberální politika*: Sborník k desátému výročí založení revue Proglas*, edited by Petr Fiala and František Mikš, 69–85. Brno: Centrum pro studium demokracie a kultury, 2000.

Pehr, Michal. "ČSL na konci komunismu." In *Josef Lux a česká politika 90. let*, edited by Milan Znoj and Michal Pehr, 27–30. Prague: Ústav politologie FF UK, 2005.

Pelinka, Anton. "European Christian Democracy in Comparison." In *Christian Democracy in Europe since 1945*, vol. 2, edited by Michael Gehler and Wolfram Kaiser, 193–206. London - New York: Routledge, 2004.

Pelinka, Anton. *Jaruzelski oder die Politik des kleineren Übels: Zur Vereinbarkeit von Demokratie und Leadership*. Frankfurt am Main: Lang, 1996.

Pélissier, Lucien. "Mounier et les communistes." In *Emmanuel Mounier ou le combat du juste*, 65–117. Bordeaux: Guy Ducros, 1968.

Peter, Matthias. *Die Bundesrepublik im KSZE-Prozess 1975–1983: Die Umkehrung der Diplomatie*. Berlin: De Gruyter Oldenbourg, 2015.
Peter, Matthias, and Hermann Wentker, eds. *Die KSZE im Ost-West-Konflikt: Internationale Politik und gesellschaftliche Transformation 1975–1990*. Munich: De Gruyter, 2012; Berlin-Boston: De Gruyter, 2013.
Peter, Matthias, and Hermann Wentker. "'Helsinki-Mythos' oder 'Helsinki-Effekt'? Der KSZE-Prozess zwischen internationaler Politik und gesellschaftlicher Transformation. Zur Einleitung." In *Die KSZE im Ost-West-Konflikt: Internationale Politik und gesellschaftliche Transformation 1975–1990*, edited by Matthias Peter and Hermann Wentker, 1–14. Berlin-Boston: De Gruyter, 2013.
Petkus, Viktoras. *Krikščioniškoji demokratija pasaulyje ir Lietuvoje*. Vilnius: Lietverslas, 1991.
Petritsch, Wolfgang. *Bruno Kreisky: Die Biographie.* St. Pölten-Salzburg: Residenz Verlag, 2010.
Pitette, Yves. *Biographie d'un journal*. Paris: Perrin, 2011.
Plato, Alexander von. "Opposition, Movements and Big Politics in the Reunification of Germany." In *The Revolutions of 1989: A Handbook*, edited by Wolfgang Mueller, Michael Gehler and Arnold Suppan, 307–319. Vienna: Verlag der Österreichischen Akademie der Wissenschaften, 2015.
Plato, Alexander von. *Die Vereinigung Deutschlands – ein weltpolitisches Machtspiel: Bush, Kohl, Gorbatschow und die geheimen Moskauer Protokolle*. Bonn: Bundeszentrale für Politische Bildung, 2003.
Pleskot, Patryk. *Kłopotliwa panna "S." Postawy polityczne Zachodu wobec "Solidarności" na tle stosunków z PRL (1980–1989).*Warsaw: IPN, 2013.
Pleskot, Patryk. *Solidarność, Zachód i węże. Służba Bezpieczeństwa wobec emigracyjnych struktur Solidarności 1981–1989*. Warsaw: IPN, 2011.
Pons, Silvio, and Federico Romero, eds. *Reinterpreting the End of the Cold War: Issues, Interpretations, Periodizations*. London: Routledge, 2014.
Popiel, Karol. *Od Brześcia do "Polonii."* London: Odnowa, 1967.
Porter, Brian. *When Nationalism Began to Hate: Imagining Modern Politics in Nineteenth-Century Poland*. Oxford: Oxford University Press, 2001.
Poulat, Émile, and René Rémond. *Cent ans d'histoire de La Croix*. Paris: Éditions du Centurion, 1988.
Povilaitis, Pranas, and Viktorija Škiudaitė. *Lietuviai krikščionys demokratai išeivijoje*. Vilnius: Leono XIII fondas, 2013.
Pradetto, August. *Bürokratische Anarchie: Der Niedergang des polnischen "Realsozialismus."* Vienna-Cologne-Graz: Böhlau, 1992.
Pradetto, August. *Techno-bürokratischer Sozialismus: Polen in der Ära Gierek (1970–1980)*. Frankfurt am Main - Bern - New York - Paris: Lang, 1991.
Préparer le concile des jeunes, audacieuse aventure. Taizé: Les Presses de Taizé, 1973.

Rabiński, Jarosław. "The Elimination of Christian Democracy in Poland after World War II." In *Christian Democracy across the Iron Curtain: Europe Redefined*, edited by Piotr H. Kosicki and Sławomir Łukasiewicz, 153–176. London: Palgrave Macmillan, 2018.
Rahner, Karl. *Strukturwandel der Kirche als Aufgabe und Chance*. Vienna: Herder, 1972.
Rataj, Jan. *O národní autoritativní stát*. Prague: Karolinum, 1998.
Rathkolb, Oliver. "An Ambivalent Attitude of Trade Unions und Political Parties." In *Solidarity with Solidarity: Western European Trade Unions and the Polish Crisis, 1980–1982*, edited by Idesbald Goddeeris, 269–288. Lanham, MD: Lexington, 2010.
Rév, István. *Retroactive Justice: Prehistory of Post-Communism*. Stanford, CA: Stanford University Press, 2005.
Rey, Marie-Pierre. "Gorbachev's New Thinking and Europe, 1985–1989." In *Europe and the End of the Cold War*, edited by Frédéric Bozo, Marie-Pierre Rey, N. Piers Ludlow and Leopoldo Nuti, 23–35. London - New York: Routledge, 2008.
Riegler, Josef, ed. *1st Round Table Europe: Vienna MS Mozart. 11-12. January 1990.* Vienna: Politische Akademie, 1990.
Riishøj, Søren. "Development of Parties and Party Systems in Central Europe 1989–2007." *Politologiske Skrifter* no. 19 (2007).
Rodríguez García, Magaly. *Liberal Workers of the World, Unite? The ICFTU and the Defence of Labour Liberalism in Europe and Latin America (1949–1969)*. Bern: Peter Lang, 2010.

Romano, Angela. *From détente in Europe to European détente: How the West shaped the Helsinki CSCE*. Brussels - New York: Peter Lang, 2009.
Rosin, Philip. *Die Schweiz im KSZE-Prozess 1972–1983: Einfluss durch Neutralität.* Munich: Oldenbourg, 2014.
Rupnik, Jacques. "Explaining Eastern Europe: The Crisis of Liberalism." *Journal of Democracy* 29, no. 3 (2018): 24–37.
Rupnik, Jacques. "The legacies of dissent: Charter 77, the Helsinki effect, and the emergence of a European Public Space." In *Samizdat, Tamizdat, and Beyond: Transnational Media During and After Socialism*, edited by Friederike Kind-Kovacs and Jessie Labov, 316–332. New York: Berghahn, 2013.

Saal, Yuliya von. *KSZE-Prozess und Perestroika in der Sowjetunion: Demokratisierung, Werteumbruch und Auflösung 1985–1991*. Munich: Oldenbourg, 2014.
Sachs, Jeffrey. *Poland's Jump to the Market Economy.* Cambridge, MA: MIT Press, 1993.
Saïd, Edward. *Orientalism*. New York: Vintage, 1979.
Sarotte, Mary Elise. *1989: The Struggle to Create Post-Cold War Europe*. Princeton, NJ: Princeton University Press, 2009.
Sarotte, Mary Elise. *The Collapse: The Accidental Opening of the Berlin Wall*. New York: Basic Books, 2014.
Saunier, Georges. "France, the East European Revolutions, and the Reunification of Germany." In *The Revolutions of 1989: A Handbook*, edited by Wolfgang Mueller, Michael Gehler and Arnold Suppan, 385–401. Vienna: Verlag der Österreichischen Akademie der Wissenschaften, 2015.
Savranskaya, Svetlana. "The Logic of 1989: The Soviet Peaceful Withdrawal from Eastern Europe." In *Masterpieces of History*, edited by Svetlana Savranskaya, Thomas S. Blanton and Vladislav Zubok, 1–47. Budapest - New York: CEU Press, 2010.
Scatena, Silvia. *Taizé: le origini della comunità e l'attesa del concilio*. Zurich: LIT, 2011.
Scatena, Silvia. *Taizé, una parabola di unità: Storia della comunità dalle origini al Concilio dei giovani.* Bologna: Il Mulino, 2018.
Schabert, Tilo. *Wie Weltgeschichte gemacht wird: Frankreich und die deutsche Einheit*. Stuttgart: Klett Cotta, 2002.
Schlotter, Peter. "Das Ende der Systemkonfrontation 1989/1990: Der Beitrag des KSZE-Prozesses." In *Deeskalation von Gewaltkonflikten seit 1945*, edited by Corinna Hauswedell, 115–128. Essen: Klartext Medienwerkstatt, 2006.
Schmidt-Schweizer, Andreas. "Motive im Vorfeld der Demontage des 'Eisernen Vorhangs' 1987–1989." In *Grenze im Kopf*, edited by Peter Haslinger, 127–139. Frankfurt am Main -Berlin - Bern: Lang, 1999.
Schmidt-Schweizer, Andreas. "Die Öffnung der ungarischen Westgrenze für die DDR-Bürger im Sommer 1989: Vorgeschichte, Hintergründe und Schlussfolgerungen." *Südosteuropa Mitteilungen* 37, no. 1 (1997): 33–53.
Schmidt-Schweizer, Andreas. "Die politischen Auseinandersetzungen am 'Nationalen Runden Tisch': Systemtransformation auf dem 'Verhandlungsweg'?" *Südosteuropa* 46, no. 1/2 (1997): 37–64.
Schmidt-Schweizer, Andreas. *Politische Geschichte Ungarns 1985–2002: Von der liberalisierten Einparteienherrschaft zur Demokratie in der Konsolidierungsphase*. Munich: Oldenbourg, 2007.
Schmidt-Schweizer, Andreas. *Vom Reformsozialismus zur Systemtransformation: Politische Veränderungsbestrebungen innerhalb der Ungarischen Sozialistischen Arbeiterpartei (MSZMP) von 1986 bis 1989*. Frankfurt am Main - Berlin - Bern: Lang, 2000.
Schollum, Esther. "Die Osteuropa-Aktivitäten der Politischen Akademie." *Österreichische Monatshefte* 7 (1989): 32-33.
Schollum, Esther. "Die Osteuropa-Aktivitäten der Politischen Akademie." In *Österreichisches Jahrbuch für Politik 1991*, edited by Andreas Khol, Günther Ofner and Alfred Stirnemann, 491–523. Vienna-Munich: Verlag für Geschichte und Politik/Oldenbourg Verlag, 1992.
Schutz, Roger. *Étonnement d'un amour. Journal 1974–1976.* Taizé: Les Presses de Taizé, 1979.
Schutz, Roger. *Fleurissent tes déserts. Journal.* Taizé: Les Presses de Taizé, 1982.
Schutz, Roger. *Lutte et contemplation. Journal 1970–1972.* Taizé: Les Presses de Taizé, 1973.
Schutz, Roger. *Niech twoje święto trwa bez końca.* Warsaw: Instytut Wydawniczy PAX, 1972.
Schutz Roger. *Passion d'une attente. Journal 1979–1981.* Taizé: Les Presses de Taizé, 1985.
Schutz, Roger. *Ta fête soit sans fin*. Taizé: Les Presses de Taizé, 1971.

Schutz, Roger. *Vivre l'inespéré. Journal 1972–1974.* Taizé: Les Presses de Taizé, 1976.
Schwan, Heribert, and Jens Tilman. *Das Vermächtnis: Die Kohl-Protokolle.* Munich: Random House, 2014.
Schwarz, Hans Peter. *Helmut Kohl: Eine politische Biographie.* Munich: DVA, 2012.
Sebestyen, Victor. *Revolution 1989: The Fall of the Soviet Empire.* London: Phoenix, 2009.
Seiler, Daniel-Louis. "Peut-on appliquer les clivages de Rokkan à l'Europe centrale?" In *Partis politiques et démocratie en Europe centrale et orientale*, edited by Jean-Michel De Waele, 115–144. Brussels: Éd. de l'Université de Bruxelles, 2002.
Seiler, Daniel-Louis. "Qu'est-ce qu'un clivage politique? Le cas de l'Europe centrale: limites et extension du modèle de Rokkan." In *Clivages et familles politiques en Europe*, edited by Jean-Michel De Waele, 79–103. Brussels: Éd. de l'Université de Bruxelles, 2011.
Service, Hugo. *Germans to Poles: Communism, Nationalism, and Ethnic Cleansing after the Second World War.* Cambridge: Cambridge University Press, 2013.
Service, Robert. *The End of the Cold War, 1985–1991.* London: Pan Books, 2015.
Siani-Davis, Peter. *The Romanian Revolution of December 1989.* Ithaca, NY: Cornell University Press, 2005.
Sjursen, Helene. *The United States, Western Europe and the Polish Crisis: International Relations in the Second Cold War.* Basingstoke - New York: Palgrave, 2003.
Škiudaitė, Viktorija. *Krikščionys demokratai Lietuvoje, 1989–2015.* Vilnius: Baltijos kopija, 2015.
Śledzianowski, Jan. *Ksiądz Czesław Kaczmarek - biskup kielecki 1895–1963.* Kielce: Kuria Diecezjalna, 1991.
Sloan, Stanley. "NATO Enlargement in the Beginning: An American Perspective." In *The Revolutions of 1989: A Handbook*, edited by Wolfgang Mueller, Michael Gehler and Arnold Suppan, 525–552. Vienna: Verlag der Österreichischen Akademie der Wissenschaften, 2015.
Slobodian, Quinn. *Globalists: The End of Empire and the Birth of Neo-liberalism.* Cambridge, MA: Harvard University Press, 2018.
Smidchens, Guntis. *The Power of Song: Nonviolent National Culture in the Baltic Singing Revolution.* Seattle: University of Washington Press, 2014.
Snyder, Sarah B. "The Foundation for Vienna: A reassessment of the CSCE in the mid-1980s." *Cold War History* 10, no. 4 (2010): 493–512.
Snyder, Sarah B. *Human Rights Activism and the End of the Cold War: A Transnational History of the Helsinki Network.* New York: Cambridge University Press, 2011.
Snyder, Timothy. *Nationalism, Marxism, and Modern Central Europe: A Biography of Kazimierz Kelles-Krauz, 1872–1905.* Oxford: Oxford University Press, 2017 edition.
Snyder, Timothy. *The Road to Unfreedom: Russia, Europe, and America.* New York: Tim Duggan Books, 2018.
Sobolewska-Myślik, Katarzyna. *Partie i systemy partyjne Europy Środkowej po 1989 roku.* Kraków: Księgarnia Akademicka, 1999.
Sobolewska-Myślik, Katarzyna. *Partie i systemty partyjne na świecie.* Warsaw: Wydawnictwo Naukowe PWN, 2010.
Soros, George. *Underwriting Democracy: Encouraging Free Enterprise and Democratic Reform among the Soviets in Eastern Europe.* New York: PublicAffairs, 2004.
Sozańska, Dominika. *Chrześcijańska Demokracja w Polsce: Przyczyny słabości i szanse rozwoju.* Kraków: Krakowskie Towarzystwo Edukacyjne - Oficyna Wydawnicza AFM, 2011.
Staniszkis, Jadwiga. *Poland's Self-Limiting Revolution.* Edited by Jan T. Gross. Princeton, NJ: Princeton University Press, 1984.
Stehle, Hansjakob. *The Eastern Politics of the Vatican, 1917–1979.* Translated by Sandra Smith. Athens, Ohio: Ohio University Press, 1981.
Steininger, Rolf. *Der Kalte Krieg.* Frankfurt: Fischer-Taschenbuch-Verlag, 2006.
Stöver, Bernd. *Der Kalte Krieg: Geschichte eines radikalen Zeitalters 1947–1991.* Munich: C.H. Beck, 2007.
Strzelecka, Małgorzata. *Między minimalizmem a maksymalizmem: Dylematy ideowe Stanisława Stommy i Janusza Zabłockiego.* Toruń: UMK, 2015.
Suk, Jiři. "Czechoslovakia in 1989: Causes, Results, and Conceptual Changes." In *The Revolutions of 1989: A Handbook*, edited by Wolfgang Mueller, Michael Gehler and Arnold Suppan, 137–160. Vienna: Verlag der Österreichischen Akademie der Wissenschaften, 2015.

Suppan, Arnold. "Austria and its Neighbors in Eastern Europe, 1955–89." In *The Revolutions of 1989: A Handbook*, edited by Wolfgang Mueller, Michael Gehler and Arnold Suppan, 419–436. Vienna: Verlag der Österreichischen Akademie der Wissenschaften, 2015.

Suppan, Arnold, and Wolfgang Mueller, eds. *"Peaceful Coexistence" or "Iron Curtain": Austria, Neutrality, and Eastern Europe in the Cold War and Détente, 1955–1989*. Vienna-Berlin: LIT Verlag, 2009.

Süß, Walter. "Die Wiener KSZE-Folgekonferenz und der Handlungsspielraum des DDR-Sicherheitsapparates 1989." In *Die KSZE im Ost-West-Konflikt*, edited by Matthias Peter and Hermann Wentker, 219–231. Berlin-Boston: De Gruyter, 2013.

Svarauskas, Artūras. *Krikščioniškoji demokratija nepriklausomoje Lietuvoje (1918–1940): politinė galia ir jos ribos*. Vilnius: Lietuvos istorijos institutas, 2014.

Szczerbiak, Aleks, and Tim Bale. "Explaining the Absence of Christian Democracy in Contemporary Poland." In *Christian Democracy across the Iron Curtain: Europe Redefined*, edited by Piotr H. Kosicki and Sławomir Łukasiewicz, 343–410. London: Palgrave Macmillan, 2018.

Szlek-Miller, Stefania. "Catholic Personalism and Pluralist Democracy in Poland." *Canadian Slavonic Papers* 25, no. 3 (1983): 425–439.

Szymański, Antoni. *Poglądy demokracyi chrześcijańskiej we Francyi, 1892–1907*. Poznań: Księgarnia św. Wojciecha, 1910.

Taras, Ray. *Liberal and Illiberal Nationalisms*. Basingstoke, UK: Palgrave Macmillan, 2002.

Taubman, William. *Gorbachev: His Life and Times*. New York: W.W. Norton, 2017.

Thatcher, Margaret. *The Downing Street Years*. London: Harper Collins, 1993.

Ther, Philipp. *Europe since 1989: A History*. Translated by Charlotte Kreuzmuller. Princeton, NJ: Princeton University Press, 2018.

Ther, Philipp. *Die neue Ordnung auf dem alten Kontinent: Eine Geschichte des neoliberalen Europa*. Berlin: Suhrkamp, 2014.

Thomas, Daniel C. *The Helsinki Effect: International Norms, Human Rights, and the Demise of Communism*. Princeton, NJ: Princeton University Press, 2001.

Thum, Gregor. *Uprooted: How Breslau became Wrocław during the Century of Expulsions*. Translated by Tom Lampert and Allison Brown. Princeton, NJ: Princeton University Press, 2011.

Tischner, Józef. *The Spirit of Solidarity*. Translated by Marek B. Zaleski and Benjamin Fiore. San Francisco: Harper & Row, 1984.

Tismăneanu, Vladimir. *The Devil in History: Communism, Fascism, and Some Lessons of the Twentieth Century*. Berkeley: University of California Press, 2012.

Tismăneanu, Vladimir, ed. *The Revolutions of 1989*. London: Routledge, 1999.

Tismăneanu, Vladimir, ed. *Stalinism Revisited: The Establishment of Communist Regimes in East-Central Europe*. Budapest: CEU Press, 2009.

Tismăneanu, Vladimir, and Sorin Antohi, eds. *Between Past and Future: The Revolutions of 1989 and their Aftermath*. Budapest: CEU Press, 2000.

Tismăneanu, Vladimir, and Bogdan C. Iacob, eds. *The End and the Beginning: The Revolutions of 1989 and the Resurgence of History*. Budapest - New York: CEU Press, 2012.

Tőkés, Rudolf L. *Hungary's Negotiated Revolution: Economic Reform, Social Change, and Political Succession 1957–1990*. Cambridge: Cambridge University Press, 1996.

Toole, James. "The Historical Foundations of Party Politics in Post-Communist East Central Europe." *Europe-Asia Studies* 59, no. 4 (2007): 541–566.

Török, Gabor. "External Influences on the Hungarian Party System." In *Democratic Consolidation – The International Dimension: Hungary, Poland and Spain*, edited by Gerhard Mangott, Harald Waldrauch and Stephen Day, 187–214. Baden-Baden: Nomos, 2000.

Tranvouez, Yvon. *Catholiques et communistes: La crise du progressisme chrétien, 1950–1955*. Paris: Cerf, 2000.

Urquijo, José Ignacio. *El movimiento obrero de Venezuela*. Lima: OIT/UCAB/INAESIN, 2004.

Vaïsse, Maurice, and Christian Wenkel, eds. *La diplomatie française face à l'unification allemande. D'après des archives inédites*. Paris: Tallandier, 2011.

Vámos, Peter. "The Tiananmen Square 'Incident' in China and the East Central European Revolutions." In *The Revolutions of 1989: A Handbook*, edited by Wolfgang Mueller, Michael Gehler and Arnold Suppan, 93–112. Vienna: Verlag der Österreichischen Akademie der Wissenschaften, 2015.

Van Kemseke, Peter. *Towards an Era of Development: The Globalization of Socialism and Christian Democracy, 1945–1965*. Leuven: Leuven University Press, 2006.

Vareikis, Egidijus. "Lietuvos krikščionių demokratų partija." In *Politinės partijos Lietuvoje. Atgimimas ir veikla*, edited by Algis Krupavičius. Kaunas: Litterae universitatis, 1996.

Varsori, Antonio. *L'Italia e la fine della guerra fredda*. Bologna: Mulino, 2013.

Varsori, Antonio. "Italy, the East European Revolutions, and the Reunification of Germany (1989–92)." In *The Revolutions of 1989: A Handbook*, edited by Wolfgang Mueller, Michael Gehler and Arnold Suppan, 403–418. Vienna: Verlag der Österreichischen Akademie der Wissenschaften, 2015.

Varsori, Antonio, and Benedetto Zaccaria, eds. *Italy in the International System from Détente to the End of the Cold War: The Underrated Ally*. London: Palgrave Macmillan, 2018.

Vaško, Václav. "Legendární professor Kolakovič." *Teologické texty: Časopis pro teoretické a praktické otázky teologie* 30, no. 4 (2007). Online at www.teologicketexty.cz/casopis/2007-4/Legendarni-profesor-Kolakovic.html. Accessed 28 October 2016.

Villaume, Pouland, and Odd Arne Westad, eds. *Perforating the Iron Curtain: European Détente, Transatlantic Relations, and the Cold War, 1965–1985*. Copenhagen: Museum Tusculanum Press, University of Copenhagen, 2010.

Voss, Lex Heerma van; Patrick Pasture and Jan De Maeyer, eds. *Between Cross and Class: Comparative Histories of Christian Labor in Europe, 1840–2000*. Bern: Peter Lang, 2005.

Wahlers, Gerhard. *CLAT: Geschichte einer lateinamerikanischen Gewerkschaftsinternationale*. Bonn: Wehle, 1990.

Ward, James Mace. *Priest, Politician, Collaborator: Jozef Tiso and the Making of Fascist Slovakia*. Ithaca, NY: Cornell University Press, 2016.

Warner, Carolyn M. *Confessions of an Interest Group: The Catholic Church and Political Parties in Europe*. Princeton, NJ: Princeton University Press, 2000.

Waterman, Peter. *Globalization, Social Movements, and the New Internationalisms*. London-Washington, DC: Continuum, 1998.

Weigel, George. *The Final Revolution: The Resistance Church and the Collapse of Communism*. Oxford: Oxford University Press, 2003.

Weinacher, Michèle, ed. *L'Est et l'Ouest face à la chute du mur: Question de perspective*. Cergy Pontoise: CIRAC, 2013.

Wenkel, Christian. *Auf der Suche nach einem "anderen Deutschland": Das Verhältnis Frankreichs zur DDR im Spannungsfeld von Perzeption und Diplomatie*. Munich: De Gruyter, 2014.

Wentker, Hermann. "Vom Gegner zum Partner: Gorbatschow und seine Politik im Urteil Helmut Kohls." *Historisch-Politische Mitteilungen* 22 (2015): 1–34.

Westad, Odd Arne. *The Global Cold War*. Cambridge: Cambridge University Press, 2005.

Wilflinger, Gerhard. "Der Mitteleuropäer." In *Erhard Busek. Ein Porträt*, edited by Elisabeth Welzig, 238–262. Vienna-Cologne-Weimar: Böhlau Verlag, 1992.

Williams, Kieran, Aleks Szczerbiak and Brigid Fowler. "Explaining Lustration in Eastern Europe: 'A Post-communist politics approach.'" *Sussex European Institute Working Paper* no. 62 (March 2003). www.sussex.ac.uk/webteam/gateway/file.php?name=sei-working-paper-no-62.pdf&site=266. Accessed on 7 April 2017.

Wohnout, Helmut. "The Klaus Era (1964–1970)." In *The Republic of Austria 1918–2018. Milestones and Turning Points*, edited by Heinz Fischer, 134–147. Vienna: Czernin, 2018.

Wohnout, Helmut. "Die Umbrüche 1989 aus der Perspektive der österreichischen Außenpolitik unter besonderer Berücksichtigung des bilateralen Verhältnisses zu Ungarn." In *Österreich und Ungarn im 20. Jahrhundert*, edited by Csaba Szabó, 325–344. Vienna: Publikationen der ungarischen Geschichtsforschung in Wien, 2014.

Wohnout, Helmut. "Vom Durchschneiden des Eisernen Vorhangs bis zur Anerkennung Sloweniens und Kroatiens. Österreichs Außenminister Alois Mock und die europäischen Umbrüche 1989–1992." In *Grenzöffnung 1989. Innen- und Außenperspektiven und die Folgen für Österreich*, edited by Andrea Brait and Michael Gehler, 185–219. Vienna-Cologne-Weimar: Böhlau, 2014.

Wolff, Larry. *Inventing Eastern Europe: The Map of Civilization on the Mind of the Enlightenment.* Stanford, CA: Stanford University Press, 1994.

Wrede, Hans-Heinrich. *KSZE in Wien: Kursbestimmung für Europas Zukunft.* Cologne: Verlag Wissenschaft und Politik, 1990.

Zabłocki, Janusz. *Dzienniki.* Volume I: *1956–1965.* Warsaw: IPN-KŚZpNP, 2008.

Zelikow, Philip. "US Strategic Planning in 1989–90." In *The Revolutions of 1989: A Handbook*, edited by Wolfgang Mueller, Michael Gehler and Arnold Suppan, 283–306. Vienna: Verlag der Österreichischen Akademie der Wissenschaften, 2015.

Zelikow, Philip, and Condoleezza Rice. *Germany Unified and Europe Transformed: A Study in Statecraft.* Cambridge, MA: Harvard University Press, 1996.

Zielinski, Michael. *Die neutralen und blockfreien Staaten und ihre Rolle im KSZE-Prozeß.* Baden-Baden: Nomos, 1990.

Ziętara, Paweł. "Christian Democrats across the Iron Curtain." In *Christian Democracy across the Iron Curtain: Europe Redefined*, edited bij Piotr H. Kosicki and Sławomir Łukasiewicz, 177–220. London: Palgrave Macmillan, 2018.

Zubok, Vladislav. *A Failed Empire: The Soviet Union in the Cold War from Stalin to Gorbachev.* Chapel Hill: University of North Carolina Press, 2007.

Żubr, Feliks. "Wenezuela." In *Akcja niepodległościowa na terenie międzynarodowym 1945–1990*, edited by Tomasz Piesakowski. London: Polskie Towarzystwo Naukowe na Obczyźnie, 1999.

Żukowski, Arkadiusz. "Republika Poludniowej Afryki." In *Akcja niepodległościowa na terenie międzynarodowym 1945–1990*, edited by Tomasz Piesakowski. London: Polskie Towarzystwo Naukowe na Obczyźnie, 1999.

Zunes, Stephen. "Estonia's Singing Revolution (1986–1991)." April 2009, www.nonviolent-conflict.org/estonias-singing-revolution-1986-1991/ (quoted December 2018).

LIST OF CONTRIBUTORS

Andrea Brait is assistant professor at the Department of Contemporary History and the Department of Subject-Specific Education at the University of Innsbruck. She publishes in the field of history didactics and on the history of diplomacy, for example, "'Vor Torschluss': Österreichs Kulturbeziehungen zur DDR 1989–90," in *Europa und die deutsche Einheit: Beobachtungen, Entscheidungen und Folgen*, edited by Michael Gehler and Maximilian Graf (2017).

Alexander Brakel currently serves as residence director of the Konrad Adenauer Foundation in Israel. Prior to that, he was deputy head of the historical division of the foundation. His publications include *Unter Rotem Stern und Hakenkreuz: Baranowicze 1939 bis 1944. Das westliche Weißrussland unter sowjetischer und deutscher Besatzung* (2009) and *Der Holocaust: Judenverfolgung und Völkermord* (2008).

Ladislav Cabada is associate professor at the Department of Political Science and Humanities at the Metropolitan University in Prague, Czech Republic. He is also permanent visiting scholar at the National University of Public Service in Budapest, Hungary. His recent work includes *Imaginäre Räume in Zentraleuropa* (with Christopher Walsch et al., 2019), *Od dunajské federace k Visegrádu ... a zpět? Staré a nové format středoevropské spolupráce* [From the Danubian Federation towards the Visegrád ... and back? Old and new formats of Central European cooperation] (with Christopher Walsch, 2017), *Balkánské komunismy* [Balkan Communism] (with Markéta Kolarčíková, 2016), and *Political Parties in East Central Europe* (with Vít Hloušek and Petr Jurek, 2014).

Giovanni Mario Ceci teaches "History of Contemporary Europe" at the Università degli Studi Roma Tre and "Terrorism: An Introduction" at IES-Rome. He is the author of several books and articles, including *Renzo De Felice storico della politica* (Rubbettino, 2008); *Moro e il PCI: La strategia dell'attenzione e il dibattito politico italiano, 1967–1969* (Carocci, 2013) and *Il terrorismo italiano: Storia di un dibattito* (Carocci, 2013).

Kim Christiaens is assistant professor and director of KADOC - Documentation and Research Center on Religion, Culture, and Society at KU Leuven. He has extensively published on international solidarity movements and transnational activism with a North-South and East-West orientation during the Cold War, including campaigns on behalf of Eastern European dissidents.

Michael Gehler is professor of Modern German and European History at the Institute of History at the University of Hildesheim, three-time Jean-Monnet Chair, former director of the Institute of Modern and Contemporary Historical Research at the Austrian Academy of Sciences (ÖAW) (2013–2017), corresponding member of the Austrian Academy of Sciences, permanent senior fellow at the Center of European Integration Research at the Rheinische Friedrich Wilhelms-Universität Bonn, and a member of the European Union's Liaison Committee of Historians. His most recent book is *Europa: Ideen – Institutionen – Vereinigung – Zusammenhalt* (Reinbek: Edition Olzog-LauVerlag, 2018).

Thomas Gronier is associate researcher at the SIRICE (Sorbonne-Identity, International Relations and Civilizations of Europe) multidisciplinary research center. His research focuses on the Holy See, Austria, Central Europe, the Cold War, communism, religious persecution, and Christianity in the twentieth century.

Piotr H. Kosicki is associate professor of History at the University of Maryland. He is the author of *Catholics on the Barricades: Poland, France, and "Revolution," 1891–1956* (Yale University Press, 2018) and editor of *Christian Democracy across the Iron Curtain* (Palgrave Macmillan, with Sławomir Łukasiewicz), *The Long 1989* (CEU Press, with Kyrill Kunakhovich), and *Vatican II behind the Iron Curtain* (CUA Press).

Sławomir Łukasiewicz is director of the Institute of European Studies at the John Paul II Catholic University of Lublin and professor at and chair of the Institute's Department of Political Science. He also serves as historian for the Lublin branch of Poland's Institute of National Remembrance and is author of *Third Europe: Polish Federalist Thought in the United States, 1940–1970's* (Budapest: Helena History Press, 2016).

Anton Pelinka is professor emeritus of Nationalism Studies and Political Science at the Central European University in Budapest. His publications include *Die gescheiterte Republik: Kultur und Politik in Österreich, 1918–1938* (Vienna: Böhlau, 2017).

Johannes Schönner is head of the Archive of the Karl von Vogelsang Institute (KVVI) and deputy director of the KVVI. He has numerous publications in the field of contemporary history and political education, among them several editions of sources regarding the history of the Austrian political parties and their formation, as well as many publications on Austrian history in general. His present research focuses on compensation settlements for the victims of the Nazi regime and political party cooperation in postwar Europe.

Artūras Svarauskas is a lecturer at the Faculty of History at the Lithuanian University of Educational Science. He is the author of *Christian Democracy in Independent Lithuania, 1918–1940: Political Power and its Limits* (Vilnius, 2014, in Lithuanian); *From Kazys Grinius to Antanas Smetona: The Relationship between Government and Political Opposition in Lithuania, 1926–1940* (with Mindaugas Tamosaitis, Vilnius, 2014, in Lithuanian), *Grade 12 History Textbook* (with Virginijus Navickas, Kaunas, 2015, in Lithuanian). His research interests include twentieth-century Lithuanian political history, social, ethnic and political tensions in interwar Lithuania, and problems of political Catholicism in Lithuania.

Helmut Wohnout is department head at the Austrian Federal Chancellery, and since 1993, director of the Karl von Vogelsang Institute. He is lecturer at the Faculty of History at the University of Graz. His publications focus on the history and politics of the nineteenth and twentieth centuries, including *Regierungsdiktatur oder Ständeparlament? Gesetzgebung im autoritären Österreich* (1993); *Political Catholicism in Europe 1918–45* (edited with Wolfram Kaiser, 2004); *Alois Mock: Ein Politiker schreibt Geschichte* (with Martin Eichtinger, 2008); *Leopold Figl und das Jahr 1945: Von der Todeszelle auf den Ballhausplatz* (2015) and *Italien und Österreich im Mitteleuropa der Zwischenkriegszeit* (edited with Maddalena Guiotto, 2018). He is a member of various scientific committees and advisory councils.

INDEX OF PERSONS

COLOPHON

Final editing
Godfried Kwanten, KADOC
Luc Vints, KADOC

Copy editing
Lieve Claes, KADOC

Lay-out
Alexis Vermeylen, KADOC

Printing and binding
Wilco B.V., Amersfoort

CIVITAS
Forum of Archives and Research on Christian Democracy
c/o KADOC
Vlamingenstraat 39
B - 3000 Leuven
https://civitas-farcd.eu

Leuven University Press
Minderbroedersstraat 4
B - 3000 Leuven
http://lup.be